PREPARING FOR WAR

IN THE SERIES

Technology/Data/War

Edited by Dr Matthew Ford

Twenty-first-century war is fought on a battlefield where digital technologies, data surveillance and algorithmic decision-making shape everyday experience. Tech giants and systems developers are scripting the future of combat and redefining the role of the officer even as soldiers go into battle with the weapons they have, not the AI platforms they're promised. Across the world, civilians are caught in the churn of information warfare, where military force and participative media have all but erased the lines between military and non-combatant. Social media platforms amplify and weaponise the public sphere, spread propaganda, manipulate perception and accelerate violence. Meanwhile, facial recognition, predictive analytics and remote sensing affect how people move, communicate, and survive, in ways that intersect with race, class and gender. Life on the algorithmic battlefield involves a constant negotiation with invisible systems that monitor, nudge and endanger individuals, often without their full awareness or consent. This is reshaping state power, eroding civil liberties and challenging the laws of armed conflict.

As series editor for Technology/Data/War, Matthew Ford welcomes submissions from authors who explore the conduct of contemporary war. He is particularly interested in the digital architectures that shape how battles are fought and the technological, organisational and socio-political challenges this creates.

OLIVIER SCHMITT

Preparing for War

Strategy, Power and Military Change

HURST & COMPANY, LONDON

First published in France in 2024 by
Humensis, Presses Universitaires de France,
This edition published in the United Kingdom in 2026 by
C. Hurst & Co. (Publishers) Ltd.,
New Wing, Somerset House, Strand, London, WC2R 1LA

© Olivier Schmitt, 2026
All rights reserved.

Préparer la guerre. Stratégie, innovation et puissance militaire à l'époque contemporaine © Presses Universitaires de France / Humensis, 2024

The right of Olivier Schmitt to be identified
as the author of this publication is asserted by him in accordance
with the Copyright, Designs and Patents Act, 1988.

A Cataloguing-in-Publication data record for this book
is available from the British Library.

ISBN: 9781805265269

EU GPSR Authorised Representative
Easy Access System Europe Oü, 16879218
Address: Mustamäe tee 50, 10621, Tallinn, Estonia
Contact Details: gpsr.requests@easproject.com, +358 40 500 3575

Printed and bound in Great Britain by Bell and Bain Ltd, Glasgow

www.hurstpublishers.com

CONTENTS

List of Figures and Tables	vii
Acknowledgments	ix
Introduction: The Challenge of Military Change	1
1. The Configuration of the International System and Military Change	55
2. The Challenge of Civil–Military Relations	103
3. Technology and Military Change	141
4. The Internal Dynamics of Military Organizations	185
5. War	235
Conclusion: Transforming Military Organizations	273
Notes	287
Index	331

LIST OF FIGURES AND TABLES

Figures

1.	Constitutive elements of military strategy	4
2.	Adam Grissom's taxonomy of military change	7
3.	Indicators of military change	43
4.	Modes of learning	47
5.	Conceptualization of military change	52
6.	Production costs for major US combat aircraft	155
7.	Stages in the adoption of a new military technology	160
8.	Strategic culture and military culture	189
9.	Learning sequence in the armed forces	266

Tables

1.	Developments and trends in military organizations	10
2.	Trends in dispersion on the battlefield	36
3.	Trend in acquisition and maintenance costs for certain French Army equipment	156
4.	Examples of contemporary organization models for the armed forces	197

5.	Characteristics of an efficient PME	222
6.	Dominant mechanisms of military change according to entity configurations	274
7.	Criteria for analyzing the evolution of military organizations	275

ACKNOWLEDGMENTS

The origin of this book lies in a workshop held in September 2011 in the Cotswolds, about two hours from London. My thesis supervisor, Theo Farrell, had invited me to be a discussant for chapters of the book he was co-editing with Frans Osinga and James Russell, to be published in 2013 by Stanford University Press under the title *Military Adaptation in Afghanistan*. My thesis was on multinational military operations, and one chapter was devoted to the intervention in Afghanistan. Theo thought it would be a good opportunity for me both to develop my professional network and to start honing my skills as an academic discussant. I was understandably flattered by the opportunity, but also terrified that I'd have to make minimally useful comments on a scientific literature—military innovation—about which I knew next to nothing at the time, and in which all the participants were internationally recognized specialists.

This first exposure to the literature on military innovation piqued my curiosity: I was still working on coalition operations, but I was beginning to take part in the seminars of the Military Innovation Research Group, which met regularly at King's College London. Indeed, the university's War Studies Department had played an important role in consolidating this scientific field. I defended my thesis in May 2014, a few weeks after Russia's invasion of Crimea. This aggression was an important moment in the evolution of my intellectual trajectory: I sensed that a major rupture in European security had just taken place, and I began to take an interest in

ACKNOWLEDGMENTS

Russian propaganda operations, the transformation of post-Cold War European armies, and the evolution of military technologies. In addition, the end of the International Security Assistance Force operations in Afghanistan provided an opportunity to study the effect of this long campaign on military change in Europe. A first step into the field of military change studies came when I was awarded two grants for a research project on learning from Afghanistan in the French and German armed forces. The project, funded by the Gerda Henkel Foundation and the Danish Independent Research Fund, led, among other things, to the publication of an article on the "selective emulation" of British and American forces by French and German troops, and a book co-authored with Alice Pannier on the transformations in French defense policy since the end of the Cold War.

In 2018, I secured further major funding from the Carlsberg Foundation for a research project on the transformation of the armed forces in the twenty-first century, of which this book is the final product. This project enabled me to take on two doctoral students, Vicky Karyoti and Michael Gjerstad, working respectively on the integration of new technologies in military organizations and the transformation of the Russian armed forces. It also gave me the means to regularly invite colleagues to research seminars, to organize two international workshops on military change, to acquire a large number of major works for the university library (the best research library in Europe on military change may be in Odense, Denmark), and to teach for three years a course on military innovation in which I tested some of the ideas presented here.

This book is the culmination of more than a decade of reflection, work and exchanges on the subject. In this respect, I would like to thank Theo Farrell, who first awoke in me an interest in the study of military change, and who probably didn't expect to continue to have such an influence on my research objects long after I had defended my thesis.

This work would not have been possible without the financial support of the Gerda Henkel Foundation, the Danish Independent Research Fund and the Carlsberg Foundation, whom I would like to thank for their trust.

ACKNOWLEDGMENTS

My colleagues at the Center for War Studies, in particular Vicky Karyoti, Michael Gjerstad, Amelie Theussen, Per Jacob Lindgaard and Sten Rynning, have been ideal partners for discussing the dynamics of military transformation. My current colleagues at the Royal Danish Defence College, many of whom work on military change, also provided inspiration when updating the book for the English version. I would in particular like to thank my colleagues at the Institute for Military Operations: it is a pleasure to work with you and to educate Danish military officers at a time when, unfortunately, Europe has to prepare for war.

For the many exchanges that have enriched my thinking over the years, I would like to thank, at the risk of forgetting some, and in no particular order: Adam Grissom, Raphael Marcus, Jean-Vincent Holeindre, Dima Adamsky, Stephen Saideman, Stéphane Taillat, Joseph Henrotin, Isabelle Dufour, Pascal Vennesson, Marc DeVore, Chiara Ruffa, Heather Williams, Jean-Christophe Noël, Olivier Chopin, Dominika Kunertova, Florent de Saint-Victor, Hervé Pierre, Beatrice Heuser, Elie Tenenbaum, Corentin Brustlein, David Pappalardo, Jean-Baptiste Jeangène-Vilmer, Stephanie Hofmann, Tsiporah Fried, Alice Pannier, Frank Hoffmann, Michael J. Williams, Thomas Crosbie, Emmanuel Dreyfus, Julien Malizard, Josselin Droff, Yohann Michel and the late Bastien Irondelle.

Stéphane Taillat, Colonel (Air) David Pappalardo and Captain (Navy) Matthieu Douillet generously agreed to proofread all or part of this book and to provide useful comments. I would like to thank them all and assure the reader that any errors they may find in these pages are my sole responsibility.

Finally, I would like to thank Michael Dwyer, from Hurst, for his confidence in the manuscript. The book was initially published in French in 2024 by the Presses Universitaires de France under the title *Préparer la guerre. Stratégie, innovation et puissance militaire à l'époque contemporaine*. This English version is more than a translation: it has been partly rewritten to take into account the feedback received during the various book presentations I gave in 2024–2025, and to include the relevant academic literature published since then.

The idea for this book was hatched long before Gabriel was born, and the English version was finally completed after Johannes had started kindergarten. My family, and first and foremost my wonderful wife Asmara, have been an unwavering support, especially during the final periods of writing. More than just my thanks, may they be assured of my love.

INTRODUCTION

THE CHALLENGE OF MILITARY CHANGE

In February 2022, the Russian Army invaded Ukraine. To the surprise of most military observers, the Russian armed forces struggled to achieve a decisive reckoning with the Ukrainian forces. Since 2008, the Russian Army had been engaged in a process of structural reform, the avowed aim of which was to improve operational efficiency, following failures regularly noted since the collapse of the USSR. By contrast, the Ukrainian Army has demonstrated that it has transformed itself since 2014, learning from its defeats and modifying its structures and practices with some success.

The operations themselves also illustrated the importance of military change. After the failure of its initial maneuver to take Kiev, and following a number of tactical errors, the Russian Army began a process of adaptation: adjusting strategic objectives (instead of a campaign comprising four simultaneous fronts, the military effort was limited to eastern Ukraine), improving coordination between air and ground forces, adjusting the chain of command, and switching from a war of maneuver to a war of position. Not to be outdone, Ukrainian forces also updated their tactics, learned to use Western equipment (notably tanks, infantry fighting vehicles and artillery) alongside what they inherited from the Soviet era, ingeniously employed commercial technologies (especially drones and communications) in the service of their military effort, and developed new approaches at the operational level to counter Russian military activities. These changes were obviously dialectical, in a dynamic of adaptation and counter-adaptation between Ukrainian and Russian forces, whose success is one of the major factors in the evolution of the conflict.[1] We see here that military change is one of the conditions of military effectiveness, which itself has major political consequences in determining the winners and losers of an armed conflict.

Moreover, in response to the shock of the conflict, most European countries announced their intention to increase their defense spending and thus modify the size and structure of their armed forces. To everyone's surprise, Germany, for example, decided to devote an exceptional 100 billion euros to modernizing the Bundeswehr, although the results have been lackluster due to the challenges of changing a military organization structurally and specific German idiosyncrasies.[2] Nevertheless, military change is at the heart of any analysis of the most important event affecting European security since the fall of the Berlin Wall.[3]

In April 2022, the newspaper *Politico* reported that some thirty former US Marine Corps generals were working together to derail the major reform initiated by the current Commandant, General David Berger, which they considered counterproductive.[4] In 2021, General Berger had initiated two strategies, Force Design 2030 and Talent Management 2030, with the aim of adapting Marine Corps structures, training and career paths to take account of the strategic context of increased competition with China and the irruption of new technologies (space, cyber, long-range missiles) on the battlefield. The drastic transformation project involved abandoning tank and helicopter capabilities, to concentrate on the amphibious assault and precision munitions more suited to confrontation in the Pacific. His opponents accused him of betraying the identity and specificity of the Marine Corps, and of overestimating the impact of new technologies. To bury the reform, former Marines lobbied the US Congress and published articles in the press (notably the *Wall Street Journal*) to influence educated public opinion. This episode illustrates the difficulty of reforming the armed forces, and the interweaving of strategic, cultural and political dimensions in the process itself.

INTRODUCTION

These examples illustrate the importance of what I refer to in this book as *military change*, defined as the modalities and processes by which armed forces evolve that affect their operational effectiveness. Indeed, military power lies at the heart of international relations. The ability to deter aggressors or violently impose one's will on adversaries shapes the structure of the international system. Of course, this does not mean that military power is the only important factor in international politics: international interactions are also shaped by economic, legal, and sociological dynamics that influence the behavior of international actors, both state and non-state. However, one specificity of international relations remains: these dynamics take place in a context where war—the use of collective armed violence for political ends—is always a possibility. As Raymond Aron wrote,

> The conduct of the diplomat-strategist, in fact, has the specific meaning of being dominated by the risk of war, of confronting adversaries in an incessant rivalry in which each reserves the right to resort to the ultimate reason, i.e. violence. [...] The theory of international relations starts from the plurality of autonomous decision-making centers, and thus from the risk of war, and from this risk it deduces the necessity of calculating means.[5]

Given the importance of military power in international politics, it is important to study the basic building block of this power: the armed forces. Numerous works in the field of strategic studies attempt to assess the balance of military power between partners and adversaries, observing the means available and the doctrines used.[6] This book adopts a different perspective, studying changes in military organizations: instead of observing a snapshot of power relationships, it sets out to study their dynamics. In particular, the study of military change raises major issues such as the adequacy of armed forces to their strategic environment, the budgetary and technological levers for improving military effectiveness, the importance of the role of civilian authorities in defining security policies, and the effect of cultural factors on military practices.

Every organization is confronted with the dialectic of stability and change: how to adapt to a changing context while maintaining regular, stable operations, a guarantee of predictability? But this difficulty is perhaps even greater for military organizations. Indeed, armed forces are highly hierarchical organizations, with a tendency to mythologize the past in order to turn it into "traditions" and identify heroic examples as a guarantee of troop cohesion. This instrumental and fantasized relationship with the past, coupled with a rigid hierarchical structure, can be a factor in preventing organizational change, leading to the commonplace notion that the military is always preparing to fight the last war. However, military organizations are also under considerable pressures for change: from the need to assess the strategic context (and in particular the capabilities of adversaries) and adapt accordingly, the integration of new military technologies within the forces, the implementation of the budgetary framework decided by political leaders, etc. The ability of the armed forces to reconcile organizational inertia with the imperatives of change determines the military power of a state. Thus, this book is fundamentally a reflection on the evolution of the distribution of power within the international system, based on an analysis of the modalities of change of the basic building block of this power, namely the armed forces. In this way, it contributes to the debate on the strategy of means which, along with operational strategy and declaratory strategy, forms the pillars of general military strategy.[7] While military strategy is about the use of military force for political purposes within the framework of grand strategy, the strategy of means establishes what kind of forces will be available, the operational strategy directs how they will be employed,

Figure 1. Constitutive elements of military strategy

and the declaratory strategy issues signals (e.g. by participation in multi-national exercises) to allies and adversaries alike.

The transformations of the global system, accelerated by the invasion of Ukraine in 2022, are clearly moving in the direction of a new militarization of international relations, after a period of relative calm represented by post-Cold War American hegemony.[8] This hegemony was historically exceptional, as all the major powers in the international system were de facto on the same side. However, with the rise of China, the return of Russia, and the emergence of other major military players (Turkey, Iran, Israel, Japan, South Korea, Indonesia, etc.), the international system is being re-hierarchized, while the multilateral mechanisms used to regulate tensions between players are being weakened.[9] The re-hierarchization of the international system is accompanied by a new polarization between competing blocs, whose precise forms have yet to be defined, but whose general contours are beginning to oppose a "Western" camp dominated by the US and benefiting from the status quo, to a "revisionist" camp dominated by China, with Russia as a second-tier partner. A third group would include countries that favor a regulated international system, as has been the case since the end of the Cold War, but are hostile to the liberal norms and values characteristic of the "Western" camp: these would include countries such as India, Indonesia, Saudi Arabia, South Africa, Nigeria and Brazil.[10] Yet, Donald Trump's reelection could further complicate the picture, since the far-right ideologies coexisting within the US administration are opposed to liberal democracy, which could lead to a further fragmentation of the "Western camp" between US ideological allies (such as Viktor Orbán's Hungary) and the remaining liberal democracies.[11]

These blocs are already engaged in fierce competition for the definition of international norms and standards (legal, technical, etc.), clash over claimed values (democracy versus authoritarianism), are engaged in a race for control of the world's critical infrastructures, and are vying for influence over third countries.[12] In addition to these geopolitical dynamics, a number of megatrends will also strongly structure the international context: the consequences of climate change, the exponential development of new technologies (including artificial intelligence and hyperconnectivity), the urbanization of the planet, and the general aging of the world's population (particularly in Europe and Asia) will have major effects, albeit impossible to predict,[13] on international security. In this context, understanding how armed forces evolve is one of the necessary entry points to understanding the international system, since the future relative power of states will depend in part on how their military organizations have changed. Indeed, the armed forces will be obliged to take the above-mentioned trends into account in their structures and planning. How can new technologies be integrated into decision-making chains? How can we continue to attract soldiers in countries with aging populations, who will be less inclined to send their youth to war? How do we think about tactics, force training and procurement for future combat in megacities? Understanding the mechanisms of military change is therefore fundamental to the study of future geopolitical dynamics.

In addition to the importance of this theme for the analysis of international conflict, understanding the ways in which armed forces change is also a political issue. The prevalence of war in international politics and the return of aggression in the international system[14] are driving up military spending worldwide, with states devoting a significant proportion of their national wealth to their armed forces. According to figures compiled by the International Institute for Strategic Studies, global military spending in 2024 amounted to $2.46 trillion in 2024, up from $2.24 trillion in 2023, including $968 billion in the US, $235 billion in China, $74.4 billion in India and $64 billion in France.[15] In a democracy, citizens and elected representatives have a right to a framework for assessing the effectiveness of defense spending. In this sense, the mechanisms of military change studied in this book contribute to providing criteria for analyzing the relative success or failure of the evolution of a country's armed forces. The book may also be of use to political or military leaders themselves involved in managing a reform process, providing them with sources of inspiration or examples of pitfalls to avoid.

INTRODUCTION

Studying military change

The scientific literature on military change is particularly rich, drawing on history, sociology, political science and strategic studies. Indeed, most military historians address, in one way or another, the question of the evolution of armed forces in peacetime as in wartime: if military history is, to a large extent, a history of military organizations and the individuals who make them up, then military change occupies a major place within it. Similarly, other disciplines are interested in the subject, using their own conceptual tools. In an attempt to categorize the field, Adam Grissom distinguishes between military innovation and adaptation. According to him, there are seven "schools" of thought that explain military innovation in terms of the

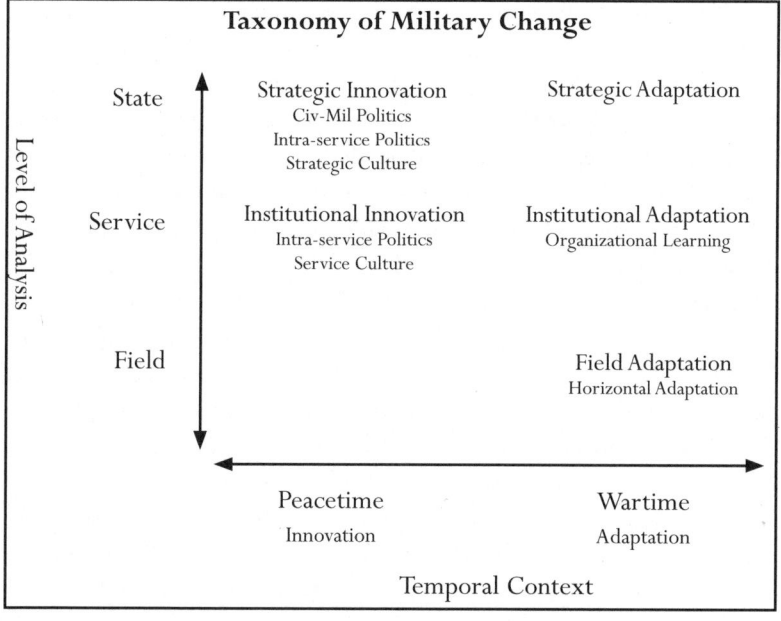

Figure 2. Adam Grissom's taxonomy of military change
(Adam Grissom, "Innovation and Adaptation," in Stéphane Taillat, Joseph Henrotin and Olivier Schmitt (eds.), *Guerre et stratégie. Approches, concepts*, Paris, PUF, 2015, p. 373)

most important factors: material rebalancing, technological change, civil–military relations, bureaucratic rivalries between services (e.g. army versus navy), internal dynamics within the services themselves, strategic culture and organizational culture. Military adaptation, for its part, can be observed at three levels: strategic adaptation, institutional adaptation and adaptation in the field. This taxonomy informs Figure 2, which summarizes the scientific literature on military change.

However, while this classification provides a good map of the state of the field, the scientific literature presents a number of problems. Indeed, any work on military change faces three difficulties.

The first is that the academic literature on the subject is divided between historical approaches, on the one hand, and attempts at theorization, often inspired by the sociology of organizations, on the other. Military historians have produced numerous works analyzing in detail the evolution of specific armed forces, and much information can also be found in works on particular conflicts.[16] However, the majority of these works, whatever their intrinsic qualities, describe rather than conceptualize the mechanisms of change in armed forces, which limits the scope for comparison between different cases. Indeed, historians are generally divided on the very meaning of the discipline: is history fundamentally an "idiographic" science, focused primarily on the study of the particular and the non-reproducible, or are generalizations possible, and, if so, how (which brings history closer to the social sciences)? Without daring to settle this thorny epistemological debate,[17] we can nonetheless observe empirically that, in the field we are interested in, most military historians who have studied changes in the armed forces devote themselves mainly to case studies, or compilations of case studies in collective works that allow identification of a few principles,[18] but without necessarily seeking to generalize and conceptualize their observations.[19]

For their part, authors mainly rooted in the field of strategic studies have developed various concepts and led a number of theoretical debates, mainly in the pages of the *Journal of Strategic Studies*. However, as Stuart Griffin notes in a synthetic overview of the field, the phenomenon of military change (sometimes referred to as military innovation, to which we return below) remains under-theorized, as conceptualization efforts are often ad hoc with the aim of explaining specific cases, and authors rarely address the major epistemological debates of the social sciences.[20] This fragmentation into empirical case studies and specific theorizations leads to a scientific field that is abundant but unconsolidated and lacking in a broad theoretical and conceptual approach. A literature review of the field published in 2018 lamented that

> The accumulated body of knowledge in the field of military innovation is not clear on the following four basic questions: Why study military innovation? What is meant by "military innovation"? How does military innovation manifest itself? And what are driving factors of military innovation? As the accumulated body of knowledge is not clear on answers to the basic questions, the foundation of frames of reference became unstable. […] Consequently, knowledge and understanding of how military organizations innovate is unclear and incomplete. More importantly, military innovation studies lack a conceptual framework that is agreed upon, which hampers scholars to study military innovation thoroughly and consistently.[21]

Finally, military sociologists also study change in the armed forces, mainly in two ways. The first, comparable to some historians' work, consists in studying specific case studies in detail, mobilizing the tools and concepts of sociology. However, as in the case of historical productions, specificity makes it difficult to generalize.[22] The second approach is a macroanalysis of major trends in the armed forces (particularly in the West), identifying ruptures and transformations in the general functioning of military organizations. Table 1 summarizes the main findings of work of this type. Nevertheless, this approach is useful for characterizing major evolutions, but it remains too general to identify precise mechanisms or combinations of mechanisms leading to military change. As we can see, the key issue is the level of analysis: we need to avoid both micro and macro approaches, and determine at the meso level the conditions for a conceptually rigorous analysis of military change.

Table 1. Developments and trends in military organizations

	Early modern period (before the Cold War)	Modern period (Cold War)	Post-modern period (post-Cold War)
Perceived threat	Enemy invasion	Nuclear war	Asymmetrical and non-military
Force structure	Mass army	Large professional army with reserve component	Small professional army
Public attitudes toward the armed forces	Supportive	Ambivalent	Skeptical or apathetic
Impact on the defense budget	Positive	Neutral	Negative
Dominant military professional	Combat leader	Manager or technician	Soldier-statesman, soldier-scholar
Civilian employees in the armed forces	Minor component	Medium component	Major component

Source: Delphine Resteigne, "Sociology of the Military," in Anders McD Sookermany (ed.), *Handbook of Military Science*, Berlin, Springer, 2022, p. 9.

To date, the main attempt to establish such a meso-level approach to military change remains that of Theo Farrell and Terry Terriff, in their 2002 book *The Sources of Military Change*. In the introduction to this collective work, Farrell and Terriff identify three "sources" of change: cultural norms, politics and strategy, and technology. These three "sources" lead to change through three possible "processes": innovation, adaptation and emulation.[23] This approach is useful, as it lays the foundations for a distinction between what we might call the "root causes" of change and the pathways through which it is implemented. However, as we shall see below, the causes identified are probably incomplete. Moreover, the book, like the rest of the literature, sometimes tends to confuse the processes and the results of change: the terms "innovation" and "adaptation," formally described as "processes," are thus sometimes used to describe the nature of the novelties introduced into the armed forces *as a result of their transformation*.

Indeed, the second difficulty, linked to the fragmentation of the literature, is the absence of a widely shared conceptual vocabulary. The term "military innovation" is typical of this difficulty. Based on a comparative analysis of a hundred or so scientific articles and books studying "military innovations," Michael Horowitz and Shira Pindyck observe a lack of consensus on the definition of the term, which prevents a systematized study of the factors and variables leading (or not leading) to an innovation.

> For example, the British development of tanks in World War I set the stage for the subsequent development of combined arms warfare by the German military and the military innovation often called blitzkrieg in the literature. However, given the range of definitions across the literature, it is not clear what aspect of and in which context the tank "counts" as an innovation or as part of an innovation. Is the tank, as a force to break through World War I trenches, a military innovation or merely a technical invention? Must an invention "succeed" on the battlefield to be a military innovation? If so, is the full innovation the tank itself, or the tank combined with the use of radios, trucks, and airplanes?[24]

The problem is compounded when military institutions themselves declare that they are adopting a policy of "innovation" (generally reduced to technological invention), with funding to match. This encourages organizations to label any change, however small, in tactics and organization as "innovation" (or any other fashionable term), in order to benefit from the available resources. The issue was highlighted, for example, when Donald Rumsfeld adopted the Transformation policy (2001–2004), which encouraged Pentagon officials to "sprinkle *Transformation*" over the initiatives they wished to see funded, thereby increasing competition for resources.[25]

Some authors also distinguish between innovation and adaptation in terms of temporality: innovation is a peacetime phenomenon, while adaptation is a wartime phenomenon. Williamson Murray argues:

In peacetime, time poses few significant challenges to the innovator: he may lack significant resources, but he has time to form, test and evaluate his ideas and perceptions. The opposite is true in war. There, those involved in combat usually possess a plethora of resources, but time is not one of them; those pursuing serious changes in doctrine, technology, or tactics in the midst of a conflict have only a brief opportunity to adapt. Adding to their difficulties is the fact that as their organization adapts, so, too, will the enemy.[26]

However, this distinction based on a temporal criterion can be criticized. Is the use of atomic weapons, developed at the height of the Second World War, really just an "adaptation"? Is every change of tactic or doctrine in peacetime an innovation? Clearly, these terms should refer to different degrees of intensity of change, and not to the time period during which the change takes place. But the question then arises of how to delimit these degrees, with no consensual definition to date in the literature. Moreover, although the temporal criterion may not necessarily help establish a clear difference between innovation and adaptation, it would be absurd to consider the contexts of war or peace as irrelevant, and dismiss this dimension out of hand.[27] After all, evidence abounds of the consequences for the armed forces of prolonged periods of peace. For example, Jim Storr aptly notes that "unfortunately, authoritarians tend to thrive in highly organized hierarchies in the steady state (such as armies in peacetime). Authoritarians tend to be bullies, which makes life unpleasant for their subordinates. The biggest problem, however, is that they are not good commanders, and may well fail catastrophically in war."[28] Andrew Gordon similarly claims that a long period of peace, "the long lee of Trafalgar," shaped the Royal Navy's organizational culture and contributed to its relative failure during the Battle of Jutland.[29] Therefore, this book aims to precisely define terms and concepts that currently denote either temporalities or different degrees of military change, reconciling these two dimensions.

Another term widely used in the literature, "military revolution," is also the subject of competing definitions. Without going back over the historiography of the notion since the original works of Michael Roberts and Geoffrey Parker,[30] one should note that the term "military revolution" is used in very different ways (and to qualify phenomena of different natures) depending on the authors and contexts. Moreover, the term "revolution" refers to very different timelines, depending on the authors: some revolutions can take place over decades, perhaps centuries. But this creates conceptual confusion which can be used to promote specific policies: "if a revolution can take decades, and we never quite know where we are on the revolutionary grade or curve, then there is always reason to promise more and better tech return in the next investment cycle."[31] Michel Fortmann distinguishes between "military revolutions," "revolutions in military affairs" and "techno-military revolutions." Military revolutions are profound transformations affecting states, societies and their ways of waging war. Revolutions in military affairs (RMAs) are changes in techniques, doctrines and ways of waging war that specifically affect the conduct of operations. A military revolution may comprise several RMAs. Finally, the military-technical revolution (MTR) "refers to a one-off phenomenon, symbolized by the impact of an innovation on the art of war."[32] This MTR can be technological, tactical or organizational, and the combination of MTR contributes to the emergence of an RMA. As we can see, Fortmann uses the terms MTRs and "innovation" interchangeably, but what he defines as RMAs are also characterized by other authors as "innovations." These few examples illustrate the need to clarify the terminology used in the field.

The third difficulty stems from a form of "positive bias" in the literature. In fact, the majority of works study reforms that have been partially or totally successful, in the sense that a change leads to an improvement in the effectiveness of the armed forces. This problem is reinforced by the positive connotation of the term "innovation," which is very present in the literature itself. Yet failures are just as important to study as successes, if the aim is to determine the conditions enabling military change. There are also cases where military change has been successful (in the sense of being effectively implemented) but damaging to operational effectiveness.[33] One of this book's aims is to minimize this "positive bias" in the literature.

The remainder of this introduction will therefore define the general framework for the analysis in this book, and introduce a conceptual model for thinking about and analyzing military change, which will serve as the basis for the subsequent chapters.

The framework: what theory of military change?

Before embarking on the study of military change proper, we need to define the ambitions of this book and clarify its scope and therefore its limits. Firstly, the question arises of the need for a specific understanding of change in *military* organizations. After all, the sociology of organizations has produced a wealth of work on change management, often popularized for the benefit of managers and taught in business schools,[34] and one might think that we already have a range of directly applicable conceptual and methodological tools at our disposal. Theoretically, this book subscribes to the general proposition that organizational change occurs when there is a reorganization of three types of structures: cognitive structures, institutional structures and relational structures.[35] Cognitive structures denote the various reasons guiding an individual's behavior and action:[36] previous socialization and habitus, cognitive frames, social capital, etc. Institutional structures denote the set of rules and regulations which incentivize specific behaviors while discouraging others. These can be legal frameworks, hierarchical regulations, codes of conduct, etc. Finally, relational structures denote "partially organized" social orders, which are related not only by network effects but also by informal relations of hierarchy and competition.[37] Relational structures fundamentally capture power relations that are not mediated by institutional structures. This distinction is particularly relevant for security studies, where power often has effects outside an international institutional framework.[38]

These three structures often interact. Institutional and relational structures shape cognitive structures. Cognitive structures shape the perception of the relational structures, but also the perception that the actors have of the resources at their disposal to initiate change. Institutional structures shape relational structures in the sense that they constitute legitimate modes of power, while cognitive and relational structures also shape institutional structures in return. Hence, the general theoretical proposition is that institutional stability and change is better understood through empirical analysis of the congruence or divergence between institutional, relational and cognitive structures.[39]

Within that broad theoretical proposition, and without denying the utility of organization studies to military studies,[40] I would nevertheless argue that the armed forces require a specific approach in order to fully grasp their change dynamics, for four cumulative reasons.

The first is that military organizations are fundamentally guided by the political context in which they operate. Of course, private companies operate within a legal and regulatory context defined by a political context, but they have the freedom to determine their broad strategic objectives (e.g. to invest in such and such an international market, or to specialize in such and such a product). Military organizations, on the other hand, have no control over the definition of their own missions and objectives, which are a matter of political choice. From this point of view, military organizations are similar to other state bureaucracies, but with one major difference: they are custodians of the means to use force, without defining the conditions of use. This is what Peter Feaver calls the central problem of civil–military relations: "the institution created to protect the political community is entrusted with the means that can destroy this political community."[41] This paradox of civil–military relations, linked to the very nature of the armed forces as organizations dedicated to the use of collective violence for political ends, marks a major difference in the way they operate from companies and other public bodies.

The second reason, linked to the first, is that armed forces can have several simultaneous missions, which do not necessarily fall within the scope of military-strategic rationality alone. We can easily deduce the main objectives of a private company: to maximize profit in order to remunerate investors, and to ensure business continuity (e.g. through investment in research and development of new products). This fundamental objective gives rise to a series of strategic decisions, both good and bad, which can be studied systematically. A theory of military change would be easier to establish if the sole objective of the armed forces was to maximize their operational effectiveness in order to defend the state they serve. General Lucien Poirier may well consider that "the purpose of military systems is, and always has been, to be capable of actually producing, or threatening to produce, effects of physical violence in several forms: effects of weakness and death, incapacitating and lethal, applied to living beings; effects of neutralization and destruction affecting natural resources, material goods, production apparatus and various branches of activity, territorial infrastructures and, of course, adversary military systems."[42] In reality and in practice, this objective is only one of many pursued by military organizations, and not necessarily the main one.[43] Depending on the case, the armed forces can also serve as a tool for internal repression, for combating terrorism, for assisting civil security or the police, for managing the country's economic activities, for taking in and training unemployed young people, for supporting defense industries, and so forth.[44] For example, one of the missions of the Soviet armed forces was to participate in agricultural work in order to support this sector, while in several Southeast Asian countries the armed forces have set up a "khaki capitalism" which serves more or less legally to ensure their self-financing, making them de facto key economic players.[45] In several Latin American countries, or in Türkiye, the armed forces have long defined one of their fundamental missions as ensuring the country's political stability.

Thus, change in the armed forces is not linked to a single fundamental objective, but to a multiplicity of sometimes contradictory injunctions, and this justifies a specific conceptual approach.

Third, the armed forces must navigate a major tension between the requirements of cohesion and the requirements of flexibility. Fundamentally, the armed forces are organizations that have become expert at creating a form of mandatory solidarity, or cohesion, to a degree unknown to civilian organizations. Creating cohesion is a requirement of military effectiveness, since cohesion is an important contributing factor to the will to fight of individual soldiers, as confirmed by several decades of study in military sociology.[46] The broad term "cohesion" is usually refined by establishing a distinction between task cohesion and social cohesion. *Task cohesion* is the shared commitment among members to achieving a goal that requires the collective efforts of the group. A group with high task cohesion is composed of members who share a common goal and who are motivated to coordinate their efforts as a team to achieve that goal. *Social cohesion* is the extent to which group members like each other, prefer to spend their social time together, enjoy each other's company, and feel emotionally close to one another.[47] The term "cohesion" is usually reserved to a relationship at the level of a primary group, which is small enough so that members can personally know each other: a crew, a squad, a platoon, etc. At the level of higher units (battalion and above), where individual members cannot realistically all know each other individually but still need to work together to achieve a common objective, the term *esprit de corps* is usually employed. Fundamentally, *esprit de corps* is the counterpart of cohesion at the level of the organization rather than at the level of the primary unit.

Both cohesion and *esprit de corps* have positive effects on individuals and are associated with better military performance. Firstly, they contribute to group pride and to a sense of collective identity: group members often describe feelings of pride and identification with their group as an entity, and this can occur even though they are unacquainted with many, if not most, of the other group members. Moreover, cohesion and *esprit de corps* also contribute to morale, understood as the enthusiasm and persistence with which a member engages in the prescribed activities of the group. Finally, they both contribute to fostering trust among members of military units. All these dimensions are important for military effectiveness, since combat requires individuals to prioritize the group's success before their own individual needs (including survival): military organizations the world over value the notion of "ultimate sacrifice," which is a celebration of putting the group's needs before one's own. In short, cohesion and *esprit de corps* are positively associated with military performance, and the armed forces have strong reasons for fostering such social bonds: it is much more effective to have soldiers willing to fight instead of having to coerce them (as has regularly happened in history).

Armed forces have three core instruments at their disposal to achieve cohesion and *esprit de corps*: collective activities (in particular, collective effort), discipline and traditions.

- *Collective activities* include military fundamentals such as training and physical reinforcement. Collective effort is a classic mechanism of human bonding, and military organizations have become very adept at using this to their advantage, for example by designing obstacles at training ranges that can only be overcome through group cooperation. Moreover, training is an important mechanism leading to task cohesion: in contemporary professional armed forces, military training is an important component of the establishment of proficiency and increased mastery of the profession of arms, from which individuals derive identity and self-esteem.[48] There is thus a virtuous circle linking task cohesion and professionalism, the two being mutually reinforcing. But other forms of collective activities also contribute to social cohesion: for example, bonding over drinks or shared meals.
- *Discipline* has two functions. In times of peace, it ensures order within the military system. It is thus an important element of civil–military relations, because it guarantees to the civilian authorities and to the population at large that those who hold military force live up to high standards of behavior and responsibility. In times of war, discipline aims at guaranteeing the obedience which is required by the realities of combat. In short, discipline is a tool of regulation and a tool of effectiveness, and it can be understood as the state of order and obedience among personnel in a military organization. It is characterized by soldiers' prompt and willing responsiveness to orders and understanding compliance with regulation. As George Washington wrote, "Discipline is the soul of an army. It makes small numbers formidable, procures success to the weak, and esteem to all."[49] Hence, discipline has meaning only when it aims at reinforcing the two objectives of regulation and effectiveness:

in order to achieve its objective, it needs to be accepted as legitimate.

- *Traditions* are, for military organizations, collective rites which ensure cohesion and *esprit de corps.* Usually, military units establish their lineage and present themselves as the heirs of glorious predecessors. Flags, symbols, ceremonies, songs and so on are different ways to establish such traditions, and help foster a sense of collective belonging, which generates pride, self-esteem and solidarity among individual members of the group.

Cohesion and *esprit de corps* are critical components of military effectiveness, but they nevertheless have a "dark side."[50] The first problem is that cohesion and *esprit de corps*, pushed to their limits, can easily become synonymous with homogeneity. However, cohesion should never be achieved at the expense of people who do not conform to the "traditional" perception of the armed forces. There is a moral reason for this (in a liberal society, there should be an equality of opportunities), but there are also three very practical justifications as well. Firstly, a very well-established finding of social psychology is that groups composed of diverse profiles make better decisions, because the diversity of background and experiences is a safeguard against "groupthink."[51] Secondly, a diversity of profiles can bring various skills that the organization may need. In the armed forces, diverse profiles can provide the language skills, technical or cultural expertise, and gender perspectives that may be required to achieve various missions (such as intelligence collection or analysis, human terrain assessment or civil–military cooperation). Thirdly, there is now ample evidence that armed forces that discriminate among their members (either by reproducing dominant societal prejudices about race and gender or by establishing their own discriminatory culture) undermine trust, fuel grievances, and lead victimized soldiers to subvert military authorities once war begins. The greater an army's inequality, the higher its rates of desertion, side-switching, casualties, and use of coercion to force soldiers to fight.[52]

The second problem is that the search for cohesion and *esprit de corps* can sometimes come at the expense of the flexibility required to confront the reality of combat operations and a changing strategic environment. Cohesion helps predict collective behavior, and is important for actual warfighting, but the armed forces have to manage the fundamental tension between cohesion and flexibility.

Finally, the fourth specificity of armed forces is the rarity and importance of the event for which they are preparing: major war. Armed conflicts occur regularly within the international system, but major wars remain rare. Major wars have three characteristics: "all the great powers in a system are involved; the wars are all-out conflicts fought at the highest level of intensity (i.e. full military mobilization); and they contain a strong possibility that one or more of the contending great powers could be eliminated as sovereign states."[53] It is beyond the scope of this book to examine the reasons for the rarity of such events,[54] but the central idea is that, although military operations may take place regularly, major war is a wholly exceptional event. And yet, even if the risk is statistically low, given the stakes of such a conflict (the possible disappearance of a state), most military organizations are tasked with preparing for it, at least partly. As a result, most of the world's military personnel spend their entire careers training for an event they will never experience. Admittedly, some armed forces conduct military operations of varying intensity and therefore experience "war," but these operations are not the sole and exclusive objective of these organizations, which continue to dedicate time and resources to preparing for a major conflict that is extremely unlikely but must nonetheless be considered. Yet, by definition, it is extremely difficult to prepare properly for an event so rare that the number of occurrences is far too limited (and the cases themselves often too old) to draw any relevant lessons. As the military historian Michael Howard wrote in a classic text: "It is as if a surgeon had to practice throughout his life on dummies for one real operation; or a barrister appeared only once or twice in court toward the close of his career; or a professional swimmer had to spend his life practicing on dry land for an Olympic championship on which the fortunes of his entire nation depended."[55] This is a major difference from a private company, which can obtain almost immediate feedback on the commercial success of a product, enabling it to adjust the price or the product itself. In contrast, the armed forces can basically only speculate on the shape of a possible major conflict, and do not have frequent and rapid feedback on the quality of their doctrine and equipment.

This problem is reinforced by the principle of deterrence, which consists in preventing an adversary from doing harm by making the cost of their actions too high in advance (deterrence by denial) or by threatening him with unacceptable damage in the event of an attack (deterrence by punishment). One of the criteria for deterrence to work is that the armed forces must be credible: deterrence is primarily a psychological phenomenon that involves convincing the adversary of the futility of their actions. However, if deterrence works, armed forces by definition have no way of knowing their "real" effectiveness, since they don't have to fight. It is when conflicts break out that the sometimes brutal adjustments between an army's reputation and its actual performance take place, and history is full of armies perceived as formidable but defeated or encountering major difficulties on the battlefield. In this sense, as Howard points out, the complexity of managing and commanding an organization as complex as the armed forces can lead commanders to neglect the ultimate objective of preparation: war itself. Consequently,

> there has often been a high proportion of failures among senior commanders at the beginning of any war. These unfortunate men may either take too long to adjust themselves to reality, through a lack of hard preliminary thinking about what war would really be like, or they may have had their minds so far shaped by a lifetime of pure administration that they have ceased for all practical purposes to be soldiers.[56]

The specificity of the armed forces, then, is that they have to prepare for a rare event, and they cannot have any real feedback on their preparation until it is too late.

Taken together, these four reasons justify devoting special effort to establishing a theory of military change.

Theory and concepts

First of all, we need to define what we understand by a "theory of military change." It is not a theory in the positivist sense of the term, which would attempt to identify immutable causal factors which, at all times and in all places, inevitably lead to a pre-identified result. Such a parsimonious approach is of limited use in understanding social phenomena. On the contrary, this is a theory in the Clausewitzian sense, i.e. an intellectual discipline aimed at clarifying observed phenomena: in this approach, the role of theory is not to dictate, but to simplify, explain and illuminate. As Clausewitz wrote, "The primary purpose of any theory is to clarify concepts and ideas that have become, as it were, confused and entangled. Not until terms and concepts have been defined can one hope to make any progress in examining the question clearly and simply."[57]

The aim here is to establish a conceptual framework to help account for the multiple political, strategic and social dynamics that intertwine in the process of military change. Concepts are the building blocks needed to construct theories, and serve to describe, by simplifying them, a class of social events. They are a heuristic tool, not an exact representation of empirical reality, but are used to organize and group together fundamentally similar events or social dynamics. The aim is to strike a balance between, on the one hand, the empirical precision found in historical and sociological studies (at the expense of generalizing the mechanisms observed) and, on the other, a parsimonious theory that is too disconnected from the complexity, and therefore reality, of the social world. I define a conceptual framework as "as a network, or 'a plane,' of interlinked concepts that together provide a comprehensive understanding of a phenomenon or phenomena."[58] The advantages of developing a conceptual framework, rather than theorizing the relationship between pre-identified variables, are its flexibility, its capacity for modification, and its emphasis on understanding (in the German sense of *verstehen*) rather than prediction.

In political science, concept analysis is generally associated with Giovanni Sartori,[59] whose work has given rise to considerable debate but is an essential contribution to the so-called scientific approach to concept construction adopted here.⁶⁰ The concept-building approach is most relevant when a large number of events are grouped together and compared, enabling the contours of the concept to be better defined. As such, most of the examples of military change given in this book are drawn from widely cited secondary sources, although it also draws on original empirical data collected as part of the Transforming Armed Forces in the Twenty-First Century project.⁶¹ While most examples come from so-called Western countries, owing to their over-representation in scientific literature, examples from other cultural contexts are given as often as possible to show that the mechanisms studied in this book are generalizable. The examples should be taken as illustrations of a class of comparable events, and not as in-depth case studies carried out according to a precise methodology (such as process-tracing): what the analysis loses in empirical depth, it gains in amplitude and, therefore, in increasing generality. The main contribution of this book is therefore to propose conceptual categories and clarify their interactions, in order to provide researchers and practitioners alike with useful intellectual tools when studying the transformation trajectory of contemporary armed forces. However, it cannot *predict* the trajectory of change in a specific military organization: this should be left to a specific empirical analysis, guided by the framework established here.

This concept-building process is rooted in a philosophical approach based on critical realism. This approach, associated with the work of Roy Bhaskar, seeks to avoid the pitfalls of subjectivism and objectivism.⁶² Critical realism considers that an external world exists objectively, independent of people's perceptions, language and imagination. This external world is said to be "real." However, our experience of the world is filtered through our experiences and perceptions, and human beings can only have access to a part of this real world: the world to which humans have access is said to be "observable." In this context, unobservable but nonetheless real factors have observable effects. For critical realists, the "real" world is not limited to material elements. Many phenomena have no material existence but are nonetheless real and have observable effects: Santa Claus is not a material entity (a priori), but he is nonetheless "real" in the sense that what is said about him has observable effects on children's behavior. In other words, like positivists, critical realists consider that the world exists outside the perceptions of the actors alone, and can be known scientifically. However, unlike positivists, critical realists do not reduce the world to observable and measurable "facts" alone, but consider that understanding the social context and perceptions is essential for analyzing social facts correctly. From this point of view, critical realists are close to subjectivists, but, unlike the latter, they do not reduce the external world to its discursive construction.[63] In other words, critical realism is realist in ontology (by acknowledging the existence of an external world) and constructivist in epistemology (knowledge is a social construct that is not independent of its producers).

Certain key concepts are associated with this philosophical approach. Firstly, reality is understood as an open system, meaning that the entities interacting to cause the observed event cannot be analyzed outside their environment. Unlike the closed system of a laboratory, which isolates the elements of experience, an open system (such as a society or organization) comprises numerous complex interactions and feedback loops that make it impossible to determine and therefore predict its future.[64]

In this open system, *entities* interact to produce social reality. An entity is something that makes a difference by itself rather than by the sum of its constituent parts: molecules, individuals or organizations can be considered as entities, depending on the level of analysis. An entity can be material (such as water, which has specific properties different from those of hydrogen or oxygen atoms taken separately) or immaterial (such as the legal framework defining the use of armed force): entities are therefore "real" in different ways. A human society is thus full of entities that are not necessarily materially real but have very concrete effects on the behavior of individuals. Water, an organization or a theocratic society can all be considered entities, depending on the level of analysis required to explain the observed phenomenon.

Entities have *powers*. Water is a molecule with the power to wet, organizations have the power to employ or fire individuals. This notion of power is important because "change often occurs when the powers of one entity interact with those of another: water can be heated by fire, teams can elect a leader, and organisations can be bought out by other organisations [...]. The social world is full of powers, whose implementation is often delayed by other powers within the open system in which they are found."[65]

Finally, powers require a *mechanism* to be implemented. The Chinese state's power to spy on its citizens requires mechanisms, including the existence of specific technologies and the obedience of the institutions responsible for this surveillance. Interactions between different entities are thus regulated by the mechanisms for implementing the powers at their disposal: within an organization, employers have the power to dismiss employees through the mechanism of labor law. However, these mechanisms are not necessarily used because of countervailing powers such as labor unions, the reality of the labor market, or the fact that employees tend to fulfill employers' expectations.

Thus, for critical realists, "reality" is made up of both material elements observable by the human senses and immaterial elements (such as mechanisms).

Conceptualizing military change therefore means establishing a framework linking entities, their powers and the mechanisms by which these powers are implemented. It also means defining mechanisms that are sufficiently general to be applicable to the greatest number of cases, and identifying the relevant entities. I have chosen to group entities into what we call *entity configurations*, which are possible aggregations of particular entities, and which condition the expression of mechanisms. The term "configuration" is inspired by the sociology of Norbert Elias, who adopts a sporting metaphor by defining a configuration as "the ever-changing field that the players form; it includes not only their intellect but also their whole person, actions, and reciprocal relations."[66] However, whereas Elias applies his concept to individuals, in order to grasp their reciprocal dependence in the constitution of society, I am here studying entities such as those defined above. In some contexts, therefore, these may be individuals, but not exclusively: the entities invoked in this work may be states, bureaucratic bodies, technological artifacts, institutions and so forth.

Five configurations of entities have been identified to form the chapters of this book: the international system, technology, civil–military relations, military organization and war. In each chapter, the entities that make up these configurations are described. In addition, four general mechanisms have been identified: circumvention, learning, diffusion and constraint, which are implemented differently depending on the configuration. These mechanisms are described below.

A large literature review of the field of organizational change has argued that there are fundamentally two approaches dominating the literature: the first looks primarily at the structural conditions and the processes that make change more or less likely, while the second looks at the role of specific actors (individuals or collective) in initiating change (institutional entrepreneurs, cause entrepreneurs, brokers, etc.).[67] Of course, the two approaches are not mutually exclusive, but researchers tend to favor one over the other. This book leans toward the first approach, namely the structural conditions enabling or preventing change. We will meet specific actors exerting agency, but the focus is primarily on the structural conditions enabling those actors to initiate or resist change.

The object of study: the armed forces

Secondly, the object of study must be precisely defined. In this book, I will be focusing on national armed forces, i.e. institutions specialized in the use of violence, whose members constitute a profession, in the sociological sense of the term.[68] Without going into the theoretical debates that have animated sociologists on the definition of a profession, we can derive from the literature a few major characteristics that allow us to define its contours. Thus, a profession requires:

- the existence of a specific body of theoretical and practical knowledge mastered by its members (e.g. operational planning in the case of the armed forces);
- a self-regulatory mechanism that defines the boundaries between members and non-members of the profession

(e.g. through specific recruitment mechanisms or exclusion mechanisms in the event of breach of a professional code);
- control over the main elements of training for entry into the profession;
- *esprit de corps*;
- the possibility of a full career in the profession;
- a specific bureaucracy allowing career progression based on merit.

The military sociologist Samuel Huntington goes even further in his definition of the military profession, associating it with a particular ethic and voluntary submission to political power.[69] Thus, for him, "by virtue of his mission, the professional soldier is pessimistic, anti-individualistic, attached to the lessons of history and to international power relations, nationalistic, and in favor of a systematic increase in military resources [...]. These characteristics do not necessarily make them the best judges of the threats facing a society: their sense of social responsibility often leads them to be alarmist and to overestimate these threats."[70]

Without necessarily going as far as Huntington's psychological portrait of the typical soldier, we can nevertheless define more precisely the object of study of this book by limiting it to national armed forces displaying the recruitment and management characteristics of a profession as outlined above. This limitation refers to the concept of "military specificity," which has been used in military sociology.[71] It is said that, when Marshal Augereau uttered the word *péquin* (slang for "civilian") to Talleyrand, the latter asked what *péquin* meant, to which the Marshal replied: "We military men call everything that is not military '*péquin*.'" "And we," continued Talleyrand, "call everything military that is not civil."[72]

Joke aside, the identification of specific characteristics distinguishing the "military" from the "civil" is an issue in itself. Military specificity, which should not be confused with a "military identity," can be defined as "the fact of having to fight collectively and violently in the name of the sovereign community, if ordered to do so,"[73] thereby distinguishing the armed forces from other organizations. It should be noted that military specificity should not be confused with mission: it goes without saying that the armed forces have many activities other than simply waging war, which they may share with other organizations (e.g. with civil relief in supporting populations after natural disasters).[74] However, the armed forces are the only organizations charged with defending the sovereignty of a political community through the use or threat of collective and organized violence.

This definition of military specificity has two consequences: on the one hand, a functional specialization of the armed forces and, on the other, a socio-political specificity of their members.

In order to achieve their objective of defending a political community, military organizations have developed certain characteristics, notably to ensure that individuals obey the orders given to them. These organizations generally combine a strong hierarchy, a high degree of centralization of decision-making and mandatory solidarity (the primacy of the collective over the individual). The first two points can be found to varying degrees in other civilian organizations, but the last point is specific to the armed forces because of its compulsory dimension. Similarly, a number of values (honor, courage, discipline, loyalty, etc.) are not as such specifically military, but within the armed forces they form a coherent system that is constantly celebrated and staged through practices such as songs, ceremonies, transmission rites or places of remembrance like war memorials.[75]

Military sociologists debate the degree of specificity of military values. Some, like Huntington, consider them to be unique to the profession and universal, to be found in all military organizations worldwide.[76] Others, like Morris Janowitz, believe that these values are specific to the profession but are influenced by the socio-political context of the societies in which the armed forces operate.[77] Finally, authors such as Charles Moskos and John Williams believe, on the contrary, that "military values" only exist within the spectrum allowed by the dominant values of societies, of which they constitute a subset destined to evolve in line with domestic transformations.[78] From this point of view, practitioners themselves have different visions. The former French Chief of Staff of the Armed Forces between 2017 and 2021, General François Lecointre, insisted on the need to preserve "military singularity," centered on the act of killing, thus implying ethical reflection and close association with political decisions.[79] However, his Danish counterpart was able to declare in 2020 that "military values are the values of Danish society transposed to a military framework."[80] If the French general was "Huntingtonian," his Danish counterpart was "Moskossian." The difference in perspective does not stem from a different relationship to the use of force, since Denmark has been an interventionist country since the end of the Cold War, and even had the highest ratio of combat casualties to population of all the countries that took part in the military intervention in Afghanistan (2001–2014).[81] However, a longitudinal study of the evolution of values in the Danish officer corps over 300 years was able to show empirically that, while certain professional values were conditioned by social evolution, the notions of discipline and sacrifice were constant over time, which would correspond to Janowitz's vision.[82] It seems quite plausible that similar results could be observed in other armed forces. Thus, the functional specialization of the armed forces is reflected in a set of traits that distinguish armies from other organizations, notably the presence of a core of values specific to the profession.

Military specificity also translates into a form of socio-political particularism. By virtue of their status, military personnel can come to create a form of "society,"[83] i.e. a group sharing common values and practices (sometimes including a rejection of civilian society). In this sense, legal status has little to do with whether or not one belongs to this society: a former soldier who has returned to civilian life can still be part of military society if they continue to share its values and practices. Conversely, not all ex-military personnel will continue to be part of "military society" if they break with common values and practices. From this point of view, it is neither difficult nor surprising to see the emergence of "military societies" in many countries,[84] which justifies the importance of the field of study of civil–military relations,[85] since it involves organizing relations between holders of political legitimacy and holders of armed force. This socio-political specificity varies from country to country and from situation to situation. For example, the contemporary German armed forces tend to erase the specificity of their soldiers, speaking instead of "citizens in uniform," to the extent that German society would most likely perceive a soldier as "a global social worker, providing worldwide aid as savior, mediator and protector."[86] In other countries, the armed forces may have statuses that are essentially distinct from civilians (e.g. military personnel do not have the right to vote in Colombia), or enjoy special lifestyles, such as military-only housing and shops in Greece, in this way establishing de facto a strict separation from civilian society.

In extreme cases, military society can perceive itself to be above the laws of the land. Between the end of the 1920s and the beginning of the 1930s, the Imperial Japanese Army took several international initiatives involving violence without consulting the civilian authorities, de facto conducting its own policy (such as the assassination of Zhang Zuolin and the Manchurian "incidents" of 1928–1929). These initiatives stemmed from a sense of military superiority over civilians:

> The army had placed its prestige above the law, justifying a cover-up in the name of national security. Generals had condoned a criminal conspiracy and assassination, tried to conceal evidence, and threatened to bring down the cabinet if the army did not get its way. A volatile mixture of the prerogative of field command, the decade-long emphasis on bold initiative and independent action, and an open contempt for the civilian cabinets and politicians became a familiar pattern in the army's continuing illegal attempts to achieve its domestic and international ends.[87]

This shows that military organizations have specific sociological characteristics that distinguish them from other organizations that use violence, such as police forces.

The decision to focus on state military organizations in this book excludes de facto the study of military change in political groupings such as alliances and coalitions,[88] in rebel groups,[89] or in terrorist groups.[90] However, it can happen that rebel groups become the main foundation of a country's armed forces: if they come to organize themselves according to the criteria already mentioned and constitute a profession, they fall within the scope of the analysis. Similarly, changes in autonomous intelligence services (such as

France's Direction Générale de la Sécurité Extérieure (DGSE) or the CIA in the US), which are institutions that work with the armed forces but are not subordinate to them, will not be addressed in this book.[91] On the other hand, military intelligence services integrated into the armed forces' chain of command fall within the above-mentioned criteria, since they perform one of the functions required by military institutions to accomplish their missions. By the same token, changes in defense industries do not fall within the scope of this study. Lastly, this book will not examine the political, economic, institutional and societal upheavals brought about by war, an area which is already the subject of a voluminous literature.[92]

The period: since 1871

My third delimitation is this: the object of study is chronologically limited to a period stretching from 1871 to the present day, i.e. since the end of the Franco-Prussian War. There are two reasons for this choice. The first is the gradual consolidation of the military profession (in the sociological sense of the term) over the course of the nineteenth century. Indeed, " the most general trend of the period was the systematic application of know-how, both organizational and technological, to problems of military effectiveness."[93] While the eighteenth century, under the impetus of the "military enlightenment," saw an attempt to systematically apply scientific knowledge (particularly mathematical and mechanical) to the military art,[94] it was during the nineteenth century that the military profession really emerged. Of course, the military *function* has existed for thousands of years, and was practiced by very different sections of the population in different societies (sometimes leading to special, often hereditary social statuses for warriors, such as Western chivalry or Japanese samurai), but the military *profession* (including specific knowledge, dedicated training, regulatory codification, *esprit de corps* and potential career) is more recent.

Huntington associates the emerging professionalization and bureaucratization of the armed forces with the reforms introduced by Gneisenau and Scharnhorst to the Prussian Army in the wake of their defeat by Napoleonic France in 1806.[95] Thus, in 1808, a law opened up the officer corps to all classes of the population (according to their level of education), putting an end to the Junkers' monopoly, while promotions were henceforth linked to a system of examination and tests of general and military culture. In 1809, the King of Prussia created a Ministry of War to regularize and systematize decisions that had hitherto been his prerogative, thus establishing a bureaucracy specialized in military matters. Finally, Scharnhorst profoundly transformed military education, persuading the King in 1810 to open several new initial officer schools (*Fähnrichs-Kriegsschulen*), but above all to create a war school for officers, the Offiziers-Kriegsschule, where Clausewitz taught and which became the prestigious War Academy (Kriegsakademie). At the same time, Prussia founded the University of Berlin in 1809 as part of a general overhaul of higher education for Prussia's elite, both civilian and military. The Kriegsakademie was conceived from the outset as an elite institution: the initial plan was to reserve it for fifty officers, but the enthusiasm aroused by the competition for entry led to this number being raised to eighty-five. However, not a single officer from the cavalry (the most socially prestigious corps in the Prussian Army) passed the entrance examination. For Scharnhorst, this was proof of their profound need for education, and he decided to admit some of them to the school, whose curriculum combined "civilian" disciplines (physics, geography, history, French, etc.) with "military" disciplines (tactics and strategy).

This transformation of the officer's career path was widely emulated, and the nineteenth century saw the massive development of institutions of professional military education (PME) at the initial level (schools for young officers) and intermediate level (mid-career war colleges). In France, the École Spéciale Militaire de Saint-Cyr, for preparing young army officers, was founded in 1802, the École Navale in 1830, and the École Supérieure de Guerre (equivalent to the Kriegsakademie) came into being in 1873, following the debacle of the Franco-Prussian War. In the US, as initial officer training schools, West Point was founded in 1802, the Virginia Military Institute (equivalent to West Point, recruiting mainly from the southern states) in 1839, and the Annapolis Naval Academy in 1845. As second-level institutions, the Naval War College was created in 1884 and the US Army War College in 1901. This development was by no means limited to Europe, and spread by the dispatch of European instructors to Russia, the Ottoman Empire and Egypt in the first half of the nineteenth century, with the same process taking place in Latin America and Japan in the second half of the century. The third level of PME, catering for senior officers (corresponding to the Centre des Hautes Études Militaires in France, the Royal College of Defence Studies in the UK or the Command and General Staff College in the US) emerged in the twentieth century, as the growing complexity of security issues revealed a need to understand the sources of national power beyond the mere conduct of operations.[96]

Over the course of the nineteenth century, this expansion of PME institutions contributed to the transformation of the officer's function from a craft learned on the job and linked to specific social conditions, to a regulated profession with a codified base of professional knowledge. By 1865, 50% of Prussian officers were nobles, with the figure rising to 80% for colonels and generals. By 1913, the proportions had fallen to 30% nobles and 52% for colonels and generals.[97] Commoners accounted for 3% of Austrian generals in 1848, 20% in 1866 and 58% in 1878, while in Russia the proportion of nobles among officers fell from 90% to 50% between 1856 and 1913.[98] By the 1870s, the professionalization of the armed forces had taken place, or was well underway, in most of the great and middle powers of the international system (which set the standard for legitimate models to be imitated).

The second reason for the choice of chronological boundaries is the transformation in the character of warfare, which began in the 1870s. A good way to visualize this evolution is to compare the experience of an American infantryman in the War of Independence (1775–1783), the American Civil War (1861–1865) and the Second World War (1941–1945).[99] In the first two conflicts mentioned, the experience was very similar: infantry marched in line, with soldiers deployed shoulder to shoulder in a practice descended directly from Greek phalanxes. These linear formations made it possible to concentrate the fire of the soldiers' muskets, partially compensating for their lack of range and precision, and facilitating command of the troops by officers through a whole series of signals: banners, colorful uniforms, shouted orders, etc. The difference in experience lay more in the degree of intensity (the Civil War mobilized greater volumes of troops and fire) than in the nature of tactical and operational acts.

The experience of the American soldier in the Second World War was obviously radically different from that of his ancestors. The "storms of steel" now present on the battlefield, owing to the volume of fire available, completely changed the tactics of infantrymen, who now had to spread out over the terrain, camouflage and cover themselves by exploiting the roughness of the battlefield (rocks, trees, etc.), and coordinate their movements with those of their comrades (e.g. by taking advantage of covering fire, which forced opponents to "lower their heads," to move). This development changed command, since officers and non-commissioned officers could no longer directly observe the behavior of soldiers, who themselves no longer benefited from the highly visual instructions of linear tactics: this raised the question of how to force or motivate soldiers to fight, when they could now escape the surveillance of their superiors and of the coercive tactics that had proved their worth for centuries.[100] Moreover, from the infantryman's point of view, the experience of war became much more individual: the battlefield seemed empty without the shoulder contact provided by his comrades in line, and without clear visibility of the adversary, who himself was dispersed and camouflaged. Finally, the time exposed to fire was considerably lengthened. Eighteenth-century battles could last less than an hour. During the American Civil War, battles could last several days (albeit interrupted by night or bad weather), though they were interspersed with long periods of encampment or marching. The Second World War front did not allow for such rest periods, with fighting continuing day and night, so that soldiers were exposed to fire (or at least to the threat of fire) for days or even weeks at a time.

The evolution described here from an infantryman's point of view was the result of a series of technological and social transformations that profoundly altered the character of warfare over the course of the nineteenth century. The first obvious evolution was the increase in the volume of fire on the battlefield and, therefore, in lethality. A Napoleonic infantry regiment of 1,000 men equipped with muskets could fire 1,000 projectiles at an effective distance of around 100 meters twice a minute. A unit of equivalent size charging this regiment with bayonets would have received 2,000 projectiles, or two bullets per man. In 1916, an infantry regiment equipped with a thousand rifles and four machine guns could fire 21,000 projectiles per minute at an effective range of around 900 meters. During an assault, a comparable unit would have received 210,000 projectiles before covering the distance necessary to make contact, i.e. more than 200 bullets per individual.[101] A Second World War GI combat group of 12 men could deliver the same volume of fire in one minute as a full company of 250 men during the American Civil War.[102] This comparison does not, of course, take into account new means of delivering fire, such as artillery (whose effective range increased from around 10 km to 50 km between 1900 and 1980) or ground attack aircraft, not to mention the superior destructiveness of the weapons involved. In addition to the volume of fire delivered, the elongation of distance made possible by advances in weaponry also led to a widening of fronts. At Waterloo in 1815, Wellington's entire army (68,000 men) defended a front line just over 3 km wide. In Normandy in 1944, this was the area that a single infantry regiment (around 2,000 men) was supposed to protect, according to the Wehrmacht doctrine: in practice, a regiment often had to protect a much wider front.[103] The profoundly structuring effect of the volume of fire available on the battlefield was a major evolution in the character of warfare, the effect of which accelerated after 1870. This elongation of distances is summarized in Table 2.

A second development was linked to the technological progress generated by the Industrial Revolution, notably the railways and the telegraph, "the only real progress in the field of communications to occur in a millennium."[104] The rail network made it possible to transport mass armies and organize their logistics. Before the invention of the railway, the size of armies was limited by a fundamental logistical problem: while soldiers could move about on their own, their food and ammunition had to be transported. The obvious solution, forage, meant that the size of armies was limited by the agricultural capacity of the land they crossed.[105] However, the railroads enabled considerable mobilization, completely transforming the morphology of the armies deployed on the

Table 2. Trends in dispersion on the battlefield

	Antiquity	Napoleonic Wars	American Civil War	First World War	Second World War	Yom Kippur War
Surface area occupied per 100,000 men (in km²)	1	20.12	25.75	248	2,750	4,000
Length covered per 100,000 men (in km)	6.67	8.05	8.58	14	48	57
Depth covered per 100,000 men (in km)	0.15	2.50	3	17	57	70
Men per km²	100,000	4,970	3,883	404	36	25

Source: Adapted from Trevor N. Dupuy, *The Evolution of Weapons and Warfare*, Fairfax, Da Capo Press, 1984, p. 312.

battlefield. For example, the largest army Napoleon commanded in 1812 numbered 600,000 men, and was 2.2 times larger than the French army of 1747, suggesting that the revolutionary levée en masse produced more numerous armies but still in the same order of magnitude as the armies of Louis XIV or Louis XV.[106] Napoleon's army at Austerlitz comprised 73,000 men, "only" 10,000 more than that commanded by Marshal d'Estrées some fifty years earlier at the Battle of Hastenbeck (1757), during the Seven Years War. Contrary to Clausewitz's suggestion, therefore, there was no fundamental transformation of the scale of warfare linked to the eruption of nationalism following the French Revolution.[107]

By contrast, the French Army of 1918 was 6.6 times larger than that of 1812. This represented a complete change in the scale of combat and was made possible by the existence of a rail network enabling troops, ammunition and food to be moved.[108] To give an idea of the logistical requirements, the Russian Army fired 87,000 rounds of ammunition of various calibers per month during the Russo-Japanese War (1904–1905), a figure considered considerable at the time. Less than a decade later, the Bulgarian Army fired

254,000 rounds of ammunition per month during the First Balkan War (1912–1913). In 1916, the French Army was firing 4,500,000 rounds of ammunition per month. In addition to the logistical requirements arising from the volume of fire delivered on the battlefield, the soldiers also needed food.

In addition to the logistics made possible by the railway, the telegraph made it possible to command the massive armies described above by providing the ability to transmit and receive orders, even though a totally centralized command system was obviously out of reach. This structural change in scale posed a particular military problem between the end of the nineteenth century and the Second World War, calling into question the "assault–envelopment–pursuit" triad that had formed the core of military art for millennia.[109] One of the great military transformations of the nineteenth century was therefore Prussia's invention, and subsequent dissemination, of the staff system,[110] whose aim was to manage the complexity introduced by the new scales of warfare, culminating in the establishment of the operational art, i.e. "the planning, preparation, synchronization and sustainment of tactics over a sustained period of time, a large geographic expanse, or both."[111] This invention "went decisively beyond the romantic heroism of the Napoleonic period [...]. Prussian officers were no longer principally fighting men and combat leaders but, in keeping with the times, highly trained professionals who practiced the 'art of war' as a science."[112]

Interestingly, the three technological trends (volume of fire, mobility and communications) that had made possible the development of mass armies also led to their decline after the Second World War, as advances in detection (e.g. by satellite) and concentration of fire made it suicidal to concentrate forces that would be quickly identified and destroyed. The attempt to counter these trends with a combination of suppression, cover and camouflage fires (and associated practices such as delegation of responsibility to elementary units, dispersion, joint combat, the need for depth and reserves) resulted in a transnational corpus of ideas on the conduct of interstate warfare, which Stephen Biddle calls the "modern system" and which was consolidated from the end of the nineteenth century and throughout the twentieth century.[113] This "modern system" is not, moreover, limited to land combat: developments in maritime combat during the industrial era, including submarines, torpedo boats, cruisers and finally embarked aviation, can be understood according to the same principles of cover, camouflage, dispersion and joint combat, and contemporary concepts such as "distributed lethality" (developed by the US Navy) are the direct consequences of the constraints imposed on naval combat by the "modern system."[114] A similar dynamic can be found in air combat, particularly from the 1960s onwards, leading to a "hider–finder" dialectic between aircraft and air defenses, where the aim is to detect the adversary without being detected oneself.[115] Since 1870, the military challenges posed by the "modern system" have spread to the land, sea and air. The specificities of military art, in the context of the "modern system" engendered by advances in fire, mobility and communications, are the second justification for the chronological demarcation of this book, as this military context creates different incentives for change from those in previous periods.

In addition to the "modern system," military art was also influenced by the second colonial wave from 1870 onwards. During these military campaigns, Western armed forces experimented with a set of practices whose longevity is remarkable.[116] In 1902, in Nigeria, 3,000 British troops controlled 775,000 km² and 24 million inhabitants, while 13,000 French soldiers were stationed in French West Africa, a region larger than Europe. It's hard not to see the parallels with Operation Barkhane, in which 5,000 French soldiers were deployed to cover the Sahel region between 2014 and 2022.

The second characteristic is the tendency to want to identify and classify local allies according to supposed ethnic characteristics. This led to the establishment of *races guerrières* in France[117] or "martial races" in the UK,[118] a tendency that may have endured in the temptation to "anthropologize" recent military interventions by Western countries,[119] for example by creating the myth of Tuareg[120] or Pashtun[121] "warriors."

Thirdly, colonial wars provided an opportunity to experiment with a range of military practices that were later transferred to Western warfare. For example, concentration camps first appeared during the Cuban War of Independence (1895–1898), when General

INTRODUCTION

Valeriano Weyler y Nicolau (an admirer of General Sherman's scorched-earth campaign in Georgia in 1864) herded a significant proportion of the Cuban population into *campos de concentración*, which led to the deaths of over 100,000 people from malnutrition and ill-treatment. Shortly afterwards, the British employed the same tactics during the Boer War, interning up to 116,000 people. A young journalist by the name of Winston Churchill, shortly after his return from South Africa, advised his American correspondents to employ the same tactic in their own conflict in the Philippines, which they did (and not just because of Churchill).[122] In any case, American troops could draw on a repertoire of brutal tactics developed during the Native American wars and reused during the Imperial Policing operation in the Philippines.[123] For its part, Germany adopted concentration camps during its brutal war against the Herero and Nama (1904–1907), in what is now Namibia.[124] Other practices, such as counterinsurgency tactics and aerial bombardment, were developed in colonized territories and sometimes subsequently reimported to home countries for population control purposes, informing military practices that continue to this day.[125]

Finally, colonial wars gradually contributed to the formation of a kind of transnational corpus of irregular military knowledge on "small wars" or "counterinsurgency," a kind of doctrinal repertoire that is regularly "rediscovered" depending on current operational activities (e.g. at the time of the Vietnam, Afghanistan or Iraq wars), and that informs military practices.[126]

Thus, the combination of the gradual professionalization of military organizations, the emergence of the "modern system," and colonial wars contributed to the creation of a coherent military-strategic context from the end of the nineteenth century onwards, which justifies the choice of 1871 as the first chronological milestone in this study, i.e. the end of the Franco-Prussian War. This choice broadly coincides with that of the military historian John France, who situates the emergence of Western military domination in the second half of the nineteenth century, under the combined effect of nationalism and the Industrial Revolution.[127] It also corresponds to the chronological demarcation made by the economic historian J. Bradford DeLong, who observes a "long twentieth century" marked by a considerable enrichment of the world's population from 1870 onwards, thanks to three factors: successive globalizations, the systematization of industrial research, and the development of the modern corporate model.[128] This chronological boundary thus provides coherence in terms of the international system (marked by Western domination), the military-strategic context, and the underlying economic dynamics (enabling the extraction of the resources needed to finance war). This is not to say that some of the mechanisms and configurations studied here do not apply to other historical periods, and I leave to others the task to apply the framework to other historical cases, but the specificity of the global politico-economic context since 1870 calls for a degree of caution in making comparisons.

Conceptualizing military change

The first challenge is to consider the very notion of military change. The idea of change is necessarily inscribed in a temporality articulating a past and a future for the organization, starting from the present. This temporality is necessarily subjective, and can be the object of conflict on the part of the players: the past is open to all sorts of reinterpretations, while the future is a blank canvas onto which players, depending on their preferences, can project selective interpretations of past experiences. Change is therefore simultaneously a matter of *perception* (for change to take place, it must be experienced as such by the players, according to their understanding of the organization's temporality) and of *potential conflict* (between players with different visions of the desirable temporality). Any organization is always evolving, but the type of change we're interested in is the one that alters actors' perception of the organization's temporality, and is likely to be the subject of interpretative conflict. This approach avoids falling into the double trap of either thinking of change as the sum of cumulative microchanges (ignoring the importance of actors) or attributing it to the visionary genius of a decision-maker (ignoring the importance of context). An intermediate approach is certainly more relevant if we accept that "consequential change comes about, not through myriads of infinitesimal changes, but as streams of related events, not dictated or planned by supreme decision makers, but through contingencies that are partially intended and partially emergent."[129]

As noted earlier, the existing literature on military change is fragmented, conceptually confused and marked by a "positivity bias." To avoid these three pitfalls, and in keeping with a critical realist ontology and epistemology, the following sections define the degrees of military change and the mechanisms that lead to them, before addressing the configurations that make these mechanisms possible, in the chapters that follow. Firstly, however, we need to define the criteria to be observed when studying military change: a military organization, like any organization, is fundamentally a sum of capabilities and skills. For the sake of convenience, these capabilities and skills are grouped here according to four criteria relevant to the functioning of armed forces: we will thus focus on observing changes in doctrines, equipment, structures and practices within military organizations.

Doctrine can be defined as "institutionalised beliefs about what works in war."[130] More precisely, it is "an intellectual construct that formulates the knowledge deemed necessary and sufficient to guide military personnel in their operational action. It prescribes the rules and optimal conditions for their conduct and disseminates them within the institution."[131] Doctrine takes the form of a corpus of texts and practices codifying and regulating the ways in which war is waged, from the smallest tactical level to the strategic, and leading to victory. Functionally, doctrine enables a military organization to save time on the battlefield by providing a shared language and symbols that allow large quantities of information to be rapidly transmitted within the organization, and practices to be unified. Doctrine is thus simultaneously:

- a tool of command (providing unit commanders with the tools and reflexes they need to accomplish their mission);
- a training tool (by enabling relatively common training of different units within an army);
- a tool for change (by indicating which practices to adapt and adopt to become more efficient); and

- a signaling tool (highlighting an organization's priorities).

Obviously, the doctrinal corpus is read and applied to a greater or lesser extent depending on the armed forces, and its size and importance can vary drastically depending on the context: while some armed forces have extensive doctrinal corpuses detailing how to conduct operations (NATO countries, Russia, China, etc.), others have much more succinct corpuses. Moreover, there are different conceptions within the armed forces regarding whether doctrine is a prescriptive or a descriptive tool, and a set of enduring principles or an analysis of future problems.[132] Despite these variations, observing the evolution of these doctrinal corpuses is an important indicator of change in the armed forces, because of the functions they perform in military organizations.

Equipment is an obvious indicator of change: the introduction of new weapons systems is often a structuring element for military organizations. Indeed, new military equipment needs to be accompanied by appropriate training for soldiers or the support required for its implementation and maintenance. The more complex the weapon system, the greater the need for organizational adaptation: the introduction of a new assault rifle (which requires adaptation of training, support and possibly tactics) is far less disruptive for a military organization than the adoption of a complex weapon system. For example, the development of a naval air capability for a navy that does not have one has far-reaching effects on doctrines of employment (a naval air group must be created, with vessels dedicated to protecting the aircraft carrier), on career paths, on training and on logistics within the organization. However, it would be a mistake to focus solely on armaments: the introduction of new technologies seen as civilian (in the sense that they are not weapons), such as radios and computers, is also changing the way military organizations operate, thus altering their effectiveness.

Organizational changes are also important: the creation of independent air forces in the twentieth century was obviously a major transformation, but smaller-scale changes can also have a major impact on the armed forces. The merger, creation or abolition of units, staffs or institutions, for example, affects the way military organizations function. Without falling into the trap of believing that the real functioning of an organization can be summed up in its organizational chart, it is nevertheless important to observe changes in structures.

Finally, organizational practices also matter. In the simplest possible terms, practices can be defined as "configurations of actions that have a certain meaning."[133] These are ways of doing things that are considered to be correct within an organization: they may be "good manners" for completing a mission report or writing an order, but also organizational rituals (ceremonies, traditions) or informal expectations in terms of behavior. But practices also include ways of "waging war," which can diverge more or less drastically from official doctrines, depending on the army and the context: doctrine provides a context, but does not determine behavior.[134] All these practices form the social cement of the organization and constitute the substratum of its doctrines, equipment and structures. This is

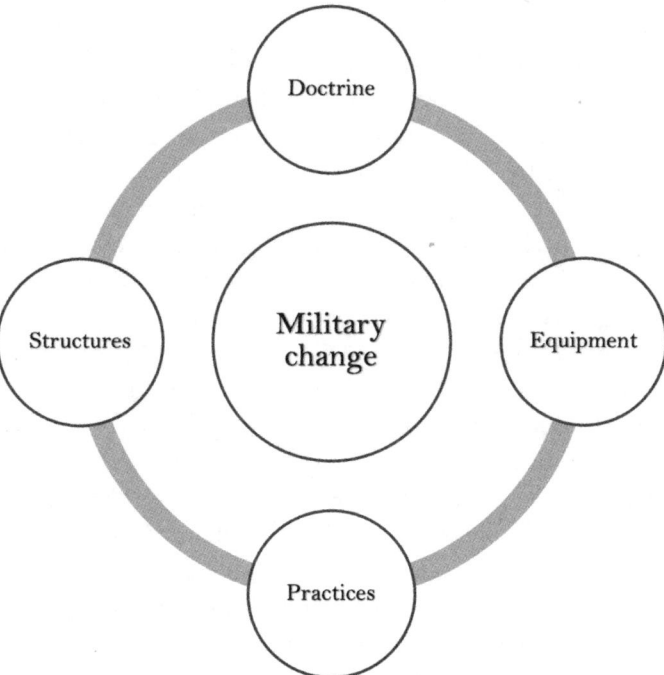

Figure 3. Indicators of military change

an important point, as the vast majority of literature on military innovation studies changes in doctrine (without necessarily taking their implementation into account), structures or equipment, but tends to forget the ways of doing things, which are at the heart of an organization's activity.

Degrees of military change

First of all, military change needs to be considered in terms of several degrees: the adoption of new types of weapon—a machine gun or an aircraft carrier—will not have the same consequences; the creation of new structures—a new office or a brand new service—does not modify the functioning of military organizations in the same way; the implementation of a new doctrine does not change combat in the same way as that of another but depends on its level of application: micro-tactical or strategic.[135]

Like all organizations, the armed forces are changing, all the time, in many different ways. But these changes are not necessarily driven by the same dynamics, nor do they have the same scope or influence on operational performance. We can therefore define four degrees of change: adjustment, adaptation, innovation and disruption. It is important to specify that the terms used are neutral and therefore have no positive or negative connotation. In this book, an adaptation or an innovation can modify the operational performance of armies *for better or worse*: the four terms used here reflect the extent of the change according to the degree of transformation they imply for the organization, but they do not prejudge the operational effectiveness of these changes.[136] These changes can also take place in both peacetime and wartime; such a position differs from that of authors who consider, for example, that innovation is a peacetime phenomenon and adaptation a wartime one, thus creating a distinction based on context, and not on the intensity of change.[137] In addition, this approach makes it possible to distinguish between novelty and innovation: an important change may be an innovation for specific armed forces, but may not be a novelty (other armed forces having already adopted an innovation). For example, the introduction of nuclear weapons in the French armed forces from the 1960s onwards was an innovation for them (given the scale of the change), but not a novelty (as the US, USSR and UK were already equipped).

The first stage is *adjustment*, which is the lowest degree of intensity of military change, with players acting directly on their own practices at the elementary unit level. The resources mobilized are internal to the unit, and the change does not require formal hierarchical validation. There is continuity, not a clean break, with previous organizational practices. Examples of adjustments may include marginal modifications to tactics, the modification of equipment and technologies to suit the needs of the players involved, minor modifications to organizational structures, and so on. Militaries, like all organizations, are in a perpetual process of adjustment: if this degree of change is the lowest, it is also the most common.

The second stage of change is *adaptation*. Adaptation presupposes a degree of hierarchical validation and the involvement of organizations or the mobilization of resources external to the unit concerned, without, however, fundamentally transforming practices. Adaptation may be requested by the actors themselves, or imposed on them by external actors. The deployment of specific equipment to deal with a particular tactical situation (e.g. the emergency deployment of mine-resistant vehicles for American and British troops in Iraq) is a good example of adaptation: it implies the mobilization of resources external to the unit concerned, but without radically changing the mission and tactics. Similarly, changes to rules of engagement, training courses or doctrine are regular examples of adaptation.

The third stage is *innovation*. This level of change requires upstream conceptualization, as well as a deployment process (including invention, incubation and implementation stages).[138] Hierarchical validation (and, often, strong institutional support) is essential, as are external resources and the coordination of several players. Innovation substantially changes the organization's practices and routines: it requires major reorganization (modification of structures and of career paths, arbitration in terms of budget allocations) and creates "winners" and "losers" in terms of the allocation of power and symbolic prestige within the organization. Examples of innovation are the development of a completely new doctrine that substantially modifies the employment of forces (such as the mechanized joint combat implemented by Germany during the Second World War) or the introduction of new capabilities that imply substantial organizational modifications (such as the introduction of aircraft carriers from the 1930s onwards, or the trend toward the creation of "cyber commands" or "space" armies in the 2010s). In this book, innovation is thus described as a *result* with major consequences for the organization, and not as a *process*.[139]

Finally, *disruption* radically changes the organization's meaning and mission. It most often comes from major external constraints, such as the introduction of a disruptive technology or a military defeat. The organization's practices and routines are completely transformed in order to adapt to a new core mission. For example, the dissolution of the USSR radically changed the Russian armed forces, forcing them to reinvent themselves; while British decolonization radically changed the Indian armed forces, which became the armed forces of an independent nation-state.

The mechanisms of military change

Once the degrees of military change have been defined, we need to identify the mechanisms linking the entity configurations and the change itself. I have identified four main mechanisms: circumvention, learning, diffusion and constraint.

Circumvention is a conscious attempt to exploit an adversary's weakness. It is linked to the dialectical nature of strategy, notably its "paradoxical dimension" as identified by Edward Luttwak following in the footsteps of authors such as Clausewitz and André Beaufre.[140] For the American strategist, the effectiveness of a strategy decreases over time, as adversaries develop circumvention strategies: in the context of strategic interaction, adversaries perpetually seek to exploit each other's weaknesses. For example, at the end of the nineteenth century, Admiral Tirpitz drew up a naval armament strategy for the German Empire based on two assumptions: that the great powers of the time would remain in competition, giving Germany the time and the space it needed for its armament policy, and that naval technologies would not undergo any major evolution.

INTRODUCTION

Both hypotheses turned out to be wrong: German rearmament led to a gradual realignment of the great powers (Franco-British agreements of 1904, then Russo-British of 1907, leading to the Triple Entente), and submarine technologies (torpedoes, mines and submarines) changed the face of naval operations. In other words, Germany's adversaries politically and technologically circumvented its naval rearmament strategy. Depending on the situation and configuration, circumvention may be implemented to a greater or lesser extent, leading to varying degrees of change in the armed forces. For example, a change in tactics or an operational plan, and a decision to acquire specific equipment to exploit an enemy's perceived vulnerabilities, are all part of circumvention.

The second mechanism is *learning*, defined as the acquisition of knowledge and skills through analysis, training, experience or education.[141]

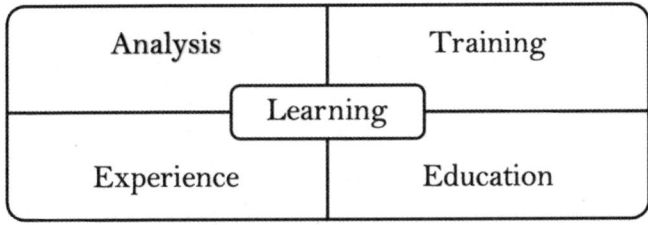

Figure 4. Modes of learning

Learning takes place at both individual and organizational levels. The armed forces invest considerable time and resources in learning, in a variety of ways. Soldiers are trained in basic tactics, while senior officers are trained in strategic issues. Officers are educated in multiple ways throughout their career, notably in defense colleges. The armed forces analyze ongoing conflicts to try to derive lessons, and apply sophisticated models of strategic analysis in order to guide their policies. They also are trained in and practice basic and advanced skills, through which they refine their procedures and understanding of modern warfare. The learning process can thus take many forms: trying to discern the future of warfare through foresight methods, analyzing the practices of foreign armed forces, observing an ongoing conflict in an attempt to draw out relevant information, testing tactical or operational concepts through exercises or wargames, and so forth. It must be noted that the armed forces are sometimes forced to "relearn" previous knowledge that had been forgotten, or replaced, notably in the context of war.[142] These learning mechanisms also take place between different armed forces, for example by sharing information between members of the same military alliance.

Generally, a socially valued way to learn in militaries is through experience. Experience is acquired by soldiers over the course of their careers to varying degrees, and its sharing is institutionalized through more or less effective "feedback" processes. Experience is also disseminated informally within military organizations through the socialization of players: a lucky young recruit may benefit from the benevolent advice of more senior non-commissioned officers, who will teach them the "tricks" of the trade; while an officer preparing for an operational deployment may rely on official documentation, and also on their own professional and friendly networks for information.

This experience-based mode of learning is not without structural problems for organizations: as a form of knowledge, experience is particularly problematic, for several reasons. Firstly, it is vivid for actors, who therefore tend to overvalue information acquired through experience over other types of information (such as analysis). Experience is also ambiguous: it is constructed by the mental and cultural preconceptions of actors, for whom it is virtually impossible to distinguish and prioritize between multiple causes. Thirdly, experience is self-justifying: actors give meaning to ambiguous experiences according to flexible interpretations that confirm their preferences at the time. Lastly, experience enables us to optimize repetitive actions with an immediate and clear return. For example, a firefighter "senses" whether a roof is about to collapse because he has seen a number of similar events over the course of his career, enabling him to build a mental model of the characteristics of a burning roof, while a doctor makes more relevant diagnoses faster over time, as she builds up a kind of mental database of patients with similar symptoms. But complex problems are ambiguous, unprecedented and without any clear feedback: in these cases, experience is a trap that will facilitate the use of bad decisions by creating false analogies with past situations, or by confirming the cognitive biases linked to the decision.[143] As a result, "learning from experience is an imperfect instrument for finding the truth [...]. Lessons are likely to be incomplete, superstitious, self-confirming, or mythic. They will characteristically lead to sub-optimal choices and are unlikely to yield valid characterizations of the causal processes underlying the experiences."[144] For military organizations, this means that tactical issues can largely be optimized with experience (an experienced soldier will "learn" that a particular tactical configuration entails particular risks and opportunities), but strategic issues are bound to be poorly handled if the response is mainly based on the experience of the players and not on rigorous analyses of the situation.

In this way, the armed forces are constantly engaged in a learning process of one kind or another, whatever the quality of the knowledge acquired and the skills mastered (it is perfectly possible to pass on dangerous practices within a unit, or to learn erroneous lessons from the observation of a conflict). In fact, the many different ways in which the learning mechanism can be applied may lead to both operational improvements and the rigidification of armies.

The third mechanism is *diffusion*, defined as the process by which (1) a military practice or technology (2) is communicated through certain channels (3) over time (4) among the members of a social system.[145] This mechanism ties in with the literature on the diffusion of public policies, which is an important field in political science. This literature generally distinguishes between transfers, which presuppose a conscious desire to import or export a public policy, and diffusion, which describes a mechanism for the circulation of a public policy, whatever the rationality and strategy leading to this circulation.[146] Diffusion depends simultaneously on:

- factors internal to the "adopting" organization;
- external and structural factors;
- and, lastly, characteristics specific to the public policy or innovation being disseminated.

Internal factors refer to the intensity of the problem to be solved (a very thorny problem encourages solutions to be found, from elsewhere too), the institutional capacity of the organization to adopt a new policy, the political or strategic culture that encourages or discourages change, and the existence of "promoters" who champion the adoption of this novelty. External factors include geographical proximity (diffusion occurs more easily between entities in close proximity) and membership of common bodies (such as international organizations), which facilitate exchanges. Finally, the specific characteristics of public policies contribute to their greater or lesser diffusion. A policy or innovation perceived as successful spreads much more easily. Everett Rogers identifies five other intrinsic characteristics of an innovation that contribute to its diffusion:

- *Relative advantage.* Is the new product perceived as better than the practice it replaces?
- *Compatibility.* Is the novelty perceived as compatible with existing standards and practices?
- *Complexity.* The more complex the innovation, the less likely it is to spread.
- *Experimentability.* If an innovation can be tested on a small scale before being deployed, it is more likely to spread.
- *Visibility.* If the results of an innovation are easily visible from the outside, it will spread more easily.[147]

In the context of military organizations, diffusion is obviously a major mechanism for change. For example, a military technology (such as a fighter jet) perceived as effective and relevant is more likely to spread. Diffusion can be voluntary, in the form of transfer (through the sale of military equipment), or involuntary, in the form of emulation (e.g. through industrial espionage). However, not all new technologies diffuse equally, for their diffusion depends on their complexity, compatibility, relative advantage and the institutional capacity of organizations to adopt these innovations.[148] This is why aircraft carriers remain the preserve of a small number of navies around the world, in view of their cost and the scale of the institutional reforms required to integrate them with the navies.

INTRODUCTION

While military organizations often seek to emulate militaries perceived as the most efficient by imitating their organizations or technologies, diffusion can also take place in a much more direct way, such as through training programs and cooperation between countries. It is also not uncommon, in the context of a conflict, for some of a belligerent's tactical and operational practices to be copied by his adversary: this comes under the heading of involuntary diffusion. Finally, diffusion can be structured within the framework of multilateral agreements, such as a military alliance. The North Atlantic Treaty Organization (NATO), like the Warsaw Pact in its day, contributes to the dissemination of military technologies and practices among its members by organizing cooperation. This diffusion can take the form of coercion (e.g. Warsaw Pact member states were obliged to supply their armies with equipment mainly designed in the USSR), emulation (due to exchanges between organizations, which contribute to the circulation of ideas and practices) or norms transfers (by recruiting certain types of profiles, and creating expectations in terms of career paths).[149]

Finally, the last mechanism is *constraint*, which is the mechanism by which entities can impose a direction of change in military organizations (by preventing or directing it). Political control of the armed forces often leads to the implementation of the constraint mechanism: depending on national legislative frameworks, political leaders can exert constraint by limiting expenditure funding or by orienting the choice of weapon system to be acquired. Constraint can also stem from the societal norms in which armed forces evolve: for example, changing gender relations have led several Western armies to introduce measures to facilitate gender equality within their forces. Of course, constraints can also arise from specific international contexts. The defeat of the German Empire in the First World War and the terms of the Treaty of Versailles exerted a strong constraint on the Reichswehr, forcing it to undergo a profound transformation. Generally speaking, defeats are often the occasion for implementing the mechanism of constraint.

These four mechanisms—circumvention, learning, diffusion and constraint—are not mutually exclusive. They are often combined in the empirical study of a specific military change. For example,

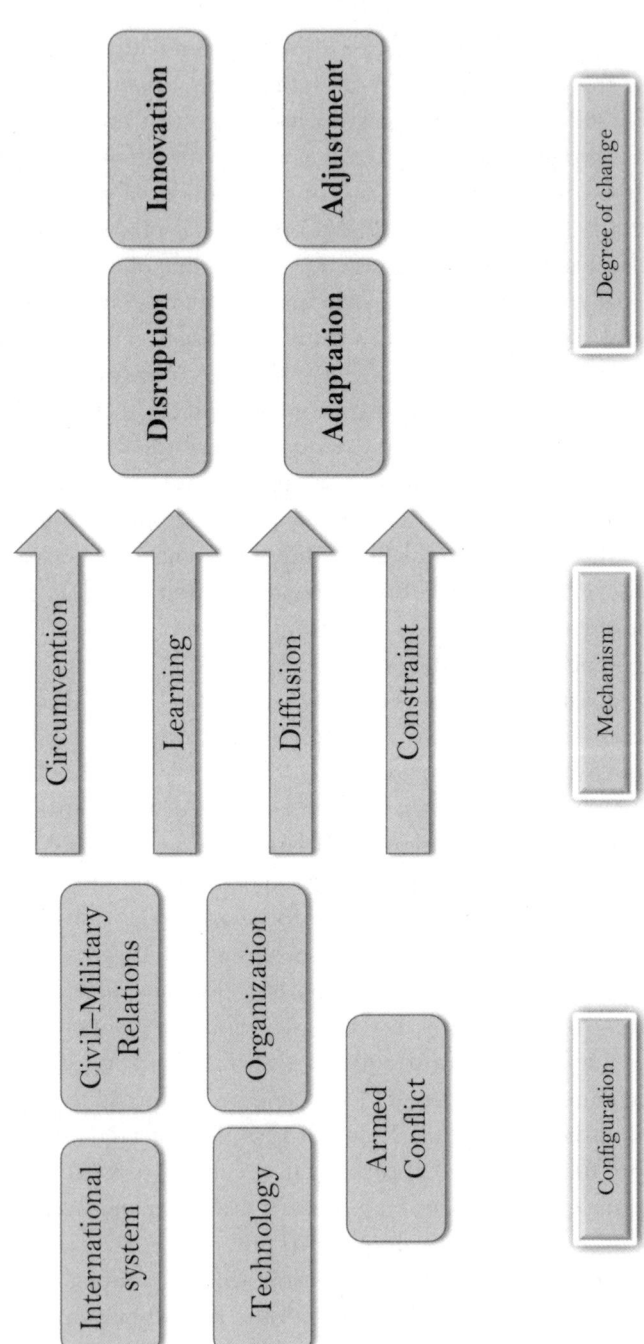

Figure 5. Conceptualization of military change

INTRODUCTION

the development of a new tactic to deal with an adversary is a case of circumvention. If this tactic is shared within a unit, and possibly codified (e.g. in a doctrine), learning takes place, to varying degrees. If this tactic is emulated by units from other countries, or even directly taught to allied units, there is diffusion. These four mechanisms need to be conceptually distinguished, but they often interact in empirical cases of military change: understanding the combinations and sequencing of their interactions is therefore an empirical question.

Finally, we can represent the conceptualization of military change graphically. Figure 5 illustrates the configurations, mechanisms and degrees of change.

The chapters that follow are devoted to studying in detail, through examples drawn from military history from 1871 to the present day, each of these configurations of entities and the way in which they are linked to degrees of change by mechanisms or combinations of mechanisms.

1

THE CONFIGURATION OF THE INTERNATIONAL SYSTEM AND MILITARY CHANGE

Traditionally, an international system is defined by the fact that the political units that make it up (notably states) recognize the risk of war between them, which leads to a certain number of strategic behaviors, such as power-balancing strategies (in the form of military development or the search for alliances). The great novelty of the twentieth century was the globalization of the international system, whereas previously there had been a European system, an Asian system and so on. This globalization of the international system was made possible by the revolution in means of communication and military force projection.

The international system can be studied in terms of two main parameters: the distribution of material power within it and the degree of consensus on dominant norms. The distribution of material power within the international system is always unequal, leading to a hierarchization of international relations.[1] For their part, dominant norms may or may not be shared by the major powers, leading to "homogeneous" or "heterogeneous" international systems, to use Raymond Aron's expression. Competition for dominant norms also plays a part in the hierarchization of international relations: some states are perceived as more "legitimate" than others, and therefore find it easier to get what they want. The Concert of Europe of the nineteenth century is a good example of a homogeneous international system, with the great powers of the time sharing a common conception of desirable norms (based on conservative monarchism). By contrast, the international system of the Cold War was heterogeneous, since competition between the US and the USSR was as much about the material instruments of power as about desirable norms and values (liberal capitalism versus authoritarian communism).

In this chapter, we will consider two major entities whose interactions determine the configuration of the international system: states and institutions of international military cooperation such as alliances. We shall see that the configuration formed by the relations between these entities has a decisive bearing on the mechanisms leading to military change. We shall therefore first look at the distribution of power between states, which conditions the configuration of the international system, before examining the effects of international institutions on military change.

The distribution of power within the international system as a factor of military change

One of the classic arguments for military change comes from the neorealist approach to international relations theory. Largely defined by the work of Kenneth Waltz and his masterwork *Theory of International Politics*,[2] the neorealist school argues that the structure of the international system, i.e. the distribution of power between states, is the best explanatory variable for state behavior. In a general context of anarchy (the absence of a superior authority capable of imposing rules and punishing deviant behavior), each state must ensure its own security, lest it becomes easy prey. For Waltz and his successors, states thus tend to *balance* the major powers or those perceived as such.[3] This balancing can take place in two ways: "externally," by creating an international alliance against the perceived threat, or "internally," by increasing available military resources. From this perspective, given the competitive nature of the international system, military change is a rational response to a transformation of the strategic environment.

States transform their armed forces in order to remain competitive and guarantee their survival: those who fail are "punished" by the system in the form of military defeats that can lead to their demise. Waltz identifies two main mechanisms of military change linked to the balance of power—circumvention and diffusion—and writes: "Contending states imitate the military innovations contrived by the country of greatest capability and ingenuity. And so the weapons of major contenders, and even their strategies, begin to look much the same all over the world."[4] He thus seems to make a clear distinction between powers that are sources of military innovation and the other states in the international system, condemned to more or less successful emulation—two mechanisms that need to be discussed.

Strategic rationality as a factor of change: offset and constraint

On the face of it, it seems obvious that a major mechanism of military change is circumvention: in principle, armies spend an enormous amount of time and energy trying to anticipate the means, capabilities and intentions of their potential adversaries, and attempting to develop doctrines and technologies to counter identified threats. This is the rational dimension of "strategic reasoning," which consists in trying to coordinate objectives and available means.[5] The advantage of the neorealist approach is that it offers a coherent intellectual framework to explain this phenomenon, based on a series of logical steps:

- The international system is competitive in view of the situation of anarchy.
- States seek to balance the power of their potential adversaries in order to protect themselves.
- Innovation and military emulation are "internal" means of balancing power (alongside "external" means such as alliances).
- States that fail to balance power are "punished" by competitive dynamics within the international system.

Military change is therefore a necessarily rational response to threats arising from the anarchic nature of the international system. On the face of it, this approach is intuitive: it seems natural that the armed forces of different states should seek to maximize their military effectiveness in the light of potential threats.

However, while military power is a major variable in the neorealist approach, few studies have focused on how it is generated, and have thus looked at the processes of military change. The first application of the theory was made by Barry Posen, who compared the evolution of military doctrines in France, the UK, Germany and the US between the world wars.[6] Adopting a positivist epistemology, Posen explicitly seeks to test the explanatory power of neorealist theory. In his book, he understands the term "doctrine" not as the codification of what a military organization deems to be "good practice" for winning a battle, but rather as a country's strategic preferences. He thus contrasts offensive doctrines (using military force to *disarm* an adversary by destroying its armed forces) with defensive doctrines (emphasizing deterrence and alliance-building to *prevent* an adversary from achieving its objectives) and theorizes that military organizations tend to favor offensive doctrines. Indeed, such doctrines are advantageous for the armed forces, as they require more resources to implement (an organizational advantage) and thus justify the military's status as holders of legitimate knowledge. Offensive doctrines are thus part of military organizations' attempt to reduce risk and control an inherently uncertain strategic environment.[7]

However, Posen observes the development of defensive military doctrines in the interwar period, one in which technological developments, on the contrary, facilitated offensive operations;[8] this he explains by the intervention of civilian decision-makers in the process of developing doctrine. These civilian policy-makers, influenced by their perception of the geostrategic environment and the balance of power, feared the military defeat that could be caused by offensive doctrines, and therefore forced the armed forces to adopt defensive doctrines emphasizing alliance-building, deterrence and defensive war plans. The adoption of defensive doctrines thus reflects the pre-eminence of the distribution of power within the international system (as perceived by political decision-makers) as an explanatory factor of military change, as opposed to bureaucratic logics privileging the interests of military organizations. For Posen, military innovation is therefore a response to the security constraints posed by the distribution of power within the international system, and requires the intervention of civilian decision-makers to force military bureaucracies to adopt new doctrines (the role of civil-military relations will be discussed in detail in Chapter 2).

Posen's analysis has been heavily debated, not least because of his empirical case studies, which show little respect for historical work on the subject, calling into question the applicability of his argument to the period studied.[9] However, the importance of the circumvention mechanism in military change can be illustrated using other examples. As one example, the militaries of sub-Saharan African countries are currently engaged in an "African revolution in military affairs," initiating a process of qualitative reinforcement of their armed forces, given the threat posed to these states by increasingly well-equipped armed rebel groups.[10]

Another major example might be the adoption by the Russian and Chinese armies of strategic and doctrinal innovations designed to counter the military practices of the US and its allies: either through offensive actions that are nevertheless below the threshold justifying a military response (sabotage, espionage, disinformation, manipulation of perceptions, etc.) or through defensive actions, known as "access denial," designed to counter the expeditionary military model developed and promoted by Washington.[11]

China is a particularly interesting case in point. According to Rush Doshi, China's international strategy since the end of the Cold War has gone through three distinct phases, all determined by the identification of the US as its principal adversary but shaped by the means available.[12] The first phase, "blunting" (1989–2008), consisted in gradually anesthetizing the sources of American power in Asia. The second phase of "building" (2008–2016) was initiated following the diagnosis by Chinese elites of an American decline revealed by the 2008 financial crisis, and aimed at laying the foundations for Chinese hegemony in Asia. Finally, the third "expansion" phase (2016–), facilitated by the fragility of Western cohesion following Brexit, the election of Donald Trump, and the coronavirus pandemic, aims to make China the world's leading power by 2049. At each of these stages, China has developed armed forces sized for the strategic objective pursued.

Thus, during the blunting phase, Chinese strategic thinking was marked by three events: the Tiananmen uprising, the Gulf War and the collapse of the USSR, which led Chinese strategists to define as the main threat an American intervention in Asia that would rely on the precision military technologies employed during the Gulf War. Faced with this threat, Beijing adopted a strategy dubbed the "assassin's mace" (in Chinese, *Shashoujian*), in reference to a Chinese folk tale in which an assassin defeats a far more powerful opponent by using this weapon to stun his enemy, instead of fighting by the book. In context, then, this strategy involved developing the means to prevent American intervention in the region. In terms of capabilities (particularly those of the Chinese Navy), this approach has resulted in the development of the world's largest submarine fleet, the world's largest stockpile of sea mines, and the development of the world's first naval ballistic missile—all so-called access denial capabilities. In contrast, Beijing underinvested in other naval capabilities such as aircraft carriers, anti-submarine warfare, air defense, maritime mine clearance and amphibious landings. The development of the Chinese Navy during this period clearly illustrates the centrality of the objective of preventing the US from operating in the region, compared with other possible uses of naval power.

This approach changed after 2008, when the US was identified as in decline, in contrast to the perception of China's inexorable upward trajectory.[13] This assessment led to an adjustment in Beijing's strategic objectives, as it no longer wished merely to prevent an American presence in the region, but now intended to protect its maritime interests and promote its territorial interests, particularly in the Indo-Pacific region. The means required to achieve these ambitions differed from those available: Beijing now needed capabilities that would enable it to *control* maritime spaces, rather than simply *deny* them to its adversaries.[14] The most notable change was the development, from 2009 onwards, of a genuine naval aviation capability program. China first acquired a former Soviet Kuznetsov-class aircraft carrier, the *Varyag*, which was lying derelict in a Ukrainian shipyard. Renamed the *Liaoning*, it was repaired between 2009 and 2011 and commissioned in 2012. The *Liaoning* served as the basis for the development of China's second aircraft carrier, Type 002, the construction of which began in March 2015, with sea trials scheduled for 2018. A third aircraft carrier, the Type 003, has been under construction since 2015 and is said to feature a flat deck (instead of a ramp) and an electromagnetic catapult. The Type 003 would not be the only one, and a series based on this model could be in development. Finally, China is working on a nuclear-powered aircraft carrier, the Type 004. The expansion of China's naval aviation program has been considerable in just a few years.

To accompany this naval air capability, China has also built up a surface fleet with advanced anti-submarine warfare and air defense capabilities. In particular, China has developed two classes of destroyers, the Luyang-III and the Type 055 Renhai, with these capabilities, and is building them at an impressive rate: no fewer than thirty destroyers have been built in less than fifteen years. Similarly, since 2008, China has been building up significant amphibious landing capabilities—the number of Type 071 landing ships has risen from one to seven—while Beijing is also developing three major Type 075 helicopter carriers (each capable of carrying some thirty helicopters). Finally, while the Marine Infantry Corps (the equivalent of the US Marines, specialized in amphibious assault) had been limited to 12,000 soldiers for several decades, it was doubled in 2017 with the aim of increasing it to at least 100,000 by 2030. This figure should be compared with the 235,000 sailors in the Chinese Navy to appreciate the scale of development of China's amphibious assault capabilities. Lastly, China is engaged in missions to secure maritime communication routes and in the development of overseas military infrastructure, the first stage of which was the creation of a military base in Djibouti in 2017.[15]

Fionna S. Cunningham also argues that China's development of information-age weapons (offensive cyber operations, counterspace capabilities, precision conventional missiles) is an attempt by Beijing to address its leverage deficit when facing the limited-war dilemma in the post-Cold War era. The limited-war dilemma results from the introduction of nuclear weapons in international politics. When two states have survivable nuclear capabilities (the ability to survive each other's nuclear attack and retaliate with nuclear strike), they are in a situation of mutual vulnerability. However, while this situation may lead to a stalemate (the fear of escalation resulting in a containment of hostilities), it may also incentivize some states to manipulate fears of escalation to achieve their aims. In that situation, a state may coerce another state by issuing nuclear threats, or by using conventional forces and counting on the target state's fear of escalation to comply with its demands. According to Cunningham, following the 1995–1996 Taiwan Strait crisis, Chinese leaders realized that they lacked conventional and nuclear capabilities that could be credibly used to resist US coercive activities. They thus developed their own solution to the limited-war dilemma by introducing information-age weapons that would increase their coercive leverage by credibly opening new pathways to escalation, which would arguably make the US pause before issuing coercive threats against China.[16]

As we can see, an identified threat (in our case, American military power) in a context of international strategic competition leads great powers to attempt to circumvent the threat and transform their armed forces. In the case of China, Beijing has developed naval capabilities in line with the perceived threat and its strategic objectives, first by seeking to prevent a possible American incursion into the region, and then by acquiring maritime space control capabilities, initially in the Asia-Pacific and perhaps globally in the future, resulting in a degree of military change corresponding to innovation. It has also developed information-age weapons that increase its coercive leverage against the US.

Identifying a threat as a mechanism for change is also important below the grand strategic level and applies to operational issues as well. The evolution of the US Air Force (USAF) since 1945 is an excellent example of this mechanism. The USAF has undergone four major successful transformations since 1945: strategic reconnaissance (1946–1972), nuclear survivability (1950–1960), SEAD, or suppression of enemy air defenses (1975–1985), and strategic precision strikes (1990–1999). What these successful changes have in common is that they are responses to operational challenges: namely, the need for intelligence (strategic reconnaissance), the development of Soviet ballistic capabilities (nuclear survivability), advances in anti-aircraft defenses (SEAD), and the need to limit destruction in asymmetric conflicts (precision strikes). On the other hand, attempts at innovation based solely on technological breakthroughs, such as close air support during the Second World War, early attempts to defeat Soviet air defenses (1960–1970) and the targeting of high-value air platforms after the Cold War (1990–2001), were failures, illustrating that correct identification of the operational–doctrinal problem is more important than technological development for successful military change: "When the Air Force leadership has identified, framed, and prioritized concrete operational problems to be solved, the service has proven to be remarkably innovative."[17]

Conversely, the misidentification or non-identification of a threat to guide doctrinal, operational and technological development can be seen as problematic from the point of view of military change. Europe's post-Cold War armed forces provide a good illustration of this. In the context of unipolarity created by the military domination of the US and its allies, and the desire for the normative dissemination of a liberal international order (based on the promotion of democracy, human rights and the market economy), security issues were gradually perceived no longer in terms of threat reduction (assuming a dialectic of opposing wills within the framework of strategic competition), but in terms of the insurance logic of risk management.[18] Threats, which presuppose adversaries with a will, have been replaced by general "risks," such as "failed states," "ethnic conflicts" or "terrorism." Against this backdrop of lack of an identified enemy, but a proliferation of vague threats, military change in Europe's armed forces has been guided more by budgetary constraints than by strategic rationality. This approach was even officially sanctioned as a planning method by the former German Minister of Defense Karl-Theodor zu Guttenberg in a 2010 speech at the Hamburg War College. The minister explicitly announced that budgetary constraints brought about by the 2008–2009 financial crisis rendered obsolete the old approach to defense planning based on financial adjustment to strategic needs.[19] On the contrary, the format of the armed forces would henceforth be determined by the available budget, and not by an assessment of the security context. To his credit, the German minister was merely making explicit what was practiced by virtually all European countries after the Cold War, even those boasting of conducting "strategic reviews," "White Papers" and the like, which often carried little weight vis-à-vis the account books of their finance ministries.

This adoption of a risk management paradigm had two consequences. The first is that it legitimized a considerable abandonment of conventional warfare capabilities, seen as relics of the past: by way of illustration, the maritime capabilities of European countries were drastically reduced after the Cold War, with certain critical segments and skills surviving only in a handful of countries.[20] As a result, it also created entire generations of officers who have only experienced a contraction in the format of their armies: European military personnel who joined the service in the late 1980s and early 1990s and now occupy the highest ranks have spent their entire careers having to manage the organizational and capability consequences of budget cuts. The second consequence is that the guiding principle behind the transformation of European armed forces has been to turn them into professional expeditionary forces, sacrificing mass for deployability, in line with the new post-Cold War political concern to use armed forces in an insurance-based logic (instead of a coercive logic of deterrence or coercion of an enemy).

As a result, European armed forces have gradually been reorganized around headquarters capable of planning and conducting military interventions, and brigades representing the relevant force size for deployment on operations.[21] This reorganization has also had the more subtle but perverse effect of increasing the size of the staffs that plan and conduct operations, leading to rank inflation in European armies due to the number of senior officers now required to run them. By way of example, the British Army in 2020 had almost as many lieutenant-colonels as in 1980 (1,731 in 2020 and 1,824 in 1980), even though its total size had meanwhile been halved. These larger staffs also take longer to plan an operation or make decisions, are much less mobile and much easier to detect (not least because of the energy requirements needed to run their IT equipment). This situation was acceptable in a context of external intervention, where the asymmetry of forces meant that European armies did not run the risk of the enemy destroying their headquarters, but it represents a real danger in the event of a conventional confrontation with a peer adversary.[22]

Interestingly, the end of the "intervention era," with the return of threats posed by the great powers (notably Russia and perhaps in the future China), seems to be bringing about a new transformation in European armed forces. They are now reorganizing around divisions (rather than brigades), and some of them have begun a process of reflection on the survivability of staffs in the context of a major confrontation with a peer adversary.

Even when the main adversary is clearly identified, the process of military change is not necessarily self-evident. This is what is called the "Goldilocks problem" in international relations:[23] like the young girl in the tale, states have great difficulty in calibrating the right response, even when the stakes seem clear. They may well under- or over-react,[24] or hesitate over the means of response, as illustrated by the case of the Imperial Japanese Army between the wars. In 1923, the international context led the Japanese Navy and Army to revise their imperial defense policy: the Russian empire had disintegrated, eliminating the threat to the north; China seemed on the verge of collapse, while the Washington Agreement of 1922 placed constraints on naval armaments; and the Anglo-Japanese alliance was due to expire in 1923. While the most likely enemy was agreed to be the US, the means of confronting it were the subject of lively debate within the army. A traditionalist current, led by Marshal Uehara, considered that Japan lacked the industrial and economic base necessary for the kind of total mobilization seen in the First World War: for them, Japan could not win a long war but had a chance of winning a short one. Indeed, the enthusiasm and courage of Japanese warriors were supposed to compensate for their material inferiority, and it was essential to maintain a large military structure in order to have the mass needed to quickly suffocate the enemy.

In contrast, the reform movement, led by Generals Tanaka and Ugaki, believed that Japan should prepare for a long war and the national mobilization required, and that this could be achieved by reorganizing the army to make it less resource-intensive. In particular, the reformers advocated re-forming Japanese divisions from square divisions (comprising two brigades and four regiments) of 21,000 men to triangular divisions (one brigade and three regiments) of 10,000 men, while a corps controlling two divisions would organize their support. Since triangular divisions were smaller, they could be deployed in greater numbers (providing more maneuver elements). Traditionalists opposed this idea, arguing that the triangular division could not operate autonomously (since it depended on the corps for support) and could not tolerate heavy losses without compromising the semblance of cohesion necessary for combat. Ugaki was appointed Minister of War in December 1923, and from 1925 he implemented a plan to reduce the size of the army that partly reflected his intentions to prepare Japan for total mobilization (notably by reducing compulsory military service from three to two years, in order to cut costs for the economy and provide a larger pool of reservists, since conscripts would leave the forces more quickly). But it wasn't until 1938, during the Sino-Japanese War, that triangular divisions were adopted.[25] As we can see, even if the enemy is identified, the means of confronting it are often the subject of bitter debate, with consequences for the armed forces. In this particular case, the Japanese Army made a number of organizational adaptations (some of them significant), before innovating as a result of the conflict (a process which will be examined in Chapter 5).

Today, many observers believe that Taiwan's choice of military equipment could be optimized. Taipei faces a clear threat: the risk of invasion by the People's Republic of China. Such a war would probably comprise three stages: an initial campaign combining air strikes, ballistic missile launches and cyber-attacks to destroy and paralyze Taiwan's defenses as far as possible. This campaign would be followed (or even accompanied) by an attempted maritime blockade of the island, to cut off trade and prevent the flow of all supplies and military support. Finally, the third phase would be an invasion proper, involving the takeover of a number of small islands as early warning posts, a delicate amphibious assault phase, and military occupation. Faced with this threat, Taiwan has so far preferred to acquire sophisticated weapons systems equivalent to China's, but obviously without sufficient mass given the disparity in resources between the two countries, with the operational principle of conducting a major existential battle (ideally with American support). Faced with the rapidly widening gap between Chinese and Taiwanese military capabilities, some authors recommend instead that Taipei adopt an asymmetrical posture of elastic denial in depth, based on capabilities that are less costly but capable of hampering or even interdicting the Chinese war effort: surface-to-air missiles in large numbers, missile boats, naval mines, drones, etc. The aim is not to wage a decisive battle, but to wage numerous delaying battles and guarantee the survival of Taiwanese forces for as long as possible, thanks to their mobility and camouflage, making the invasion effort too costly for the Chinese.[26] To date, Taiwan has not yet reversed its posture: while the enemy may be clear, the response may not necessarily be so.

As we can see, the strategic rationality of armed forces seeking to evolve in order to gain an advantage over their adversaries is expressed through a more or less successful circumvention mechanism. But the international context can also lead to military change through a mechanism of constraint. These constraints are of two kinds: political and geophysical.

Firstly, international power balances can impose limits on a state's military development. The most famous example is probably that of the Reichswehr following the Treaty of Versailles, whose army was limited to 100,000 men, whose navy could not exceed 100,000 tons and 15,000 sailors, and which could not have an air force. German military leaders worked to mitigate the impact of these measures as far as possible (with the help as well of the USSR, to which we return below), but the overall framework was constrained by the balance of power resulting from the First World War. As another example, the collapse of the USSR in 1991 led to the partition of its army in a process whose exceptional dimension should not be overlooked:

> The Soviet military was not destroyed by invading armies. It did not attempt to seize political power from the disintegrating Communist party and Soviet state, not even as a desperate act of self-preservation. Nor did it launch a foreign war to rally domestic support for the imperiled regime. Sitting on the largest nuclear weapons arsenal in the world, it made no threats to use them. Instead, the Soviet Armed Forces went complaining but passively into the dustbin of history, to use Trotsky's phrase.[27]

Here again, military change (involving disruption in both cases) was imposed by international power relations.

Another example of the mechanism of constraint is provided by conventional or nuclear arms control agreements, which limit or prohibit certain types of weaponry. Political leaders then make strategic choices that are binding on armies, by banning certain types of weapons from their arsenals: consider, for example, the Convention on Cluster Munitions, which came into force in 2010 and has 108 signatories among UN member states. Similarly, international treaties governing international humanitarian law (IHL), i.e. the lawful means of conducting military operations, influence the evolution of armed forces. For example, the proliferation of IHL rules has led Western armies to set up legal advisors (LEGADs), who are in constant dialogue with those in charge of operations, to ensure that actions comply with international law and thus modify military practices where appropriate.[28] In addition to this organic dimension, the structuring effect of IHL is also reflected in training curricula (military personnel receive more or less in-depth presentations on the main principles of IHL) and in planning practices. Of course, not all armies are equally sensitive to the need to respect IHL, for this depends on the choices made by their political leaders, and the application of IHL can vary within the same military organization depending on the moment and the context.[29] Like any norm, the standards of international humanitarian law can be violated, but to date they seem on the whole to be rather robust,[30] and are therefore forcing a certain number of armed forces to adapt their practices.

Another type of constraint is imposed by the geophysical environment. Over centuries, military organizations have developed a body of military knowledge specific to their environment, known as "military geography," which includes (but is not limited to) cartography and the study of the physical characteristics of theaters of operation.[31] Defense planning therefore not only takes into account the adversary's military capabilities and intentions, but must also integrate the specific characteristics of the environments in which operations may be conducted, which in turn guides capability development. One can observe this at present in the gradual recognition by armed forces (particularly in the West) of the effect of climate change on theaters of operation (e.g. by accelerating wear and tear on equipment or causing soldier fatigue due to extreme heat) and on the potential for triggering conflicts, leading to the gradual integration of this dimension into defense policy.[32] For example, in 2022, France approved a Climate and Defense strategy to prepare its armed forces for the consequences of climate change.

One factor to take into account is the under-reported yet significant carbon emissions from the global military sector, estimated at up to 5% of total global emissions. Duncan Depledge has introduced the concept of "low-carbon warfare" to describe a future in which militaries are forced to adapt to the realities of net-zero commitments. He explains that this emerging shift is not just about greening military infrastructure but involves a deeper transformation in how armed forces are structured, equipped and deployed in response to geopolitical, societal and environmental pressures.[33] While early military interest in reducing carbon emissions was primarily driven by operational efficiency and fuel cost concerns (e.g. in Iraq and Afghanistan), today's motivations are increasingly rooted in climate policy and public accountability. There are several implications for future conflict: whether military decarbonization can be achieved without compromising operational effectiveness; how technological innovation might enable or hinder this shift; and whether a more sustainable form of warfare could paradoxically make the use of force more palatable.

Another implication of climate change is the shifts in oceanic conditions (such as rising temperatures, changing salinity and altered current patterns) that are significantly reshaping the underwater soundscape which submarines use to conceal their presence and which sonar systems depend on for detection. It turns out that detection ranges are generally shrinking, making sea-based military activities an attractive option. The implications of this shift touch on global security, particularly the credibility of submarine-based nuclear deterrence and the strategic calculus of nations such as the US, China and Russia.[34] Here, again, we see how external factors provide incentives to point the evolution of armed forces in a specific direction.

Thus, strategic rationality is a factor in military change, whether it involves circumventing an adversary or reacting to external political or geophysical constraints. Fortunately, one might say, it is normal for an organization to try to perform rationally in a given context by offsetting its adversaries' capabilities. However, as we have seen, these attempts at offset do not necessarily mean successful military change. This leads us to study the second factor discussed by Waltz: emulation.

Emulation: the unintended diffusion of military power

As mentioned in the introduction, emulation is fundamentally an "involuntary" diffusion: one actor decides to imitate the military practices, doctrines or equipment of another, but without the latter's direct help (and sometimes against its will). The emulation of military practices is apparently common within the international system,[35] which can be explained simultaneously by strategic rationality (adopting what "works"), by the existence of internationally desirable standards of military behavior, by the intrinsic characteristics of the emulated military practices or technologies, and by the emulating country's capacity to adopt the technology.

Several neorealist authors have studied cases of emulation. João Resende-Santos, for example, argues that the military transformation of Argentina, Chile and Brazil between 1860 and 1935 can be explained by a dangerous security environment: several wars took place during this period, such as the Pacific War (1879–1884) between Chile, Peru and Bolivia; the Acre War between Bolivia and Brazil (1899–1903); and the Colombian–Peruvian War (1932–1933), which led the states of the region to draw inspiration from foreign military models deemed effective.[36] Thus, while most of these countries were inspired by France before 1870, the defeat of the French Second Empire made Prussia the military model to imitate, leading them to import a model of mass army and universal conscription that was far removed from their previous military practices. Posen also argues that the adoption of mass armies from the nineteenth century onwards, and the encouragement by governments of the nationalist sentiment required to build them up, was a rational response by states to ensure their survival: "As in any competitive system, successful practices will be imitated. Those who fail to imitate are unlikely to survive. [...] The mass army is a successful practice from the point of view of state survival in international politics."[37]

Obviously, such emulation of military practices identified as effective can be observed throughout history: for example, between 1600 and 1900, countries as diverse as Russia, China, the Ottoman Empire and Egypt all transformed their armed forces by explicitly drawing inspiration from European models deemed militarily effective.[38] Another example of emulation is the evolution of the American Army between 1812 and 1941, which was strongly influenced by French military thinking,[39] perceived as generally leading to military victories (despite Sedan) until the defeat of 1940. Among other consequences of this inspiration, the organization of American staffs was copied from the French structure and differed from the historical organization of British staffs. These organizational differences, involving divergent planning and command practices and routines, led to regular friction between Americans and British during combined operations in the Second World War.[40]

An important instrument in the emulation process was the defense attaché. From the nineteenth century onwards, the function of military attaché developed as a logical consequence of the "invention of diplomacy" and the gradual professionalization and ritualization of states' external activities.[41] The role of these military attachés included facilitating cooperation between partners, as well as intelligence and observation.[42] Between 1860 and 1870, Russia developed an extensive network of defense attachés, whose reports (and in particular their observations of the French defeat at Sedan) fed into and legitimized the transformation efforts of war minister D. A. Milyutin.[43] Similarly, the reports of American defense attachés in Japan, Germany and the UK between the world wars contributed to the evolution of tank organization and employment doctrine, and to the development of landing craft.[44]

While strategic rationality may seem an obvious factor in one country's decision to emulate another, it is far from the only one. Indeed, the existence of international norms influences desirable military changes, which cannot be reduced to the emulation of effective practices. Norms can most simply be defined as "a standard of appropriate behavior for actors with a given identity."[45] Theo Farrell argues that two broad categories of norms influence the development of armed forces: norms relating to common ideas of military effectiveness, which provide the basic prototype of what a military organization "should" look like, and norms relating to humanitarian law, which influence what is morally acceptable in terms of the use of force and legitimate means.[46] A striking example of this "military isomorphism," based on a particular idea of what military efficiency represents, is the post-Cold War diffusion of the American military model based on technological domination of the adversary. As a result the world's armed forces, or at least those of the countries who want to be seen as part of the "Western" camp, have gradually come to resemble one another.[47] Similarly, under apartheid, the South African regime saw itself as a white bastion, and made a point of acquiring Western weapons (despite an embargo) and imitating them through a process of reverse engineering, in order to be seen as part of the "club" of white, Western powers.

Indeed, the process of emulation according to the perceived dominant norm of "proper" armed forces organization is not necessarily rational from the strict point of view of military effectiveness, as the example of the Irish Army shows. Between 1920 and 1941, this army prepared a conventional defense against what was perceived as the main threat: invasion by the UK. Irish planners were aware that this conventional defense was suicidal in the face of British superiority, but rejected the obvious alternative, namely to prepare a defense that would have taken into account the guerrilla experience gained during the Anglo-Irish war of 1919–1921. The reason lies in the fact that, in building the Irish armed forces, those in charge had forged their idea of military professionalism and of what an army "should" be by imitating the British model, which was then taken as the international standard of quality. This shows how emulation can lead to defense planning that is ill-suited to a country's strategic situation.[48]

The third factor that makes emulation possible is the intrinsic characteristics of the technology or military practice being emulated.

THE CONFIGURATION OF THE INTERNATIONAL SYSTEM

Some military practices or tactics are easier to implement than others, and some technologies are simpler to emulate. For example, the US remains the world leader in advanced military technologies more than thirty years after the Cold War, and despite massive industrial espionage by China, because of the intrinsic—and growing—difficulty of imitating these technologies. There are several reasons for this. Firstly, whereas military technologies of the early twentieth century could benefit from economies of scale thanks to their use of civilian technologies, the most advanced military technologies of the twenty-first century are more often than not domain-specific. Whereas a car manufacturer at the beginning of the twentieth century could relatively easily convert to the construction of tanks or aircraft, given its expertise and industrial capacity (Renault produced tanks, Cadillac made bombers during the Second World War), the advanced military technologies of the twenty-first century are not based on civilian industrial needs: stealth, material resistance, electromagnetic warfare capability and systems integration require specific, cutting-edge expertise. Moreover, because of their growing complexity, the share of "tacit knowledge" (as opposed to codified knowledge) in the development of these technologies is significant, requiring experience acquired by engineers and workers over many years. This tacit knowledge, which varies from company to company, explains, for example, the differences between the designs proposed by Lockheed (the angular F-117) and Northrop (the rounded B-2) to develop the stealth capability of American aircraft.[49]

This intrinsic evolution in the complexity of military technologies probably explains why Germany succeeded in just a few years in copying the design, revolutionary for its time, of the Dreadnoughts launched by the Royal Navy in 1906, whereas contemporary China, despite almost thirty years of effort, still doesn't seem capable of developing fighter aircraft of comparable quality to those deployed by the US.[50] However, it must be noted that Beijing seems to have acknowledged that its defense industry could not fully compete with the most advanced Western companies, and seems to conceive for its J-20 fighter an operational role different from that of the US F-22 and F-35, with which the Chinese plane is often unfavorably compared. The limitations of emulation or involuntary diffusion may be compensated by a circumvention mechanism.[51] Conversely, technologies that are easy to imitate, such as those for small arms (assault rifles, handguns, etc.), are much more easily disseminated.

Finally, it is the ability of armed forces to adopt a military technology or practice that determines its potential for dissemination. This adoption capacity is determined by two main factors: the financial intensity required to deploy the technology or military practice concerned, and the organizational capital required. The level of financial intensity obviously refers to direct and indirect costs (maintenance, training, etc.), while organizational capital relates to the scale of organizational change required. In addition to the cost of the ship, the integration of an aircraft carrier within a navy is particularly complex: not only does the carrier have to be operated, but also the necessary aircraft (an aircraft carrier without aircraft loses its appeal) and the crews trained to operate a complex weapons system. The implementation of the aircraft carrier itself calls for a major reorganization, with specific training programs, career paths, logistics and infrastructure. But an aircraft carrier doesn't operate on its own: it must be part of a naval air group made up of different types of vessels (frigates, destroyers, refueling tankers, attack submarines) to ensure its protection and autonomy at sea. A navy that decides to acquire an aircraft carrier in effect acquires a whole new way of conducting naval operations, with drastic consequences for its organization. The financial intensity and demand for organizational capital required to operate a carrier battle group explain why this military capability is not widely used.

Conversely, some military capabilities or practices are inexpensive and require little organizational capital, which explains their easy diffusion.[52] A good example is chemical warfare capabilities, which diffused rapidly in the aftermath of the First World War, before being gradually banned by multilateral conventions that helped curb their proliferation. Obviously, an organization's capacity to adopt is a function of its resources, its size and also its culture (as we shall see in Chapter 4), and not all military organizations are equal when faced with the challenge of adopting a military technology or practice. In particular, small states need to implement specific strategies, adapted to their own strategic context, in order to successfully adopt foreign capabilities.[53]

As we can see, emulation is also an a priori logical response to the assessment of the strategic context: we can't always try to circumvent the practices of our adversaries, and it is sometimes less costly and simpler to copy what others do best. However, this is not necessarily a rational phenomenon, and it is often the result of imitative logic linked to competition between states for international status. Finally, emulation is conditioned both by the intrinsic characteristics of the technologies or practices emulated and by the adoption capacities of the military organizations themselves.

The limits of the power distribution explanation of military change

Despite the elegance of the neorealist approach's predictions, it is very easy to find a multitude of historical examples contradicting the theory's predictions regarding the dynamics of innovation and emulation of armed forces. Thus, in 1904, Japan won a major naval battle against Russia at Port Arthur, eventually emerging victorious in 1905 in the Russo-Japanese War for control of Manchuria.[54] This conflict is particularly interesting as it provides a counter-example to the dynamics of military change as described by neorealist theory. Firstly, Tokyo's victory reveals an absolutely colossal effort to transform its armed forces in the space of a few decades.[55] When Commodore Perry forced the commercial opening of Japan in 1853, the country had no permanent armed forces, only numerous samurai units that lacked the characteristics of Western armed forces: unified command, structured organization and professionalized staff. And yet, in 1895, the Japanese armed forces won their first victory in a modern conflict against China, twenty-six years after the end of the Boshin Civil War (1868–1869) and eighteen years after the Satsuma Rebellion (1877), which saw the crushing of the last samurai furious at the loss of their social status during the Meiji era. Admittedly, Chinese forces were not militarily comparable to European armies, but Japanese troops had by then reached a level of professionalization that made them well-trained, well-equipped and efficient—in short, fit for modern combat. Ten years later, these same troops won their war against a European adversary. This major transformation of the Japanese armed forces was carried out with the support of certain European armies (France created a school for non-commissioned officers and an officers' school modelled on Saint-Cyr; Germany contributed to the creation of a staff college; while the navy was advised by British officers), involving a mixture of innovation (notably doctrinal) and emulation.

However, while neorealist theory predicts that the security environment should be the main source of motivation to innovate, the dynamics of transformation in the Japanese armed forces had much more to do with a desire to imitate Western "best practices" in order to enable Tokyo to be recognized as a fully fledged great power in the international system of the time, than with an objective threat: the quest for international status was a far more important motivation than responding to the strategic environment.[56] Moreover, while neorealism predicts that states seek to imitate the most successful military practices (as revealed by the success of their weapons), emulation of the French model persisted even after the defeat of Sedan in 1870. Although Japan officially adopted the Prussian military model in 1878, no German instructors arrived in Japan until 1885, and even after this date French influence remained strong. Indeed, French troops had been advising the Shogun's armies since 1865, and the Yokohama language school (established at that time) had by then produced a cadre of officers capable of communicating with French instructors: this situation was an important factor in the Meiji government's decision to continue employing these instructors despite the defeat of 1870. The major (and successful) transformation of the Japanese armed forces thus contradicted neorealist predictions: it was carried out in the absence of any major threat defining Tokyo's security environment, and it continued to draw inspiration from military models that had nevertheless been defeated in battle.

According to the emulation dynamic described in neorealist theory, following Russia's defeat in 1905, other international powers should have drawn inspiration from the Japanese armed forces, since they had demonstrated the superiority of their military model. The

Russo-Japanese War provided a wealth of tactical and operational lessons, which were widely noted by Western observers of the conflict (such as military attachés and journalists).[57] The Battle of Mukden (20 February – 10 March 1905) saw the participation of 600,000 soldiers, making it the largest battle ever fought, while the Battle of Tsushima (27–28 May 1905) was the most important naval battle since Trafalgar. A number of factors stand out in the analysis of the battles, and they are often echoed in the accounts written by observers: the inordinate importance assumed by firepower on the battlefield, rendering dense infantry formations obsolete and leading to trench warfare, which limited maneuver; the usefulness of infantry support weapons (grenades, trench mortars) for assaults; the crucial role of artillery fire in reducing fortified defenses in support of the infantry; and the usefulness of the machine gun as both an offensive and defensive weapon. These observations were taken into account by the Western powers, to varying but generally limited degrees, in the reform of their armed forces,[58] thus demonstrating a lack of emulation. Austria-Hungary and France did not believe in the importance of dispersing formations: General Foch argued, for example, that the lessons of the Russo-Japanese War were of no interest, and General de Négrier believed that the moral qualities of the French soldier were capable of overcoming any technological obstacle (though the UK, Germany and the US partially revised their employment doctrine in favor of more dispersed formations). These countries also missed out on the development of grenades and trench mortars, despite their proven usefulness in this war: the British Expeditionary Corps of 1914 had neither grenades nor trench mortars, and was forced to acquire them as a matter of urgency. French and German troops also rediscovered the lessons of the Russo-Japanese War in 1914. The situation was the same for machine guns: while Japanese troops ended the war by equipping each regiment with 3 to 6 machine guns, the lessons were very differently interpreted by Western countries: Germany began the 1914 war with 4,900 machine guns in its inventory, France had around 2,500, and the British Expeditionary Corps 108.[59]

As we can see, effective military practices are not necessarily emulated, contrary to the predictions of neorealist theory, and we could multiply the examples of states failing to reform their armed forces (through innovation or emulation) despite proven threats, thus constituting cases of the "under-balancing" of power within the international system.[60] Examples here are Brazil and Argentina facing Paraguayan expansionism (leading to the 1864–1867 war), France and Great Britain facing Nazi Germany, and contemporary Ukraine facing Russia.[61]

How, then, are we to explain the difficulties of the neorealist approach in reconciling its elegant conceptualization with empirical observations of state behavior? Firstly, it must be admitted that Kenneth Waltz himself has always maintained that neorealism is not a theory of foreign policy, but a theory of the international system. In other words, his approach is supposed to account for the structural incentives that weigh on the behavior of states: this does not mean that all states respond optimally to structural incentives, nor that, empirically, all states are motivated by security. Quite simply, those that are not will end up being "punished" by the logic of the system. Neorealist theory therefore predicts long-term trends, in particular a balance of power within the international system, and not specific behaviors.[62] However, as Peter D. Feaver pointed out in 2000, this so-called punishment is under-theorized, and it is unclear under what conditions it is supposed to be exercised and what forms it might take. In any case, it seems that, statistically, states adopting policies of "under-balancing" power are no more victims of aggression than others, which suggests a major conceptual problem for the neorealist approach.[63]

Indeed, "power," the central variable of the neorealist approach, is an incredibly ambiguous notion and therefore particularly difficult to measure.[64] The classic approach is to list a set of resources that are supposed to provide a preponderant military advantage to the states that possess them. For example, Hans J. Morgenthau lists geographical position, natural resources, industrial capacity, military capabilities, population size, national character, morale and diplomacy as key characteristics of power.[65] Raymond Aron attempts to both contextualize and generalize the sources of power, and thus identifies first the *space* occupied by political units, then the *materials available* and the *knowledge* that enables them to be transformed into weapons, the *number of men* and the art of transforming them into soldiers (*or again the quantity and quality of tools and combatants*), lastly, the *capacity for collective action*, which encompasses the organization of the army, the discipline of combatants, the quality of civil and military command, in war and in peace, and the solidarity of citizens in the face of hardship, good fortune or bad.[66]

However, by seeking to emphasize context, Aron makes his criteria so general that they become unmeasurable and cannot serve as an a priori estimate of a state's power. This leads him to give a highly inoperative definition of a collectivity's power as dependent on "the scene of its action and its capacity to use the resources, material and human, given to it."[67] In fact, Aron is much more concerned with defining strategy than power. For his part, John J. Mearsheimer believes that power can be measured in terms of population size, economic wealth, and naval, air and land capabilities, as well as the possession of nuclear weapons.[68]

These resource lists seem intuitively convincing and reflect the criteria of power, but in fact they pose several problems. Firstly, these lists of resources and capabilities may have a heuristic virtue but, as William Wohlforth points out,[69] no criteria for assessing their relevance are given: in the absence of such relevance criteria, anyone can draw up his or her own list and deduce a hierarchy of powers from it. Even if a list is correct at one point in time, the relative importance of the elements of the list may vary over time. For example, "national character" is present on Morgenthau's list but not Mearsheimer's. Is this an indicator that may have had historical importance but is now outdated? We can't know, because neither provides a criterion for assessing when an indicator is relevant or outmoded. In other words, the lists establishing the indicators of power fail to provide the fundamental criterion or criteria by which the indicators are identified, and thus they come to resemble a kind of divination exercise combined with the author's intuition.

In addition to the lack of rigorous criteria for establishing indicators of power, the gap between the measurement of the material attributes of military power and the actual outcome of armed conflict is particularly striking. As Stephen Biddle writes, "the standard capability measures at the heart of all this are actually no better than coin flips at predicting real military outcomes. An enormous scholarly edifice thus rests on very shaky foundations."[70] Thus, the four standard indicators of military power (GDP, population size, size of armed forces and military expenditure) fail to account for the outcome of armed conflict more than 60% of the time, where pure chance would have led to 50% success. Consequently, Patricia Sullivan notes,

> the vast majority of military doctrine is predicated on the assumption that troop strength, firepower, and military effectiveness determine war outcomes. Recent scholarly research is inconclusive—alternatively pointing to war-fighting capacity and military effectiveness, military strategy, or the strategic selection of "winnable" wars as the most important determinants of victory and defeat. But none of these factors can fully explain why powerful states frequently fail to prevail in the armed conflicts they initiate against materially weak targets.[71]

Other attempts to measure material resources more accurately do not significantly improve their ability to predict military outcomes in armed conflict.[72] As we can see, basing the dynamics of military change on the concept of power is intellectually problematic.

This is a very real problem for military organizations. Indeed, assessing the power of one's adversary in order to develop circumvention strategies is extremely difficult due to the structural challenges posed to intelligence collection: adversaries conceal their capabilities, making information partial, and this same information is processed according to the doctrinal presuppositions and inevitable ethnocentrism of the military organization.[73] In fact, "short of the costly and perilous audit of war itself, the problem of estimating the likely performance of one's armed forces against one's potential enemy is the most intractable problem of defense planning."[74] A good example is the overestimation of Nazi Germany's military capabilities by French military intelligence in the 1930s: the units responsible for intelligence on Germany overestimated industrial production, as well as the armaments and units actually available. These errors of assessment, which led to the almost systematic raising of available estimates, were the result of two factors: on the one hand, the memory of the 1914–1918 war and the anguish about the "manpower wall" faced by the French high command at the time, and, on the other, a fantasized, culturalist vision of "eternal Germany," which led to the "German" being seen as intrinsically disciplined, efficient and combative.[75] Conversely, the declaration of war on the US, which constituted the Third Reich's greatest strategic error and sealed its inevitable military defeat, was based on a reasonable and rational—but false—estimate by Nazi leaders of the relative military potential of Berlin and Washington.[76] By 2022, most Western militaries had overestimated the military capabilities of the Russian Army and underestimated Ukrainian military capabilities, and some countries were also mistaken about Moscow's intentions (it should be noted that Russia itself was self-deluded about its own and Ukraine's military capabilities).

The problem is compounded by the fact that intelligence services tend to assess intentions based on an analysis of military capabilities, whereas their political masters tend to assess adversaries' intentions based on their personal interactions with their counterparts and their own prior convictions.[77] It is therefore not uncommon for political decision-makers and military experts to have divergent assessments of adversaries' capabilities and intentions (a good example being the disagreements between US political leaders and the intelligence community over the USSR in the 1970s): the idea of a pure and perfect intelligence cycle that would supply political decision-makers with the pure and perfect information they need is a fantasy, as decision-makers already have prior convictions and non-intelligence information channels to forge their convictions. Examples of this type are innumerable and, in fact, inevitable.[78] After all, if all states had perfect information about each other's capabilities, there would be no need for war: rationally, the weaker would systematically give in to the stronger to avoid the destruction associated with armed conflict. War takes place, among other reasons, because both belligerents believe they have a reasonable chance of winning, and war thus serves as a revealer of each other's capabilities and intentions.[79]

It could then be argued that it's not so much "real" power that counts but "perceived" power, and that armed forces still react by offsetting and emulating what is perceived, rightly or wrongly, either as a threat or as an effective procedure to adopt.[80] Some authors suggest, for example, that leaders react to the perceived levels of relative power and the perceived trends of relative power (are their countries in decline or are they progressing?), which shapes their objectives and, eventually, their defense strategies.[81] This is partly true, but it tends to overlook the fact that leaders may be in denial about their own country's relative decline.[82] Moreover, the uncertainty and lack of information inherent in strategic relationships also have a more subtle effect: decision-makers know what they know, but they also know what they don't know.[83] And the knowledge of the existence of an unknown part of the adversary's intentions and capabilities regularly leads them to want to minimize risks by avoiding a firm commitment to a single military strategy. In other words, most decision-makers not only react to the power (real or perceived) of their adversaries, but also incorporate the unknown element into their strategic assessment, prompting them to diversify their policies of military change. To borrow terms from the field of economics, decision-makers are not faced with an environment characterized by risk (i.e. an environment in which events and their relative probabilities of occurrence are known and therefore quantifiable), but one characterized by "radical uncertainty" (i.e. an environment in which future events are impossible to know and their probability of occurrence impossible to determine).[84] In this type of environment, players cannot optimize their behavior, but simply try to cope, notably by envisaging a multiplicity of scenarios, for which they develop more or less versatile military capabilities. As a result, the real or perceived power of other strategic players is never the only factor triggering military change.

Moreover, military organizations generally do not have the luxury of preparing for just one type of mission or having to counter just one adversary. The spectrum of use of military power is broad, ranging from show of force to high-intensity warfare, through intimidation, stabilization or coercion operations. These operations require different capabilities and skills, which are not necessarily fungible. In addition to the difficulty of assessing adversaries' capabilities and intentions, military organizations also have to prepare for a multiplicity of tasks: even if one of them is prioritized at a given moment (notably according to threat assessment), the others do not disappear altogether. The present-day Danish Army provides a good illustration of this dilemma: after spending twenty years being optimized for counterinsurgency operations, it has been engaged since 2014 in a process of ramping up so as to be capable of conducting high-intensity operations, at the risk of forgetting that it still participates, in a more limited way than before, in stabilization operations that require specific skills.[85] Given the context of radical uncertainty and the demands of the multiple uses of military force, armed forces cannot structurally be optimized, in the economic sense of the term, in the face of a threat. In other words, to be effective, armed forces cannot be completely efficient: redundancies and reserves are needed if they are to conduct a broad spectrum of operations and reduce the risks associated with uncertainty. Obviously, the more limited the resources, the more intense the dilemma, but even the US armed forces would not have the resources to simultaneously conduct counterinsurgency operations (such as in Iraq or Afghanistan), a major conflict in Europe and a war against China: organic choices are therefore always imperfect attempts to resolve the challenges posed by uncertainty and mission diversity.

As we can see, the distribution of power within the international system provides a context for military change, as well as stronger or weaker incentives: in the event of an imminent threat, for example, the circumvention mechanism is more likely to operate. Nevertheless, there are many other factors that come into play to explain change in military organizations, and these require an understanding of the role of other entities or configurations of entities. Within the international system, cooperation between political actors is another powerful factor in military change.

Alliances and military cooperation

An alliance can be understood as a political and military structure in which actors join forces with other actors pursuing similar objectives, in response to a common security interest, notably to confront a common enemy or threat.[86] The alliance is thus characterized by the mutual security guarantee (often a mutual defense clause) that the allies grant each other. The alliance is thus directed outwards, toward an adversary from whom protection is required. This distinguishes it from other forms of security and defense cooperation, notably collective security organizations (such as the Organization for Security and Cooperation in Europe, or OSCE), which aim to manage disputes among their members and are therefore inward-looking. Similarly, other forms of military cooperation, such as arms transfers or multinational military exercises, play an important role in structuring international relations (notably by signaling convergence or divergence of interests), but they do not constitute "alliances" unless accompanied by mutual security guarantees. Finally, military coalitions (such as the coalition set up during the Gulf War) are temporary and ad hoc, whereas alliances are supposed to have greater longevity.[87]

Alliances vary in format and degree of institutionalization: they can be bilateral, "minilateral" (between three and five allies) or multilateral. They can also be highly institutionalized, with an international secretariat (like NATO), or not. There is also a difference between symmetric and asymmetric alliances.[88] Symmetric alliances bring together partners of comparable power, while asymmetrical alliances unite a major power with secondary allies. NATO, and in general all US alliances, as well as the Warsaw Pact, are thus asymmetric alliances. The format of the alliance is important, as the choice to join implies that a state must choose between its autonomy and its security. In an asymmetric alliance, the major power may agree to reduce its security (by pledging to protect weaker powers) in order to maximize its autonomy, through concessions promised by secondary powers. These concessions may, for example, include the construction of military bases in strategic locations for power projection, trade agreements or some form of control over the secondary power's domestic policy (e.g. the USSR intervened militarily in Hungary and Czechoslovakia). In exchange for these concessions, which reduce its autonomy, the secondary power increases its security.

Finally, it is important to mention the concept of the "alliance security dilemma" in order to understand their internal politics.[89] This concept refers to a tension between, on the one hand, the fear of certain states of being caught up in a conflict they do not want, due to the irresponsible behavior of one of their allies ("the trap"), and, on the other hand, certain states which are afraid of being abandoned by their allies in the event of a conflict ("the abandonment"). Alliances deal with this dilemma in different ways. For example, the rules of access to NATO stipulate that the candidate country must have settled any territorial disputes (to avoid a "trap" for other allies), and NATO's operations include regular reassurance measures, such as the deployment of French, American, German or British troops in the Baltic states as part of the "reinforced forward presence" action plan (to allay the fear of "abandonment" felt by some allies).

It is therefore important to distinguish between alliances and defense cooperations, as the mechanisms leading to military change for armies involved in these international commitments may be of a different nature.

Alliances as an incentive for military change

Understanding the importance of alliances for military change means taking into account the transformation of military cooperation within alliances as a result of the changing nature of warfare discussed in the introduction. The First World War led to an initial qualitative leap toward more advanced cooperation. Prior to the conflict, even nominally allied states such as France and Russia, or Germany and Austria, maintained suspicious relations with each other and were reluctant to initiate military coordination.[90] This trend was reversed after 1909, as joint military exercises between allies became more frequent (helped by a worsening international context), but the continuing inadequacy of military coordination was demonstrated from the start of the Great War by the recriminations of the French against the Russians (and vice versa) or of the Germans against the Austrians.[91] The gradual and painful establishment of a genuine inter-allied coordinating body under the command of General Foch was an essential factor in the Entente's victory, but it required difficult negotiations on chains of command and the degree of political control exercised over the French general, which were only resolved at the beginning of 1918.[92] The conditions of the war, with its unprecedented volume of fire, number of men involved and size of theater of operations, highlighted the growing need for military integration and coordination. This lesson was not taken on board by the victors, as the French and British waited until 29 March 1939 to discuss possible military coordination in the event of war.[93] During the Second World War, the stakes of the conflict forced the Allies to coordinate their military strategies as much as possible, in particular under the growing impetus of the American Joint Staff, which acquired political weight far beyond its military functions, despite the persistence of sometimes profound political differences.[94] Nazi Germany's inability to ensure equivalent coordination with its Central European allies, the Italians and the Japanese prevented the Third Reich from fully mobilizing its military and political resources.[95]

A major example of the effect of alliances on military change was the "Lend-Lease" program of support for allies initiated by the US after its entry into the war. Between 1941 and 1945, Washington sent the UK, the USSR and other allies goods and equipment worth a total of $50 billion at the time (around $608 billion in 2020 dollars): $31 billion to the UK, $11.3 billion to the USSR, $3.2 billion to Free France, $1.6 billion to China, and $2.6 billion to other allies. The aid was obviously significant in keeping the UK in the war, which was a major strategic objective for Washington, but it also played a major role in the USSR's war effort. Much of the Red Army's logistical support was provided by the Lend-Lease program. Washington sent 2,000 locomotives and 12,000 railcars, as well as half the rails used by the USSR: in all, 92% of the wartime production of railway equipment was supplied by the program. By the end of the war, 33% of the Red Army's vehicles had been distributed under the Lend-Lease program, including 400,000 trucks and jeeps (33%

of the Soviet fleet), 18,200 aircraft (30% of the Soviet fleet) and 13,000 battle tanks (10% of the Soviet fleet). In addition, the US supplied the USSR with 38,000 machine tools and a number of materials essential to industrial production, including 55% of the aluminum and 80% of the copper used by Moscow during the war, as well as 57% of the fuel used by Soviet aircraft. With the USSR having lost a significant proportion of its agricultural land to the German invasion, the US also sent a total of 4.5 tons of food.[96] The program was thus an important factor in the resilience of the USSR and contributed to the evolution of the Red Army during the Second World War.[97]

This trend toward integration continued after the Second World War, as a result of the changing nature of warfare: the exponential multiplication of firepower, mass and speed prompted members of the two main alliances (NATO and the Warsaw Pact) to develop historically unique internal planning mechanisms.[98] Indeed, the need to coordinate large volumes of forces belonging to different countries presupposed common principles of employment and increasing interoperability between the weapon systems of different countries, and therefore relative convergence in defense policies.

NATO and the Warsaw Pact, both asymmetric alliances with a lead state (the US and the USSR respectively), resolved these problems in different ways. Early on, the USSR adopted an authoritarian model for managing its allies, imposing subordination to the war plans determined by the Soviet General Staff. Three months after the creation of the Pact, a document providing for the complete domination of the USSR over its allies was sent to the Eastern Europeans, without even pretending to consult them: in practice, the system of Soviet "advisors" placed with the armed forces of their allies was the main control mechanism. The Pact played no part in the onset of the Berlin crisis in 1958, but the American willingness to support West Berlin, underestimated by Khrushchev, paradoxically led to a transformation of the alliance: as the risk of conflict increased, the USSR began to steer the Pact toward much more operational planning and preparation for conflict, thus changing it from a political tool for managing allies to a military machine ready to conduct a potential conflict. One of the main results of the Berlin crisis was to firmly establish the plans and mechanisms needed for high-intensity combat against NATO forces.

However, greater military integration was the prelude to a political crisis within the Pact. In January 1966, Moscow proposed a reform of the Pact's command structures, centralizing decision-making around Soviet forces, and formalizing the relegation of members to mere advisors (a profound departure from NATO, where the North Atlantic Council and the Military Committee are places for negotiation). This reform was very poorly accepted by Moscow's allies: Romania questioned the principle of the alliance, in particular the subordination of national armed forces to the Supreme Soviet Commander; Czechoslovakia wanted a Military Council modeled on NATO's Military Committee (i.e. a body for coordination and negotiation); Poland tried to transform the Pact into a kind of NATO by creating the equivalent of the North Atlantic Council. The crisis was temporarily averted, however, as Moscow decided in 1966 to postpone military reform in favor of political coordination within the Pact, in particular in respect of the response to relations with China, the Vietnam War and the Six Day War of 1967. But the invasion of Czechoslovakia in 1968 was a clear signal of how the alliance was being managed by Moscow: the new socialist government in Czechoslovakia demanded a share in political decision-making and clarification of the Pact's military doctrine. The aim was not to leave the Pact (as Hungary had threatened to do in 1956), but to try to reform it. This socialist heresy was not tolerated by Moscow, which intervened militarily: although the operation was formally led by the Pact, it was in fact Soviet troops who largely dominated. The intervention enabled the Pact's structures to be reformed in the direction desired by Moscow: the new coordinating institutions rewarded loyal allies by giving them greater scope for expression, but maintained the decision-making power of the USSR.

In addition to this forced integration, which had direct consequences for the doctrine of Moscow's allies, the USSR also organized industrial cooperation within the Pact in order to guarantee a degree of interoperability between allies (and establish its political dominance). In practice, certain allies were authorized to produce under license (and export) military equipment created in Russian design offices: Czechoslovakia, for example, was allowed to produce most Soviet tanks (except the most modern), enabling it to lay the foundations of a defense industry. Nevertheless, this cooperation was conceived as vertical integration, based on a model of controlled, coercive distribution: war materiel was designed in the USSR before being offered to the Warsaw Pact allies.[99] The problem of interoperability was thus resolved in an authoritarian manner, with the degree and pace of doctrinal and capability change for Pact forces more or less imposed by Moscow.

As a "liberal" alliance,[100] NATO tried to solve the problem of integration in a different way, leaving states in control of their own defense policies, but creating common standards for practical interoperability (by unifying planning procedures) and technical interoperability.[101] In the 1950s, given Europe's dependence on American military aid, the NATO bureaucracy tried on several occasions to be more intrusive in coordinating member states' defense planning (sometimes leading to forms of specialization by state), which was one of the factors behind French frustration with the Alliance.[102] In fact, French military reconstruction after the Second World War was highly dependent on American aid, in terms of both transfers of equipment and know-how, and the technological building blocks needed to rebuild a defense industry (with a different effect depending on the sector: limited for land armaments, vital for the navy, decisive for aeronautics).[103] This dependence, which also existed for other European countries, led to American attempts to coordinate military capabilities and thus to intrude into national defense planning. However, relations between states were redefined as a result of the rise in European capabilities, the political clarification brought about by France's withdrawal from the integrated military command in 1966, and the growing trust that military organizations placed in each other,[104] leading to a management approach to military integration based on the quest for interoperability. In concrete terms, this interoperability takes the form of STANAGs (standardization agreements), which are prescriptive documents expressing the agreement of all or some NATO nations on the implementation of a technical or procedural standard.

One of the major aspects of NATO is that it functions as a producer of military standards which influence the development of national armed forces. It should be noted that this production of standards influences not only Alliance members, but also those aspiring to join: before joining the Alliance in 1999, Hungary, the Czech Republic and Poland had committed themselves to converging their armed forces toward NATO standards, and had taken steps in this direction (with varying success).[105] Drawing on the experience acquired during this first enlargement, the convergence trajectory was formalized by NATO from 1999 onwards in the program known as the Membership Action Plan, which does not prejudge the final decision but constitutes a process of support for candidates, and which was implemented in particular for the 2004 enlargement. However, the convergence effect varies according to country size. For example, smaller countries lack the institutional resources needed to develop their own approach to the use of military force. Moreover, while their contribution to multinational operations signals support for a cause or solidarity with an organization (such as NATO), their contribution is too small to be decisive: their operational experience thus differs from that of larger countries. As a result, the strategic doctrine of small states becomes disconnected from operational concerns, but it serves to signal their goodwill to allies through the adoption of a common vocabulary, by importing military concepts from the "big" countries. Here we see a case of conceptual diffusion, which varies according to the size (and therefore institutional resources) of countries, but which, in the name of doctrinal convergence, can sometimes be counterproductive for certain countries if they fail to take into account the specificity of their operational needs.[106]

However, NATO's liberal philosophy allows those countries that so wish (and have the capacity) to develop a national defense industry, capable of offering products that compete on the NATO or international market. This is why, during the Cold War, NATO battle tanks were designed and produced in the US (M-48, M-60, M-1), France (AMX-30, Leclerc), Germany (Leopard 1 and 2) and the UK (Chieftain and Challenger), whereas Warsaw Pact battle tanks (T-55, T-62, T-64, T-72 and T-80) were all designed in the USSR (and some, like the T-72, produced under license by other Pact members). The same observation could be made for many other items of equipment: the existence of national defense industries within NATO is in accord with the alliance's philosophy of functioning as an instrument of coordination, not constraint. To take a French example, Dassault Aviation could not have existed within the Warsaw Pact: that is the difference between an asymmetrical alliance based on coercion and an asymmetrical alliance based on compromise (but which does not exclude competition between allies for the export of their equipment).

This general non-coercive philosophy does not exclude the fact that, as an asymmetrical alliance, not all allies have the same capacity to define standards within NATO. Clearly, as the US is both the most militarily powerful and the most technologically advanced country, American standards regularly become NATO standards, diffusing American ways of doing things to other countries in the alliance. This dynamic is particularly visible in the current acquisition by many European countries of the F-35 fighter: the concern for interoperability coupled with the desire to give political guarantees to the main military ally is leading to the accelerated diffusion of this American aircraft.[107]

Moreover, even without coercion, multilateral relations can lead to pressure on certain states to acquire certain types of equipment. A good example is Canada's acquisition of German Leopard 1 tanks in the 1970s. As early as 1951, Canada had deployed a brigade of sixty Centurion tanks to Europe to contribute to collective defense. However, when Prime Minister Pierre Trudeau came to power in 1968, he expressed doubts about both the deployment of this brigade and the size of the defense budget. Between 1969 and 1973, the brigade was halved in size, and the government announced that heavy tanks would be replaced by lighter combat vehicles (fire support vehicles). This replacement was not absurd: tanks were extremely expensive and, because of their size, Canada could only deploy them in Europe and not in territories where the USSR might have attempted an (admittedly improbable) incursion, such as the Arctic. Moreover, they were considered unusable for domestic operations. In fact, Ottawa was participating in collective defense with equipment that could be used almost only in Europe. Yet, despite earlier announcements, the Canadian government decided in 1975 to continue deploying heavy tanks and, in 1976, acquired 128 Leopard 1 tanks. In the meantime, Canada's European allies had put pressure on Ottawa, arguing that only heavy tanks provided the requisite credibility in the face of the USSR, and that alliance cohesion could be negatively affected by Canada's decision to deploy fire support vehicles. The European NATO countries found a sympathetic ear with the Canadian armed forces and the Department of Foreign Affairs, helping to put pressure on the government. We can see here how multilateral policy within the alliance can help influence the trajectory of national armed forces, in this case by defining the acquisition of a certain type of military equipment (with the doctrinal and capability possibilities and constraints that go with it).[108]

However, power relations between member states alone are not sufficient to explain all military changes. This can be illustrated by the debate on the adoption of a standardized caliber for small arms in the armies of NATO member countries in 1979–1980. In the 1950s, NATO member states had agreed to equip their soldiers' assault rifles with 7.62mm-caliber ammunition. However, a number of developments in the 1960s and 1970s called this consensus into question. Firstly, in 1964, the US adopted a new assault rifle, the M-16, firing 5.56mm ammunition. This new assault rifle was originally reserved for "non-NATO" operations (including the Vietnam War), but was generalized to the entire US Army after the expiry of the first STANAG on ammunition calibers in 1968, while the choice of caliber reflected prevailing conceptions of "lethality" in the US.[109] At the same time, the Bundeswehr was dissatisfied with the 7.62mm caliber for assault rifles, and felt that the caliber should be reserved for machine guns mounted on combat vehicles, while infantrymen's assault rifles should be equipped with a lighter caliber to reduce recoil and increase accuracy. This assessment reflected Bundeswehr doctrine: to protect the plains of West Germany from Soviet invasion, German troops preferred to fight close to their armored vehicles. Once the vehicles were close to the objective, the troops had to disembark and engage the enemy at close range with light automatic weapons: for the Bundeswehr, these weapons had to be built to fire ammunition optimized for combat under 300 meters. Germany therefore began work on a smaller ammunition than the 5.56mm, resulting in a 4.75mm ammunition concept.

For the UK, the problem was different. In the 1960s, the British Army was looking for a munition that would be useful both in the event of a Soviet invasion and in the context of the wars of decolonization. Staff decided that an ammunition capable of engagement up to a range of 600 meters was a good compromise (compared with the 450 meters permitted by the M-16's 5.56mm), and began work to establish an ammunition with a caliber between 6mm and 6.5mm. However, the Defence Review of 1968 and 1974 established British participation in NATO as a clear priority, relegating stabilization missions in the former Empire to the background. As a result, British operational analysis converged with that of the Bundeswehr, resulting in a 4.85mm ammunition project.

In 1975, a NATO panel agreed on the criteria for evaluating ammunition, and in particular its ability to inflict wounds. During the 1960s, the US had gradually become convinced that expected kinetic energy (EKE) was the best measure of a munition's wounding power. EKE was an approximation of the energy transfer between bullet and victim, measuring the probability of a bullet remaining in the body given the decelerating forces acting on them. The formula was always contested, since it was based on modeling and it was impossible to obtain and verify all the necessary data, but the Europeans had not sufficiently invested in the field of "lethality science" in the 1960s and had no valid arguments to oppose the American results. It was therefore the American criteria (which had validated the 5.56mm ammunition already in service) that were used to evaluate the various munitions. However, while these criteria enabled the US to confirm its choice of caliber, they were unable to control the entire process. In fact, at the end of the tests, the chosen ammunition was the SS109 model developed by Belgian manufacturer Fabrique Nationale: unlike the Germans and British, who had developed new calibers, FN realized that the US had already adopted the 5.56mm caliber, and that the best way to win the market was to optimize their ammunition. The choice of the Belgian manufacturer thus forced the US to spend $110.5 million on rechambering their M-16s, and to speed up development of the M-16A2. This simplified story[110] of the adoption of STANAG 4172 illustrates the complexity of the effect of an alliance like NATO on military change: this includes incentives for standardization, different operational problems, power relationships between states, and the struggle to define common standards, as well as opportunities for the "little guys" to optimize their strategy and influence the "big guys."

Finally, an alliance can serve as a privileged cooperation framework for joint military equipment development programs. States have three main options for acquiring military equipment: national development (which presupposes the existence of a capable defense industry), development through international cooperation, or off-the-shelf purchasing. We have already seen that membership of an alliance produces a normative alignment effect, leading to a preference for certain suppliers for off-the-shelf purchases. But this effect also extends to industrial cooperation. States can make the political choice to develop cooperation with a partner, "forcing" national manufacturers to cooperate. The development of the Franco-German Tigre combat helicopter is a good example of this type of effect. The initial choice to develop the aircraft in cooperation was deeply political, in order to demonstrate the gradual Franco-German convergence, even if the program did experience a number of difficulties.[111] In the same vein, the signing of the Lancaster House Treaties (2010) by France and the UK had consequences for industrial cooperation between the two countries (notably in the missile industry),[112] while the American–Japanese alliance influenced the forms of Japanese rearmament after the Second World War and the development of its defense industry (e.g. by producing the American F-15 fighter under license in Japan, or developing the F-2 fighter as a derivative of the American F-16).

As we can see, alliances provide a specific incentive for military change, due to the demand for integration. Depending on their internal policies, the balance of power between states, the transmission of knowledge and industrial needs lead to doctrinal and material convergence between allies. We therefore need to think of an alliance not only as a political framework for security cooperation, but also as a normative framework within which practices and know-how circulate, leading to changes in armed forces through processes of dissemination and sometimes coercion.

Defense cooperation

Alliances, as mutual defense commitments, are not the only institutional framework for military cooperation: multiple formats exist and serve as channels through which military change takes place.

A particularly striking example is German–Soviet cooperation after the First World War. The normalization of relations between the two states under the Treaty of Rapallo (1922) was also the occasion for particularly intense secret military cooperation, with important consequences for the development of both the Reichswehr and the Red Army. Yet this cooperation was far from self-evident: the Soviet leadership made no secret of its contempt for the German Army (suspected of being a den of aristocratic counter-revolutionaries described by Lenin as "savages" and "predators"), while the role of the Social Democrats in suppressing attempted communist revolutions in 1918–1919 was obviously a deep irritant for the Bolsheviks. For their part, German officers and NCOs were overwhelmingly opposed to Bolshevism, which is not surprising given that a significant number of them came from the right-wing and far-right veterans' associations that had helped crush the 1918–1919 insurrections.

Yet a convergence of interests was identifiable: the USSR, devastated by war and internationally isolated, needed technical expertise, financial capital and military technology, which only Germany was willing to provide. In return, German leaders saw cooperation with the USSR as the best way of circumventing the constraints imposed by the Treaty of Versailles, which had ended the First World War. In particular, the terms of the treaty prevented Germany from developing modern means of warfare (in particular tanks and combat aircraft): partnership with the USSR was the way around this prohibition. The first contacts were established in 1919, and formalized following the Treaty of Rapallo. Hitler's accession to power in 1933 put an end to this period of collaboration, but the links were never completely severed: economic exchanges continued, Soviet envoys regularly sounded out the Germans on the possibility of relaunching cooperation, while several German diplomats and military officers pleaded in the same direction. It is undeniable that the ties forged over a decade between Germany and the USSR facilitated the signing of the non-aggression treaty (known as the "Ribbentrop–Molotov Pact") in 1939.

German–Soviet cooperation between 1922 and 1933 was profound. The Red Army encouraged the German defense industry to relocate experts and industrial production banned by the Treaty of Versailles to the Soviet Union: several factories producing combat aircraft and other military technology were set up in the USSR by Germany. The German Army also acted as an intermediary between the Soviet state and German industry, attracting investment and skills transfers to key sectors of the Soviet defense industry. The Red Army and Reichswehr also set up joint structures, including a flying school, a mechanized warfare training camp, and two chemical weapons factories. At the peak of cooperation, between 1928 and 1932, hundreds of Germans and Soviets worked side by side in bases, military academies, laboratories and so on.

This cooperation enabled Germany to develop and test the new generation of tanks, combat aircraft and chemical weapons, which in theory were forbidden by the Treaty of Versailles.[113] It was experiments in the USSR that led to the development of portable radios for coordinating tank and aircraft formations, a key element of the Blitzkrieg. The prototypes and concepts tested in the USSR led to the weapons used by Germany in the Second World War: the Panzers I, II, III and IV would never have seen the light of day without cooperation with the Soviet Union. For the Soviets, cooperation with Germany made possible the acquisition of knowledge and know-how, either through exchanges or by stealing and spying on German activities (involuntary transfer and dissemination). The T-24, T-26, T-28 and T-35 tanks benefited greatly from the knowledge acquired through contact with the Germans. Soviet aviation also benefited from exchanges: the first generation of Soviet heavy bombers were such copies of German models that an imprudent engineer working for the German Army attempted to sue the USSR in an international court for patent infringement (much to the dismay of the Reichswehr and the German government, which did not wish to draw attention to cooperation with the Soviet Union).

In addition to technological development, cooperation also led to doctrinal evolution: the experiments and tests carried out at the mechanized warfare training camp led Germany to completely reassess the role of tanks in joint combat, culminating in the development of the Panzer IV. Luftwaffe doctrine was also extensively developed and refined in the USSR. In return, the Reichswehr took part in the training of hundreds of Soviet officers, including the Red Army's main future cadres: among the Soviet officers who studied in Germany were two chiefs of staff, two of the Soviet Union's five field marshals, an air force chief of staff, and the directors of the mechanization and chemical weapons programs; as well as the country's leading military theorists and several directors of military academies. Cooperation also led the Red Army to draw inspiration from the German command model, organized around a centralized joint staff.

As we can see, German–Soviet military cooperation was absolutely central to the development of both countries' armed forces, providing a framework for learning (experimentation) and dissemination (transfer and emulation) mechanisms: "it was German rearmament that would pose the greatest problem to European stability and lead directly to the events of September 1939. If Hitler had not initiated a European arms race in 1933, a new war would have been unlikely. And it was work conducted in the USSR that laid the foundations for that rearmament program."[114]

A strange example of cooperation is the Franco-Israeli affair known as the "Cherbourg missile boats." In 1965, France and Israel signed a contract for the sale of twelve Sa'ar III missile boats for the Israeli Navy. The ships were built by Constructions Mécaniques de Normandie (CMN), a shipyard in Cherbourg, and the weapons systems were to be assembled in Israel. However, in June 1967, shortly before the outbreak of the Six Day War, General de Gaulle decided to impose an embargo on arms sales to Israel because of the imminence of the conflict. This selective embargo initially concerned only offensive weapons and did not affect ships, but was later extended after the Israeli raid on Beirut airport in December

1968. The first missile boat was launched on 11 April 1967, and five were delivered before the embargo. Two others, undergoing trials at the time of the embargo, managed to reach Israel. The five remaining ships were moored in the commercial port, from where they were exfiltrated by Israeli intelligence services on the night of 24–25 December 1969. It is possible that France chose to let the operation take place, making use of the opportunity to formalize arms contracts with Arab countries including Egypt, Saudi Arabia and Libya. It is therefore a rather strange case of simultaneously voluntary and involuntary diffusion, but one which had important consequences for the Israeli Navy.[115]

If German–Soviet cooperation is a case of cooperation between comparable powers, many forms of asymmetrical cooperation (between significantly different powers) also exist, serving as a framework for military change through the diffusion mechanism. In 1924, China founded the Whampoa Military Academy with the support of the USSR, and adopted the Soviet system of political control of the army. Foreshadowing China's later break-up, Whampoa's first commandant was Chiang Kai-shek, and its political commissar Zhou Enlai (who would go on to become a prominent communist leader). The Chinese instructors had mostly been trained in Japan, and were accompanied by Soviet instructors: "although not fully Western in European and American eyes, the Soviet advisers were able to convey to their Chinese students the basic core of Western military strategy and tactics."[116] This is an interesting case of a multiplicity of cross-influences (Japanese, Soviet, Western) in the development of the Chinese Army at the beginning of the twentieth century, and of the complexity of the mechanisms of diffusion.

Today, the institutional forms of what is known as security force assistance (SFA) are numerous: they can take the form of an instructional detachment, the deployment of experts, a training offer in the host country's military schools or an invitation to participate in national military curricula. This type of cooperation is an important means of disseminating military practices, with varying degrees of success depending on the capabilities of the host countries and the compatibility of the partners' objectives. A simple form of military cooperation is the invitation to different countries to host some of their officers in national military courses. Depending on the capabilities of the host country, this international socialization can have more or less widespread effects. For example, the École Supérieure de Guerre in Paris was an important node in the network that disseminated the French doctrine of "counter-revolutionary warfare" between 1955 and 1975, welcoming a growing number of foreign officers and making possible the creation of international professional networks that facilitated the circulation of the doctrine.[117] Obviously, the effect is all the greater when the host country is perceived as having "something to offer" according to the principle of desirable standards of military organization set out above: in the context of the Cold War, "counter-revolutionary warfare" intrigued a number of countries who feared having to deal with communist insurgencies and were curious to learn from the French experience in Algeria. A state's international reputation is thus an important aspect of its ability to disseminate military practices.

Other, more intrusive forms involve direct military support, with experts seconded to target countries. Again, this is not a new practice, but it has been widely employed in recent years at great expense in Africa as a means of strengthening states in the fight against terrorism, with very mixed success. For example, following the Mali crisis of 2012, a myriad of programs aimed at reforming the armed forces were put in place: Operation Barkhane (commanded by France) and the European Task Force Takuba both had an operational training dimension, while the European Union Training Mission in Mali and the EU Capability Building Mission (EUCAP) had a broader objective of reforming the governance of the armed forces and security services, to which we should also add the mandate of the United Nations Mission for Mali (MINUSMA) and initiatives taken by civil society players such as the Geneva Centre for the Democratic Control of Armed Forces (DCAF). Besides this institutional overlayering that diluted competencies and responsibilities, a major factor in the failure to reform Mali's security forces was the disconnect between "programs to reform and restructure states' defense and security systems, and the actual functioning of these systems," in particular "the combination—and often conflict—between legal-rational approaches on the one hand,

and informal dynamics on the other."[118] Very often, programs aimed at improving the legal-rational efficiency of the armed forces are to the detriment of informal logics of power relations that benefit particular actors, who therefore have no incentive to implement them. This brings us back to the idea set out in the introduction that, depending on the country, the armed forces can fulfill a multitude of functions (including the acquisition of positions of power), which do not boil down to defending the country against external threats.

The diffusion of external military practices can also have perverse effects on the missions of local armed forces and on political dynamics. In Niger, military-operational partnerships have led to the creation of a special forces command (following a general trend since the end of the Cold War toward the diffusion of such units in the world's armed forces)[119] and the development of "hybrid" civil–military units. However, these changes have led to tensions within the armed forces: battalions under the new Special Operations Command compete for the best equipment, and seek to attract donations from different international partners, both weakening inter-unit cohesion and complicating logistical support. For their part, hybrid units are in institutional competition with more traditional security tools such as the police.[120] Similarly, the creation of elite units under Western instruction in Cameroon poses a more fundamental problem of governance, since these units can easily be used as a tool of repression against ethnic minorities, thus reinforcing the autocratic dimension of the regime. The same is true of the Iraqi "Golden Division" or the Somali "Danab," thus posing a fundamental problem for Western countries: the only way to prevent the political and repressive use of these elite units would be to remain indefinitely in the host country and ensure their direct command.[121] The Soviets had already set an example with the Somali forces between 1960 and 1977: in just fifteen years, Soviet military assistance had made them the fourth most powerful army in sub-Saharan Africa. However, following a political U-turn, the Soviets were expelled from the country, leaving Somalia's armed forces logistically and financially unsustainable for the country, corrupt, but embedded in a repressive state structure.[122] Military partnerships are also not necessarily very effective in contributing to the dissemination of human rights standards: if these standards conflict with the institution's interests in maintaining its cohesion, they are regularly violated by the armed forces receiving Western military training.[123]

Finally, we must not underestimate the effect of these partnerships on the suppliers themselves, which generally involves the creation of units dedicated to the training and education of foreign armies.[124] The UK, for example, created a Specialised Infantry Group comprising five battalions dedicated to these missions; the US has set up Security Assistance Force Brigades; France has created the Centre Terre pour le Partenariat Militaire Opérationnel; and Italy has created a dedicated center within its infantry school. Cooperation encourages military change in both directions and, in particular, institutional evolution. However, as we have seen, change initiated within the framework of asymmetrical partnerships often comes up against the limits of the target countries' capacity for adoption, with the diffusion of practices remaining limited and the effects sometimes even counterproductive.

Conclusion

The configuration of the international system—and, in particular, the distribution of power and the institutional relationships established between states (alliances or defense cooperation)—is the first configuration that influences military change. Military change takes place through two main mechanisms: circumvention (the attempt to gain an advantage over a strategic competitor) and diffusion (voluntary through transfer or involuntary through emulation), even if constraint and learning sometimes come into play. However, as we have seen, it is illusory to think that these mechanisms obey a pure and perfect rationality. Many armed forces attempt to strategically offset their adversaries, but multiple constraints make the exercise particularly complex, especially as it is always a gamble on the future: at the end of the day, the true test of military effectiveness is war itself. Attempts at strategic circumvention are therefore always marked by the nagging question of the effectiveness of the adopted measures in the event of conflict.

This permanent uncertainty leads to attempts to reduce risks, for example by emulating a country considered to be the "international standard" at a given time, sometimes at the risk of being counterproductive, as illustrated by the Irish example. Here, again, emulation is not "pure and perfect"; it is also a matter of social logic linked to relative prestige, which fluctuates over time.

Finally, institutions play an important role in the processes of military change, whether through mechanisms for coordinating defense policies and developing interoperability within the framework of an alliance (mechanisms which may be more or less coercive, depending on the alliance's internal political management) or through defense cooperations which encourage the diffusion of military practices. As we can see, the configuration of the international system—and, in particular, the power held by entities such as states and international organizations—constitutes an important context for military change, even if it is far from the only one. But it was essential to begin our investigation with this dimension in order to fully understand the general environment within which political and military decision-makers operate in their defense planning.

2

THE CHALLENGE OF CIVIL–MILITARY RELATIONS

Having studied the importance of the international system for military change, we need to change the level of analysis and take into account the various configurations and relationships between political entities and armed forces. First of all, we need to clarify a point of terminology. In English-language literature, the term "civil–military relations" actually covers two meanings: on the one hand, the study of institutional relations between political and military powers, raising the question of political control of the armed forces; and on the other, the analysis of links between the norms, values and dispositions of civil society and the armed forces. For the first type of questioning, I use the term "political–military relations," and "armed forces–society relations" for the second.

The entities involved in civil–military configurations are therefore different from those studied in the first chapter. They include the executive and legislative branches of government (with the specific actors varying from country to country), the armed forces' directorates and main services, and civil society associations. We can also add non-material entities such as the economic system or the dominant norms of society. In each case, the configurations between these entities influence the nature of military change. We will therefore begin by examining political–military relations, before turning to the issues of the political economy of defense and the links between civil society and the armed forces.

Politico-military relations

The relationship between political power and the armed forces is an important determinant of the process of military change. As mentioned in the previous chapter, Barry Posen, in his book on doctrinal change, laid the foundations for the analysis of power relations between civilians and the military, arguing that the intervention of civilian authorities is necessary to force the armed forces to evolve their doctrines.[1] His insights were subsequently complemented and qualified by other works.[2]

The role of political power

In a classic work, Deborah Avant compares the evolution of British and American counterinsurgency doctrines, arguing that the different institutional configurations between the US and the UK made the British armed forces more flexible, and more capable of developing a successful counterinsurgency doctrine during the Boer War and in Malaya, than the American Army in Vietnam.[3] In the US, institutional control of the armed forces is divided between the executive and legislative branches: the presidency decides on political and strategic orientations, and Congress votes on budgets and validates certain senior officer appointments. The British parliamentary system, on the other hand, concentrates control powers in the executive, since the first-past-the-post system gives a clear majority, usually an absolute one, to the party that comes out on top in the elections, which then has free rein to form a government that will be supported by the parliamentary majority. These different institutional configurations influence the institutional development of military organizations: the separation of powers has enabled the American military to professionalize with little institutional control, and thus to create an autonomous sphere of claimed expertise, hostile to outside intrusion. Indeed, the President can only exercise his ability to promote or dismiss officers if Congress validates their decisions—something that is far from guaranteed, being dependent on the political situation. In the event of a threat of executive control, the armed forces can always turn to supporters in Congress who will oppose the executive's choices. In addition, the armed forces have a variety of bureaucratic and institutional tools at their disposal to try to minimize the effect of political decisions: in addition to appealing to Congress (and other civilian allies with clout in the public debate), military decision-makers can try to control the agenda-setting of issues (by deprioritizing the demands of politicians) or strategically raise the specter of legal and constitutional constraints that would prevent them from implementing the instructions given to them.[4] In other words, the American armed forces can more easily resist outside intrusion by playing the two branches of government off against each other, which in turn increases their resistance to change.

However, these tactics are limited to slowing things down, and the US armed forces obviously submit to major reforms when they are imposed by political authority. The example of the Goldwater-Nichols Act of 1986 (named after its promoters in the Senate and House of Representatives) is revealing, since it is a legislative act imposing jointness on the US armed forces under the aegis of a joint chief of staff, where parallel, army-specific bureaucracies had previously existed—a good example of innovation imposed by civilian authorities.[5] The same configuration can, however, prevent a change desired by the armed forces. The significant role Congress plays in the equipment decisions of the US armed forces leads to a politicization of equipment procurement: members of Congress can thus force the US armed forces to continue acquiring certain types of equipment, particularly if they are produced in their electoral strongholds (thus fueling the local economy).[6] Since the 2010s, the US Air Force has been trying to retire the A-10 "Warthog," but Congress regularly opposed this move (until 2023), notably under pressure from elected officials in Arizona. Indeed, Davis-Monthan Air Force Base, near Tucson, is the main base for the A-10s and contributes nearly $2.5 billion annually to the local economy, a windfall that elected officials do not wish to deprive themselves of. Here, political constraint prevents the armed forces from changing.[7]

In contrast, the British armed forces developed under strong institutional constraints, and are more flexible owing to the habit of external government intervention in their day-to-day operations. According to Avant, these institutional practices explain why the British Army, under pressure from the cabinet, was quickly able to develop counterinsurgency doctrines during the Boer War and in Malaya, while the US Army was able to resist the wishes of the Kennedy administration and maintain a doctrine based on destroying the adversary more than protecting the population in Vietnam. However, even in a system such as Britain's, in which political control is easier, the military tries to retain autonomous areas of legitimate expertise. Thus, recent British doctrinal developments, and in particular the emphasis placed on notions such as "multi-domain integration" or "integrated operating concept," can be seen as an attempt to develop a particular jargon, opaque to the uninitiated outside the Ministry of Defence, but which enables them to claim a specific competence in the field of the future of military operations.[8] The doctrinal change can thus be interpreted in this case as the result of a mechanism for circumventing not a potential external adversary, but civilian rivals in the civil–military division of powers.

In India, civil–military relations are characterized by an "absent dialogue."[9] In some areas, the Indian armed forces actually enjoy considerable autonomy, ceded in practice by politicians and civil servants who have neither the expertise nor the motivation to exert an effective control. Elsewhere, it is hampered, mainly by bureaucrats who hold the purse strings, and by institutional arrangements that stifle and inhibit action and reform. In areas where greater civilian participation could genuinely improve the army's effectiveness, it is absent; in areas where civilian participation can inhibit, it is stifling. The armed forces retain a high degree of control, even in areas where greater civilian involvement would actually be beneficial. In the field of capability development, both bureaucrats and officers, often at loggerheads, lack the expertise needed to make the right decisions in a system that is distorted anyway by lack of accountability, corruption and political interference. Inter-service cooperation is also compromised, largely due to a lack of civilian understanding of its importance and a tendency on the part of civilians to avoid getting involved in internecine wars between services, a tendency exacerbated by the autonomy enjoyed by the armed forces in organizational and operational matters: an Indian-style Goldwater-Nichols Act seems a long way off. Professional military education could also benefit from greater civilian involvement, provided that the civilians concerned are better informed about military and strategic affairs and recognize the need for officers to study in the best programs abroad. As things stand, the system remains "in-house" and inadequate, focusing on what officers know best—operations and tactics—and neglecting the development of critical and strategic thinking. When it comes to promotions and appointments, civilians have had more impact, but a lack of expertise also affects this area, as does the tendency to defer to the opinion of uniformed leaders and let their sectoral interests take precedence over the system. Defense planning also suffers from these and other shortcomings, notably the inability of successive governments to give binding assurances on the availability of funds, on the one hand, and the abdication of agenda-setting power to the armed forces, on the other. We can see here how dysfunctional political–military relations and the siloed separation of responsibilities are actually holding back military change.

The importance of institutional arrangements is also evident in other countries. In France, the constitution of the Fifth Republic enshrines the central role of the executive, and in particular of the President of the Republic, in defining military doctrine and its implementation (in practice this tends to reduce the role of the Prime Minister, despite the fact that he or she is constitutionally responsible for national defense).[10] This reaffirmation of the role of the executive obviously follows on from the problematic relations between civilian authorities and the military during the Algerian War, which led to a progressive distrust of political leaders by the army. In 1960, before the putsch of the generals in 1961, Raoul Girardet noted that "everything seems to be happening as if the armed forces considered themselves to have a kind of political right of arbitration or veto. They believe they are entitled to exercise this right of arbitration or veto in the face of a decision or change in civilian power that would immediately threaten what they consider to be the major requirements of national destiny."[11]

Faced with this form of conditional obedience, which could easily tip over into a putsch, General de Gaulle was determined to reassert the pre-eminence of politics, especially as he intended to take advantage of the nuclear project begun under the Fourth Republic to radically change French strategic doctrine. In 1961, de Gaulle gave a major speech in Strasbourg, in which he developed his vision of defense policy.

> For the Head of State, France's armed forces must have three functions. Firstly, they must be equipped with modern weaponry, including (and above all) nuclear weapons. Secondly, given the globalization of conflicts, troops must not be concentrated in a single region, but be ready to fight (almost) anywhere. Finally, they must provide "immediate defense," and therefore be based on national territory. In this presentation, we can recognize the three pillars of force structure that would later be developed (strategic nuclear–intervention–territorial defense), and we can already glimpse the concept of an "all-out" defense that would reappear in the 1960s.[12]

According to the then Minister of Defense, Pierre Messmer, the speech was received very coldly, if not with hostility, by the forces, who feared that funding for conventional means would be cut in favor of a nuclear capability whose usefulness was still unclear and whose doctrine was undeveloped.[13] However, it was the French President's desire to provide France with a nuclear deterrent capability that led to a profound change in the organization and doctrine of the French armed forces, equipping them with new resources against their will. Indeed, nuclear capability was a strong identity marker for General de Gaulle, who was preoccupied with his quest for France's "greatness": in 1964, he reportedly confided to his close friend Alain Peyrefitte: "We make atomic bombs and their delivery systems, and we will continue to do so. We're doing it less to face up to a threat than because we want to regain our sovereignty. Regaining our independence is the main purpose of our nuclear force. And then, of course, there's defense. If we're not threatened now, we could be one day."[14] This policy was initially organized by Pierre Messmer, who undertook a reform of his ministry's structures with a view to building up the deterrent capability.[15]

Subsequently, all major developments in French doctrine were driven by a reconfiguration of civil–military relations, with the President remaining the cornerstone of the main changes.[16] A good illustration of this is Jacques Chirac's decision to suspend national service in 1996–1997. The figure of the President of the Republic was central to the decision: "the reform of the armed forces was decided and led by Jacques Chirac. [...] A failure to elect Jacques Chirac to the Presidency of the Republic would very probably have led to the extension of the mixed army and the maintenance of national service."[17] It was indeed Jacques Chirac's choice that gradually imposed itself on the Ministry of Defense, whose preference was to revamp and optimize the mixed system (comprising a proportion of professional troops and a proportion of conscripts). The narrative that professionalization was somehow the inevitable consequence of the changing strategic context of the post-Cold War era is an a posteriori reconstruction, which rationalizes the decision while concealing the divergent preferences of the civilian and military powers of the time. This decision obviously had major consequences for the format of the armed forces themselves, but also for the ways in which authority was regulated internally: in particular, the ways in which command was exercised were largely adapted to take account of the transition from a military population made up mainly of conscripts to an exclusively volunteer population.[18] We can see here how the ability of civilian authorities to impose change (a mechanism of constraint) can lead to innovation: the two most profound transformations of the French armed forces under the Fifth Republic did not come from the armed forces themselves, and were more a matter of political preferences than reactions to threats.

The imposition of change by civilian authorities is not limited to doctrine and capabilities, but also concerns norms within the institution. Since the attempted coup of 2016, the Turkish regime has imposed a number of organizational reforms aimed at institutionalizing Islam within the armed forces, leading to a number of changes in daily practices: prayer, takbir, the place given to piety, the end of certain forms of discrimination, and so on. This institutionalization does not mean the disappearance of Kemalist practices but is indicative of a political desire for greater control over the armed forces, in order to facilitate convergence between the values of the Turkish armed forces and the dominant values of civil society.[19]

Conversely, in contemporary Latin America, the armed forces take on a significant number of internal security tasks (police missions, border control, public health functions such as garbage collection, and sometimes even tasks like providing hairdressing services in isolated communities or offering rudimentary education). On the one hand, this is a pragmatic response to the lack of institutional capacity in the region's states, which are thus able to draw on existing resources. However, in addition to the fact that recourse to the armed forces constrains the development of civilian capacities, military organizations also benefit from this, since these functions enable them to continue to play a pre-eminent political and social role, corresponding to their own conception of their role as guardians of the state and the *patria*. However, this politico-military configuration has prevented any significant reform and modernization of these armed forces, to the detriment of their military effectiveness.[20] In certain contexts, and depending on their position within the state apparatus, the armed forces may indeed actively refuse to reduce their politico-social role. In Algeria, for example, the so-called Hirak protest movement began in 2019, one of whose demands was the establishment of a "civilian, non-military state." This slogan was completely rejected by the military authorities, with the 2020 constitutional revision even enshrining the army as guardian of the country's "vital and strategic interests" (art. 30, para. 4), the exact opposite of one major demand of the Hirak.[21] Similarly, following Marshal Sissi's seizure of power in Egypt in 2014, the Egyptian Army gradually extended its hold over multiple economic, political and social sectors of the country, gradually creating a "neo-militarist" society, without any increase in operational effectiveness (particularly in the fight against terrorism); indeed, quite the contrary.[22]

The importance of political preferences

Obviously, political preference is not necessarily independent of threat perception itself: policy elites can construct different paradigms (e.g. crisis management versus territorial defense), which are more or less shared and whose implementation can guide defense reform.[23] The evolution of Chinese military doctrine since 1949 is an interesting example. Three major and four minor changes can be identified in China's military strategy during this period. The so-called strategic or forward defense of 1956, which emphasized the defense of coastal areas against a possible American invasion, represented a major change from the military strategy of the civil war, and was followed by a minor change in 1960; the "active defense" of 1980 was a major change aimed at countering a possible Soviet invasion from the north, and was followed by a minor change in 1988; and the "local wars under high-tech conditions" doctrine of 1993 was a major change that shifted the emphasis south and east along China's coastal zone, and was followed by minor changes in 2004 and 2014. According to Taylor Fravel, the extent of these doctrinal changes can be explained by the interplay between two variables: the perception of a change in the character of war and the degree of unity of the Chinese Communist Party.[24] When either of these two factors was absent, changes in military doctrine were minor or non-existent. For example, the 1956 strategy, according to Fravel, resulted from the lessons of modern warfare drawn from the study of the Second World War and the Korean War, and was implemented by a party united by the leadership of Mao Zedong. The 1980 strategic shift resulted from a study of the change in the conduct of warfare that manifested itself in the 1973 Arab–Israeli war, and was implemented by a party just unified by Deng Xiaoping after the divisions of the Cultural Revolution. The 1993 strategy, Fravel continues, resulted from the study of the 1991 Gulf War, with its high-tech precision strikes, air dominance and advanced weaponry, and was implemented by a party recently united after the divisions caused by the Tiananmen Square massacre. In each case, the main strategic changes affected operational doctrine, force structure and training. Here we see the importance of a political variable (namely party unity) in military change.

Another particularly illustrative example of this importance is provided by the USSR and, later, Russia. Specialists have long noted the influence of the siloviki, the members of the armed forces, secret services (FSB, SVR) and paramilitary forces of certain Russian ministries (interior ministry, border guards, presidential guard, prosecutor-general's office, government communications and information agency in particular) within the state apparatus, since they make up around a quarter of the governing structures at all levels of the Russian administration and more than 60% of the Kremlin staff. The importance of the siloviki is nevertheless part of a long history of civil–military relations in the Soviet Union and, later, in Russia.

Thus, according to Tom Nichols, the Soviets never succeeded in establishing a military institution that was guided by the political sphere, rather than being tempted to intervene in it.[25] As a result, the Party and the Red Army were in fact simultaneously partners and competitors, with Soviet defense policy the subject of fierce competition between civilians and the military, rather than being defined by civilians and implemented by the military, as in Western democracies. Nichols also argues that the Red Army was in fact more ideologized than the Party itself, with the Marxist-Leninist rigor of the military often pitted against a more pragmatic Party.

Four phenomena contributed to this situation of permanent tension. Firstly, the ideological question is fundamental. Steeped in Marxist-Leninist ideology, Soviet officers saw their loyalty as being to the state and the Party conceived in the abstract, and therefore saw no contradiction in defending the Party while criticizing its leaders. This specific aspect of Soviet military culture blended with the traditional Russian imperial conception of Moscow as the "Third Rome," with everything that was good for the Party necessarily being good for the whole world. Secondly, the question of control over doctrine was a major one. Contrary to Western practice, Russian military doctrine was conceived as a Marxist-Leninist science and therefore implied Party participation in its elaboration: Soviet doctrine went far beyond the armed forces, and had consequences for all aspects of life in the USSR (education of young people, location of production industries, scientific exchanges with the non-communist world, etc.). By its very nature, control of the doctrine implied control of significant resources and was therefore a political issue. The problem was that, since the Party was the source of Marxist-Leninist science, the military could not question the doctrine without questioning the Party itself. Unlike in the US, where the President is at the top of the chain of command but not in charge of determining doctrine (and the military can therefore debate it), opposition to doctrine in the USSR was necessarily a challenge to the Party. Thirdly, and in line with the weak constitutionalism of Soviet political culture, there was no legal regulation of civil–military interactions. This not only allowed Stalin's strong intrusion into military affairs during the totalitarian phase of the USSR, but also enabled the military to attempt to influence the security agenda after Stalin's death, thus participating in a competition with the Party already made possible by ideology and the struggle for control of doctrine. Finally, the participation of many military personnel in civilian bodies such as the Central Committee, the Supreme Soviet and sometimes even the Politburo helped to shift the civil–military conflict into the political arena itself. The armed forces were no longer simply at the service of the state, but also of specific career interests, with some divisional commanders being deputies or holding other elective offices.

These four factors have influenced the Red Army since 1917, starting with the strong opposition between Leon Trotsky and Mikhail Frunze over the definition of what a Soviet military doctrine should be, with the latter arguing that military doctrine should be scientifically based on Marxist-Leninist theory. Stalin pushed this logic to the limit, since as First Secretary (and therefore the Party personified), he was the only one who could formulate doctrine.[26] After Stalin's death, Khrushchev tried to maintain relatively strong control over the military, but, as he was not Stalin, latent tensions between civilians and the military began to emerge. And, in fact, the Brezhnev period was marked by the gradual withdrawal of civilians and the military domination of the definition of Soviet defense policy, a situation that Andropov and Chernenko had neither the time nor the will to change. The real attempt to regain control was led by

Gorbachev, but was ultimately unsuccessful due to bureaucratic resistance and other political priorities of the moment, notably management of an economy on the brink of collapse. Here we see a fundamental question raised by civil–military relations: what to do with a social class accustomed to not being controlled by civilians, ideologized to the point of identifying its interests with those of the state, and predisposed to intervene in politics by virtue of the elective positions held by some of its members?

Zoltan Barany provides the answer, linking the state of civil–military relations to the failure of Russian democratization after the collapse of the USSR.[27] For Barany, the Russian military was "departified" after the fall of the USSR, but not depoliticized, as was the habit under the Soviet regime, adopting behaviors that were problematic from the point of view of the functioning of civil–military relations, such as the involvement of active officers in electoral competition (with the support of their superiors), acts of insubordination to political power that were rewarded rather than sanctioned, opposition to certain state policies, and practices clearly aimed at lying to civilian authorities. Three main events have contributed to the impossibility of establishing democratic control of the armed forces in Russia. Firstly, Gorbachev's invitation to the active military to participate in electoral politics set Russian civil–military relations on a dangerous course. The second moment was the acceptance of this situation by Yeltsin, who was dependent on the support of the army after the 1991 coup attempt, and even more so after his (theoretically forbidden) dissolution of parliament in 1993. The "Afghans" generation, followed by the "Chechens," tried to gain electoral positions, often on lists run by ultra-nationalist parties opposed to Yeltsin. These attempts were met with limited success, but they legitimized the existence of a class of military officials in office who openly and publicly opposed the defense policy. As a result, the third formative moment was Putin's determination to integrate these military officials into the state apparatus by appointing them to political posts (as provincial governors, or to senior positions in the Kremlin or ministries). This clientelist policy eliminated the military from the competition for legislative posts (which in any case were of less and less importance owing to the gradual concentration of power in the hands of the executive initiated under Yeltsin and strongly accentuated under Putin), but it made possible the maintenance of a class of "military politicians," this time direct clients of the Putin regime. There are several examples of military personnel advocating reform of the armed forces or opposing Putin who mysteriously fell silent once they obtained positions of responsibility. A caricature of this co-optation policy could be seen in the promotion of those responsible for the Kursk submarine tragedy, four months after their initial dismissal from the armed forces, and despite the fact that the Russian commission of inquiry had found them responsible for negligence and lies.

This political presence of the military has had important consequences for Russian defense policy. In the early 2000s, Russian security doctrine saw international terrorism as the main threat, while the military doctrine established by the General Staff (populated by officers who had not really accepted the end of the Cold War) still saw NATO as an existential threat. In other words, the doctrine established by the military was in deliberate contradiction with the foreign policy priorities established at the political level. We can certainly see the definition of NATO as the main enemy from 2010 onwards in Russia's security doctrine as a victory for the military and a consequence of their growing weight in the apparatus of power. It is also understandable that all the attempts at cooperation made by the West (financing the securing of Russian nuclear arsenals, the NATO–Russia Council, invitations to participate in the NATO missile defense shield, cooperation in the fight against terrorism, arms sales and the Obama administration's effort to "reset" relations) were ultimately unsuccessful: in a vision of the world as a zero-sum game, where anything bad for the West is necessarily good for Russia, the Russian military benefited from these policies (to modernize their armaments, obtain intelligence and influence within NATO, and legitimize their brutal policies in the Caucasus) but never had any intention of establishing deep cooperation.[28]

This configuration of powers explains the difficulty of reforming the Russian military, and in particular its continued insistence on conscription, heavy armaments and mass, despite regular efforts to modernize.²⁹ The Russian military found itself in a situation where it was incapable of reforming itself, but had sufficient power to block attempts at reform initiated by the civilian authorities.³⁰ Thus, it is notable that the most significant attempt to reform the Russian Army, initiated by Anatoly Serdyukov when he was Minister of Defense (2007–2012) and based on a fight against corruption, transformation of conscription and increased professionalism among officers and NCOs, was strongly resisted by the armed forces, culminating in his dismissal by Putin in 2012.³¹

Finally, it should be noted that the authoritarian drift of the Russian regime, and the concentration of power in the hands of the President, prevent the emergence of reliable information for the *Duma* (the Russian parliament) on the state of the Russian armed forces, of which no one, not even senior military officials, the defense minister or Putin, has a clear picture. It seems that this structural problem, which poses command and coordination problems between political and military leaders, manifested itself during the Russian invasion of Ukraine in 2022. In fact, "the advantages of democratic systems do not lie in their ability to avoid bad decisions, whether on the part of the government or commanders. [...] The advantages lie in their ability to recognize mistakes, to learn and to adapt,"³² something that authoritarian regimes do not allow. We can see here the importance of the configuration of political–military relations, in this case in an authoritarian and kleptocratic state, for change (or the absence of change) in the armed forces: while incremental improvements are possible under the effect of new doctrines or new technologies, profound reforms of practices (in particular, the end of corruption or systematic bullying against new recruits, the infamous *dedovshchina*) is impossible because of the way the regime functions.³³

Political intrusions in the military

The configuration of political–military relations can lead to innovations (as in the case of the imposition of nuclear deterrence in France) and an increase in military effectiveness, but it can of course have the completely opposite result. The most striking example (and probably an extreme one) is the arrest and execution of thousands of Red Army officers between June 1937 and November 1938. In all, 35,000 officers were imprisoned or executed, including Mikhail Tukhachevsky, hero of the Russian Civil War and certainly one of the most outstanding Soviet strategists, who contributed greatly to both the doctrinal and capability development of the Red Army.[34] These arrests were a pivotal moment in the unleashing of the "Great Terror," during which over a million Soviet citizens were imprisoned in labor camps and at least 750,000 were executed. This purge of the Red Army, which had a lasting effect on the institution, had its origins in the October Revolution and the Bolshevik unease with a hierarchical institution inherited from Tsarism. This original unease (which had led to military experiments such as "soldiers' committees," before Trotsky took over and relied on Tsarist officers) was, over time, coupled with Stalin's obsession with the enemy within, leading him to become convinced of the existence of a conspiracy within the military and, more broadly, within Soviet society. The purge of the Red Army had a disastrous effect on its cohesion: "Part of the Red Army indulges in an orgy of denunciations. All loyalties are shattered. There is no esprit de corps, no self-defense reflex in the institution. Most officers huddle in their shells, keep contact with the outside world to a minimum and wait for the storm to pass."[35] Indeed, the elimination of many military cadres during this period is generally put forward as one of the factors explaining the poor Soviet performance against Nazi troops in the early stages of Operation Barbarossa. Similarly, the purge could explain the absence of an alliance between France, the UK and the USSR against Nazi Germany before the start of the Second World War, as the scale of the violence of the Great Terror horrified politicians in London and Paris, who saw Stalin as an unreliable and dangerous leader with a weakened army.[36]

Without reaching the brutality of the great Soviet purges, the fear that leaders may have of their own armed forces does appear to be an explanatory factor for certain military changes. Thus, Caitlin Talmadge argues that elites facing strong external threats but few or no internal challenges will strive to increase the capacity of their armed forces to maximize operational efficiency. Specifically, they will ensure that officers are promoted on merit rather than because of political connections, that soldier training is comprehensive and realistic, that command and control structures are unified and rationally organized, and that information management protocols facilitate the rapid flow of data and intelligence throughout the forces. The calmer politico-military context allows these elites to know that the operational effectiveness of their armed forces—necessary to ensure national defense—is not in danger of being turned against them. By contrast, according to Talmadge, elites facing strong internal threats and few significant external challenges are likely to undermine the tactical and operational capabilities of their armies by prioritizing political loyalty over competence in officer selection and promotion, downplaying soldier training, creating multiple, tangled chains of command, and complicating intra-military communication. This makes it more difficult for armies to launch coups of their own accord or to serve as an effective tool for opposition civilian elites in their efforts to depose those in power. The fact that the resulting forces are likely to be ineffective in combat is relatively unimportant, since the scarcity of external threats reduces the chances that they will be called upon to fight. Elites faced with a mix of internal and external threats are likely to follow one of two paths: they can either strive to adapt the army so that it responds to what they see as the most pressing threat (usually internal) and keep their fingers crossed for the other challenge (usually external), or they can create a mixed force in which the bulk of the army is structured so that it represents only a small internal threat, and selected units are reinforced so that they are able to operate effectively on the battlefield.[37]

A good illustration of this is the Iran–Iraq War. Neither Iranian nor Iraqi leaders felt secure during the war and, as a result, both adopted policies and practices that undermined the conventional combat effectiveness of their armies. Iran, however, fared better than Iraq at the start of the war, as a large proportion of its regular forces still enjoyed the advantages in leadership and training derived from the Shah's period. This competence eroded over time and, from 1982 onwards, the Iranians regularly failed to demonstrate basic tactical competence or execute complex operations. Iraq, on the other hand, exhibited marked tactical and operational improvement by the end of the war, after struggling to fight properly for six years.

Talmadge shows that this change can be attributed to the fact that President Saddam Hussein of Iraq changed his threat perception. In particular, Saddam Hussein increasingly feared growing internal threats stemming largely from the military's dissatisfaction with the way the external threat posed by Iran was being managed, and, to relieve the pressure, he reluctantly authorized improvements in officer selection, training and command structures in the Republican Guard and some regular army units.[38]

As we can see, the configuration of political–military relations provides a context of prime importance for understanding military change. Depending on the degree of trust and cooperation between political and military powers, change can be initiated by a mechanism of constraint, which can sometimes lead to innovations (as in the case of nuclear deterrence or the Goldwater-Nichols Act) or to brutal disruptions (as in the case of the Great Purges). But we can also observe a mechanism of circumvention, with political and military authorities sometimes competing for positions of power. Hence, it is necessary not only to look at the institutional regulations and normative practices framing political–military interactions, but to also consider the armed forces as political actors, engaged in some form of military politics.[39] The outcome of these political competitions shapes the way the armed forces evolve.

The sinews of war: the political economy of military change

The *condottiere* (and marshal of France) Gian Giacomo Trivulzio is reported to have told King Louis XII: "To sustain war, three things are necessary: money, money and more money." In fact, the ability of armies to finance themselves directly determines their form and, therefore, their evolution. In his book on *The Wealth of Nations*, Adam Smith had already observed that defense funding was a government responsibility, not least because defense is a public good. A public good benefits all citizens equally, whereas private goods are consumed individually and only by those who own them: when a public good like defense is "produced," it applies to all citizens, whether they have participated in its production (e.g. through taxation) or not. Smith argued that it was the state's responsibility to finance defense properly, not least because the cost of warfare was increasing as a result of technological development:

> The great change introduced into the art of war by the invention of fire-arms, has enhanced still further both the expense of exercising and disciplining any particular number of soldiers in time of peace, and that of employing them in time of war. Both their arms and their ammunition are become more expensive. A musket is a more expensive machine than a javelin or a bow and arrows; a cannon or a mortar, than a balista or a catapulta. The powder which is spent in a modern review is lost irrecoverably, and occasions a very considerable expense. The javelins and arrows which were thrown or shot in an ancient one, could easily be picked up again, and were, besides, of very little value. The cannon and the mortar are not only much dearer, but much heavier machines than the balista or catapulta; and require a greater expense, not only to prepare them for the field, but to carry them to it. As the superiority of the modern artillery, too, over that of the ancients, is very great; it has become much more difficult, and consequently much more expensive, to fortify a town, so as to resist, even for a few weeks, the attack of that superior artillery. In modern times, many different causes contribute to render the defence of the society more expensive. The unavoidable effects of the natural progress of improvement have, in this respect, been a good deal enhanced by a great revolution in the art of war, to which a mere accident, the invention of gunpowder, seems to have given occasion.[40]

Charles Tilly has shown how the rising cost of war, and therefore the need to systematize its financing through the bureaucratic capacity to raise taxes or mobilize soldiers, contributed to state consolidation in Europe,[41] even if this was not the case everywhere in the world, notably in Asia (where state consolidation is thought to be mainly due to emulation of the Chinese model).[42] Similarly, the Industrial Revolution of the nineteenth century can be at least partially explained by the development of the British arms industry, linked to the country's imperial ambitions.[43] In all cases, the gradual generalization of the model of the state as a sovereign political entity and the basic unit of the international system over the course of the nineteenth and twentieth centuries helped to make the financing of war a public good, financed by the state, in most regions of the world (although geographical and temporal variations can be observed).[44] As a public good, defense funding obviously competes with other types of public expenditure, and the political choices made naturally shape the evolution of the armed forces.

Funding defense

In the first place, states have several ways of financing their defense effort, all of which are more or less costly for citizens: forced labor, forced savings plans, direct taxation, war bonds, indirect taxation, floating debt, issuing money, austerity measures, existing savings, indebtedness to foreign creditors, international donations, or plundering foreign resources.[45]

When it comes to choosing a defense funding method, decision-makers have to choose between several conflicting incentives. A direct resource extraction method, because of its compulsory nature, makes citizens particularly aware of defense issues, even if it makes possible rapid funding (depending on whether the state has sufficient administrative capacity to impose the process). Indirect resource extraction is less visible to the public but, depending on the instrument chosen, may entail risks such as incurring inflation. Finally, the extraction of foreign resources is painless for citizens but can make the state dependent on foreign creditors. Historically, states have adopted a combination of these instruments, depending on the situation, in an attempt to meet defense needs while minimizing the economic and political risks of their decisions.

The choice of financing method has important consequences for the structuring of armed forces, and for certain capability and doctrinal choices. Military power can be regarded as the combination of two production factors: capital (armaments, munitions, human capital acquired through training, etc.) and labor (number of soldiers, sailors, airmen serving in the armed forces). One factor of production can partially replace another, albeit imperfectly: for example, the development of a nuclear deterrent capability by

France can be understood in economic terms as a preference for the capital factor over the labor factor. All other things being equal (and, in particular, without taking into account the prestigious aspect of possessing a technology seen as the preserve of a very small number of states), it is less costly for France to equip itself with a nuclear deterrent than with a conventional deterrent: it would be necessary to mobilize a considerable number of soldiers under the flags (labor factor) to achieve the same degree of deterrent credibility as that offered by nuclear deterrence (capital factor). However, the two factors are not completely substitutable: the possession of a nuclear deterrent capability does not cover all modes of force employment, for which conventional means are always necessary.[46]

It is easy to observe that the armed forces of Western countries are highly capital-intensive, while the labor factor is less important (smaller armies, fewer conscripts). To get the full picture, we need to look at the political economy of these countries. Indeed, most of them have weakly regulated labor markets (there is a free market for workers to find a job), which generally forces armies to compete with other employers for the recruitment and retention of skilled workers: even Western armed forces that rely partly on conscription need career soldiers. In fact, there is a significant correlation between labor market flexibility and the political choice to have relatively small professional armed forces,[47] and competition for workers leads these armed forces not only to adapt their recruitment practices, but also to anticipate career trajectories (notably by providing skills that can be reused for a civilian career).[48] Moreover, most of these countries are democracies, a regime that forces elected officials to implement the preferences of the average voter,[49] and this average citizen is reluctant to pay the cost of war. As a result, an excellent way to finance the cost of defense in a democracy is through debt (which is less costly for the average voter than taxes) and to favor force structures reliant on capital (high-performance military equipment) rather than labor (number of soldiers). In Western democracies, these financing methods mean that the average voter pays comparatively less for defense than citizens elsewhere, but they also influence both the format of the armed forces and their doctrines of employment. In the US and Israel, for example, the average electorate is generally associated with greater support for the use of force. On the other hand, there is no obvious link with perceived threat: if the average electorate is more supportive of the use of force, the reason is not that they feel more threatened by the outside world, but that they do not pay the cost associated with the use of the military instrument.[50] In the case of the US, the transition from tax-based to debt-based defense funding since the Korean War, coupled with the professionalization of the armed forces since the Vietnam War, has led to a relative lack of interest on the part of citizens in defense issues, thereby diminishing democratic control over the military choices made by the executive branch.[51]

Of course, satisfying the average voter is not the only political economy consideration with consequences for the size of armies. As Adam Smith already envisaged, the rising cost of armaments has a structuring effect on the evolution of armies themselves and on their employment. For example, Britain's grand strategy between 1904 and 1969 was an attempt to adapt, in a politically acceptable way, to growing inflation in the price of weapons systems (which was rising faster than British GNP), while maintaining its international role. From the eighteenth to the twentieth century, the British strategy was one of blockade and attrition, preferably avoiding heavy Continental commitments of land forces but with substantial subsidies to allies in Europe. This strategy was associated with the financial capacity to sustain relatively long conflicts, but was ultimately favorable economically in terms of opening up new markets. The First World War changed this configuration. As a proportion of national income, Britain spent scarcely more on defense in 1914 than it had in the years following the Boer War. This prudence was not the result of short-term structural limitations in the economy, but rather of a concern for fiscal orthodoxy and the desire to correlate military spending with taxation. This link between taxation and military expenditure was abandoned in 1916, making London partially dependent on the US for funding, and entirely dependent on Washington for its stock of foreign currencies. After the war, the link between defense spending and taxation was re-established, but the financing of the British armed forces suffered from a drop in tax yield due to other charges to be paid: notably debt servicing, and unemployment and housing benefits. It was not until 1935 that the government again decided to finance defense through debt. After the Second World War, the UK adopted a defense policy that favored military capital and, therefore, smaller armed forces with advanced technologies and weapons systems. This helped to strengthen the strategic relationship with the US, particularly with a view to reducing production costs.[52] The question of how to finance defense thus has consequences for the direction taken by military change (notably through a mechanism of constraint), and new avenues of financing are regularly explored. In 2023, for example, specialists proposed making better use of the colossal resources of the American capital market in order to finance the armed forces of the US.[53]

Financing instruments

In addition to the general economic and political context, which influences a country's defense funding model, it is important to look at the public policy instruments used to implement these choices. A public policy instrument can be defined as "a technical and social device that organizes specific social relationships between the public authorities and those for whom it is intended, based on the representations and meanings it conveys."[54] In the case of France, the main public policy instrument responsible for organizing defense funding is the military programming system, notably through the Military Programming Law (abbreviated in French as LPM). Over the long term of the French state budget, the trend is toward the "normalization" of defense spending, through a three-pronged movement to unify and clarify defense spending (to avoid accusations of "debudgetization"), institutionalize multi-annual programming, and eliminate heterodox budgetary practices.[55] The case of programming is particularly interesting, since it concentrates the tensions between military and financial imperatives, and highlights the role of public policy instruments in military change. In France, the principle of an annual vote on public expenditure (the annualization principle) was consolidated in the nineteenth century. However, military programming required a form of multi-annualization, owing to the scale of expenditure involved, particularly in armaments programs. Before the Second World War, several legal means of derogating from the annualization principle were tried out, and were consolidated in several stages after the Second World War. A law of 30 March 1947 created the principle of program authorizations (in French, AE, which are authorizations to incur expenses) and payment credits (CP, which are the actual funds available to cover the AEs), while the constitution of the Fifth Republic provides for the possibility of a "program law" and a financial ordinance of 2 January 1959 enables program authorizations to be grouped together. The various instruments required for multi-year programming of defense spending were thus consolidated under Gaullism through the LPM. The LPM is fundamentally a programming tool invented not only to provide for major multi-year investments, but also to indicate a trajectory for the armed forces: programming by cycle provides relative visibility to the evolution of formats. However, as the basic principle of French budgetary law is annualization, the LPM is not normative in nature: it must be transposed each year into the annual Finance Acts, which are legally binding.

The first LPM, which ran from 1960 to 1964, was aimed at equipping the French armed forces with a nuclear arsenal (against their will, as we have seen), while the next two LPMs, even if they included an increasing share dedicated to conventional forces, were aimed at finalizing the equipment of the three components of the French nuclear deterrent.[56] But the objective of having such an instrument was a political one:

> Programming is a tool of military Gaullism, a way of governing the armed forces rather than a strategic doctrine. LPMs helped the executive to impose its will on the staffs and members of parliament. Moreover, in the wake of the military rebellions in Algeria, programming also helped the civilian authorities to regain control of the military. Finally, politicians set the course through planning and programming. In so doing, it defines higher interests and common objectives.[57]

This multi-year programming, together with the increasing standardization of budgetary practices, has de facto led the Ministry of Finance to take a closer look at defense spending, which necessarily has consequences in a context of budgetary restraint. Since the end of the Cold War, the French Ministry of Defense has been comparatively more affected by budget restrictions than other ministries,[58] which has led to successive adjustments in the size of the armed forces. In order to minimize the effects of these budget cuts, managers used three types of compensatory strategies: generating exceptional (and therefore uncertain) revenue, for example by selling off the ministry's real estate assets; re-categorizing equipment purchases (which were supposed to be part of a multi-year program) as off-the-shelf emergency purchases (in order to benefit from exceptional funds linked, for example, to overseas operations); and postponing armament programs.[59] The last-mentioned compensatory strategy has two components. The first is to reduce the volume of orders and spread programs over time. However, this approach generally leads to an increase in the unit cost of the weapon system (as economies of scale are reduced), which diminishes the effectiveness of the measure. For example, France was initially scheduled to acquire seventeen FREMM multi-purpose frigates, a figure reduced to eight in the 2009–2014 LPM. This reduction in the overall volume increased the unit cost of a FREMM, with the program to acquire eight FREMMs remaining about as costly as that for seventeen. Admittedly, personnel and maintenance costs are necessarily reduced, and savings are therefore made over the entire life cycle of the frigate, but the immediate financial gain is far from obvious. The second component is simply a deferral of expenses, which consists in postponing spending that cannot be carried out in the current budget year, something generally referred to as the "payment hump."[60] In the 1990s, this "payment hump" increased as a result of late payments for five major programs: the Rafale aircraft, the Tiger helicopter, the M-51 missile, the new-generation nuclear submarine and the Leclerc tank. Thus,

> in 2007, a study by the French Ministry of Defense estimated that between 40 and 70 billion euros would be needed to achieve the *Armées 2015* model, due to the growth of the "hump." This realization weighed heavily on the work of the 2008 White Paper

commission, which made a major reduction in the size of the armed forces in an attempt to bring the military model into line with available funding capacities.[61]

In fact, 54,000 jobs were slated for elimination at the Ministry of Defense, with operating expenses cut in an attempt to safeguard equipment spending as much as possible. Similarly, budgetary constraints led to a number of innovative organizational changes, such as the creation of *bases de défense* (BDD), which centralized support for several units, but at the same time reduced the room for maneuver and authority of the commanders of these same units (e.g. the commander of a regiment), who became dependent on external players. As one colonel put it, "I can't even get the walls painted or a light bulb changed without the BDD."[62] This shows how defense funding instruments can be used to implement a constraint mechanism that brings about change in the armed forces.

Budgetary ideologies

Finally, we need to consider the normative weight of the zeitgeist in shaping economic-political configurations and their consequences for military change. For example, the outsourcing and privatization movement, which has led to a significant reduction in the skills and size of the US armed forces since the end of the Second World War, is directly linked to the consolidation of neoliberal ideology and the belief in the superior efficiency of the private sector. Indeed, a movement emerged aimed at revitalizing private enterprise and diminishing the influence of the federal government. While certain military decision-makers expressed skepticism regarding the purported advantages of privatization, others actively endorsed the initiative; more commonly, however, officials adopted a stance of ambivalence as they proceeded with the implementation of outsourcing reforms.[63] Privatization took place in two phases. The first, from the end of the 1940s to the 1970s, saw the transfer to the private sector of skills in arms production, land and property ownership, and some basic services previously held by the armed forces. The second phase, from the 1990s onwards, privatized social welfare (including assistance for families and veterans) and logistical support. This anti-state ideology had deep roots in American history and, according to Aaron L. Friedberg, could even partially explain American strategic choices, which in the early 1960s settled on a doctrine of "flexible response." This had the advantage of representing a compromise between building a credible capability against the USSR without requiring too great an increase in the role of the state (notably by limiting its role of direct resource extraction).[64] Thus, the transformation of the US armed forces has often been portrayed by its advocates as the inevitable outcome of rational economic decision-making; in reality, however, it has more closely resembled a "political campaign."[65]

In France, the transformation of the role of the state began when François Mitterrand came to power in 1981, but it accelerated sharply under the presidency of Nicolas Sarkozy (2007–2012), with the implementation of the General Reform of Public Policies (RGPP) process, which also affected defense.[66] Support services were particularly targeted, notably catering and clothing, although outsourcing was eventually abandoned in favor of an internal rationalization method known as *régie rationalisée optimisée* (RRO).[67] Similarly, a growing proportion of the operational maintenance of military equipment has been outsourced to private companies, again with a view to rationalization and efficiency, and despite the complexities this entails. In France, as in many other NATO countries, the same logic has governed the flow management of ammunition supplies, thus preventing the building up of stocks, whose usefulness has been demonstrated by the war in Ukraine.[68] Generally speaking, the logistical support of Western armies is said to have fallen victim to the adoption of a "post-Fordist" approach, inspired by the civilian world and characterized by the centralization of management control and the simultaneous decentralization of production processes, resulting in flattened hierarchies; the replacement of the mass workforce by a highly skilled core and a less-skilled periphery; the outsourcing of non-essential functions; and the development of a networked approach to supply and knowledge. Although more efficient, this system nevertheless makes Western armies more vulnerable to strategic shocks, as their logistical supply lacks both volume and resilience.[69]

These examples illustrate how dominant economic beliefs also play a role in military change.

Armed forces and civil society

A third type of configuration is possible, this time between the armed forces and their country's civil society. Every soldier is first and foremost a civilian who is progressively militarized, i.e. socialized in an institution whose norms, rites and values he or she learns (despite the mythical biography that some invent for themselves by associating their identity with their profession). The "Triomphe" ceremony at Saint-Cyr, the French Army's officer training school, is a good example of this gradual socialization: at the end of their first year, the new cohort of cadets receives its name, during a traditional sequence marked by the famous command "Men: on your knees ... Officers: stand up."[70] The armed forces are thus engaged in a continuous process of militarization of their recruits, creating de facto interfaces with civil society, whose debates, norms and values do not stop at the barracks' door.

Thus, the massification of the armed forces brought about by conscription had one very direct effect at the end of the nineteenth century in Europe: the need to select, sort and rank the young men who would be declared fit for service. Military physicians were thus obliged to define fitness assessment criteria based on the dominant representations of masculinity at the time. These criteria made it possible to build up a veritable body of statistical knowledge on the height, torso width and average physical abilities of the soldiers of the time, which were very quickly interpreted, in an anthropomorphic perspective, as revealing the "good health" (or otherwise) of their nation. The statistics collected by the armies served as a basis for broader socio-political mobilizations, notably the development of sports and hygiene practices, which were first experimented with in the armies. At the same time, while European military physicians had difficulty in defining a standard of "fitness," colonial experiences made this universal standard in fact of little relevance, and multiple selection practices coexisted depending on whether service was to take place in Europe or in the colonies. Here we see the interpenetration of social issues (notably concerns about national characters) and military practices.[71] In fact, the question of how to match identified military needs with civilian recruitment possibilities regularly arises. For example, the contemporary US Army is facing a major recruitment problem due to the obesity epidemic in the US: only 23% of young adults (aged 17 to 24) are physically fit for service, and only a small fraction of them want to join the armed forces. To avoid missing recruitment targets, the US Army has set up a pre-recruitment program dedicated to potential recruits whose body mass index is up to 6% higher than the prescribed upper limit. These recruits follow an eighty-four-day program combining physical exercise and education in balanced nutrition, to help them lose enough weight to be integrated into the classic military training curriculum: changes in society inevitably condition the type of recruits available, forcing armies to adapt.[72]

Demographic changes are also a challenge for the armed forces: in Japan, the structural aging of the population, coupled with very restrictive immigration rules (which severely limit the possibility of becoming "Japanese" and therefore of serving in the armed forces) and gender norms that remain very strongly male-dominated (limiting the possibility for women to serve in the armed forces), is creating a real recruitment crisis for the Japanese Self-Defense Forces and limiting their transformation.[73]

Another example is the adoption of compulsory military service in France in 1872, which revived the republican myth of the "citizen soldier" obeying the institution out of love of country. Yet the French Army of the late nineteenth and early twentieth centuries had to contend with the consequences of the general rise in the population's level of education, a process initiated by the Guizot law of 1833, continued by Victor Duruy under the Second Empire and completed by Jules Ferry under the Third Republic. One's level of education came to be adopted by the armed forces as a means of distinguishing between officers, non-commissioned officers and soldiers; in this way, the armed forces pragmatically integrated the republican principle of meritocracy into their selection methods. However, the result was an army organized by caste, with officers largely drawn from secondary school alumni and non-commissioned officers and soldiers mainly from the working classes and with a primary school education. These castes had different skills and socializations, leading to a stiffening of everyday military practices in a pernicious process. Officers sought to maintain the social distance between themselves and the rest of the military, and this was achieved through strict maintenance of the hierarchy ("hierarchy is an exact science"). As Marc Bloch noted, observing the survival of stratified social practices:

> Career officers already form a small society, characterized by many traditions, which is undoubtedly the most appropriate for restoring to our relatively leveled civilization the image of what was in ancient France, the notion of "order" rather than "class" [...]. Today, even a general, even one of the most star-studded, if he enters the room where a modest second lieutenant is working, cannot fail to offer him his hand without breaching the most elementary courtesy. Confronted with a non-commissioned officer, let alone a private, it would take the most exceptional circumstances to prompt him to make this gesture.[74]

Faced with these practices of social distancing and hierarchical observance, NCOs, limited and constrained in their autonomy, established themselves in a role of social control of the trooper, which enabled them to minimize the risks to their own function: if the regulations were applied to the letter, they could not be punished. Soldiers were therefore the victims of constant harassment by NCOs, which was in fact a protective strategy for the latter. The various military manuals and regulations were memorized, and competence was measured by the ability to recite them. In this way, a military catechism developed, in which practical knowledge (such as shooting and maneuvering) was backed up by theoretical knowledge, with cadet corporals having to be able to recite "the speed of each movement in handling the weapon" or the means of "deploying riflemen in half-sections." For Mathieu Merly, this stratification, which stems from the distinctions created by the school system, goes some way to explaining the resistance to change and inflexibility of the French armies prior to the outbreak of the First World War:

The officers, in a position to impose their interests, find a real advantage in this organization, despite critics urging them to reduce the distance between themselves and the troops. As for non-commissioned officers, they have no choice but to play the game imposed by military discipline. For this reason, Republican barracks struggled to meet the challenges imposed on the army at the end of the 19th century. Disciplinary inertia stood in the way of the evolution in hierarchical relations demanded by tacticians and supporters of the officer's educational role, sensitive to the sociological evolution of the contingent and the need to build "moral strength" by seeking consent.[75]

We can see here how a change in recruitment methods for the armed forces, resulting from political decisions but having to take into account the sociological evolution of the country, leads to a rigidification of practices and hierarchies.

Another particularly illustrative example of the interpenetration between the dominant norms of civil society and the evolution of practices within armies is the evolution of the management of soldiers' sexual relations, and more generally of gender issues, by the American armed forces over the course of the twentieth century. In the first place, a classic issue for armies was to minimize sexually transmitted infections (STIs), which affected soldiers who might be sent into combat. During the First World War, military officers and doctors were keen to keep young men in combat, while American society was concerned about the effect of war on the morality of its youth. Visits to brothels were banned, religious groups distributed pamphlets extolling the benefits of abstinence, recreational and sporting activities were organized to keep soldiers busy away from the front, while strict punishments (including stays in forced labor camps in the event of contamination) were meted out by officers. Despite this, the US Army lost seven million days of active service to STIs between its entry into the war in 1917 and the armistice in 1918. The question of how to regulate the sexual behavior of male soldiers led to numerous experiments over the years. The idea that young men had a "right to sexual relations"[76] led some Second World War commanders, for example, to provide them with prostitutes or to encourage relations with local women of "good reputation."

Control over reproductive practices has also evolved considerably. Overall, regulations during the First and Second World Wars allowed men to be married and have children, and the need for personnel (e.g. military medical staff) led to women being allowed to serve in the armed forces but without the right to have children. Female servicemen who became pregnant during service were thus demobilized. After the Second World War, regulations reflected the imaginary nuclear family and the desire to protect it: young Americans married early and had children quickly. In such situations, the priority for women was seen as caring for the home. Thus, once married, military nurses could no longer serve in the active army but only in the reserves. In the forces, married women could continue to serve, but regulations encouraged them to break their contracts as soon as possible after marriage. This policy was very costly for the armed forces: during the 1950s, 70–80% of women left the forces before the end of their contract, which meant that the US military had to replace 40–50% of female troops (the "women's corps") every year. In addition, an executive order signed by President Truman in 1951, and interpreted very broadly, authorized the discharge of women who became pregnant. These regulations were gradually lifted in the 1970s in the wake of the feminist revolution and the adoption of laws promoting gender equality (notably the Civil Rights Act of 1964 and the Equal Rights Amendment of 1972). In 1974, the Secretary of Defense demanded that all regulations allowing women to be discharged for marriage or pregnancy be abolished, much to the dismay of some military officials. However, a court of the Second Circuit agreed, ruling in *Crawford vs Cushman* in favor of a young Marine who had been discharged because of pregnancy. Since then, women serving in the US military have enjoyed the same marriage and parentage rights as their male counterparts, including their gradual integration into combat units, with the ban on women serving in such units lifted in 2015.[77]

A similar dynamic can be observed with regard to the right of homosexual (gay and lesbian) and transgender people to serve. The ban on homosexuals joining the forces dates back to the Second World War, when most psychiatrists considered homosexuality a form of mental deviance. Legally, Article 125 of the Uniform Code of Military Justice made sodomy punishable by court martial. In the early 1980s, a directive made demobilization compulsory for people openly homosexual, in the name of military efficiency: gays and lesbians would have been a hindrance to mission accomplishment. Following his election, President Clinton promised to lift the ban on service, which led in 1993, after discussions with Congress, to the DADT (don't ask, don't tell) policy: the armed forces were not to ask their members about their sexual orientation, and they were not to publicly disclose it. During the 2000s, the general attitude of the American population shifted largely in favor of greater inclusion of homosexuals (with several states adopting same-sex marriage provisions), and in opinion polls a large majority of the population (including conservative segments of opinion) announced that they were in favor of homosexuals being able to serve in the armed forces without having to conceal their sexual orientation. In 2010, President Obama announced the end of DADT, specifically mentioning that the policy discouraged homosexuals from joining the armed forces, thereby depriving them of potential resources of talent and skills. In the case of transgender people, the ban on serving by openly revealing this identity was lifted in 2016, but the policy was reinstated in 2018 by President Trump. It is notable that tolerance for transgender people is lower than tolerance for gay people in American society, which may explain this variation.[78]

We could go on and on offering examples of how changes in the dominant norms of society shape the evolution of practices and institutions within the armed forces. For example, following the professionalization of the French armed forces, a recruitment issue arose: the armed forces moved from a flow management rationale to an incentive rationale, becoming an employer among other possible employers. In this context, the armed forces have pragmatically tried to attract candidates from Muslim populations, very often the descendants of immigrants from the Maghreb. These populations often have an ambivalent perception of the armed forces: for some, it may be synonymous with colonial oppression, but others see it as a space still regarded as "truly meritocratic," in which promotion is based on performance and which nurtures values deemed positive of virility, cohesion and surpassing oneself.[79] To take these populations into account, the armed forces created a Muslim military chaplaincy in 2005, joining the Catholic, Protestant, Jewish and Orthodox military chaplaincies. One of the first measures taken by the chief chaplain for the Muslim faith was to reintroduce halal combat rations, which had been introduced in the 1990s but discontinued for no explicit reason. By 2020, the number of military personnel of Muslim faith could be estimated at 10–12% of the armed forces (Muslims represent around 8% of the French population).[80] Other studies have also shown that the shift to the right of Israeli politics over time has also had an impact on the military practices of Tsahal (the Israeli armed forces), notably in terms of increasing—and unpunished—violence against Palestinians, due to the growing influence of ultranationalist settlers and religious extremists within the armed forces.[81]

To adapt to societal changes, some military organizations are adopting specific institutional practices. For example, the Indian armed forces recruit from a population marked by great religious diversity (Hindus, Sikhs, Muslims, Christians and Buddhists serve side by side) and by regular inter-religious conflict. To minimize conflict, the Indian armed forces have adopted a number of institutional measures, such as forming units on an ethnic, non-denominational basis; encouraging officers to be discreet about their religious beliefs; institutionalizing respect for all religions through training, symbols and ceremonies; and maintaining an apolitical stance.[82] Still on the subject of adapting to societal norms, when Sweden decided to reintroduce conscription in 2017 (having abolished it in 2010), the rhetoric justifying the new model was based no longer on the previous myth of the "citizen soldier" but on values now widespread in Swedish society: voluntarism, individualism and gender equality.[83] A major challenge for recruitment in many armed forces will therefore be to ensure that they are able to attract the skills, particularly technological skills, needed to conduct future operations. This could give rise to questions about career models (is a linear trajectory for officers still necessary, or should lateral integration be allowed in all ranks?), hierarchy (can a specialist in a field be paid more than his or her superior in rank to ensure that he or she stays with the institution?) and command styles.

What also happens is that the spirit of the times permeates the evolution of strategic discourses and doctrines. A good example is the development of theories on strategic bombing between the First and Second World Wars, notably by the Italian Giulio Douhet, the Briton Hugh Trenchard and the American William (Bill) Mitchell. While the details of their theories diverge, all three authors agree that aerial bombardment can have major strategic effects. For Douhet, the targeting of civilian populations should lead them to rebel against their leaders, thus bringing the conflict to an end; for Trenchard, the air weapon is so impressive that it should lead to a psychological collapse of the civilian populations; and for Mitchell, the damage caused by bombing on critical infrastructures should push civilian populations to put pressure on their leaders (unlike Douhet, Mitchell does not recommend the direct targeting of civilian populations, but theorizes that their suffering will have a similar effect of challenging the leaders). Although they differ in certain respects, all three theories of strategic bombing are based on a fundamental assumption of the moral collapse of civilian populations, perceived as weak and lacking in resilience. However, this hypothesis corresponds to a zeitgeist imbued with the "science of crowds," which tends to see populations as impressionable and manipulable: according to these theorists, in certain circumstances the individual would disappear in favor of a regression toward a collective personality (what Gustave Le Bon, in the spirit of the times, called "the unchanging heart of the race" or "the soul of the race").[84] Accordingly, strategic bombing could be used to manipulate crowds and achieve political effects. In this sense, these theories are typical of the anxieties of European elites in the interwar period, faced with the emergence of democratic, nationalist and communist movements following the collapse of the Central European empires: how to deal with this "molten people"[85] and its new demands? Apart from the psychologizing tendency of the time, it cannot be denied that, at least for Douhet and Mitchell, their perception of crowds was influenced by their own political preferences, themselves rooted in the debates of the time. Douhet associated with the Fascist movement out of bureaucratic calculation in order to promote the air force, but his political views were close to the proto-fascist modernist movement celebrating the machine and glorifying the fighter at the expense of the weak civilian—a creed forcefully expressed for example by d'Annunzio.[86] For his part, Mitchell belonged by marriage to the American upper middle class, wrote in a context of heightened racial tensions in the US marked by the second period of the Ku Klux Klan (the Tulsa massacre took place in 1921), and made no secret of his preference for a social order characterized by a hierarchy of races. In 1935, for example, he wrote: "whether the culture of the white race is to continue as the world's greatest force, or whether Asiatic culture will dominate, will be determined from the American continent, by air power."[87] Thus, "the hypothesis of the moral weakness of populations by these authors is based on a limited empirical sample, but above all reflects a hierarchical perception of social classes on the part of members of the bourgeoisie of their countries and the political convictions of some of them."[88] We can see here how a change in practice and doctrine is rooted in the socio-political debates of the countries concerned.

Another fascinating example of this dynamic is the development of what Dmitry Adamsky calls a "faith–nuclear nexus" in Russia since the end of the Cold War.[89] Adamsky distinguishes between three main models of the relationship between faith and military duty. The first model, known as "enabling faith," refers to institutional arrangements that allow military personnel to practice their religion while continuing to perform their military duties. The second model, "faith as enabler," describes an organization in which religion is interwoven with nationalist ideology and becomes a synonym for patriotism. Finally, the third model is that of military theocratization, in which faith shapes the strategic thinking and operational practices of military organizations (as was the case in Iran).[90] According to Adamsky, contemporary Russia falls into the second category, with gradual signs of tipping into the third. This is particularly true of the branch of the armed forces tasked with operating nuclear weapons, which the Russian Orthodox Church has made a particular effort to penetrate by theologically justifying nuclear deterrence as the key to protecting the Russian homeland; by developing new rituals mixing religious and military aspects (e.g. displaying relics at military ceremonies, or blessing military sites named after Orthodox saints);

and by generally encouraging religious practice, with the support of the state. This interpenetration is obviously mutually beneficial, with the Putin regime gaining an ideological ally and the Russian Orthodox Church reaping substantial material benefits. But the formation of this "faith–nuclear" nexus raises questions about the evolution of military practices themselves. As Adamsky writes: "The more the priesthood is involved in operational issues and the keener its professional contacts with the operators, the greater the likelihood that a demand for nuclear Orthodox jurisprudence will emerge. [...] The closer the situation approaches a protracted geopolitical crisis, the more prominent the role and involvement of the nuclear priests in the decision-making might become."[91]

For Adamsky, this situation poses medium- and long-term structural questions for military practices and doctrines within the Russian armed forces. In addition to the possibility of a shift toward a military theocracy mentioned above (which would imply a much greater role for the Orthodox Church in doctrinal definition), we must not rule out the possibility of a falling out between the church and the civil authorities (of which Russian history provides numerous examples), the consequences of which are difficult to foresee given the current entanglement of the Orthodox clergy with Russia's nuclear forces.

Conclusion

As we can see, the configuration of civil–military relations is often critical in explaining military change. Whether we are talking about politico-military relations, the political economy of defense or the interactions between armed forces and society, it is clear that military change is part of socio-political dynamics that go far beyond the armed forces. As a result, the main mechanism by which military change takes place within politico-military configurations is constraint: whether it be the constraint imposed by political decision-makers in choosing a strategic orientation, the constraint exerted by the politico-economic environment, or the normative constraint emanating from transformations (and sometimes demands) in society.

This mechanism of constraint regularly leads to military changes that, because of their scale, can be described as innovations: think of Charles de Gaulle's imposition of a nuclear deterrent, the gradual integration of women and homosexuals into the American armed forces, or the evolution of British strategy as a function of defense funding. This civil–military configuration is therefore essential to understanding the trajectories taken by armed forces.

3

TECHNOLOGY AND MILITARY CHANGE

Technology has penetrated our lives to such an extent that we often no longer realize how much our daily lives depend on it, whether for our livelihood (mechanization of agriculture), our travel (cars, planes, public transport), our communications (telephones, internet), our health (medicine, surgery and pharmacology) or our leisure (television, video games, cinemas). Technology creates our world and shapes our relationship with it.

For the armed forces, technology is obviously seen as an efficiency multiplier, and has been since prehistoric times: the oldest weapons ever found may be the "Schöningen spears" (unearthed in present-day Germany), 300,000-year-old assegais probably used for hunting as well as warfare. Remarkably, these spears are shaped like a modern javelin, with the weight distributed toward the tip to ensure stability of trajectory once launched. Over the long term, the history of warfare has been characterized by long phases of technological stagnation punctuated by sudden accelerations triggered by various drivers.[1]

The importance of technology for the armed forces can be measured by a thought experiment: if a great general of antiquity (Alexander the Great, Julius Caesar, Hannibal, Scipio Africanus, Alaric) were suddenly brought into the twenty-first century and given the task of leading a military campaign, what would their reaction be? There's no doubt that these military leaders had at least an intuitive understanding of the main principles governing the use of military force, which are still relevant today: defining the objective, mass, economy of effort, maneuver, unity of command, surprise, security, simplicity, etc. They would probably have to adapt to much more codified staff procedures and a very different cultural and normative environment. But we can certainly imagine that the biggest shock would come from the multiplicity of means of destruction made possible by technology: how would they react to fighter planes, artillery tubes, satellite links, radios, precision-guided munitions and so forth? A classic parable is attributed to Albert Wohlstetter: if, on a medieval battlefield, a knight miraculously received an assault rifle fitted with a bayonet, how would he use it? After manipulating the magazine, the trigger and the firing mode selector, would he understand that this was a weapon enabling him to aim at targets some 300 meters away; would he attempt a charge using the bayonet; or would he simply reject this block of metal and return to his sword and shield, which he knew how to use?

These two short fictions serve to illustrate two central ideas. Firstly, technology is a major factor in the changing character of warfare, with Martin van Creveld going so far as to write that "war is completely permeated by technology and governed by it."[2] Secondly, technology is by no means "self-evident": it is understood and employed according to the norms and contexts in which it is embedded.

So we need to start by investigating what a "technology" is. Following W. Brian Arthur,[3] a technology serves first and foremost to fulfill a human purpose. For some technologies the purpose is obvious and fixed (oil refining), for others it is multiple and changing (computers). A technology can be a method, a process or a tool, and it can be material or immaterial (a computer program). Secondly, we need to think simultaneously about the technology itself and the practices surrounding its use. As it aims to accomplish a human goal, technology generally responds to a desire or need, but in turn it modifies the practices and behaviors of individuals. Thirdly, technology is characterized by hierarchy and recursivity. This means that a technology is itself made up of other embedded technologies, whose interactions produce the desired effect. Take the example of a car, which is made up of a multitude of "technological blocks" (motorization, propulsion, steering, electrical signaling, etc.) whose combination results in the ability to transport humans, faster and with less effort and discomfort than an oxcart. Military technologies are very often good examples of embedded technologies: the extreme example is, of course, an aircraft carrier, which carries aircraft (themselves particularly complex technological artifacts embedding multiple technologies), while navigating, delivering fire, communicating with the outside world and so on. We can see here how technology serves humans, as much as humans serve technology: maintenance is obviously essential to fulfilling the initial objective of the technology. Because of this hierarchy, we need to distinguish between different types of technology according to the magnitude of their effect. Economists use the term "general-purpose technologies" to designate technologies, such as electricity, that have three characteristics: a high potential for continuous improvement, their ubiquity in a large number of industrial sectors, and their complementarity with other technologies.[4] These versatile technologies require a well-developed civilian industrial base to be properly exploited, but have a far greater effect on military practices than specialized technologies.

Finally, a technology is always based on a phenomenon, or set of phenomena, that can be exploited and used. A hammer uses gravity; a truck uses the principle that chemical substances (such as gasoline) produce energy when combusted, and that rolling objects move with much less friction than flat surfaces; a modern computer uses electron transfer within semiconductor materials to create electronic circuits that function as an electrically controlled on/off switch to perform fundamental logical calculations.

In a military context, technology can be understood as the totality of means of destruction (weapons, explosives), means of mobility (missiles, vehicles) and means of control (communications, observation). Of course, some weapons systems combine these different functions: a modern fighter jet is a means of mobility as well as a means of destruction and control.

Logically, a technological artifact is the result of a set of compromises and choices created by incompatibilities between different phenomena. These compromises and choices are, of course, themselves dependent on the cultural and normative context, and on the objective assigned to the technology. This is why "technology" cannot be studied outside the social context in which it is produced, from which it emerges and which it influences in return.[5] Thus, numerous studies in the field of sociology of science and technology (STS) have shown that technological development is linked to a particular momentum (a new technology is not developed in isolation but as part of a wider technical system that simultaneously has social and technological components); that technological progress in one field is often held back by stagnation in related sub-fields (e.g. video game developers are constrained by the computing power of the consoles or computers used by potential customers); and that users often reinvent the uses of a specific technology by attributing new functions or meanings to it. The study of the role of technology in military change can therefore only be carried out by taking into account the social context of production, reception and use of these technologies.[6]

The configurations of entities to be studied imply a greater degree of precision than in previous chapters: we need to focus not only on specific political or military leaders, but also on hitherto little-mentioned entities such as defense industries or research ecosystems (including universities). We will also look at technological imaginations and the artifacts themselves, which are often not the end result but simply an important stage in a process of changing practices and doctrines. Here, we consider artifacts (such as weapons systems) as entities: they are non-human actors in a socio-technical network, which nevertheless have an effect on this network through the dependencies and stakes they create for other actors (this is similar to the concept of "actants" developed by Michel Collon and Bruno Latour).[7]

Strategic imperatives and technological development

For the armed forces, the most immediate stake in technological development is obviously the tactical advantage provided by weapons systems that are comparatively better than those of the adversary. Very prosaically, "Armies that could reach further, hit harder, and get there faster usually won, while the range-restricted, less well-armed, and slower armies lost. For this reason a vast amount of human creative effort has been poured into extending the range, increasing the firepower, and accelerating the speed of weapons and the armies."[8] The armed forces are thus regularly engaged in a process of incremental improvement of their equipment in order to gain a potential tactical advantage. This is all the more true given that the period considered in this book corresponds with the advent of the era of industrial warfare: "Napoleon still fought Julius Caesar's war. The war of 1914 is industrial and democratic."[9]

Military modernization or arms race?

It is no secret that armed forces seek to maintain or incrementally improve the equipment at their disposal. This dynamic is sometimes referred to as the "dialectic between sword and shield," to explain the cycle of interactions between offensive and defensive weaponry. Think, for example, of small arms such as assault rifles, which can cause considerable damage to enemy troops, while body armor can offer protection against projectiles. Another example of this dynamic can be seen in the relationship between ships and torpedoes. Ships have long been the cornerstone of military fleets, offering high transport capacity, considerable firepower and protection against enemy attack. In response, torpedoes were developed to sink enemy ships. This cycle of development and counter-development led to increasingly sophisticated torpedoes, with shaped-charge warheads and precision guidance systems. In response, ships were equipped with countermeasures such as decoys, jamming systems and acoustic detection devices. Similarly, airplanes have been a key tool in military operations since the early days of aviation, offering reconnaissance, close air support and strategic bombing capabilities. In response, anti-aircraft defenses were developed to shoot down enemy aircraft and deny them access to the airspace above the battlefield. This cycle of development and counter-development led to a variety of anti-aircraft weapons, from simple machine guns to surface-to-

145

air missiles and advanced radar systems. In turn, specific weapons and tactics were developed for SEAD (suppression of enemy air defense) missions. The examples could be multiplied almost ad infinitum, since the dialectical relationship between offense and defense is such an important factor in military modernization. When these improvements are routine and incremental, they correspond to what we called "adjustment" in our introduction,[10] and are a permanent activity of the armed forces, corresponding to a kind of precautionary principle. The circumvention mechanism is at work here, but it is not necessarily linked to a particular adversary, and the intensity and tempo of these adjustments are limited.

On the other hand, depending on the political context, these modernization dynamics can accelerate and become arms races, which have an impact on the equipment of armies. An arms race can be defined as "intense competition between opposed powers or groups of powers, each trying to achieve an advantage in military power by increasing the quantity or improving the quality of its armaments or armed forces."[11] Arms races are generally considered to have seven characteristics in common.

- They are motivated by international rather than national imperatives.
- They are generally bilateral.
- They are intense in terms of effort and speed.
- They are associated with high levels of political tension.
- They cover specific operational needs.
- They are indicative of important strategic issues.
- They are understood by the players as an arms race.

The speed with which weapons are acquired is a necessary condition for an arms race, but it is not a sufficient one. There must also be a real or perceived intention to use these increased capabilities against other states, and thus to engage in a dynamic of circumvention. We therefore need to imagine a spectrum of strategic interactions, ranging from minimal adjustment as part of routine modernization to a complete and intense arms race. For example, some observers believe that the naval modernization underway in the Asia-Pacific region, with China, India, Japan, South Korea and the US investing heavily in their navies, is still a modernization process and has not yet reached the threshold of an arms race.[12]

We generally identify three main "models" to explain[13] arms races: the technological imperative model, the domestic incentives model, and the action-reaction model.

The technological imperative model sees scientific and technological development as an autonomous force driving arms races. For example, advances in naval artillery and ammunition in the nineteenth century enabled ships to fire farther, with unprecedented power and accuracy, prompting navies to reinforce ship protection by armoring their hulls and optimizing their construction and the structure of their machinery. According to this model, technological advances in warships led to competition for battleships in the first half of the twentieth century, until the introduction of embarked naval aviation rendered them obsolete. Technological development thus creates external pressure on armed forces, which have to keep constantly up to date or risk being left behind and leaving their country vulnerable to aggression.

The domestic incentives model focuses on analyzing a state's domestic policy to understand the reasons behind its decision to acquire more armaments than it needs for its own defense. According to the traditional argument of this model, authoritarian regimes manipulate the fear of external threats to justify their choice to arm themselves, thus creating an internal consensus. For example, historians have applied this model to explain the naval arms race between Imperial Germany and Great Britain prior to the First World War. More recent research on the influence of domestic structure focuses on the concept of "military-industrial complexes," which refer to informal coalitions of military, political and industrial elites that promote increased defense spending to protect their interests and improve their position within the state apparatus.

The action-reaction model explains how states arm themselves in response to the arming of their rivals, leading to a cycle of armed rivalry. According to this model, the security of each state is threatened by the arming of other states, creating a security dilemma[14] and an illusory quest for military security. This situation leads to perpetual competition for military advantage, which in turn stimulates a reaction from other competitors. For example, before the First World War, the great European powers competed by building ever more powerful battleships and developing mass armies, while during the Cold War the US and the Soviet Union competed by accumulating nuclear weapons beyond what was necessary to defeat each other.

The three models are complementary but have different explanatory powers for analyzing strategic competition, which we have considered here in the form of an arms race.[15] The technological imperative makes it possible to understand competitive military modernization programs, since armed forces that fail to improve themselves risk being defeated by better-equipped adversaries in the event of conflict. However, technological evolution alone is not enough to generate widespread military competition of the kind seen during the Cold War. In fact, human autonomy is a decisive factor in political decision-making and in the implementation of armament policies. Political leaders and state institutions must take the decision to invest in armaments, and provide the necessary means, particularly financial. In other words, technology does not autonomously constrain human decisions. The model of domestic structures explains why arms races persist once launched, as arms production and the pursuit of the race become institutionalized in the state bureaucracy of competing countries. During the Cold War, for example, the armed forces of the superpowers and their industrial suppliers sometimes sought to acquire weapons systems in order to maintain their industrial base and keep future procurement contracts, which in turn pushed the other side to arm itself more quickly and thus fueled the arms race. The action-reaction model is the only way to understand the underlying reason why states arm themselves against each other. Arms races are dictated by political objectives: states seek to arm themselves rapidly in order to achieve military conditions favorable to their political goals, whether they aim to change the international order in their favor or to defend the status quo against potential rivals. States compete to impose their will through threats or the actual use of military force.

An interesting example of the dynamics of the arms race, which helps to explain the evolution of armed forces in the Middle East, is the military rivalry between Israel and the Arab countries.[16] This competition has undergone several transformations over the years, reflecting changes in the security environment and the nature of warfare. One major change has been the shift from a race focused on high-intensity conflicts to one focused on low-intensity conflicts, such as the Israeli–Palestinian conflict and the conflict in Syria. This evolution has led to changes in the types of weapons and technologies developed and used. Moreover, the arms race has evolved from a bipolar competition between Arabs and Israelis to a regional one, with the participation of other players such as Iran and Turkey, making the security environment more complex and competitive. The regional arms race has thus shifted from a conventional to an unconventional one, owing to the changing nature of warfare and the growing importance of asymmetric warfare. The development of unconventional weapons, such as medium- and long-range missiles and cyber capabilities, has also made it easier for states to target critical infrastructure and civilian populations, increasing the risk of escalation and instability in the region. Although the shift toward low-intensity conflicts and the development of new technologies may have reduced the risk of large-scale wars, the arms race remains a major challenge to regional security due to increased instability and the risk of escalation, and it partly determines the format and acquisitions of the region's armed forces.

What this shows is that military change can be explained by threat perception interacting with the nature of available technologies and the desire to circumvent an adversary. However, we must be wary of any determinism in this area: there are multiple circumvention possibilities, and the one chosen is not necessarily the only one available. A good example is the absence of mobile intercontinental ballistic missiles in the US. During the Cold War, the US, China and Russia invested massively in the protection of their intercontinental ballistic missiles (ICBMs) by means of large silos. In theory, these were potentially vulnerable to a massive strike, which could have nullified (or greatly reduced) the second-strike capability necessary for the credibility of nuclear deterrence. To overcome this vulnerability, consideration was given to making the ICBMs mobile, to guard against surprise first strikes in the event of nuclear war. The US Air

Force was particularly interested in this concept because of concerns about Soviet advances in ICBMs and because of competition with the US Navy and its submarine-launched ballistic missiles (SLBMs). In 1979, President Jimmy Carter proposed deploying 200 MX missiles in underground shelters linked by routes known as "racetracks," to make it difficult for Soviet ICBMs to target them all. However, this proposal was cancelled by President Ronald Reagan in 1981 owing to controversy and landowner concerns. The US Air Force had studied various options for mobile ICBMs—such as basing them on trains, trucks, aircraft, ships and submarines—even before deploying its first ICBM, and continued these investigations right up to the end of the Cold War. Despite these studies and proposals, the US Air Force never deployed mobile ICBMs, partly because the success of the US Navy's SLBM force, and the effectiveness of siloed Minuteman missiles compared with earlier ICBM designs, diminished the interest in portable ICBMs in the 1950s and 1960s. In the 1970s and 1980s, US decision-makers had differing views on the vulnerability of ICBMs, which prevented the crystallization of a durable coalition of interests in favor of the solution provided by mobile ICBMs.[17] This shows that the dynamics of circumvention are not univocal, and that several options are generally possible: technological development is, above all, a matter of choice.

Technological prestige

In addition to circumvention, it should also be emphasized that states' quest for prestige and status leads to the diffusion of military technologies: certain weapons or weapons systems sometimes become symbolic markers of the status and rank of the states that possess them. These states then adopt an attitude of "conspicuous consumption," acquiring military capabilities because of the status they confer. Take, for example, Brazil's decision to acquire the French aircraft carrier *Foch*, whose strategic utility was unclear, mainly because it enabled Brasilia to join the closed "club" of aircraft carrier owners. Similarly, countries seeking status and recognition have recently tended to acquire armed drones, with this weapon system gradually becoming a symbol of mastery of military modernity.[18]

This phenomenon of conspicuous consumption also explains, at least in part, the commercial failure of the F-20, a fighter developed by the US in the late 1970s and positioned as a low-cost export product: the calculation was that a number of countries would find it more attractive, because it was cheaper and better suited to their needs, than the F-15 and F-16 fighters, which were at the cutting edge of American technology at the time. However, many countries preferred to buy fewer of the most technologically advanced fighters rather than to build up a larger fleet at lower cost: the prestige associated with possessing the latest technological symbols was the decisive factor in the decision (even if it was rationalized and justified in different ways).[19]

The search for prestige can also explain certain technological choices, such as in the field of nuclear weapons. For example, China's perceived insecurity was a key factor in its decision to acquire a nuclear deterrent capability. However, security considerations are not always the only determining factor in the choice of the type of weapons to be developed. China has sometimes allocated significant resources to one weapon system rather than another, even when the security benefits were uncertain. China's limited resources require trade-offs, and decisions come with security or opportunity costs. China chose to absorb these costs on the assumption that the weapons chosen would bring it greater prestige. The examples of the hydrogen bomb, the neutron bomb and the underwater ballistic missile illustrate this argument. The hydrogen bomb, for example, has clear security advantages over the atomic bomb, due to its greater destructive power. However, these advantages are mitigated by China's no-first-use policy and the need to be able to threaten its adversaries with a second strike. Instead of allocating funds to hydrogen bomb technology, China's security would be better served by investing in long-range weapon delivery systems. Similarly, with the neutron bomb, China has financed a weapon useful on the battlefield, whereas its nuclear strategy rules out nuclear war. In this case, China's pursuit of the neutron bomb was motivated more by prestige than by security considerations. Finally, while a new fleet of sea-based nuclear weapons strengthens China's nuclear deterrent, more mobile ICBMs could achieve similar results and be a more reliable option, given China's past difficulties in developing SLBMs. Prestige helps to explain these decisions to varying degrees. The case of the neutron bomb is the most convincing example of the explanatory power of prestige, as China had little to gain from its development in terms of security. The case of the hydrogen bomb shows a more complementary relationship between prestige and security, with prestige playing a slightly more important role. The search for new-generation sea-based nuclear weapons is less obvious in terms of security benefits, but prestige probably played a predominant role in China's decision to launch its SLBMs when it did.[20]

It is clear that certain weapons systems sometimes benefit from a fad that outweighs their real strategic utility. A good contemporary example of this is the development of so-called hypersonic weapons, which are becoming an object of competition for the relative prestige of states. Hypersonic weapons are weapons systems capable of exceeding Mach 5 speed. In practice, this is already the case for ballistic missiles, but their trajectory remains predictable. The systems currently under development in the US, China, Russia, France and North Korea (among others) fall into two broad categories: hypersonic glide vehicles (HGVs), which are powered by ballistic missiles that enable them to reach the desired speed, and hypersonic cruise missiles (HCMs), which are powered by a superstar jet engine for part of their flight.[21] The advantage of these systems is that their trajectories are difficult to estimate, making interception particularly complex for missile defense systems. Their strategic utility therefore lies in the fact that they guarantee the credibility of nuclear deterrence, increase the possibility of deep conventional strikes, reinforce denial-of-access postures, and can be used for strategic signaling.[22] All these functions are already fulfilled by current systems, and hypersonic weapons are in fact an improvement on existing systems, corresponding to an adjustment. And yet, according to the rhetoric put forward by certain states, the acquisition of hypersonic weapons is proof of their technological superiority.[23]

The most obvious case is that of Russia, which communicates widely about its "hypersonic weapons" already in service, with an ardor reminiscent of the Nazi propaganda surrounding the *Wunderwaffen* during the Second World War. For example, on 19 March 2022, Russia conducted an intense communications campaign around the alleged firing of a Kinzhal airborne ballistic missile at an ammunition depot in Ukraine, even calling a press conference to insist that a "hypersonic" weapon had been fired. However, the missile was used in exactly the same way as a conventional ballistic missile, with absolutely similar effects: the operational added value of the "hypersonic" munition was therefore nil, but it does reflect the search for prestige linked to the apparent mastery of a showy technology (coupled with a small propaganda effect designed to intimidate Western civilian populations who are ignorant of the technical details but easy to impress).

This fascination with novelty is a potential risk for military organizations. They can be seduced by technologies and weapons systems deemed promising, which the defense industries (and certain players within armed forces) have an objective interest in promoting, to the detriment of technologies deemed older but nonetheless indispensable. In an important book, *The Shock of the Old*, the historian David Edgerton shows the extent to which the effects of fashion focus attention on supposedly disruptive technologies but blind us to the reality of fundamental, often ancient technologies that are essential to the functioning of societies.[24] The same is often true of the armed forces: new technologies can have a much greater seductive effect than their actual strategic utility.

The cost of military technology

Logically, technological development capabilities are limited by government resources. In fact, one of the challenges facing military technologies is financing the rising cost of armaments. As far back as 1953, an international group of specialists expressed concern that

> The considerably higher cost of modern weapons today makes it very difficult for nations with populations of less than 150 to 200 million to equip their armed forces with a complete and balanced range of armaments. Firstly, combat units are

much better equipped today than they were in 1939 (at least three times as much). Secondly, the cost price itself has risen considerably. In 1945, the P-51 "Mustang" used on the European front already cost the equivalent of 24 million francs. In 1952, the F-86 "Sabre" cost almost 200 million francs. On the same basis, infrastructure expenditure increased by a factor of around 5 over the same period. The 13-ton light tank, for which production has begun in France, will cost at least 50 million francs; an American heavy bomber of the latest model, almost 2 billion. The bombing sight alone cost $60,000 in 1945, or around 20 million francs at today's exchange rates. Its 1953 successor, far more efficient and accurate, cost $250,000, or almost 100 million francs. A master radar costs 2 billion francs. Complete radar coverage of the French territory would require, at the very least, 100 billion francs. An aircraft carrier costs 30 billion. The cost of setting up and supporting an armored division is in the order of 150 to 200 billion francs, not including infrastructure; annual maintenance requires around 45 billion. There's no doubt that the price of modern equipment has a lot to do with this considerable increase in military costs. But let's not delude ourselves: most of the above-mentioned prices apply to mass production, involving quantities sufficient to keep production costs within reasonable limits. However, for countries that can no longer afford to order large series of rapidly obsolete equipment, these prices are infinitely higher still: it is especially in the aeronautical sector that the situation is taking on a truly dramatic character.[25]

The ever-increasing costs of military technology were famously formalized by Norman Augustine in 1983, when he was CEO of Lockheed Martin. In a guide for his company's managers, he listed a series of principles for managing major weapons programs. The most famous of these is probably the "law of impending catastrophe," in which Augustine establishes a relationship between time and unit cost, asserting that the costs of certain high-tech equipment increase mechanically over time, independently of other technical factors such as speed, weight or maneuverability. For example, the unit costs of high-performance fighter jets increase fourfold every ten years, while other equipment such as ships and tanks experience cost growth of twice every ten years. This increase in the unit costs of defense equipment at a higher rate than the growth in national defense budgets leads to the famous prediction that by 2054 the US defense budget will only be able to buy one aircraft. This aircraft will have to be shared by the Air Force and Navy three and a half days a week, except in leap years, when it will be made available to the Marines for an extra day. This prediction also applies to other countries, but on different timescales. For example, the UK would reach this situation two years earlier than the US.[26]

We can find partial empirical confirmation of Augustine's argument. Figure 6 illustrates the increase over time in the production cost of major American combat aircraft.

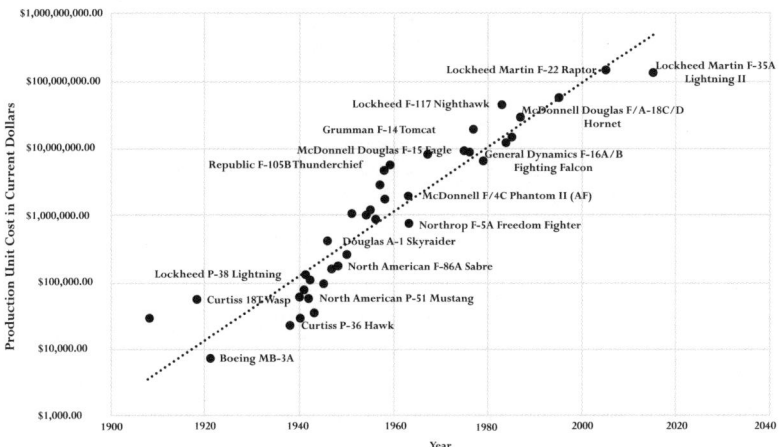

Figure 6. Production costs for major US combat aircraft (From Daniel R. Lake, *The Pursuit of Technological Superiority and the Shrinking American Military*, Basingstoke, Palgrave, 2019, p. 31)

Similarly, the (real) unit cost of British fighter aircraft has multiplied by 244 in seventy years. The cost multiplication factor between the Gladiator (Spanish Civil War) and the Spitfire (Second World War) was 1.5, then 2.4 between the Spitfire and the first Meteor jet model (1946). It then rose to 2.6 between the Meteor and the Hunter (1955), to 3.3 between the Hunter and the Lightning (1959), and to 7.9 between the Lightning and the Typhoon (2003).[27]

This phenomenon can be seen in many other cases: let's take the example of three relatively recent items of French Army equipment, the Rafale fighter jet, the Tiger helicopter and the NH-90 helicopter, which replace equipment from the previous generation, respectively the Mirage 2000 fighter jet, the Gazelle helicopter and the Puma helicopter. As Table 3 shows, both acquisition and maintenance costs are multiplied.

Table 3. Trend in acquisition and maintenance costs for certain French Army equipment

	Previous generation	Current generation
	Mirage 2000	Rafale
Acquisition costs	€9.4m	€50m
Maintenance costs	€5m per year	€15m per year
	Gazelle helicopter	Tiger helicopter
Acquisition costs	€25.5m	€75m
Maintenance costs	€1.5m per year	€15m per year
	Puma helicopter	NH-90 helicopter
Acquisition costs	€24.7m	€50m
Maintenance costs	€4m per year	€10m per year

Source: Data taken from Sophie Lefeez, "Toujours plus chers? Complexité des armements et inflation des coûts militaires," *Focus Stratégique*, no. 42, IFRI, 2013. Figures are orders of magnitude.

Obviously, the new equipment outperforms the old in many areas, and the comparison between the Rafale and the Mirage 2000 is incomplete without taking into account the fact that the Rafale is designed to provide the French Air Force with a single aircraft that replaces several types of aircraft from the previous generation, thus reducing training and maintenance costs. Nevertheless, each generational change means an infinitely higher multiplication of equipment acquisition and maintenance costs, which cannot be explained by the rate of inflation. Several cumulative reasons have been put forward to explain this seemingly inexorable rise in the cost of acquiring new weapons systems: the inability to invent new designs for platforms (the general architecture of a fighter aircraft, a battle tank or an aircraft carrier has been the same since 1945);[28] the continuing decline in production volumes, which reduces or even cancels out economies of scale; poor management of development and procurement processes, combining underestimation of costs and regular changes in order volumes;[29] rising costs of an increasingly specialized workforce and, more generally, of production factors; and greater complexity of the systems themselves, which have to concentrate an entire set of capabilities in a single platform. The combination of these factors, which are more or less important depending on the system and the country, certainly explains the trend observed by Augustine.

For the armed forces, this rise in equipment costs translates directly into a reduction in the volume of equipment. For example, the New Zealand Air Force sacrificed its fighter aircraft capability in the early 2000s by opting not to replace its A-4K Skyhawks, as the option of leasing F-16s from the US was deemed too costly. Without necessarily going so far as the outright elimination of capabilities, the obvious solution to rising acquisition costs is often to reduce equipment fleets. In Western countries, for example, there has been a steady decline in aircraft fleets and in the number of tanks and ships available. This effect has been particularly marked since the end of the Cold War, as it combines with a fall in defense budgets to create particularly significant downward pressure, but even with a constant budget, volumes would have been progressively reduced due to rising unit costs. We can see here how technological progress exerts a constraint on military change, leading to ongoing adjustments to the target format of armies. If the scale of the adjustments to be made becomes too great (as in the example of the New Zealand Air Force), we can speak of innovation.

This downsizing is in fact creating a crisis of military effectiveness, which raises (again) the question of the utility of the use of force and the modern possibility of victory.[30] In a 2007 article, the French historian and colonel Michel Goya diagnosed a "crisis in the Western model of limited, high-tech warfare," noting that "in July–August

2006, despite the commitment of the equivalent of the French Army and Air Force, the Israelis failed to defeat a few thousand men in Lebanon, entrenched in a rectangle measuring 45 km by 25 km."[31] In fact, Western military inefficiency has been demonstrated in Iraq, Afghanistan and the Sahel: the tactical gains offered by technological progress are cancelled out by the strategic impossibility of occupying the terrain (normally the comparative advantage of the land domain),[32] as a result of the military mass being too small. Strikingly, Russia, which had committed itself since 2007 to reducing the size of its armies in order to guarantee their modernization (including technological modernization), was unable not only to occupy Ukraine, but above all to destroy its armed forces. The war in Ukraine thus saw both Russia and Western countries remobilize old equipment to replace that destroyed on the battlefield, resulting in a "high–low-tech" mix that illustrates the performance–mass dilemma and the constraint that technology places on the format of armed forces. For example, the ever-increasing cost of advanced weapons systems, against the backdrop of a diffusion of long-range precision firing capabilities and the widespread use of inexpensive, easily accessible platforms (drones),[33] has led some analysts, particularly in the US,[34] to call for an overhaul of force structure and technology development processes. The aim would not necessarily be to have the best (which is also the most expensive), but to think in terms of systems that are less expensive than traditional platforms and capable of having effects that may be individually less important, but collectively superior due to the mass created by savings on individual platforms.[35]

Moreover, it seems that contemporary military operations require ever more sophisticated software for data processing, whose progress is outstripping that of platforms. This calls for a new way of thinking about capability development, disaggregating sensors, effectors, platforms, software, data and applications, which may also be a way of thinking differently about the production costs of weapons systems.[36] Identifying the calibration of the "right technology," which will enable forces to win tactically without creating an operational, strategic and financial impasse, is an absolutely major challenge, for which there is as yet no truly appropriate response. This will probably involve identifying new military practices that have yet to be invented: more than the technological race, the ability to invent effective military practices at the right cost will probably be the main differential between the great powers in the twenty-first century. From this point of view, the autonomization of certain platforms and systems could contribute to lowering the cost of certain missions[37] (e.g. by saturating the skies with prowling munitions to ensure air defense missions rather than employing fighter planes). Technological progress is inseparable from a reflection on practices.

Developing new military technologies

The dynamics of military modernization (which can escalate into an arms race depending on the intensity of the circumvention mechanism) and financial constraints partly explain *why* military technologies are advancing within the armed forces, but they certainly don't explain the *how*.

Stages of technological development

Weapon system development comprises several phases and stages, each with its own context. The first two stages are the invention and development of a particular technology. An invention is generally linked to a new way of exploiting or using a phenomenon. This invention must then go through a development phase to ensure the best means of implementing it, often through new engineering processes. Once developed, the technology must be accepted: it must correspond to uses and not call into question existing practices (and their associated social status) too much. It can then be deployed, after a test phase. A new phase begins when the technology is actually used in armed conflict: it is not uncommon for the uses initially envisaged not to correspond to combat conditions, and to need to be adapted to the conflict in progress. A new stage then begins, involving the discovery of unforeseen uses, the evolution of the technology to meet changing combat conditions, and finally its exploitation, as the technology ceases once and for all to be "new":

it is now both adopted and tested on the battlefield. These stages are summarized in Figure 7.

Novelty	• Invention • Development
Adoption	• Acceptance • Deployment
Employment	• Discovery • Evolution • Exploitation

Figure 7. Stages in the adoption of a new military technology (Adapted from Vincent P. O'Hara and Leonard R. Heinz, *Innovating Victory: Naval Technology in Three Wars*, Annapolis, Naval Institute Press, 2022)

Firstly, it must be recognized that "throughout the modern era the dominant corpus of scientific ideas has been reflected in contemporary theories and practices of warfare in the Western world."[38] During the Enlightenment, scientific advances in force, motion and geometry were applied to the concepts of drill, order and discipline. Military theorists also sought to apply the laws of nature to warfare so as to guarantee victory. In the nineteenth and early twentieth centuries, discoveries about energy and entropy influenced ideas about mass mobilization, motorization and industrialization in military strategies. In the twentieth century, ideas linked to cybernetics and complexity theories were also transcribed into a military context. One example is the use of cybernetic theories during the Vietnam War, in which the search for a highly efficient feedback loop and the application of systems analysis led to a conflict that prioritized statistical assessments and control over adaptable tactics to counter an elusive and unpredictable enemy. The implementation of a rational, technological approach to warfare, orchestrated by a military hierarchy that emphasized techno-scientific expertise, ultimately resulted in military failure. Cybernetics eventually fell out of favor and was increasingly replaced by chaos theory, which was imported into scientific and military contexts.[39] This approach, based on network science,[40] which is reflected in the terms "network-centric warfare" and in concepts in vogue in Western armed forces (such as "multi-domain operations"), nevertheless often results paradoxically in greater control over tactical units. Scientific and technological development thus creates certain specific imaginaries of how society, organizations and individuals function; these are regularly transcribed into the military context in an ever-renewed and always disappointed hope of imposing a form of control over the chaos of war. These scientific imaginaries can be more or less important within different military organizations: the US armed forces, for example, are reputed to be more techno-fetishist than those of other countries.[41]

Within this general context of scientific imaginaries, the development of military technologies is linked to specific social contexts to do with the relative status of expert communities. For over fifty years, since the development of nuclear-tipped ICBMs, the US has sought a means of defending itself against these missiles. These efforts have evolved through a variety of strategies and technologies, from nuclear-tipped rockets to ground-based kinetic interceptors and space-based laser weapons. Missile defense requires rapidly identifying the launch of a hostile missile, tracking thousands of warheads on their ballistic trajectory and directing interceptors to the right location, all in less than thirty minutes. From the outset, designers turned to computers to perform the complex calculations quickly. However, missile defense presented an additional difficulty: any error would be catastrophic. Computers might fail to intercept approaching missiles, leaving civilian populations defenseless, or, worse still, might misidentify an approaching threat and respond to a non-existent attack, thus mistakenly triggering nuclear war. Missile defense planners initially viewed computers as the pinnacle of speed and reliability, as opposed to slow and fallible humans, but then came to see them as potential causes of catastrophic failure.[42]

Physicists initially dominated the missile defense debate because of their position as high-level advisors. They tended to overlook the difficulty of software, seeing computers as mere tools rather than a new science, and programming as more production than research. Physicists also sought simplicity, with unified laws based on idealized models, and thus based their arguments in favor of missile defense on the constraints imposed by the laws of nature. This approach contrasted with that of computer programmers, faced with the complexity, uncertainty and messy interfaces imposed by human institutions. Computer experts argued that there was no way to test missile defense software under realistic conditions, and that it could not simulate Armageddon. They tempered their faith in technological progress by admitting that complex software could have limitations. In short, they struck a balance between human reason and human fallibility.

In the late 1960s, a sense of crisis developed among programmers owing to their inability to write infallible code, prompting them to develop a discipline, software engineering, in the 1970s. This new disciplinary status emboldened software engineers to make software complexity and catastrophic failure a central issue, and to argue that missile defense should be seen more as an information systems problem than a physics one. Public debate on the Strategic Defense Initiative launched by President Reagan largely focused on exotic projects such as the space-based X-ray laser championed by Edward Teller, whereas the main obstacles actually lay in more mundane technologies: infrared sensors, radar and computers. Today's systems face a much smaller threat than the Soviet arsenal, but they must defend against a wider variety of potential attacks and launch sites, from North Korea to Iran. Programmers are faced with the dilemma of writing software that is both functional—i.e. proven by testing— and adaptable. As soon as they adapt it to a new situation, it is no longer tested. This example shows that technological development is linked to the way in which technical judgments acquire authority, to the way in which experts assess risks, and to the question of who chooses the experts. These social configurations constrain the directions in which weapons systems are developed and, ultimately, the hardware that equips armies.

Similarly, the development of stealth technologies for US fighter jets shows how technological choices depend on scientific communities and environmental constraints, and are not predetermined. The history of stealth technology revolves mainly around the efforts of Lockheed Martin and Northrop engineers, who were commissioned by the US Department of Defense in 1979 to develop a stealth bomber.[43] However, tensions soon arose between the aeronautical and electrical engineers of the two companies: the challenge of deflecting and absorbing radio waves was primarily an electrical problem, but the aeronautical engineers refused to relinquish their status as lead aircraft designers. The serendipitous discovery of the work of Soviet physicist Pyotr Ufimtsev proved to be a significant breakthrough for Lockheed, as his equations for predicting the reflection of electromagnetic waves off two- and three-dimensional objects provided the basis for the design of an aircraft composed of radar-reflecting facets. In 1981, the Lockheed F-117A stealth fighter was unveiled, equipped with state-of-the-art precision-guided munitions and computer-controlled systems that made it possible to pilot an inherently unstable aircraft: Lockheed won the initial contract for the stealth fighter. Meanwhile, Northrop continued its efforts to develop a long-range, high-altitude stealth bomber to complement the aging B-52 and B-1 bombers, drawing on lessons learned from the development of the Tacit Blue, a battlefield surveillance aircraft that was eventually abandoned. Building on this experience, the Northrop team discovered that well-designed curved surfaces could also deflect radar. Founder John K. "Jack" Northrop's fascination with "flying wings," characterized by the absence of a defined fuselage and vertical tail, proved decisive in this research. The flying wing design, highly aerodynamic by nature, was considered ideal for a long-range, inherently unobservable aircraft. As a result, Northrop successfully delivered the B-2 bomber in 1989, based on a completely different stealth philosophy from that of the F-117.

Interactions between civilian and military technologies

Technological development within the armed forces is therefore inseparable from the national and international scientific context. Here, we need to consider the general effects of the transformation of societies brought about by the Industrial Revolution on the conditions for the production of armaments and other military technologies: armed forces become one of the players in a whole comprising industries, research centers, political decision-makers and military organizations. The First World War marked a major turning point in the blurring of differences between civilian industries and military needs: to fuel the gigantic *Materialschlacht* of the great battles of the conflict, armaments had to be mass-produced. As a result, "The Great War was part of a major intensification of the industrialization of European societies [...]. Women's work, production lines, Taylorism—all these developments began before the war. But it was the considerable efforts made by warring societies that enabled them to reach an essential milestone."[44]

One of the first consequences was a steady search for ways to integrate civilian technologies into combat. An excellent example is barbed wire, patented in 1874 by an Illinois farmer and later an indispensable instrument of military practice in the First World War.[45] This accelerated industrialization redefined the role of armed forces in the identification and production of military technologies, with significant differences according to national contexts. In the UK, the Vickers and Armstrongs companies enjoyed a high degree of autonomy in the conduct of their industrial policy (sometimes extending to an autonomous foreign policy); this was acquired during the Edwardian period, before a gradual rapprochement with the state took place from the late 1930s.[46] In the US, the combination of private companies, public arsenals delegated to private operators and state-controlled arsenals that existed at the end of the Second World War was gradually "rationalized" in favor of private industry during the Cold War.[47] In fact, many studies show that the Cold War saw a strong intensification of links between civilian and military actors in technological development. The US government worked with government agencies, independent laboratories and contract firms to develop important technologies during this period. These organizations solved complex problems by working together to develop cutting-edge technologies in fields such as computing, satellites, nuclear power, and chemical and biological technologies. The Army, the Atomic Energy Commission, the Office for Naval Research, the CIA and NASA all contributed to the funding and supervision of these projects.[48]

In the USSR, the Soviet regime set up a system of military industry control via the Military-Industrial Commission (VPK in the Russian abbreviation), an agency of the Council of Ministers responsible for coordinating the various army, Party and government organizations involved in arms acquisition and production. The VPK's remit was to examine proposals submitted by the defense industries on the basis of their technical feasibility, production requirements and impact on other sectors of the economy, as well as financing, production and schedules. VPK decisions were subject to approval by the Council of Ministers. Industrial production was handled by companies operating under different ministries, such as the Ministry of Medium Machinery Construction (for nuclear warheads) or the Ministry of General Machinery Construction (for ballistic missiles and space vehicles). Unlike arrangements in Western defense industries, design and production were kept separate. However, the main missile design bureaus were linked to specific missile production plants (the Progress plant in Kuibyshev, the Yuzhmash plant in Dnepropetrovsk and the Khrunichev plant in Fili). Although new projects were initiated by the design bureaus, it was the military services themselves that were behind most of the requests for new or improved weapons systems. The General Staff played a key role in the weapons procurement process. As a rule, it did not initiate proposals for new weapons, nor did it give final approval. Rather, its role was to review all proposals, adapting them to overall acquisition budgets and military policy, and thus serving as a forum for resolving conflicts within the armed forces over resource allocation. Design bureaus exerted considerable influence over weapons programs and the types of technologies to be developed. There was considerable competition between design bureaus, and before a production decision was taken, prototypes produced by different design bureaus were tested, and several options may have been available.[49]

In China in the 1950s and 1960s, a group of military scientists and bureaucrats played an important role in promoting a techno-nationalist development strategy. This strategy aimed to link the development of strategic weapons to the overall national program of technological and economic development. Unlike the conventional weapons program and the rest of Chinese society at the time, this approach was collaborative, non-hierarchical and depoliticized. Marshal Nie Rongzhen was the acknowledged leader of this group, which achieved two decisive breakthroughs during the Mao years. Firstly, he set up a flexible and efficient organizational structure, the National Defense Science and Technology Commission (NDSTC), to oversee strategic projects. Secondly, he formulated a techno-nationalist vision that justified the allocation of enormous resources to a few advanced weapons systems, arguing that this was the only way for China to become a truly international power.

Under Deng Xiaoping, the Chinese leadership adopted the organizational innovations of the NDSTC, but shifted the emphasis from nuclear programs to conventional armaments and civilian technologies. The new generation of those championing strategic weapons sought to respond to the enormous political, economic and security changes by championing a critical technology acquisition plan, the 863 Plan, which is still in place today. This plan has led to major advances in fields such as biotechnology, automation, information technology, energy and space, with both military and civilian applications. Thus, although China began to demilitarize its priorities in the late 1970s, the techno-nationalist vision continued to play an important role in technological planning aimed at increasing international economic competitiveness as much as national security.[50] This willingness to interface is reflected today in China's discourse of "civil–military fusion."[51]

Another case in point is Israel, which has created a particularly responsive and innovative defense technology ecosystem, facilitated by the conscription system, which enables links to be created and maintained between civilians and the armed forces, even after conscripts have completed their service. There are many examples of knowledge networks that have facilitated military cooperation, notably in the development of Israeli drones, observation satellites and the Merkava tank.[52]

These growing links between civilian research, military laboratories and the armed forces have meant that the last-mentioned have had to adapt their needs definition practices and enter into constant dialogue with a multiplicity of interlocutors. This has led to the multiplication of capability programming and monitoring positions in the military staffs, and to ever-renewed attempts to "capture civilian innovation" by increasing the points of contact between armed forces and civilian players, whether public or private. This mechanism corresponds to a form of learning on the part of military organizations, which, with varying degrees of success, provide themselves with the means to interact with other scientific players. This dynamic has been reinforced over the past decade by the perception of a possible "Fourth Industrial Revolution," which is characterized by the fusion of the digital, biological and physical worlds through technologies such as artificial intelligence (AI), robotics, genetic engineering and quantum computing (among others),[53] and in which the civilian sector is at the forefront. Initiatives as diverse as the Defense Innovation Agency (AID, in France), the Defence and Security Accelerator (DASA, in the UK) or the Defense Innovation Marketplace (DIM, in the US) all share the same underlying philosophy of a renewed need for civil–military cooperation, which is in fact helping to change the practices and organization of the armed forces. It should be noted that these multiple forms of cooperation can have unexpected consequences, even for the armed forces. For example, after the Second World War, Norway developed the Terne anti-submarine missile, despite the fact that the Norwegian Navy had expressed no need for it. The missile was thus developed by the Norwegian Defense Research Establishment (FFI), which had managed to secure government funding for the project through a skillful combination of rhetoric about the inevitability of a need in this field, support from prestigious partners in the US and the UK, and a certain amount of bureaucratic skill. The Norwegian Navy thus found itself equipped with a missile it didn't want, but which it eventually adopted.[54]

An important contemporary development is the gradual reliance on smartphones, and the infrastructure enabling their use, for the prosecution of modern warfare. It means that warfare is ever-increasingly data-centric in view of the desire to constantly improve targeting, and that the armed forces are increasingly dependent upon private actors (companies or citizens), which become participants in war in different ways: through providing direct support to a military campaign by sending data (such as pictures or video feeds) used for targeting, by contributing to narrative struggles and propaganda campaigns, or by becoming consumers of images and videos about a specific conflict.[55]

The challenge of international cooperation

The question of the multiplicity of interlocutors for armed forces is even more pronounced in the case of international cooperation for the development of weapons systems. In principle, states have several options for obtaining armaments: national production, off-the-shelf purchasing, licensed production of foreign systems, development and production in cooperation with one or more other states, leasing, or simply not acquiring a capability. However, since the end of the Cold War, international cooperation in the field of armaments has multiplied. Within the European Union, for example, the European Defence Agency was created in 2004 to coordinate the efforts of states in the production and acquisition of armaments. In theory, armaments cooperation is expected to generate considerable economic and military benefits. By pooling research and development (R&D) expenditure between partners, states can save on the sunk costs inherent in the development of new weapons. In addition, the production of a larger number of units should enable states to benefit from greater economies of scale, thus reducing the unit cost of the weapons acquired. If each state contributes components with distinct comparative advantages to a collaborative project, the final product should be superior to what each state could have developed individually. In short, the aim of international cooperation in arms production is to reduce development and production costs for states, while at the same time outperforming their strictly national equivalents in military terms.

However, international cooperation is often inefficient and difficult to implement. The fundamental difficulty with collaborative armaments projects is that they suffer simultaneously from the "agent–principal" problem inherent in defense procurement[56] and from the collective action problems characteristic of international collaboration. As with defense procurement in general, agents (i.e. defense companies) seek to extract excessive profits or use public funds to acquire resources that will enable them to win future contracts. And in an international context, the fear of suffering losses in relation to one's partners strongly dissuades states or companies from investing in the actions needed to make collaboration effective.[57] Moreover, interactions between governments and defense contractors can vary from country to country, thereby complicating the dynamics of cooperation. Depending on the governance of defense companies (public or private) and the market shares controlled by these companies, states will prefer projects based on economic or military considerations, and on whether or not they involve significant technology transfers.[58] In fact, there is a trilemma between the desire for independence (in order to guarantee control of technologies and systems deemed critical), economic spin-offs, and control of development and production costs:[59] the trade-off between these three dimensions depends on national political preferences at any given time.

In the case of France, Samuel Faure has analyzed the various choices made by the state in the acquisition of armaments: sometimes through European cooperation ("with Europe") and sometimes through national production or off-the-shelf purchases, particularly from the US ("without Europe"). According to Faure's argument, it is the nature of the interactions between the French armaments elites at any given time that explains the choice of production or acquisition mode for any given item of equipment. Faure identifies two main variables to explain these configurations: the industry's degree of autonomy from the state and the interdependence between French and European armaments elites. Depending on the interaction between these variables, four types of configuration emerge: "exclusive," "disembedded," "amalgamated" and "inclusive." The "exclusive" configuration is characterized by a low degree of industry autonomy vis-à-vis the state, and strong interdependence between French and European elites, leading to bilateral cooperation choices. The "disembedded" configuration combines a high degree of industry autonomy and strong interdependence between French and European elites, and leads to multilateral partnerships. The "amalgamated" configuration covers a low degree of industry autonomy and a low level of elite interdependence, leading to "made in France" programs. Finally, the "inclusive" configuration denotes low industry empowerment and high elite interdependence, and leads to off-the-shelf purchasing of equipment produced in allied countries (especially the US). For Faure, these interactions explain the choices made to produce military equipment alone or in cooperation, as illustrated by the European A400M transport aircraft ("disembedded" configuration), the Rafale fighter jet ("amalgamated" configuration) and the purchase of the American Reaper drone ("inclusive" configuration).[60]

This means that armed forces have to take into account equipment that sometimes imperfectly matches their expressed needs, quite simply because they are only one of the players contributing to the definition of the weapon system's characteristics and its acquisition. In fact, a national military organization is only one member of a decision-making network that also includes the defense industry (national and international), political leaders, and other military organizations when equipment is developed in cooperation. Difficult compromises must therefore be found between partners. Current Franco-German cooperation projects are a good illustration of this tension. Paris and Berlin are at present engaged in two major projects: a new air combat system centered around a new fighter aircraft to replace the French Rafales and German Eurofighters (the FCAS program, or Future Combat Air System), and a new battle tank to replace the French Leclercs and German Leopards (the MGCS project, or Main Ground Combat System). However, the two countries are finding it difficult to reconcile their objectives. As far as the MGCS is concerned,

> the capabilities required by France to replace the Leclerc tend to focus on intervention, especially in North Africa—which implies a light weight, facilitating mobility. However, the successor to the "Leo" is intended for continental warfare in Europe, and would therefore be a heavy tank, in line with the German doctrine of "joint combat" (*Gefecht der verbundenen Waffen*). [...] The question is therefore whether and how a common system can come into being.[61]

TECHNOLOGY AND MILITARY CHANGE

Similarly, under the FCAS program conducted in partnership with Spain, France aims to deepen Franco-German and Franco-Spanish cooperation, renew its capabilities, adapt to new threats, preserve French and European strategic autonomy, guarantee interoperability and project its forces abroad. For its part, Germany is seeking to strengthen its aeronautics industry, contribute to NATO in close cooperation with the US, increase its strategic autonomy and offset the decline of the automotive industry. Finally, Spain aims to raise the technological level of its aeronautics industry, pursue cooperation with European countries and renew the capabilities of its air force. Therefore:

> All these motivations are good reasons to move forward with the SCAF [i.e. FCAS] program, but some of them may conflict with certain aspects of the program or with the motivations of other partners. For example, the desire to improve skills in certain areas is not necessarily compatible with the "Best Athlete" principle, which consists in entrusting industry with what it knows best. Similarly, the desire to continue to be a leading player within NATO may lead to unfavorable choices being made with regard to a program aimed at European strategic autonomy. From the German point of view, France's desire for strategic autonomy may also conflict with the desire to share the industrial benefits of the program fairly. A compromise therefore needs to be found between strategic autonomy, desired above all by the French, and the development of the German aeronautics industry, desired from the other side of the Rhine.
>
> Furthermore, the SCAF program is not perceived in exactly the same way by all our partners. For France, the SCAF is essential for its major industrial players, who cannot afford to remain without a combat aircraft or engine project. German and Spanish manufacturers are not quite in the same situation: it's more a question of increasing their expertise in these fields.[62]

This shows how, as a result of compromises that take into account differing political, industrial and strategic interests, armed forces may have to implement weapons systems that only partly meet their needs, in a context in which the rising cost of armaments makes industrial cooperation increasingly essential.

Adopting and implementing new technologies

Acceptance of innovation is a major issue. Historically, many civilian innovations have created public controversy because they challenged established hierarchies or interests: electricity, printing, agricultural mechanization, mechanical refrigeration, etc., which are completely taken for granted today, all had difficult beginnings, sparking public debate and fears for health, employment and the sense of community.[63] The same applies to military organizations: the integration of new technologies creates winners and losers. A new capability will attract resources, which are usually drawn from other existing capabilities. Managers therefore have a vested interest in minimizing the importance of a new technology. Moreover, depending on their effect and nature, new technologies can pose a threat to hierarchy and status within the armed forces. Like all organizations, armed forces are structured not only according to positions and resources, but also according to the prestige attached to certain attributes. All other things being equal (ranks, responsibilities, skills), two officers will not necessarily be perceived in the same way; this may vary depending on the specialty or service to which they belong. In particular, exposure to fire, associated with courage and heroism, is seen as more prestigious than other attributes. Thus, in many armies, the so-called combat arms (infantry, cavalry, etc.) are perceived as more prestigious than the so-called support arms (signals, training, equipment, etc.).

These perceptions of relative prestige shape recruitment practices (by attracting the most ambitious or promising candidates) but can be challenged by new technology. The most famous example is the introduction of the battle tank, which rapidly rendered traditional cavalry missions obsolete. In most European armies, cavalry was perceived as the heir to chivalry, owing to its close relationship with the horse, historically a symbol of wealth, power and nobility.[64] As a result, cavalry officers in several European countries opposed the introduction of the tank, arguing that it could never match the performance and utility of traditional cavalry, in order to protect their prestigious status within military organizations.[65] Without going into the details of how the tank was adopted in the interwar period,[66] we can observe that its integration was often achieved by adapting a set of traditions (e.g. in a military unit's symbols) and maintaining old customs and practices, in order to present the adoption of the tank as an evolution of the cavalry officer's status, rather than as a transformation.

The American "combat aviation brigades," which are responsible for conducting air–land combat from helicopters, have traditionally descended from cavalry units, the argument being that reconnaissance and charge missions from helicopters are in fact cavalry tasks, and only the mount is different. Similarly, the technological evolution of three generations of American fighter jets (F-86E Sabre, F-4C Phantom II and F-15A Eagle) has led to greater automation of piloting tasks: the complexity and increasing speed of these aircraft would have required far too much effort on the part of the pilot. However, this automation was regularly challenged by the pilots themselves, who had created a myth of air chivalry, combining aggressiveness, individualism and pride in mastering the machine. The gradual automation of tasks was seen as an attack on the identity of what constituted a "good pilot," even if the technology was objectively an aid to improving their combat efficiency.[67] The most prominent and famous proponent of the pilot myth was Colonel John Boyd, who tried to influence the development of the F-15s and F-16s: for Boyd, these aircraft were too heavy, because a pilot had to engage his adversary in a spinning gun battle. The remote engagements made possible by the radar–missile pairing on board the F-15s and F-16s, which profoundly altered the face and distance of aerial combat, were seen as threats to the fighter pilot's identity by Boyd and his colleagues in the "fighter mafia."[68]

The integration of new technologies is thus a risk for those with high status within the armed forces, who will tend to retard or hinder their development and integration. Consequently, Terry Pierce argues that when a new technology is too disruptive, strongly challenging established hierarchies or practices (thus corresponding to an innovation), it is often more effective to "disguise" it as an adaptation by pretending that it is merely an evolution of existing practices.[69] The acceptability of new technologies is an issue in itself, and military leaders must take into account the organization's culture and practices to ensure the effective integration of new systems.

Mastering technology

In fact, the introduction of a new technology necessarily changes military practices through a learning mechanism: the institution needs to devote resources to ensuring mastery of a technology and optimizing its combat potential. Depending on the technology, changes can be either adaptive or innovative. For example, the introduction of a new assault rifle requires adaptation: specialists need to test the weapon's limits of use, identify the gestures that enable it to be reloaded or disassembled and reassembled while optimizing both speed and safety, and possibly adapt existing tactics marginally to take account of new capabilities (e.g. longer range). The comparison between the old weapon and the new one will be a topic of discussion for several months, some manuals may have to be rewritten, and there will be a need to "train the trainers" who will then be responsible for disseminating best practice, but the scale of the change remains limited for the organization. Of course, the introduction of the tank, for example, is on an altogether different scale: we now have to create new channels for new professions (pilot, gunner, tank commander), reorganize logistical support around what is now vital equipment, equip entire units with expensive equipment, and, above all, rethink operational concepts to take account of the new technology.

Another example is the gradual emergence of combat information centers on US Navy ships in the early twentieth century. Communication and coordination in navies are a long-standing problem, historically addressed in a variety of ways, including the use of flags or various visual signals. From the late nineteenth century onwards, the growing complexity of warfare at sea, due to technological advances such as steam propulsion, affected commanders' ability to receive information and control their ships and fleets. Steam propulsion brought significant tactical advantages, but it also increased the complexity of maritime operations. Commanders had to find new ways of signaling to ships operating beyond the visual range of flag hoists. Although signal rockets and searchlights showed promise, they remained as vulnerable to weather and misinterpretation as traditional flags. The introduction of radio on board warships further complicated command and control. At the beginning of the twentieth century, fleet commanders not only had to manage units scattered beyond their visual field and operating in three dimensions, but also had to cope with increasing quantities of information circulating at speeds beyond the cognitive capabilities of the most experienced captain or admiral. The solution found by the US Navy was the creation of the CIC, where sailors used technology to understand the complex, dynamic environment and provide commanders with a clear tactical picture. This development required senior officers to compromise on the traditional hierarchy and draw on the expertise of petty officers and sailors to develop an effective command and control system. Integrating machines and people into the CIC demanded collaborative efforts, moving decision-making away from the bridge and drawing on the skills of officers who didn't fit the stereotypical profile of the American naval officer. Thus, "CICs gave naval commanders a metaphorical second brain. Inside this human-machine mind, relatively junior personnel made time-critical decisions, sometimes so quickly that the information reached an officer in tactical command or commanding officer only after the fact. In social-scientific terms, cognition at sea was socially distributed;"[70] this represented a significant change in the practice of war at sea. At the outset of the Second World War, CICs were rudimentary and faced limitations in large-scale coordinated attacks. However, the introduction of combat operations centers in late 1942, which managed information from a variety of sources during combat, greatly improved the US fleet's air defense capabilities. The Battle of the Philippine Sea, nicknamed the "Great Marianas Turkey Shoot," demonstrated the effectiveness of the new system, which successfully intercepted hundreds of Japanese aircraft.

Technology and organizational friction

However, the introduction of new technologies, in particular information management technologies, carries with it the risk of increasing friction. In fact, warfare in the twentieth- and twenty-first centuries has gradually been intermediated by technologies enabling the commander to represent an operational situation: first counters on maps, then visualizations on screens synthesizing information from an ever-increasing number of sensors. This progressive technologization regularly leads to the hope of being able to "pierce the fog of war": the idea is that ever-increasing numbers of high-performance sensors would provide the commander with a complete, real-time picture of the situation on the ground, giving them a decisive advantage in conducting their maneuver.[71] However, the challenge for any military organization is to manage the incompressible gap between the actual situation on the ground and its representation for the benefit of the commander, the management of this gap being ensured by informational practices within the organization: "if a military is unable to connect its internal representations to external realities, then it cannot know where to aim, it cannot hit the things it aims at, and it receives poor feedback about what it hits and misses."[72] There is thus a great risk that an organization will structure the data and the representations it makes of it to serve its own bureaucratic interests and conform to its own cultural codes. For example, in the province of Anbar in Iraq in 2007–2008, US Navy Special Forces were engaged in a process of continuous elimination of suspected insurgents, aimed at emulating the "find, fix, finish, exploit, and analyze"[73] (F3EA) practices developed by the Joint Special Operations Command (JSOC) and its commander, General Stanley McChrystal, which are said to have helped put some 12,000 suspected insurgents out of action between 2003 and 2008 (killing around a third of them). However, the politico-military situation in Anbar province was probably not conducive to a campaign of this type at the time, and an approach based on protecting the population would probably have been more appropriate. But the data collected by the US Navy's Special Forces and their processing highlighted the identification of new targets (thus legitimizing the Special Forces mission), while obscuring other types of socio-cultural data that could have been used to help stabilize the province.[74] The multiplication of sensors and representations of information on the battlefield can thus have both positive and negative impacts on military effectiveness, depending on the way in which the organization collects, manages and represents data. Adaptive management of informational practices to solve operational problems will tend to have a positive effect, while an attempt to manage information without questioning the organization's institutional and cultural preferences will tend to create friction and limit military effectiveness.[75]

More generally, the introduction of a new military technology, especially an advanced one, generally increases complexity within a military organization and reduces its resilience. The quest to reduce uncertainty in constrained environments (e.g. cost and time factors) results in increasing organizational complexity. The number of different organizational units, the number of connections between them and the interdependence of specialized knowledge in separate units tend to increase, making the organization more complex. Paradoxically, complex technologies are adopted in order to control uncertainty, and organizational structures are made more complex in order to adapt to and control new technologies. Complex organizations and technologies—and their interaction—thus tend to produce unpredictable effects, as shown by the example of the introduction of the M-1 Abrams tank in the US Army.[76]

The M-1 Abrams tank was born of the strategy of countering quantity with quality. American military planners had calculated that an army equipped with highly sophisticated weapons could defeat an enemy equipped with a greater number of less sophisticated weapons. The M-1 tank was thus equipped with complex technology designed to offer a high degree of speed and precision when attacking the enemy. Achieving these improvements required sophisticated computer technology both on board the tank and in the test and repair units. Complex test equipment was required to analyze faults, and highly skilled technicians were needed to diagnose and repair system irregularities. The new M-1 and its associated test equipment therefore required a large number of highly sophisticated maintenance personnel at a time when the Army was not receiving enough recruits capable of acquiring the necessary skills. It became necessary for the Army to differentiate the types of knowledge available at different levels of the organization. In the field, for example, maintenance personnel had to remove and replace damaged components and send them to the rear for more sophisticated testing and repair.

One of the organizational consequences of the new technology was that tank units at the front became more closely dependent on repair units at the rear. Previously, combat units could carry out repairs in the field and continue to operate. The new technology has forced repairs to be carried out by rear support systems. This closer coupling between rear and front units can lead to friction and surprises, as technological complexity begets organizational complexity. Both are conceived as rational control mechanisms, but they can lead to unpredictable events that weaken the organization's resilience. The problem becomes even more acute when several interdependent technological systems are introduced simultaneously, as the Army attempted to do with the Future Combat Systems program in the early 2000s. The aim was to introduce a whole range of military capabilities (combat vehicles, transport vehicles, mortars, artillery, drones, etc.) operating in a network to gain rapid superiority over the enemy. The program was too complex, with multiple delays and cost overruns, and the Army finally decided to cancel it in 2009.[77]

Technology and theory of force employment

In fact, a military technology is only useful in so far as it contributes to a theory of force employment. A good example of this dynamic is the introduction of radar among the Western powers in the 1930s. The principle of radar (a term coined by the US Navy meaning radio detection and ranging) was perfected between 1922 and 1941 by an international community of scientists, based on a number of advances in engineering and physical science. The basic principle of radar is simple to understand: radio waves are sent to an object (illumination), which reflects these waves back to the point of origin. The position of the object is thus determined by measuring the characteristics of the reflected waves. Repeated illumination of the object determines its velocity and vertical position. However, it was the detailed understanding of a number of physical principles that enabled the emergence of today's radars. These principles are

> 1) that electromagnetic (EM) radiation can be used to find remote objects when employed at high radio frequencies, 2) that such radiation can be transmitted in pulses so that it is possible to detect disruption in the signal, 3) that returning signals and disruptions can be accurately captured at the point of origin, 4) that the frequency of pulses can be used as an indication of distance to an object hit with EM radiation, and 5) that antennae can be utilized to determine the direction of an object.[78]

These principles were understood and mastered within a few years of each other in the UK, France and the US, but the integration of the technology in the three countries was very different. The most exemplary case was the UK, where radar made possible a change in strategic posture. Until the mid-1930s, Britain's strategic posture was determined by a doctrine of retaliatory deterrence against Nazi Germany, built around a fleet of strategic bombers. The idea was that hostile action by Germany could be deterred by the threat of aerial bombardment of civilian and military targets, which would make the cost unacceptable. The premise of this reasoning was that, in the absence of effective anti-aircraft defense, "the bomber will always get through," and that the best defense was attack. Of course, the weakness of this reasoning lay in the fact that there was nothing to stop Nazi Germany from doing the same: developing a fleet of strategic bombers that would threaten the UK and deter it from intervening in European affairs.

The possibility of integrating radar technologies was conceived in this strategic context. Properly employed, radar would make possible the development of a deterrent by denial that would significantly increase the cost of an offensive: this time, the bomber would no longer get through, as it would be detected and intercepted. Radar was a key technological development that led to a reconceptualization of British strategy. It was no longer a question of developing a fleet of strategic bombers, but of a genuine combat network comprising sensors (an infrastructure of radar installations on British territory enabling the detection of threats), effectors (fast-fighting aircraft designed to intercept aggressors, including the famous Spitfire), and a command center for aggregating and visualizing the information provided by the sensors in order to direct the effectors. From then on, the British war effort was directed toward the development of this "combat network." This was of course put into practice during the Battle of Britain,[79] and it constitutes a major innovation in the art of warfare in the twentieth century, since its philosophy still permeates contemporary military operations.[80] On the other hand, France saw the use of radar as only one of several possible methods of establishing an early warning system in the event of invasion, and the US saw no obvious use for it in their doctrine.[81] The Italian Navy even entered the war in 1940 without having equipped its ships with radar: given that the identified enemy was the French Navy in the Mediterranean, the Italian admiralty had judged that the cost of integrating a new technology was too high in relation to the expected benefits.

Thus, any technological development should ideally be accompanied by doctrinal debates to rethink the practices of armies, their theory of victory, and the expected benefits of a new weapon system. For example, at the turn of the 2010s, a major theoretical debate was taking place in Russia between three schools of thought on the role of technology in warfare. Traditionalists believed in the simultaneous maintenance of high technology and large forces. They argued that developments in information technology and precision weapons did not fundamentally change the character of warfare. They saw no reason why the purchase of new technologies should be at the expense of manpower. Traditionalists felt that Russia had to respond asymmetrically to the Western technological challenge, given its technological backwardness and limited resources. They argued that Russia should concentrate on developing new tactics and strategies to counter Western technology, rather than try to match it directly. The modernists, on the other hand, were willing to exchange manpower for technology. They felt that Russia should focus on developing advanced technologies to compensate for its lack of manpower. Modernists argued that Russia should prioritize the acquisition of new technologies, such as drones, precision-guided munitions and electronic warfare systems. They believed that Russia should invest in the development of new tactics and strategies that take advantage of these technologies. The modernists argued that Russia should respond asymmetrically to the Western technological challenge, focusing on the development of new technologies that would give Russia an edge over the West. They also prioritized technology over manpower. They believed that Russia had to respond in kind to the West's technological challenge in order to defend its sovereignty: the country had to invest massively in cutting-edge technologies and modernize its army to match the West. In their view, Russia should focus on developing new technologies that could give it an edge over Western countries, such as hypersonic missiles, artificial intelligence and robotics. They argued that Russia should adopt a more aggressive stance toward the West and be ready to engage in high-tech warfare. For them, Russia should respond symmetrically to the West's technological challenge by aligning itself with the latter's technological capabilities.[82] The difficulty of deciding between these different debates, and the obsession with "circumventing" the armed struggle (by technological means too), certainly help explain in part Russia's failures in Ukraine from 2022.[83]

In principle, some technologies may never reach the "employment" stage: they may be accepted and deployed in the armed forces, but not used if the opportunity does not present itself. Similarly, deployed technologies may see their usefulness drastically reassessed during the employment phase. A good example is the development of searchlights prior to the Second World War. The ships of the main belligerents invested heavily in this technology, which promised to be able to detect and target enemies, even at night, thereby providing a decisive tactical advantage. However, once in combat, searchlights proved to be a vulnerability: they could indeed detect and aim at the enemy, but also provided the latter with a superb target. Searchlights had a very specific application, notably in anti-submarine warfare, but their use was actually limited during the Second World War, and the technology was virtually abandoned by the end of it. Similarly, some developments are driven by pure techno-fetishism, on the assumption that more technology is necessarily better. An amusing example is the adoption by the US Army in 2004 of "pixelated" camouflage for its fatigues, in the belief that a design inspired by digital shapes would be more disturbing to a human observer than one inspired by natural forms. However, in use, the camouflage, which was supposed to make soldiers less visible, actually made them easier to spot: the Army recognized its mistake and abandoned the camouflage in 2011.[84] Once again, there is a learning mechanism for assessing the real effect of a new technology in combat.

What this shows is that there is a specific time frame for a military technology to be exploited to its full potential. While tanks were introduced to the battlefield during the First World War, the first signs of the possible mechanization of armies appeared at the end of the nineteenth century. The first visions of their possible use can be found in the short story "The Land Ironclads" published by H. G. Wells in 1903, and they only achieved spectacular results and maturity in terms of both technological mastery and concepts of use during the Second World War.[85] Similarly, naval mines were invented in 1776 by an American engineer, but were first deployed, after engineering problems had been solved, during the First Schleswig War (1848–1851) to mine the port of Kiel, before being used by the Russians to defend Kronstadt during the Crimean War (1854). Even then, mines were seen as an unglamorous weapon, and only as a defensive tool, on a par with coastal defense batteries. It wasn't until the Russo-Japanese War of 1904–1905 that navies realized that mines were not just a means of defending an area, but could also contribute to modifying and reshaping the geography of the area of naval engagement. After this discovery stage had been reached, a process of evolution during the First World War led to full exploitation during the Second World War.[86]

Sometimes, certain technologies only become fully exploitable after another technology has been deployed. This is the case with the torpedo, which was invented in 1866, but which only acquired real doctrinal and operational maturity after the deployment of submarines at the end of the nineteenth century. The two technologies had been conceived and designed separately, but it was their combination that enabled their optimal exploitation. Similarly, the possibility of "remote warfare" from the mid-2000s onwards was only made possible by the combination of several technologies and practices: "equipping *Predator* with laser designators, arming them with *Hellfire* missiles, linking them with the various players in the battlespace and intelligence community, and controlling them across continental distances."[87] It was indeed the combination of different technological "bricks" developed separately over a period of some fifty years that made possible the emergence of a new military practice.

In practice, given limited resources, these technological breakthroughs and recombinations leading to changes in military practices are highly dependent on initial choices often made years or even decades beforehand and thereafter maintained and perpetuated because of "path dependency" (an initial decision leads to others in the same direction, while closing off alternatives) and loss aversion, once sunk costs have been incurred.[88] Thus, it is important to think of technological development and its effect on armed forces in a long-term perspective: many military technologies are used in ways that differ from their initial concepts of employment, but it is only over time that optimal uses may emerge, owing to (unforeseen) combination with other technologies or under the pressure of conflict. There is thus an incalculable element of chance in supporting technologies that may or may not have operational relevance three or four decades later.

Conclusion

Technology plays a key role in the conduct of warfare, as it has the potential to transform military practices and strategies. As we have seen, technological development raises many issues for military change. In particular, it creates incentives for circumvention but also constraints for armed forces: modernizing equipment to maintain a tactical advantage, reacting to changes in potential adversaries (with the risk of being drawn into an arms race), cooperating with a multiplicity of actors, notably civilian and foreign, and so forth. These constraints may come up against internal resistance, particularly in the event of a change in relative status within the organization or a challenge to its fundamental institutional beliefs. The third main mechanism at work is learning: military organizations must learn to cooperate with multiple players and learn to use technology to its full potential. Finally, we have observed diffusion mechanisms, notably in the search for emulation of certain "prestigious" weapons within the framework of international cooperation. Depending on the context, these mechanisms lead to the full range of change: from adjustment to disruption. Above all, this chapter illustrates the difficulty of predicting which technologies will be "effective" for an organization: some technologies will only be useful after an unforeseen combination with existing technologies, while others will only be recognized by the military organization as a function of its organizational culture and force employment doctrines. The "right" technology does not exist in absolute terms.

The technologies associated with the "Fourth Industrial Revolution," in particular artificial intelligence and performance-enhancing technologies for cognition and physical capabilities,[89] will raise a series of questions linked to their acceptability and the degree of disruption they entail in the practices and routines of military organizations. How these questions are answered will be an important dimension of the scale of change in military organizations in the twenty-first century.

4

THE INTERNAL DYNAMICS OF MILITARY ORGANIZATIONS

This chapter is devoted to the military organizations themselves: by refining the granularity of the analysis once again, new configurations emerge, particularly when we study in detail the dynamics between the different components of the armed forces.

The entities studied in this chapter are both material (such as the various institutions making up a country's armed forces, or particular individuals) and immaterial. Indeed, like any organization, the armed forces have their own particular cultures, which shape the way in which change takes place. It is the interactions between these material and non-material entities that enable certain mechanisms to operate. This chapter is divided into four parts. The first examines the distinction between strategic culture and military culture, and how these create a context within which military change does, or does not, take place. The second discusses the competition for resources and missions between different components of the armed forces, and the effect of this competition on innovation. The third deals with the need to think about future warfare, the epistemological limits of the exercise, and how armed forces can nevertheless organize themselves to stimulate innovation. Finally, the fourth part analyzes the training, experimentation and knowledge transfer mechanisms within the armed forces, and their effect on change.

The organizational context: strategic culture and military culture

There is a classic joke going around the Pentagon. One day, the Secretary of Defense asks the Chiefs of Staff of the Army, Navy, Air Force and Marines to "secure a building." Each interpreted the order differently: the Army set up a defensive perimeter around the building, controlling access and creating checkpoints to verify comings and goings. The Navy sends sailors into the building, who turn off the lights, make a note in the registry and lock the doors before leaving. The Air Force negotiates a five-year lease with an option to purchase with the building's owner, and identifies a subcontractor to air-condition the building. Finally, the Marines locate the creek closest to the building, conduct a doctrinally flawless amphibious assault, take the building by force and plant an American flag on the roof. In their own way, they have all "secured" the building.

Strategic culture and military culture

The different components of the American armed forces react differently to the same order, reflecting in this way their individual institutional cultures. The term "culture" is particularly complex to handle in the social sciences, and the subject of endless debate. For our purposes, we can probably distinguish between strategic culture and military culture. The notion of strategic culture formally emerged in Anglo-Saxon political science, in the 1970s to be precise, although earlier works had already studied the influence of so-called cultural factors on strategic behavior (think, for example, of the term "ways of war" explored by the British strategist Liddell Hart).[1] Jack Snyder's first definition of strategic culture, given in 1977, is "the sum total of ideas, conditional emotional responses, and patterns of behavior that members of the strategic community have acquired through instruction or imitation and share with each other."[2] This definition has been widely accepted for a decade within the strategist community, but it is potentially tautological, since it fails to distinguish between ideas and behaviors. Are ideas the variable that explains behavior, and, if so, how are they formed? Or do socialization and behavior create a repertoire of action that becomes binding?

The constructivists of the 1990s contributed to the debate by making culture an explanatory variable. Alastair Johnston thus understands strategic culture as a system of symbols (e.g. argumentative structures, languages, analogies, metaphors) that acts to establish influential and enduring strategic preferences by formulating conceptions of the role and effectiveness of military force in interstate affairs, and veiling these conceptions in such an aura of factual reality that the established strategic preferences appear the only realistic and effective ones. This approach to strategic culture allows us to make it an independent variable, and to distinguish it from the dependent variable to be explained: the strategic choices of a given country.[3] Making strategic culture an independent variable also ensures the falsifiability of the theoretical model by comparing the explanatory value of strategic culture with other independent variables, as positivist epistemology requires. Johnston's approach was criticized by Colin Gray, one of the first strategists to take an interest in the notion of strategic culture in the 1980s, who contested the possibility of differentiating culture from action, and thus of establishing a causal link between the two, as Johnston does. He then defined strategic culture as comprising the ideas, attitudes, traditions, mindsets and preferred methods of action that are persistent (but not eternal), socially transmitted, and more or less specific to a geographically determined security community with a necessarily unique historical experience.[4]

After this debate between positivists and constructivists, a new generation emerged at the turn of the 2010s, calling for the disaggregation of strategic culture to avoid considering it monolithic,[5] and showing that the actors themselves were aware of the different facets of their own strategic culture, which they could mobilize "strategically" as required to justify their own political choices.[6] For example, French strategic culture is made up of at least two constantly competing subcultures: a messianic "soldier of the ideal" tradition (as Clemenceau put it) and a realist tradition dating back at least to Richelieu. These two traditions compete, coexist and dominate in turn, depending on the political moment.[7] Raymond Aron perfectly perceived this contradiction in General de Gaulle, about whom he wrote:

> If foreign policy is a jungle—I'm willing to subscribe to this view without illusion—it's hard to see why France should claim this or that satisfaction, either in the name of its past, or in the name of its historical role, or in the name of its human quality. The difficulty with General de Gaulle's foreign policy is that it always oscillates between a conception of traditional Machiavellianism and claims that are rather difficult to justify within the framework of this very Machiavellianism.[8]

Thus,

> Like all social phenomena, strategic culture is subject to transformation and change according to socio-political contexts. Moreover, most of the works mobilizing the concept of strategic culture fail to distinguish between different levels of analysis, namely *preferences* in favor of the use of force and the *modalities* of its application. In short, it is crucial to distinguish between political-strategic and tactical-operative levels. Finally, the term "culture" (in itself problematic, as it can give the illusion of an irremovable uniqueness) must be divided into several components for the purposes of analysis. Firstly, *narratives* need to be studied: both political narratives about what the country's international role should be, and military narratives that serve to constitute a professional identity (for example, chosen models of courage or heroism). Secondly, we need to consider the *institutional arrangements* that enable the use of force, both constitutional provisions and the bureaucratic routines of the military institution. Thirdly, it is important to study the *practices*, in the sociological sense of the term, associated with the use of force. These include political practices and societal tolerance of armed force, as well as "military heuristics," i.e. what the armed forces consider to be the ideal way of employing force, whether codified officially in doctrine or shared informally within

the forces. All these elements are in constant interaction and influence each other, together constituting a strategic "culture," itself evolving over time.[9]

We propose here to reserve the term "strategic culture" for the politico-strategic level, and to use the term "military culture" to denote the tactico-operational level and, in particular, military heuristics and associated practices. Military culture can thus be defined as "a core set of beliefs, attitudes and values which, through processes of socialization, become deeply embedded within an army and guide the way in which it manages its internal and external lives, interprets its tactical and operational objectives, and learns and adapts."[10] It is these military cultures that explain why the US Air Force, US Navy, US Army and US Marine Corps react differently to the same order in our imaginary example.[11] We can also refine the granularity and identify military subcultures according to specialties (infantry, cavalry, submarine, fighter aviation) or other historical subdivisions specific to each armed.[12] We can also identify military subcultures that do not exactly coincide with institutional distinctions. Brian

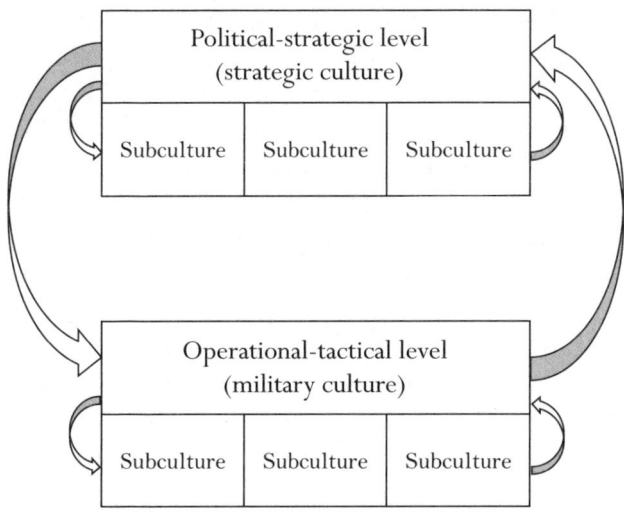

Figure 8. Strategic culture and military culture

McAllister Linn identifies three military subcultures within the US Army: "guardians," "heroes" and "managers." All three have different understandings of the institution's past, the challenges facing the US and, above all, the means to address them.[13] What emerges is a cameo or mosaic of different military cultures coexisting within the same military organization, that organization itself being one of the components of the country's strategic culture. These cross-interactions are summarized schematically in Figure 8.

In this way, military culture is both a factor and an object of change: it can facilitate (or hinder) military change, but it is itself the object of change. This section also looks at how national strategic culture influences military culture and thus the armed forces. By contrast, feedback analyzing the effect of military culture on national strategic culture is outside the scope of this book on military change.

However, we must be careful to avoid the pitfall of culturalism, i.e. reducing behavior to the expression of an essentialized culture. This is a recurrent pitfall in attempts to understand societies seen as "other." For example, translations made of Sun Tzu in the West sometimes reflect the preoccupations of the translators rather than an engagement with the author's thought.[14] Sun Tzu was thus often perceived in the West as the "Chinese" thinker par excellence, whose reading would enable us to understand an Asian "mentality" in general, or a Chinese one in particular.[15] The same tendency toward culturalism can be found in superficial pseudo-reflections, such as "the Chinese play go and we play chess," which are supposed to "explain" Beijing's strategic approach. Besides the fact that chess is a Persian game, Vladimir Putin is also supposed to be a master of it, which is seen as a quality in the mouths of his admirers: is playing chess therefore a handicap or a strategic quality? True, it is also sometimes pointed out that Putin practices judo, as if the key to Russian grand strategy were to be found in an understanding of *sen* (initiative) and *kuzushi* (imbalance). It remains to be explained how France's predilection for *pétanque* and *belote* helps us understand General de Gaulle's foreign policy ...

Culture and military change

In the first place, national strategic culture infuses and guides military cultures. Dimitri Minic shows how the conspiratorial view of the world held by post-Cold War Russian elites, and in particular their perception of a permanent American plot to bring down Russia,[16] influenced Russia's military elites,[17] leading them to see Washington's hand in every international event and to imagine a permanent American doctrine of subversion. Russian military thinkers have coined terms such as "color revolutions" or "controlled chaos" to describe what they imagine to be an American plan. In fact, this vision of the world holds that

> contingency does not exist in international relations: a coup d'état in Africa is thus necessarily linked to the global competition between the great powers, who have chosen a new battleground for their confrontation. It's easy to see how, in this vision, a revolution such as that of Euro-Maidan is inevitably interpreted as part of a wider competition between the United States and Russia, thus denying the demonstrators any autonomy and denying the social dynamics specific to an internal political crisis in the Ukraine.[18]

Yet Russian military thinkers have tried to imitate the American doctrinal chimera they imagined, adopting a vision of war that attempts to circumvent armed struggle—a vision that has shown its limits in Ukraine.[19] Here we see the link between national strategic culture and military culture.

Military cultures themselves are also used to explain organizational change or changes in practices. In her book on the French and British armies, Elizabeth Kier highlights the influence of norms on the very structure of military organization.[20] To explain why the French Army abandoned an offensive doctrine in favor of a defensive one in 1928, Kier argues that this change was a response to the introduction of a conscription period reduced to one year by the "Painlevé" law. The French Army placed no particular value on a defensive doctrine, but adopted it because French officers felt that conscripts were incapable of effectively implementing an offensive doctrine. Kier's study highlights how norms define an organization's capabilities and activities. Surprisingly, despite Germany's extensive and successful use of reserve forces during the First World War, French officers, trapped in their organizational culture, remained blind to the offensive capabilities of conscripts. Kier points out that of the thirty-four corps that attacked France in August 1914, twelve were reserve units, and all were deployed in the front line of the attack. Despite the German example, French officers continued to underestimate the conscripts' offensive capabilities, being blinded by their organizational culture.

Kier demonstrates how norms orient actions by shaping the way actors represent problems to themselves, and the way they solve them. Moreover, norms play an essential role in enabling actors to construct identities that give meaning to their own actions and those of others. In other words, actors not only ask themselves, "What is the nature of this situation?" and "What am I supposed to do?" but also, "What are my responsibilities as an officer in the French Army?" For example, Craig Cameron shows how the operations carried out by the First Marine Division in the Pacific during the Second World War were influenced by their self-representation as a warrior elite and by a simultaneous process of dehumanization of the Japanese.[21] According to Cameron, Marine operations, characterized by costly frontal assaults and unnecessary brutality toward surrendering Japanese soldiers and civilians, were a direct consequence of the First Division members' self-identification and perception of the enemy.

Another example is provided by the concept of the "revolution in military affairs" (RAM) in the USSR, the US and Israel.[22] In the 1970s, US and NATO defense planners became aware of a potentially devastating problem. In the event of conflict in Europe, NATO forces could initially cope with the Warsaw Pact's first-tier formations, but they would be at a disadvantage in the race to deploy reinforcements across the Atlantic. Third-echelon Soviet forces, made up of less well-prepared reservists and maintained at less than half their peacetime strength, could probably outmatch what would have survived of the NATO forces. The US and its allies had to find a way to stop this third echelon. The solution lay in a host of new technologies that would enable NATO to carry out precise strikes against Warsaw Pact assembly areas, depots, transport centers and armored formations, located hundreds of kilometers behind the front line. In the mid-1980s, the US launched initiatives such as the Assault Breaker and the Smart Weapons Program, while NATO explored the "follow-on forces attack" concept. At the same time, the US Army developed a new air–land battle doctrine, laying the foundations for a "reconnaissance-strike complex" capable of transforming high-intensity conventional conflicts. The Soviets were the first to recognize these new developments as a "military-technical revolution," observing that the emergence of a reconnaissance-gun complex would transform conventional combat. Soviet strategists realized that precise long-range strikes could annihilate enemy forces as well as critical supply, communications and command elements, deep in the adversary's rear, creating the conditions for a catastrophic theater-wide collapse. They saw that conventional, rather than nuclear, munitions could become the weapon of choice against many targets, rendering massive tank and infantry formations ineffective.

American planners, on the other hand, took a much less holistic view of the new technologies, seeing them simply as a means of preventing third-echelon Soviet forces from reaching the central front. The Israelis adopted an even less strategically articulated approach to the new technologies, although they were the first to implement all the elements of a reconnaissance-strike complex during their air operations in the Bekaa Valley in 1982. Ironically, the Soviet Army, although the least able to implement these new technologies, was the best able to understand their impact on warfare.

The variation in national capabilities in understanding and implementing new technologies is influenced by the way culture shapes problem-solving styles. For example, the Soviet Army placed great value on the intellectual skills of its senior officers and offered them many opportunities to debate doctrine. By contrast, the US Army had few structures for such debate: although doctrinal change did take place under the impetus of TRADOC (see below), it did not achieve the conceptual breadth imagined by the Soviets. As a result, most of the essential concepts relating to the application of information technologies to warfare were developed by the Soviets by observing the weapons systems used by their adversaries.

Once formalized in the US, this RMA spread within NATO from the 1990s onwards. But here, again, there are many differences in terms of adoption, reflecting different cultural and institutional preferences depending on local strategic and military cultures.[23] For example, the UK adopted the key elements of the RMA with a view to optimizing operational effectiveness (consistent with the pragmatic culture of the British armed forces), while the German armed forces adopted the vocabulary and concepts in their doctrine without fundamentally modifying military practices, seeking legitimacy with American allies rather than combat effectiveness.[24]

Despite these variations between countries, there is nevertheless a similarity in thinking within military organizations, which Ben Zweibelson attributes to the prevalence of a mechanistic and sequential approach to conflict. According to Zweibelson, the epistemological framework of the vast majority of military organizations is a "simple loop," non-reflective, used to identify problems, objectives and the means to achieve these objectives based on the problems and resources available. This mechanistic approach permeates the methodological tools that military organizations develop, including doctrine, operational planning procedures (such as NATO's Comprehensive Operations Planning Directive), and conceptual tools for analyzing reality such as "centers of gravity" or SWOT (strengths, weaknesses, opportunities, threats) and CARVER (criticality, accessibility, recuperability, vulnerability, effect, recognizability) matrices. All these tools and techniques derive from a Newtonian and mechanistic conception of reality, according to which a system is a closed, static entity, but they fail to take into account feedback loops and complex causality phenomena on the part of both the enemy and the organization itself.[25] To overcome these intellectual and methodological limitations, a movement promoting so-called design approaches and offering new planning tools has been developing over the past two decades, with strongholds in Israel, Canada, Australia and, gradually, the US, despite resistance at a conceptual level from a number of military organizations.[26]

We can see here that strategic or military cultures operate mainly through a mechanism of constraint on military change, by filtering information, attitudes and preferences deemed legitimate or not within the framework of this culture. But these strategic and military cultures are also subject to change, even if this can be difficult. For example, both German Admiral Tirpitz and Soviet Admiral Gorshkov attempted to develop naval cultures in their respective countries. However, "the most immediate challenge faced by both men was an internal one, namely that they sought to create large ocean-going fleets in countries that were close to being landlocked and, more importantly, dominated by Army-centric strategic cultures."[27]

In fact, there are different degrees of change in military and strategic cultures: adjustments and adaptations are frequent, innovations and disruptions much rarer.[28] Social science literature tends to consider that for change to take place, there must be "critical conjunctures," i.e. moments of crisis and political failure, often triggered by external events, which introduce novelty or uncertainty.[29] Chiara Ruffa explains the development of the military cultures of the French and Italian armies in terms of these critical conjunctures and, in particular, the Second World War. In Italy, for example, the armistice of 8 September 1943 gave rise to a profound rethinking of relations between the state, society and the armed forces, and redeployed the myth of the Italian military as "bad soldiers but good people" that had taken shape after the First World War. "Good people" gradually became "good humanitarians" in Italian military culture, leading to specific preferences in terms of use of force and contact with populations. In France, two "critical conjunctures" played a fundamental role: the defeat of 1940 and the attempted putsch of 1961. These two events shaped political–military relations and, in particular, the armed forces' acceptance of a subordinate role vis-à-vis politics. According to Ruffa, these events led the armed forces to evolve from their traditional military culture of engagement and assertiveness on the battlefield, to a military culture based on "controlled assertiveness."[30]

Critical junctures are thus a privileged moment for the evolution of strategic and military cultures. When they are faced with the failure of previous policies, these moments open up new opportunities:

other actions or new standards suddenly become possible. But for this window to be used, norm entrepreneurs are needed.[31] It is their interpretation of the critical moment that opens up new possibilities: neither the state nor the agents of society can react to material changes until they have interpreted them using various frameworks of understanding. In other words, a discursive process accompanies crises: the way in which key players frame the debate and mobilize specific symbols and discourses is very important to the process of change. Changing strategic and military cultures thus requires both a material and an ideational dimension: events must occur that call into question existing presuppositions, and require a new normative framework provided by norm entrepreneurs.

The evolution of Japanese strategic and military culture from the early Meiji era to the present day is a particularly interesting case in point. The centralization of power and accelerated modernization of Japan from this era onwards created a social demand for ideological and nationalist reinforcement, which took several forms, not least the "invention of tradition"[32] of the *bushido* (or "samurai way") from the late nineteenth century onward. As the samurai disappeared as an organized social class, their past and way of life were mythologized in order to provide an ideological substratum for the new era and the armed forces: a number of values (honor, loyalty, discipline) supposedly characteristic of the samurai way of life were put forward as a means of ideological cohesion. This mythologization had a direct impact on Japanese military practices, particularly during the Second World War, contributing to the ideologization of the conflict from the Japanese point of view.[33] Obviously, defeat provided a new critical conjuncture, rearticulating the relationship between the army and society, and imposing a form of constitutional pacifism that influenced the development of Japanese self-defense forces. It is interesting to note that the rise of China, and the possibility of a direct threat against Japanese territory, could constitute a new critical conjuncture, which, depending on the positioning of norm entrepreneurs, may lead to a new evolution in Japanese strategic and military cultures.[34]

Once again, the main evolutionary mechanism seems to be constraint.

The Internal Dynamics of Military Organizations

Inter-service competition as a driver of military change

As mentioned, a military organization is not monolithic, and is made up of institutional subdivisions, which have their own interests and may come into conflict. In modern armed forces, these subdivisions are generally associated with functional specialization in a particular environment or mission. Indeed, the growing complexity of conflicts has led many armies to go far beyond the historical distinction between army and navy. Table 4 illustrates the diversity of solutions found by different countries, showing the armies (or "services" in American jargon) directly under the command of a joint chief of defense.

Table 4. Examples of contemporary organization models for the armed forces

US	UK	France	Russia	China
Army	Army	Army	Ground forces	Ground forces
Navy	Navy	Navy	Navy	Navy
Air Force	Air Force	Air and Space Force	Aerospace forces	Air Force
Marine corps*			Strategic rocket forces	Strategic Support Force
Coast Guard			Airborne forces	
Space Force			Special Operations Forces	
National Guard			Logistics support	

Note: The Marines depend administratively on the Department of the Navy (as does the US Navy) but remain an independent service and are not subordinate to the Navy. Similarly, the Coast Guard depends on the Department of Homeland Security in peacetime but transfers to the Department of the Navy in wartime, although it too remains an independent service.

Obviously, these functional divisions according to environments or missions are an attempt at bureaucratic rationalization in terms of a logic of specialization, which is often confronted with the difficulty of precisely distinguishing in reality between attributions and environments. For example, as we shall see below, the creation of independent air forces (and their separation from land forces) was justified not only by a logic of domain (the air environment requiring specific equipment, training and doctrines), but also by a logic of mission (air forces were intended to carry out strategic bombing, theoretically justified by the writings of authors such as Douhet, Trenchard or Mitchell). However, at a time when distances between potential combatants have been greatly increased by the use of missiles, and when ground forces can de facto operate in the third dimension, some authors advocate "reattaching" the American Air Force to the Army, by imitating the Navy model (which has its own embarked air force). The logic here is that of the mission: land forces should have at their disposal the full spectrum of resources, including those in the third dimension.[35] Of course, the counter-argument is the same one that justified the creation of independent air forces: the environment and the mission would be so specific as to require a dedicated organization.

This type of friction obviously arises at the interfaces between domain and missions: who should control the observation drones that provide intelligence before and during an operation? The army, which is the primary beneficiary of this intelligence? Or the air force, which has control and expertise in the air? Should nuclear deterrence capabilities be attached to different services, depending on the domain (e.g. the navy controlling submarines), or should we create a service specifically dedicated to this mission, bringing together nuclear capabilities operating in different domains? Who should control operations in cyberspace? Does outer space require a dedicated service (the choice of the US), or should it be subordinated to the air force (the choice of France)? And so on.

Inter-service competition and military change

In practice, these tensions are unavoidable: every organization is, in reality, an attempt to simplify the characteristics and dynamics of reality to make possible a form of institutional rationalization. But the consequence is that conflicts between institutions over resources, missions and functions are also inevitable. The challenge is to understand how this competition affects military change.

The creation of independent air forces is a good example of this dynamic of functional specialization. The world's first independent air force was the British Royal Air Force (RAF), created in April 1918, following the creation of the Ministry of Air in January of the same year, and merging elements from the Royal Flying Corps (RFC, which was part of the Army) and the Royal Naval Air Service (RNAS, which was part of the Navy).[36] This was a wartime innovation (see Chapter 5), which can be explained by a combination of three factors: defeat, cost rationalization and the weight of public opinion.[37] The first major steps toward the creation of the RAF were taken between the summer of 1915 and the summer of 1916, during the so-called Fokker scourge following Germany's deployment of the Fokker Eindecker E.1 aircraft, which represented a major advance in aerial combat. At the same time, Zeppelin airships were regularly bombing British soil, particularly London, with apparent impunity. This German air dominance generated enough public concern to lead to the creation of a parliamentary commission of inquiry, as well as a working group within the War Ministry. One of the issues at stake was that the RFC and RNAS were not cooperating in the development and acquisition of new aerial technologies, leading to delays, additional costs and redundancies; and that they were also experiencing difficulties in delimiting their zones and perimeters of intervention. In 1917, Prime Minister Lloyd George asked General Jan Smuts to suggest an institutional solution to the air weapon problem.[38] In his two reports, Smuts proposed the creation of an independent ministry, which would run an air force that would itself be independent, created from the merger of the RFC and RNAS. This solution was, of course, opposed by the First Lord of the Admiralty, Eric Geddes, who was not opposed to a Ministry of the Air, but wished to retain control of RNAS, thus foreshadowing the British Navy's position on the RAF between the wars.

Indeed, the new RAF's first challenge was to ensure its institutionalization and continuity.[39] Right from the end of the war, the Admiralty was careful to repeat regularly that an independent RAF could not meet the air defense needs of the Navy, a message shared, albeit with less open hostility to the new service, by the Army.[40] Moreover, in 1919, the Air Ministry and RAF premises were placed at the intersection of Kingsway and Aldwych. Although these buildings are now located between the London School of Economics and King's College London, in a lively area frequented by students, they were described at the time as "gloomy." Above all, they were located almost twenty minutes' walk from Whitehall (the heart of the British government), putting the RAF at a disadvantage compared with the Army or Navy, whose premises were much closer to the heart of the seats of power.

Faced with these political and bureaucratic challenges, the RAF's first Chief of Staff, Hugh Trenchard, developed the idea of creating an "air force spirit" in his 1919 memorandum on the permanent organization of the Royal Air Force, which served as the basis for the RAF's development in the years following the First World War. Trenchard's strategy for creating a culture within the RAF was based on the creation of specific institutions and structures, which helped generate a culture enabling the RAF to establish itself as it faced up to the challenges posed by other service arms. Trenchard had a very clear idea of the culture he wanted to instill in the RAF, which could be summed up as "independence and control of the air."[41] Independence referred to the notion that RAF officers no longer belonged to the Navy or Army, but had to truly acquire an "air culture." This meant inventing traditions derived from or inspired by those of the Navy and Army. Control of the air was a doctrinal proposition (referring, of course, to the notion of "sea control" in the work of American Admiral Mahan), which served to justify the RAF's existence as an independent force. Trenchard advocated the use of air power to support the Army in a joint campaign, or as an interdiction tool targeting critical infrastructure. But, above all, he argued that the air weapon was the most effective in the psychological field: for him, the moral effects of bombing outweighed the material effects by a ratio of 20 to 1.[42] This doctrinal proposal was subsequently consolidated and disseminated through the creation of military teaching institutions within the RAF, notably the RAF Staff College.[43]

This shows how competition between services and, in this case, direct threats to the survival of a young institution can force it to innovate in its structures, practices and doctrines. This institutional competition is not the only explanation for the RAF's survival in the interwar period,[44] but it does go a long way toward explaining the RAF's change through a circumvention mechanism.

Similarly, institutional competition (or the perception of it) largely explains the evolution of the US Marine Corps between the US's entry into the Second World War and the start of the Vietnam War. It was during this period that the Marines built their public image, defended their existence and positioned themselves as the rapid reaction tool for defending American interests around the world, perfecting a public relations and lobbying system far more developed than those of the other services. For Aaron O'Connell, this system is the result of a siege mentality present within the corps, making Marines believe that they were perpetually under threat of dissolution.[45] As a result, the Marines built a dual image based on tradition and values. On the one hand, the Corps was presented as the quintessence of aggressive masculinity, transforming suffering into value, an image of themselves that the Marines were able to confirm during the Pacific campaign and the Korean War. This aggressive vision is reflected, for example, in the motto "First to fight," but it also enabled the Corps to reject an all-technological version of the future of warfare (unlike the Air Force or Navy) by putting forward a more romantic vision based on heroism and group solidarity. At the same time, the Marines built up an image, aimed at the general public, of tough but fair and caring men, which responded perfectly to the American anxieties of the 1950s, marked by the "crisis of virility" and the fear of rising juvenile delinquency. Through programs such as the Devil Pups (training camps for at-risk teenagers) or Toys for Tots (toy drives distributed to orphans at Christmas), the Marines positioned themselves with the general public as defenders of family values and traditional communities. This dual image enabled the Corps to present itself as the guardian of both the interests and the values of the US. Here, again, the evolution of a service's practices was very directly linked to a strategy of circumvention aimed at developing its difference from other services (in this case, the Army and Navy), and thus justifying its existence.

Competition between services is a regular factor in military innovation, as illustrated by the development of the Polaris missile by the US Navy in the late 1950s.[46] Polaris marked the launch of the fifth ballistic missile program under the Eisenhower administration. The Air Force's ballistic missile program had begun with the Atlas program, which owed much of its development to civilian intervention by the Secretary of the Air Force. Shortly afterwards, the Titan and Thor programs were added to Atlas. For its part, the Army's ballistic missile program was centered on the Jupiter system, the fruit of missile development efforts by the Army's missile branch at Redstone Arsenal. The underlying reasons for these two ballistic missile programs can be attributed respectively to a civilian constraint (in the case of the Air Force) and to competition within the Army between the branch in charge of ballistic missile development and the artillery. However, the development of Polaris cannot be explained by these dynamics, and it is all the more remarkable in that it established itself as the only missile system sufficiently innovative to make it through the early 1960s and become an important part of the US nuclear force structure.

Unlike the Army, the Navy did not have an in-house branch specifically dedicated to ballistic missile development. Although there were ballistic missile advocates within the Navy, they focused on the development of liquid-fuel missiles and were just as interested in space thrusters as in missiles, if not more so. Like the Air Force, the Navy had a guided missile program that focused mainly on cruise missiles, while being heavily controlled by the aviators—naval aviation being the branch most threatened by missile development in general. All the established branches within the Navy were opposed to ballistic missile development, and those who advocated it lacked a solid organizational base to counter this opposition. In addition, the Navy did not experience early and consistent civilian intervention in favor of missiles, as had been the case with the Air Force's ballistic missile program. Conversely, civilians were opposed to the Navy's ballistic missile program, deeming it unnecessary in view of the four Air Force and Army programs already underway in 1955. However, during this period, the Navy was involved in intense inter-service conflicts over roles, missions and budget allocations, which intensified in the mid-1950s with the downsizing that followed the Korean War.

Within Naval Command, two opposing views emerged on how to approach these conflicts. The first was that the Navy should avoid confrontation with the Air Force and preserve its existing share of the budget by avoiding battles. The second view argued that unless the Navy developed its own system superior to that of the Air Force, it would see its resources reduced, as the ballistic missile programs of the Air Force and Army would absorb a larger share of the defense budget. This would inevitably lead to the inter-service battle that the first group sought to avoid. The second view prevailed, championed by Admiral Arleigh Burke, Chief of Naval Operations (CNO), who began the arduous process of pushing the Polaris program forward despite near-unanimous opposition from civilian officials in the Office of the Secretary of Defense (OSD) and internal Navy branches. The decision to develop Polaris was triggered by inter-service competition, and logically intensified these conflicts, particularly with the Air Force. As the first solid-propellant missile (a technological innovation in its own right), Polaris prompted the Air Force to re-evaluate its own solid-propellant missile program. Quickly, and without substantial civilian support, the Air Force redirected its resources to the Minuteman solid-propellant intercontinental ballistic missile program, with the aim of protecting its programs from the "Polaris threat." Together, Polaris and Minuteman quickly replaced the previous four liquid-fuel missile programs, by offering greater efficiency and survivability. The success of Polaris and Minuteman gave the US armed forces greater operational capability, which led to the cancellation or withdrawal of other less successful Air Force systems, including the Snark, Navaho, Skybolt, B-70 and B-47. Above all, this rationalization led to the stabilization of US nuclear capabilities around a "triad" of Polaris strategic sea-to-surface ballistic missiles (SLBMs), Minuteman intercontinental ballistic missiles (ICBMs) and an air component consisting of nuclear-armed B-52s. This triad formed the technical-military basis for the transition from a doctrine of massive retaliation to one of graduated response.[47] Here we see how competition between the various services has had positive effects on technological development (the adoption of solid rocket missiles) and doctrinal evolution.

Another striking example is the development of an airborne combat capability (made possible by an impressive fleet of helicopters) by the US Army between the 1950s and 1960s, giving the US Army more aircraft than either the Air Force or the Navy. A series of agreements signed between 1948 and 1966 governed the weight and capabilities of Army aircraft. The Air Force aimed to limit Army aviation to logistics and communications in a specific area of the battlefield, while imposing restrictions such as a maximum weight of 5,000 lb (2,300 kg) for fixed-wing aircraft. However, at the time the Air Force was neglecting its close combat support responsibilities, as its leaders believed that strategic bombing was its primary mission. Although some senior Army officers accepted these agreements, preferring to allocate financial resources to equipping ground forces or seeing no practical use for light aircraft within the Army, many officers understood the potential advantages of light rotary-wing and fixed-wing aircraft for essential tasks such as artillery fire guidance, casualty evacuation, transport and close air support of ground troops, missions not fulfilled by the USAF. Consequently, at the operational level, there was considerable independent experimentation. Army officers took advantage of opportunities that arose, such as using Piper Cubs (light, single-engine aircraft) borrowed from local flying clubs to direct artillery fire, or modifying helicopters by adding guns to assess their fire support viability.

In the early 1950s, these efforts were sporadic and uncoordinated. Over the course of the decade, however, various groups began to collaborate, forming what Frederic Bergerson calls a "bureaucratic insurgency" characterized by non-compliance with official agreements limiting the Army's role in close air support.[48] This insurgency gained momentum when Robert McNamara became Secretary of Defense in 1961. McNamara's team showed a keen interest in Army aviation and served as influential advocates of the insurgency's goals. Shortly after taking office, McNamara initiated the establishment of a high-level Army "council," headed by General Hamilton Howze, to conduct a comprehensive review of the air mobility concept. In 1963, the Army received authorization to develop its first armed helicopter, the Cheyenne, which marked a major milestone. Subsequently, the use of helicopters in Vietnam from 1965 gave impetus and validation to the Army's aspirations, leading to a remarkable expansion of the fleet. By 1970, Army Aviation had succeeded in consolidating its position, and its existence was no longer threatened.

Here we see the combination of several mechanisms: an attempt at bureaucratic circumvention, which is supported by civilian leaders before being legitimized by operational use. Of course, the joint level is essential for coordinating the various programs and ensuring that each service's employment concept fits into a relevant overall concept: competition has its limits. It should also be noted that there are cases of inter-service cooperation, leading to innovations, such as when the USAF adopted the "battlefield air interdiction" concept in support of the "air–land battle" doctrine promoted by the Army.[49] But as long as it remains under control and does not risk the collapse of the whole, joint competition can be quite beneficial to innovation. Indeed, the risk of compulsory cooperation is that it may encourage the status quo: "New operational concepts directly or indirectly create classes of 'winners' or 'losers,' with respect to particular capabilities, force types, and structures, as well as within the subcultures of the military service in question. With innovative concepts, these effects are magnified. Mandating consensus is a sure way for those who envision themselves as 'losers' in the new way of war to block changes."[50] As we can see, the role of the joint level is a complicated one, as it has to strike a balance between healthy competition within armies, which is a factor of innovation, and the risk of fragmentation, to the detriment of unity of operational effort.

Imagination in power: thinking future war

Most military organizations devote resources and energy to trying to discern the contours of the future of warfare, in the hope of being better prepared for it. The intensity of this effort varies, but it is clear that in most cases the imagined future casts a shadow over the organization's present.

Military history and defense planning

Nevertheless, the attempt is particularly difficult, for a number of reasons. In the first place, defense planning takes place in a context of ambiguity, in which decisions have to be taken in advance of wars that can only be imagined.[51] The institutional response is usually to turn to more or less recent military history, in an attempt to discern similarities and analogies that would enable us to identify relevant lessons for the future. However, two main problems arise when trying to draw lessons from past wars for future planning. Firstly, wars are difficult to compare owing to their dissimilarity, making it difficult to draw meaningful comparisons. The limited availability of comparable data further complicates military analysis. There are few battles or wars in any historical period that lend themselves to empirical analysis, making comparisons and generalizations difficult. Specific factors such as technologies, leadership capabilities and context further hamper the accuracy of comparisons, especially when going back in time. Secondly, the complexity of the factors explaining the outcome of combat makes it impossible to state with certainty why one side prevails in a conflict, making it hard to extract relevant lessons. Military outcomes are probabilistic and subject to random factors. Yet hindsight bias often leads to the assumption that the outcome was determined from the outset, regardless of the probabilistic nature of victory. The natural tendency is to overemphasize the actions of the winners and the mistakes of the losers, thus skewing the analysis.[52] Yet Clausewitz warned that studying the past requires analysis of why decisions were difficult, not whether they were right or wrong.[53]

This instrumental relationship between military history and defense planning is quite understandable. In the absence of abundant data on the nature of future conflicts, planners fall back on the available data—past events as they think they know them. Yet social scientists are well aware of the epistemological difficulty of generalizing from a limited number of cases, in which causal mechanisms are themselves particularly ambiguous, and in which contingency and chance play an important role in the outcome of battles—something identified long ago by Clausewitz (who made chance one of the elements of his "second trinity").[54] Jean-Luc Leleu gives the example of the "Meyer" battle group in the German Army, which had to face the Allied assault during the D-Day landings on 6 June 1944, and spent the day going back and forth along the coast:

> The use of this battle group illustrates the difficulty of acting in a crisis situation. Considered one by one, the decisions to engage it were logical at the time each one was taken during the morning [...]. This episode puts into perspective the value and degree of legitimacy that can be attributed a posteriori to an action's success or failure. Throughout the day, the 352nd Division's staff functioned perfectly [...]. In retrospect, however, its actions appear ineffective in the light of the final balance sheet.[55]

What lesson or tactical principle can be drawn from an analysis? Should it be positive (the troops acted professionally) or negative (but the outcome was poor)? Wouldn't the lesson, commonplace and of little use to the institution, be precisely that it is very difficult to determine the factors of combat effectiveness? Here we see the epistemological difficulty of identifying strategic and tactical principles. But necessity is law, and military organizations often function as institutions for the reduction of chance, through rationalization and an instrumental reading of the past that tends to reduce the role of contingency. Moreover, a certain interpretation of the past can serve to cement the cohesion of the institution, for example around a common doctrine: indeed, "the creation of military doctrine is an exercise in highly selective historical interpretation."[56] The result is often problematic: in a remarkable book on what he calls the "seduction of battle," the historian Cathal J. Nolan shows how the heroization of decisive battles and the role of "great captains" in Western military thought have led to an overestimation of the strategic significance of these great engagements. As a result of this mythologization, military leaders have often been convinced that they could win a war quickly thanks to winning a major battle, but the reality is that these battles are very rarely decisive, and war most often degenerates into a long, devastating conflict of attrition for the belligerents.[57]

In fact, historians are well aware that every event is unique (a subject of endless controversy with social scientists who try to identify possible generalizations) and, above all, that history as a discipline is not the past but what historians say about the past: interpretations and knowledge are never set in stone, and to hope to draw generalizable lessons is to take a major intellectual risk. Michael Howard thus believed that for military history to be useful to the armed forces, it had to be studied in breadth, depth and context,[58] in order to provide officers (as a priority) with an intellectual repertoire enabling them to grasp the nuances, contingency and temporality of events. Pierre Grosser rightly points out that the point of history is to "provide a few keys to understanding the soil in which a crisis could arise, or the world that could arise despite crises, enabling us to reflect on the world in which we live."[59] Similarly, this kind of approach allows us to be sensitive to the unspoken, the implicit and the "common sense" that forms the basis of decisions: "When we think historically, we understand that, in our own times, as in the past, our actions are often influenced by shared understandings that we don't make explicit, common viewpoints so obvious 'they needn't be said.' These shape both how we see and act in the world."[60] In fact, acquiring the historical method raises awareness of continuities, ruptures and contingencies, and thus develops a form of strategic empathy,[61] which is certainly useful for armed forces.

The problem is that this approach requires specific training that takes time and resources, which few armed forces can afford to devote to the training of their officers. The result is often a partial and instrumental use of military history that poses risks of over-interpretation and mythologization of events, and thus the identification of the wrong lessons for the future.

The use of history by the armed forces may be analyzed according to the two "systems" of thought described by Daniel Kahneman.[62] "System 1" is the rapid, quasi-automatic reflex mode of thinking. These reflexes can be both innate (grimacing at an unattractive image) and acquired (a professional chess player knows thousands of combinations by heart and plays certain moves "automatically" according to the situation). "System 2" is the deliberate, sequential mode of thinking that applies an analytical method to a situation (and is therefore slower). Properly used, the historical method in the armed forces falls under "system 2": it is particularly sensitive to the strategic context. Used superficially (without adequate training or without the necessary time being devoted to it), it risks feeding "system 1," i.e. providing a repertoire of ready-made analogies that serve more to justify decisions taken than to understand the strategic environment.[63] During the Vietnam War, the historical analogy preferred by decision-makers proved the best predictor of their policy recommendations, as these analogies functioned as intellectual shortcuts enabling them to make sense of the situation: they thus applied preconstructed reasoning to a particular situation (system 1) instead of using history as an awareness of the nuances of the context (system 2).[64]

This tendency is even more pronounced when an organization relies on a mythologized and little-questioned past. French military leaders in the Serval and Barkhane operations regularly referred to Marshal Lyautey's "oil stain" approach as an inspiration (the former Chief of Staff of the French Armed Forces, General Lecointre, even explicitly claimed to be inspired by it during a hearing at the French National Assembly), while completely decontextualizing the realities of the process and failures of French colonization.[65] In this case, history actually served as a unifying myth, helping to construct a rationality and an imaginary continuity of practices for the organization. This mythification can be dangerous, as it gives the organization a sense of superiority ("we know how to do it because we've done it before") and prevents it from grasping the particular context by attempting to impose practices derived from other sociopolitical contexts[66] at all costs: the geographical similarity of theaters of military operations does not mean the similarity of socio-political contexts. For example, at the start of the interventions in Iraq and Afghanistan, the British Army had created a myth of "excellence" in counterinsurgency,[67] and had identified objectively contradictory lessons from its historical experiences of the Anglo-Afghan wars and the wars of decolonization (notably Malaya). These contradictions were rationalized by deliberately refusing to resolve inconsistencies between tactical, operational and strategic practices,[68] at the cost of obvious operational failures.[69]

Even without falling into the mythologizing of one's own past, studying other conflicts can also be problematic if methodological precautions are not taken. For example, it seems that the Chinese People's Liberation Army (PLA) took a particular interest in the Pacific campaign during the Second World War, and in particular the battles of Midway, Guadalcanal and Okinawa, in order to learn from them in the event of conflict with the US. It would appear that Chinese analysts have drawn relevant lessons in terms of intelligence, logistics, the establishment of forward bases and the targeting of opposing logistics. But "the lessons from the three battles, as the Chinese understand them, may reveal as much, if not more, about what the PLA values—or does not value—as the quality of the historiography."[70] Thus, PLA analysts tend to attribute Japanese decisions to arrogance or hubris, and thus to a create of immutable Japanese "national character" (which corresponds to a classic perception of Japan in China), while neglecting the underlying rationality of decisions or institutional explanations (e.g. on the lack of adaptation of the Japanese armed forces). Similarly, Chinese military literature on the period focuses almost exclusively on the operational aspects of battles, but neglects their strategic consequences. For example, analyses seem to suggest that Japan should have initiated an early air–land offensive during the Battle of Okinawa, which would have pushed American forces back into the sea and greatly weakened the US Navy, but without necessarily justifying how this offensive would have been conducted or why it would have had the effect predicted by analysts. It seems that this counterfactual reveals more the doctrinal preferences of the PLA, which since the 1930s has emphasized the concept of "active defense," i.e. rapid offensive actions (including pre-emption) with a strategic defensive objective. The analysis of the Battle of Okinawa (and also of the 1991 Gulf War) could well be a justification aimed at confirming a well-established doctrine within the PLA.

Imagination, foresight and science fiction

Historically, the second option has been to turn to the imagination, often in the form of literary or artistic explorations of the future of warfare. From the early nineteenth century onwards, armies turned to the fields of aesthetics and the arts to think about technologies and operations, thus initiating the creation of genuine "martial aesthetics"[71] and importing into strategic thinking the Romantic discourse of the time on "military art," "genius" or the "coup d'oeil" (the intuitive insight into a complex situation). Literature—and science fiction in particular—is regularly called upon to help armies think about the future. In recent years, the work of authors such as Tom Clancy,[72] August Cole and Peter Singer,[73] or projects such as the "Red Team" in France,[74] represent attempts to use literature as an illuminating lantern to dispel the darkness of the future of war and draw consequences for defense planning. Since the nineteenth century, attempts by both the military and artists to predict the future of conflict have more often than not proved false,[75] even if they have influenced the evolution of armed forces.

Should we then fall into a nihilistic crisis in which all prediction is impossible and defense planning is useless because it is doomed to error? Probably not. Intellectual effort is in itself valuable and indispensable because, as Clausewitz held, it educates the mind and gives it the intellectual flexibility needed for the inevitable adaptation required when real war comes. Moreover, even if we know that the predictions will be wrong, there are degrees of error: the aim is not to anticipate completely correctly, but to anticipate as little wrongly as possible, which is immediately much more achievable. Indeed, thinking about future warfare falls into a particular category of uncertainty: namely, events for which it is impossible to have an answer, and for which it is impossible to assign a probability. As Donald Rumsfeld put it in a much-mocked but highly relevant classification, we can distinguish three types of information. The first is "known knowns," i.e. facts that can be known and are known by the organization. The second category, "known unknowns," refers to facts which can be known, or for which a probability can be assigned, but which are unknown to the organization. For example, the performance and full technical details of the Chinese J-20 fighter jet are knowable (they exist), but this does not mean that the CIA is aware of them.[76] Similarly, it is possible to assign probabilities to specific events over a closed time horizon ("who's going to win the election next week?"), and it is possible to develop this skill.[77] On the other hand, the third category, "unknown unknowns," refers to information that nobody can have, such as "how long will the Chinese Communist Party stay in power?" The future of warfare falls into this category of knowledge: the aim is not to make an absolutely accurate forecast, but to arrive at an anticipation that serves as a guide to the evolution of armed forces, based on a plausible assessment of the future and leaving sufficient room for adjustment to correct trajectories in the event of new information. In fact, any strategy necessarily requires a vision of the future, either to make it happen (positive future) or to prevent it (negative future). Despite their inflexible limitations, anticipation and foresight exercises are an indispensable first step in establishing a strategy.

Bureaucratic struggles and the theory of victory

So how do visions of the future of warfare emerge and take hold in armed forces? One important mechanism of military change, particularly doctrinal change, seems to be circumvention. For Stephen Rosen, it is senior officers who are respected members of their organization (and thus possess significant social capital), driven by visions of future warfare, that lead innovation campaigns within their organization. These campaigns depend on innovation strategies that have both intellectual and organizational components.[78] As mentioned, military organizations are made up of professional communities or subgroups. These groups have overlapping and evolving capabilities, and as a result a degree of debate is formally introduced over the allocation of doctrinal tasks. Doctrinal innovations occur when one element succeeds in asserting itself in an internal political struggle for power over the organization's future. For Rosen, innovation involves more than a simple transfer of resources from one subgroup to another: it requires an "ideological struggle" that results in a new theory of victory. Once this "theory of victory" has been formalized and accepted, its implementation is ensured by the creation of new career paths enabling the promotion of young officers specialized in the organization's new tasks or functions.[79] Innovation is therefore not necessarily a rapid process, as it requires these young officers to be promoted, to sponsor each other and to obtain positions of responsibility. Similarly, in her study of the Soviet armed forces, Kimberly Marten argues that innovators are more likely to be "Young Turks" who have not been fully socialized into the organization, or "old hands" who are secure enough in their careers to take risks. She also argues that changes in the composition of communities can affect this innovation: for example, the inclusion under Gorbachev of civilian defense experts in debates on military doctrine led to radical new proposals for doctrines.[80]

In the People's Republic of China, at the turn of the 1980s, a group of military intellectuals was formed, who published their work in various specialized journals. This group of officers, some of them well connected with the Chinese Communist Party apparatus and therefore often protected, set out to change the focus of the PLA, and in particular its preparation for an imminent all-out war against the USSR. On the contrary, they introduced a notion of long-term planning (which was politically validated by the 1985 strategic shift toward an "army of peace"), developed methodological tools to aid defense planning (often inspired by those developed in the US), and studied the effect of technological upheavals on the future of warfare. When the 1991 Gulf War occurred, the Chinese community was surprised by the American military performance[81] (as were most of the world's experts), but they already had the intellectual tools needed to take into account the changes observed in the conduct of operations, and in particular the integration of reconnaissance and strike capabilities. These officers were thus able to propose a Chinese version of the "revolution in military affairs," which contributed to the transformation of the PLA from the 1990s onwards.[82]

However, the "ideological struggle," as Rosen calls it, is not necessarily based on a rational-scientific debate about concepts and theories of victory. In fact, military organizations tend to rely on "folk theories," which, unlike scientific theories, have plausibility and ostensible validity but are ambiguous and have unquestioned premises fitting existing organizational beliefs. These "folk theories," such as "complexity" in modern Western armed forces, provide an intuitive master narrative guiding the development of military concepts, but they lack systematic examination of cause and effects.[83]

For example, the writing of the now famous FM 3-24 doctrine on counterinsurgency was a time-driven compromise between the various authors and their views on the nature of insurgency, and not a proper scientific debate on the causes of rebellion and the effects of military force.[84]

However, there is a real challenge in reconciling conceptual development and organizational logic. Over the past forty years, the US Army's conception of "information operations" has oscillated between a technical and a psychological understanding of the term "information," resulting in an internal contradiction:

> The resulting doctrine employed information as a tool for affecting perceptions, but held an implicit understanding of information—and an information organizational infrastructure—that was based upon information as data. Moreover, the new inform and influence activities [IIA] concept was poorly aligned to both the prevailing institutional culture and the micro-organizational culture of the information operations community, which favored discrete, measurable, and technological solutions to information problems. The result was a doctrine that was widely misunderstood, poorly executed, and short-lived, despite its overall appropriateness for the strategic environment in which the Army found itself.[85]

We can see here that bureaucratic issues within the same organization (who defines and executes information operations?) influence the conceptualization of the organization's very role, and that doctrinal evolution is constrained by the match between operational needs and the dominant military culture.

The need for military incubators

We can see that the identification of a new "theory of victory" by military thinkers is a key factor in innovation, but how can a military organization configure itself to facilitate the emergence of these officers? A good way would seem to be to establish incubators—informal sub-units outside the chain of command—that provide professionals with the intellectual space in which to think about future warfare and necessary reforms. Secondly, for the concepts born in incubators to become doctrines, they must circulate in large-scale, multi-level defense networks, and military leaders must defend, socialize and protect the new concepts, as Rosen noted.

In 1973, for example, a series of events forced US Army leaders to reorient the institution. The end of conscription and the advent of a fully professional force altered the composition of the US Army, while the end of combat operations in Vietnam meant that troop numbers were half what they had been at the height of the conflict. In addition, the short-lived Yom Kippur War highlighted a radical shift in the range, accuracy, lethality and logistical support requirements of modern tank warfare, while underlining a fundamental change in the role of tactical air power. General William E. DePuy, who would become the first head of TRADOC (Training and Doctrine Command) and personally oversee the rewriting of Army doctrine, stepped into the breach. He set up a working group of senior officers and thinkers to draft the various chapters and act as a sounding board for the new ideas, which were then field-tested in corps-level exercises. The group soon realized that adequate close air support would only be possible with air supremacy, which meant that the army would not only need air support, but also an air campaign in the early phases of a conflict to suppress the enemy's air defenses. The resulting doctrine, dubbed "active defense," radically changed the Army's theory of conflict in Europe, from a force tasked with stalling the Soviets until reinforcements arrived, to one whose mission was to win the first battle. Throughout the development phase, DePuy personally presented the new findings to key Army and Pentagon stakeholders, North Atlantic Treaty Organization (NATO) allies and members of the think tank community, helping to "socialize" the new ideas and facilitate their adoption.[86] In the US, an important incubator was the Office of Net Assessment (ONA), created in 1973 and substantially transformed by the Trump administration in 2025. Long headed by the legendary Andrew Marshall, it played an important role in creating new methodologies for assessing military power relationships, as well as in identifying the effect of new technologies on warfare. One of the advantages of ONA was the quality of the personnel assigned to it, as well as Marshall's willingness to open up to the civilian world, working in particular with academics, in order to acquire methodologies, concepts and ideas that would not have emerged in the bureaucratic structure of the Pentagon.[87]

Here we see the importance of these incubators, which can take several forms: units separated from the chain of command and hierarchically protected; a community organized around military journals promoting debate and discussion; doctrine centers with strong institutional latitude and links to civilian expert communities; and so on. For example, between 1964 and 1992, France had the Centre de Prospective et d'Évaluations (CPE), followed by the Groupement Permanent de Planification et d'Études Stratégiques (GrouPES) and the Délégation aux Études Générales (DEG), which carried out a great deal of original work, such as strategist Lucien Poirier's thoughts on nuclear deterrence. For example,

> In creating the CPE, Pierre Messmer broke with the long-established practice of entrusting the military apparatus with the prerogative of theoretical and doctrinal thought. This was all the more innovative and daring in that the CPE worked on the margins of the general staff, enabling it to escape the competition and pressures of the three armed forces, but also to produce objective thinking unlike that of the various general staffs, due in particular to their continual competition for their respective budgets.[88]

But these structures tend to be absorbed into the formal bureaucratic machine, either by becoming annexes to the minister's office, or by becoming an institutional player and thus losing their originality. An alternative could be to provide doctrine centers with specific resources and protect them from the hierarchical chain. But to attract the best officers, these centers need to be perceived as prestigious positions, which is not always the case, particularly in countries where operational experience is a source of internal prestige and a major factor in promotions. Finally, the possibility of free operational debate, notably through quality military magazines, is an important factor in the emergence of new ideas and theories of victory. Otherwise, military organizations tend to fall into the routine of incremental adjustment of what already exists.

A final possibility is to rely on external organizations, particularly universities or think tanks. In the US, the field of security studies was consolidated after the Second World War in universities (particularly Princeton and Yale), in conjunction with decision-making circles. Similarly, the consolidation of US nuclear doctrine was mainly the work of researchers (notably Albert Wohlstetter, Bernard Brodie and Herman Kahn) affiliated with the RAND Corporation, a think tank originally created to advise the US Air Force.[89] In the UK, the Royal United Services Institute (RUSI) was founded in 1831 to advise the British armed forces, while the International Institute for Strategic Studies (IISS) was founded in 1958 to focus initially on nuclear deterrence issues. On the academic side, the Department of War Studies at King's College London and the Chichele Chair in Military History at the University of Oxford also have a tradition of cooperation with institutions, if only because of the number of their students who go on to pursue careers in the public sector.

However, the relationship between researchers and practitioners is structurally tense for several reasons. Firstly, career incentives are different. Academics, in particular, generally derive no professional benefit from cooperation with decision-makers: especially at the beginning of their careers, promotion is based on scientific tasks (research and specialist publications) and teaching, which are fundamentally the core of the profession. This is not a problem in itself: there is no obligation for researchers to take an interest in a field for reasons other than pure intellectual curiosity, and this is, moreover, a prerequisite for unexpected discoveries.[90] However, these divergent incentives can lead to a disconnect between the concerns and even the vocabulary of researchers and decision-makers.[91] Secondly, the way in which issues are framed often leads to misunderstandings: decision-makers generally expect precise answers to a specific issue that will enable them to implement a public policy, while researchers will often emphasize the complexity of a situation. Thirdly, the time frame is different: when a new issue emerges, decision-makers want immediate answers (or as quickly as possible), whereas research (especially when it concerns a new topic) is usually conducted over several years. Finally, the issue of asymmetrical power relations is central, particularly when the subject of the research is dependent on funding, as in the case of project-based research. In this situation, the client may tend to shape the results or dismiss results that do not suit them, particularly by threatening not to renew a grant. The temptation is even greater when the possession of expertise is a power issue within the bureaucratic apparatus. In France, for instance, attempts to create a field of "strategic studies" under the Fifth Republic have been regularly met with hesitation on the part of senior civil servants, who alternate between attempts to structure expertise through state funding and fears that the results of this expertise will call into question public policy choices and, ultimately, their own competence and social status within the state.[92] In the case of authoritarian regimes, the question does not even arise, as the vast majority of think tanks become de facto instruments of public diplomacy serving to promote the regime's policies.

As we can see, reliance on external bodies is complicated for the armed forces, particularly when expertise becomes a power issue, which is often the case. Relations therefore fluctuate depending on the country and the moment. External researchers nevertheless offer three fundamental advantages: the ability to conduct more substantial studies than those of an administration that has to manage day-to-day affairs; knowledge of scientific methods which guarantee results that are far more valid than the analytical skills of the vast majority of decision-makers; and, when the power relations allow, the ability to express problems freely without fear for one's career. Given that the structural tension between researchers and decision-makers is fundamentally irreconcilable, the relationship between the armed forces and research centers is always evolving, with the latter able to act as military incubators to a greater or lesser extent depending on the situation.

Preparing for war: training and learning

An important mechanism for change within military organizations is learning. This can be achieved in a number of ways: through training and education (particularly for officers), through experimentation and training, or through the institutionalization of experience.

Military training and education

Officer training and education is an important element in the possibility—or otherwise—of change: it serves both as socialization, by transmitting the values of the institution to its executives, and as training, by attempting to provide ideas and practices relevant to the profession of arms. The content of training and education is therefore an important element in a military organization's ability to change. A comparison can be drawn, for example, between the training of American junior officers at West Point and its German equivalent, the Hauptkadettenanstalten, in the interwar period.[93] At West Point, cadets followed a four-year program focused on mathematics and science, while adhering to bureaucratic rules that emphasized submission and the making of obedient junior officers. In contrast, German *kadetten* received a university-like education, fostering critical thinking with no guarantee of promotion. While American officers studied theory, application and approved doctrinal responses, German officers embraced *Auftragstaktik*, a superior–subordinate relationship that emphasized mission-driven leadership without rigid supervisory oversight. German officers, when given orders, were responsible for working out the details, and were even allowed to disobey if circumstances warranted.[94]

These different systems gave rise to contrasting intellectual approaches to problem-solving. American commanders with infantry and armor resources planned and executed attacks within the limits of approved doctrine, often lacking innovation. Only a few officers were creative, adapting to rapidly changing situations. By contrast, German commanders, who had the time and freedom to take the necessary measures without strict restrictions, were more aggressive in their approach and effectively managed the operational and tactical chaos.

Interestingly, despite these differences, Germany ultimately lost the Second World War, while the US and its allies emerged victorious. One of the reasons for this outcome was that German senior officers, educated to value operational and tactical freedom and to accept change, failed strategically. The mandates imposed on them by their leaders contradicted the principles of *Auftragstaktik*.

To survive in the German military-political system, most generals abandoned their training and conformed to the regime.[95] For their part, American commanders in the field were allowed to deviate from the guidelines if the situation warranted, and the more astute among them did so. While the German top brass succumbed to pressure and ultimately lost the war, the American generals were successful because they used their intelligence and worked within the system, rather than blindly adhered to doctrine.

This flexibility was certainly made possible by a second military educational institution, the Command and General Staff School (CGSS) at Fort Leavenworth, Kansas, offering training for captains or commanders destined to serve as regimental commanders or in staff operational planning positions.[96] The main focus was on commanding division- and corps-level formations, a role which could only be acquired through education, as army peacetime experience was mainly limited to regiment-sized units. Officers aspired to attend the CGSS, as it was seen as a prerequisite for securing important assignments at the Army War College and the General Staff. The CGSS program was developed on the basis of lessons learned from the First World War. It emphasized the operational transition from a "stabilized front" (trench warfare) to more mobile "open warfare." The success of these operations depended on the collective efforts of all branches of the Army and on the superiority of fire. CGSS graduates, who served at division or army corps level during the Second World War, applied this doctrine effectively. Although there was no specific adversary on which to focus, the school's curriculum cultivated mental flexibility to compensate for this.

However, the CGSS study program had certain shortcomings, particularly in the areas of mobilization planning, logistics and air–ground operations. In addition, technological advances were not always fully taken into account in the doctrine, particularly the role of aviation. To make matters more complex, shortly before the war, the US Army switched from square to triangular divisions. The abolition of two brigade headquarters, each overseeing two regiments, posed challenges in terms of command and control of the division, with commanders facing increased difficulties in managing their responsibilities. Solutions to these problems were found through practical experience in North Africa and during the early stages of the invasion of Sicily, rather than by relying solely on training at Fort Leavenworth. Nevertheless, the US Army demonstrated its adaptability as a learning organization, and Fort Leavenworth played an important role in developing the Army's ability to learn and adapt quickly.

Probably one of the essential missions of professional military education (PME) for the armed forces is to equip officers with the technical skills that will enable them to fulfill their role (depending on their rank), and also (or even more importantly) to give them the intellectual tools that will enable them to analyze, understand and therefore adapt to the unforeseen situations that arise in absolutely all wars. The adoption of PME systems differs from country to country, but the trend since the nineteenth century clearly shows a positive relationship between the development of PME institutions and military performance, particularly when these encourage critical thinking within the armed forces and do not merely serve as tools for inculcating the organization's norms and values.[97] Through this learning mechanism, the role of PME is to contribute to the organization's flexibility, not its rigidity. One institutional solution is to make time for training in officer careers, and to make such training desirable in order to attract the best candidates. The curricula themselves need to distinguish between what is training (the acquisition of specific professional skills and practices) and what is education (the acquisition of concepts and intellectual habits that strengthen officers' analytical skills). In fact, left alone, "the military is more likely to focus on training instead of education."[98] The question of the presence of civilian teachers in military curricula is thus an important one, even if it regularly creates anxieties linked to status within the armed forces. Anit Mukherjee distinguishes between "effective" and "weak" PME institutions.

These two models constitute ideal-types, and the two ends of a spectrum concerning training within the PME. Thus, there is a multiplicity of "hybrid" models which integrate civilians to varying degrees (as ad hoc contributors, as a complement to a training-based curriculum, as a legitimizing tool vis-à-vis civilian institutions, etc.), but which do not constitute an effective PME model.

Table 5. *Characteristics of an efficient PME*

Features	Effective PME	Weak PME
Composition of the teaching staff	Permanent civilian teachers are essential members of PME institutions	No permanent civilian teachers
Curriculum focus	In addition to operations, training is organized around subjects related to diplomacy and the use of force, including international relations, organization theory, area studies, constitutional law, military history and security studies.	Mainly focused on training and operations.

Source: Anit Mukherjee, "Educating the Professional Military: Civil–Military Relations and Professional Military Education in India," *Armed Forces and Society*, 44/3, 2018, p. 480.

Training and experimentation

The second way of learning is through training and experimentation. Before the First World War, the British Army conducted several large-scale exercises to test concepts and train its troops and staff. In 1904, it landed an entire division in an assault on the Essex coast, while other formations tried to defend themselves; and in 1912, it simulated a major battle of movement, with both sides led by the promising officers Douglas Haig and James Grierson. The Army drew useful lessons from this, notably on aerial reconnaissance and the role of cavalry. As Simon Batten notes, the pre-war maneuvers demonstrated that the British Army had made substantial advancements in professionalism and operational competence since the Boer War. The primary issue was not a failure of the pre-1914 exercises to prepare the Army for the initial phase of the conflict, which involved mobile warfare. Rather, the challenge lay in the fact that this phase was brief and, from October 1914 onward, gave way to protracted static trench warfare—a form of combat for which the British were no more or less prepared than their French and German counterparts.[99]

Similarly, in the 1970s, a transformation movement within the US Air Force's Tactical Air Command (TAC), led by a group of young officers, initiated a revolution in military practices by designing highly realistic training exercises, including the famous "Red Flag" exercise.[100] The effectiveness of Soviet anti-aircraft defenses posed a major threat. Moreover, Soviet aircraft had demonstrated comparable technological capabilities and superior maneuverability to their American counterparts. Moreover, TAC pilots were tasked with a wide range of missions, which limited their skills in one specific area, namely aerial combat. This was partly due to the fact that, in the 1950s and 1960s, the needs of Strategic Air Command (SAC) bombers had been given priority over those of the TAC. After the Vietnam War, Major Richard "Moody" Suter, a member of the Air Force staff, developed a new training concept that progressively increased the level of difficulty by simulating encounters with Soviet-type aggressors in a realistic environment. This approach emphasized the testing of new command structures, with a single air component commander in control of the battle. New aircraft such as the F-16, A-10 and F-117 were subjected to scenarios that improved their survivability. In addition, John Jumper of the Fighter Weapons School advocated the development of new tactics, training and evaluation. Pilots were trained to destroy integrated air defense systems, and then to carry out deep attack missions. The effectiveness of these skills was validated during the major El Dorado Canyon operation against Libya in 1986. During this period, air power theorists such as John Boyd and John Warden made a valuable contribution to the development of air campaigns. In the 1990s, for example, the dichotomy of "tactical" and "strategic" was deemed inadequate to describe air power: the Gulf War had elevated tactical aviation to a strategic role in the fight against Iraq, by redirecting targeting toward enemy centers of gravity deemed more relevant than ground forces. As a result, TAC and SAC were merged to form Air Combat Command. Here we see how specific training and exercises can contribute to doctrinal and organizational innovations.

Exercises have a dual role to play: they are intended not only to train troops and consolidate staff practices, but also to experiment with new concepts and practices. The difficulty for the organization is to avoid falling into the trap of the exercise serving "only" as a choreographed and therefore necessarily perfect maneuver, and to avoid discarding lessons that do not go in the expected direction: given the cost and time required to prepare a major exercise, the temptation is often strong to use the exercise as a validation tool. For example, the French Army's *grandes manœuvres* prior to the First World War may partly explain the failures of the first months of the conflict: "these major maneuvers may even have had a negative effect on the representations of the generals who took part in them. The distribution of army corps roles was carried out several months in advance, and the effects of combat were softened by exercises without noise, confusion, excessive fatigue or fear. They undoubtedly contributed to keeping old generals under the illusion of exercising effective command."[101] The temptation is all the stronger in that certain exercises can serve as a strategic signal to an adversary (or partners),[102] and that the political objective can outweigh the organizational stakes.

Another well-known form of experimentation and training for armies is the wargame. With a long history, these games (which come in a variety of forms) were consolidated as a planning tool by Prussia from the nineteenth century onward.[103] Some of these wargames have achieved almost legendary status: for example, the wargames organized by the Naval War College in the 1930s are credited with helping the US Navy prepare for the war against Japan, by experimenting with the importance of aircraft carriers in a campaign and mentally preparing officers for operations.[104] Thus, "the object of the wargame is to explore the dynamics of war, not its minutiae, but it is also to examine the mechanisms, which can shed new light on what happened."[105] The wargame can serve as a tool for strategic research, allowing options to be simulated or conflict dynamics to be modeled,[106] and as a training tool. Properly used, wargames can help influence decisions on doctrine and equipment. However, it should be stressed that wargames cannot be considered as conclusive evidence and should not be used as such. Their true value lies in their ability to shed light on important issues and create a space in which potential solutions can be explored. Wargames, in essence, are abstract representations based on a set of assumptions.

While their usefulness derives from the unscripted, semi-organic interactions between players, it's important to note that wargame designers introduce elements that influence the course of the game. Erroneous or misleading assumptions can thus mislead players into drawing inaccurate conclusions, either because they reinforce the organization's prejudices or because they serve the agenda of the game designers themselves. For example, in January 1941, Soviet commanders met to simulate the forthcoming campaign against Nazi Germany, in particular by trying to identify the axis of German effort, which in turn would enable them to organize the Red Army's posture. The exercise "validate[d] the Ukraine option of deploying the bulk of the Red Army in 1941, as the most favorable basis for penetrating southern Poland. This [was] the essential result of the *Kriegspiel*. And the one with the most far-reaching consequences, since the main German forces would attack 400 km to the north, in Belarus."[107] Depending on the rules and the way the game is run, the wargame, like the exercise, runs the risk of becoming nothing more than a tool for validating the organization's preconceptions. Like the French Army in 1939–1940, the Wehrmacht fell into this trap before the landings on 6 June 1944.[108]

Lessons learned

Another way of learning is through the institutionalization of experience, a process known as lessons identified/lessons learned (LI/LL). Obviously, gathering information on one's own practices with a view to improving them is an important factor in change. Armies, for example, generally have widely standardized LI/LL processes, which help to disseminate certain practices deemed relevant.[109]

Nevertheless, we need to disaggregate the LI/LL process, which has several dimensions. Firstly, as we mentioned in the introduction, experience in itself is often a weak guide to identifying mechanisms and social phenomena in general. It is subject to an availability bias (actors overvalue what is present in their minds), and important elements are filtered through the actor's understanding of events. And this understanding is inevitably partial. Consider how the Battle of Waterloo was experienced by Fabrice, the hero of *The Charterhouse of Parma*:

> A sharp cry rang out close to him; two hussars fell, struck by bullets, and when he looked at them, they were already twenty paces behind the escort. A sight which seemed horrible to him was that of a horse, bathed in blood, struggling on the ploughed earth, with its feet caught in its own entrails. It was trying to follow the others. The blood was pouring over the mud. "Well, I am under fire at last," he thought. "I have seen it!" he reiterated, with a glow of satisfaction. "Now I am a real soldier!" The escort was now galloping at full speed, and our hero realized that it was shot which was tossing up the soil. In vain he gazed in the direction whence the fusillade came. The white smoke of the battery seemed to him an immense way off, and amid the steady and continuous grumble of the artillery fire he thought he could distinguish other reports, much nearer. He could make nothing of it at all .[110]

We can easily imagine that an LI/LL analysis written by Fabrice wouldn't necessarily help us understand the battle or identify the causal mechanisms behind Napoleon's defeat. We are deliberately exaggerating here, but the problem remains: individuals who are closest to the action are not necessarily in the best position to analyze and, above all, explain the why behind a socio-technical phenomenon, in this case a combat action. Multiple explanatory factors may escape their observation, and they themselves have intellectual biases which overdetermine the explanation they will give to events (confirmation bias) or which prevent them from understanding a situation altogether (false beliefs). When exposed to painted tablets depicting believers who had prayed and survived a shipwreck, Diagoras of Milos disputed the hasty conclusion that prayer was the cause of their salvation. Instead, he questioned the absence of portraits depicting those who had prayed but nevertheless lost their lives. In other words, "what we see does not necessarily reflect what we do not see."[111] As a result, care must be taken when identifying lessons based on experience, as it is quite possible to learn the wrong lessons: military institutions need to take methodological precautions in their LI/LL process. A famous example is the 1936 Spanish Civil War, which was used as an example by many European forces of the difficulty of conducting combined arms maneuver on the modern battlefield. Only some European officers disagreed and kept pushing for the use of tanks, one of them being Heinz Guderian, who ended up being vindicated.[112]

Jeannie Johnson has shown that in its LI/LL process, the Marine Corps retained what favored the institution's cultural prejudices about the use of force, and that many important lessons were in fact forgotten very quickly.[113] The risk is multiplied when the experience becomes mythologized, particularly following a victory: the temptation to think that since we won, we were right to do what we did is perfectly human. But it is subject to now well-known biases: confirmation bias (the tendency to explain events by coherent stories, excluding divergent factors), overestimation bias (the tendency to assign actors a role and importance greater than reality), and inertia bias (thinking that trends continue inexorably, without taking potential ruptures into account). French military thinking after the First World War provides a striking example of this inertia. The 1936 *Instruction sur l'emploi tactique des grandes unités* (Instruction on the tactical employment of large units) states:

> Without ignoring the importance of the progress made since 1921 in the field of combat and transport equipment, the Drafting Committee nevertheless felt that this technical progress did not significantly alter the essential rules established by its predecessors. It therefore accepted that the body of doctrine, objectively laid down in the aftermath of victory by eminent leaders who had just assumed high command, should remain the charter for the tactical employment of our major units.[114]

Here we see a concentrated version of all the biases presented above: the illusion of an "objective" collection of lessons of the conflict, overestimation of the role of individuals and underestimation of contingency, mythologization of past actions, and inability to identify ruptures. Thus, "a genuine slowdown in French military thinking can be identified, before moving on to what the American historian Robert Doughty has termed a fixed 'doctrinal straitjacket' for the second half of the 1930s."[115] The problem is not specific to interwar France. In fact, states that have recently experienced military victories tend to cling to outdated military concepts, leading to a disconnect between military strategy and grand strategy.[116]

This is just as true when observing foreign wars, the difficulty being compounded by the fact that the observing organization is not necessarily directly involved.[117] In fact,

> To successfully learn, a military organization requires access, objectivity, interpretation, and generalizability. In short, access means being there and having good data. Objectivity is exactly what it sounds like and this is often where attempts to learn stumble. Interpretation requires the organization to understand what is happening and why. It also requires an understanding of how and whether events and developments are significant. Finally, generalizability happens if the observation can be transferred from its context to projected future scenarios.[118]

We can therefore understand the difficulty inherent in identifying relevant lessons from experience: having the right data, analyzed and interpreted in the right way (which cannot be improvised and which should ideally require advanced training in the human and social sciences), and assessing whether or not this data is generalizable. This is in fact a similar problem to that of the use of military history mentioned above: in the absence of a large number of observable wars (fortunately), organizations are forced to study existing conflicts, at the risk of patchy data and lessons that are in reality not very generalizable, or to study past conflicts at the risk of current preferences being imposed on historical examples.

The second problem relates to the institutionalization of the lessons themselves: lessons identified are not lessons learned. There's no point in producing LI/LLs if they don't change the institution's policy. NATO doctrine has established a formal approach to LI/LL. NATO's Joint Analysis and Lessons Learned Centre (JALLC) has established a sequential process for conducting lessons learned activities. The first sequence is composed of *observation* (of a military activity that needs to be improved) followed by *analysis* (of the seriousness of the process and of remedial actions to take). After the analysis phase, a lesson is deemed "identified" (LI). The second sequence is the "implementation phase" and has three components: approval of the LI and the tasking of a specific body (1) that will be in charge of implementing the identified remedial actions, which have to be validated by the commander (2). After the formal validation, a lesson identified becomes a "lesson learned" (LL). The final action (3) is the dissemination of the LL among relevant stakeholders.[119] However, the formal lessons learned process described in doctrine explicitly applies to "learning from experience": it is fundamentally a self-assessment and auto-correcting mechanism to improve on already ongoing actions and activities.

However, for this process to be successful, military organizations require a number of organizational capabilities:

- *Knowledge acquisition capability* (to effectively acquire information and knowledge from the operational environment and alliance partners).
- *Knowledge transformation capability* (the ability to effectively combine existing and new knowledge).
- *Knowledge dissemination capability* (the distribution of lessons learned).
- *Knowledge management capability* (the storage and retrieval of information).[120]

Depending on their own institutional setting, military organizations are more or less equipped in order to conduct the LI/LL process. Moreover, the organization may sometimes have compelling reasons *not* to learn. For example, even before the end of the American withdrawal from Vietnam, the US armed forces began to reflect on the lessons they could learn from this experience. The 1970s were marked by a rejection of the counterinsurgency experience and an attempt to define the Army's identity as an organization exclusively dedicated to conventional combat. One of the instruments of this attempt was the Training and Doctrine Command (TRADOC) placed under General William E. DePuy. He undertook to reformulate American military doctrine and the teaching system in favor of conventional combat, which implied a partial erasure and a specific interpretation of the Vietnam experience. FM 100-5 *Operations* (the Army's doctrinal document describing its conception of the conduct of military operations) was updated in 1976 under DePuy's direction. DePuy wrote a letter to the Army Chief of Staff, General Fred C. Weyand, in which he described his approach as "taking the Army out of the rice paddies of Vietnam and placing it on the battlefield of Western Europe against the Warsaw Pact."[121] Significantly, the passages in the 1968 edition of FM 100-5 dealing with stabilization operations were deleted, apart from a few purely technical remarks concerning the difficult terrain (jungle, mountain) in which operations were to be conducted. One of DePuy's concerns was that the US Army had concentrated too much on light infantry because of Vietnam, and was in danger of being overtaken by the advances in weaponry and fire intensity seen during the 1973 Yom Kippur War. Within American forces, this conflict very quickly took Vietnam's place as the main source of "feedback" and as an insight into the future character of conflict. Simultaneously, counterinsurgency experiences were selectively erased from the American doctrinal corpus: the FM 31-16 counter-guerrilla manual was withdrawn from service without replacement in 1981, and the 1972 edition of FM 31-23 on stability operations was replaced in 1974 by a new manual, FM 100-20, which dropped the term "stabilization operations." Even the heart of American-style counterinsurgency in the 1970s, the JFK Special Warfare Center and School at Fort Bragg, was affected, with all counterinsurgency training files destroyed, apparently by order of the command.[122] Courses on counterinsurgency were drastically reduced or disappeared from the curricula of military schools such as the Artillery School, the Intelligence School, the Command and General Staff College, and the Army War College.

As an organization, the US Army thus engaged in a voluntary deletion of part of its institutional memory, the aim of which was to ensure that a military intervention of the counterinsurgency type would never happen again, so that it could concentrate on responding to the Soviet threat (which led to the development of the air–land battle doctrine). However, such an oversight could only be effective if accompanied by a specific reinterpretation of the Vietnamese experience. In 1975, the Strategic Studies Institute of the Army War College undertook a study to draw lessons from the American intervention, the final eight-volume report of which was submitted in 1979, after a consultant (BDM Corporation) had come on board.[123] The report challenged the conventional wisdom that Vietnam was a "tactical victory and a strategic defeat," arguing that the US armed forces had lost far more battles than they were willing to admit, and criticized the reliance on a model of warfare combining intensive use of technology and firepower. Between the lines, the report argued that the Army's poor performance was due to the fact that it was too prepared for conventional warfare to deal effectively with an engagement like Vietnam, and that a strengthening of counterinsurgency capabilities was necessary, simply because there was little chance of this type of conflict disappearing.

This conclusion was exactly the opposite of the Army's transformation, whose generals wanted to ensure that it would no longer have to engage in counterinsurgency experiments. The Commandant of the Army War College therefore commissioned one of his officers, Colonel Harry Summers, to write another study.[124] This was published in 1981, and was an attempt to change both the memory and the lessons of Vietnam. Summers presented his study as a Clausewitzian approach to the American decision-making process during the conflict. For the author, the war would have been "winnable" if the US had not succumbed to the counterinsurgency fad, and if civilian decision-makers had been willing to make a greater military commitment while limiting civic protest on US soil. The problem, for Summers, was not the overuse of military force, but its overly constrained use, not least because of an overemphasis on counterinsurgency. *On Strategy* was immediately adopted by senior Army officers: it was placed on the Army Chief of Staff's recommended reading list (where it remained until 2004), and became required reading at the Command and Staff College, the Naval War College and the National Defense University. Articles on Clausewitz became fashionable in the professional journal *Military Review*, while articles on Vietnam or counterinsurgency became rare. However, according to David Fitzgerald, the officer corps was quite divided in the 1980s. While generals (then in charge of Army reform) were very much in agreement with Summers's conclusions, junior and senior officers were generally much more reticent, and while *On Strategy* was widely read, its conclusions were controversial among younger officers (who ironically agreed with the conclusions of the BDM Corporation study without having read it).[125]

The ghost of counterinsurgency resurfaced in the 1980s, this time in the form of a reflection on the concept of "low intensity conflicts" (LICs) following the American engagement in El Salvador. Some officers, wishing to see LICs become part of official doctrine, set out to study American military history through the prism of US involvement in "small wars." For these officers, history showed that the Army had conducted successful counterinsurgency operations in the past, and that the failure in Vietnam was a failure in the application of this doctrine, not a fundamental strategic failure as claimed by Summers.[126] LICs made a modest appearance in US military doctrine: they were mentioned in the 1986 edition of FM 100-5 (which was mainly devoted to air–land battle) and were even the exclusive object of the doctrinal document FM 100-20, updated in 1986 and 1990. However, despite this attempt, the balance of power within the Army at the end of the 1980s was the same as at the beginning of the decade. It favored high-intensity conventional missions, relegating counterinsurgency to secondary missions to be avoided wherever possible: the institutionalization of LICs was therefore limited and had little impact on changes within the Army. But this debate of the 1980s began a modest revision of the dominant memory of the Vietnamese experience. Andrew Krepinevich's account has nothing to do with Summers's, showing a battle for the strategic use of the "lessons" of Vietnam, which served to justify the Army's main orientations and thus the evolution of its structure, doctrine and force model.

As we can see, the learning mechanism is particularly important within military organizations as a factor for change, and involves training, practice, experimentation and the codification of experience. Each of these approaches has its advantages and limitations, and they work best in combination. The major challenge is to make the military organization a "learning organization":[127] it is through the interaction between different learning mechanisms that new concepts, or doctrinal or organizational innovations can emerge, contributing to military effectiveness. Such a learning organization presupposes specific institutional arrangements (intellectual incubators, military debate organized in journals, rigorous intellectual training for officers, experimentation and training facilities, reasoned and cautious analysis of experience, etc.). These are costly, and can easily be devalued as unglamorous, but they are in fact the guarantee of flexibility and resilience in the face of the unexpected.

Conclusion

In military organizations, the two main mechanisms for change seem to be circumvention and learning. Circumvention takes place in two ways. Firstly, depending on circumstances, the different components of the armed forces may compete for resources and missions. As we have seen, this competition can be an important driver of innovation, but it must be regulated to avoid undermining overall coherence. The second type of circumvention is the attempt to anticipate future warfare (or at least to reflect on its characteristics). Here, again, for the mechanism to be effective, the institution must be structured in such a way as to encourage "incubators" of thought and, in general, debate on military issues. Otherwise there is a risk of intellectual and doctrinal stagnation, which can lead to a disconnect between threats, available technologies and practices.

The second mechanism is learning. Armed forces organize learning systems on a large scale and in a variety of ways: training, education, feedback, experimentation. The accumulation of these learning mechanisms does not necessarily mean that the military organization is a learning organization: this requires the development of a culture of continuous improvement and questioning. If this is not the case, learning mechanisms serve only to validate the institution's presuppositions, contributing to its rigidity.

The two mechanisms mentioned here interact in the context of the country's strategic culture and the organization's military culture, which act as a constraint on change. As we have seen, changing these strategic and military cultures takes time and requires specific conditions. The responsibility of military leaders is therefore important when it comes to developing institutions that support circumvention and learning, while minimizing the constraint imposed by the organization's cultural context.

5

WAR

What is obviously most important for military organizations is the trial of combat: it is here that the effectiveness of their training, doctrine and equipment passes or fails the ultimate test. The prospect of war is the ultimate horizon for peacetime organizations, and combat is the great revealer of the value of decisions taken.

The configuration of actors we shall discuss here is once again different from that of the other chapters. It includes the various components of the armed forces: tactical units directly exposed to fire, intermediate echelons of coordination, and higher echelons making strategic decisions. As we shall see, the informal, vertical and horizontal networks linking these three echelons are important for understanding military change in wartime. But the configuration now includes an acting enemy, who seeks to impose its own will and adapts itself to the evolution of combat. This interactionist dimension, characteristic of strategic activity, obviously exists in peacetime, but it is magnified in wartime, since confrontation accelerates mutual adaptation. Consequently, the main mechanisms explaining military change in wartime are constraint (exerted by the enemy), circumvention (to gain the upper hand) and learning (to institutionalize the solutions identified during the circumvention process). Military change is highly prevalent in wartime, with adjustments and adaptations abounding and almost constant, but there are also regular instances of innovation. Of course, war can also lead to the disruption of an organization, particularly in the event of a major military defeat. In fact, war is a great accelerator of military change, which is essential in wartime, but this is obviously made much more difficult by the particular context of confrontation, which exerts phenomenal pressure on the organization.

The importance of combat

War is a means of resolving conflict through organized and collective violence, and is thus fundamentally a means of communication between adversaries. War remains a very rare event in the international system: the vast majority of conflicts do not degenerate into war, simply because war is extremely destructive and unpredictable. One of the factors that explain the outbreak of conflict is the lack of mutual information on the capabilities and intentions of the players involved. By definition, if the relative power of each actor were perfectly known, there would be no war: to avoid the disastrous costs of conflict, the weakest would systematically give in to the strongest. Wars occur when states have different estimates of their relative power. War thus serves as a revealer of information: it reveals real capabilities, as well as the intensity of preferences (how far are actors willing to go to get what they want?).[1] As Margaret Atwood writes in her poem "The Loneliness of the Military Historian": "I don't ask *why*, because it is mostly the same. / Wars happen because the ones who start them / think they can win."[2] Violence in warfare is thus, from a strategic point of view, a form of communication with the adversary, signaling each side's capabilities and intentions.

But, of course, the use of violence is anything but harmless for the military organization itself, which may find its concepts and doctrines validated or else completely inadequate. It is also subject to destruction on a scale that can have a structuring effect on the armed forces, eventually leading to their collapse. To avoid this, many adaptations and innovations generally take place during a conflict. But the use of violence also changes organizational practices and can lead to disinhibition, lowering the tolerance threshold for cruelty within the forces. It is therefore important to study the different effects of combat on the dynamics of military change.

The weight of attrition

The first dynamic to study is obviously the attrition created by combat itself. Modern warfare is particularly violent, owing to the destructive potential of the technologies employed. Any so-called high-intensity combat is bound to be highly destructive, as illustrated by the neo-imperialist war of aggression waged by Russia in Ukraine since February 2022. Credible estimates put the number of Russian casualties at around 950,000 since the start of the invasion (including up to 250,000 killed) against 400,000 Ukrainians (including up to 100,000 fatalities). The material damage is also immense: visually confirmed Russian tank losses in June 2023 amounted to 2,988 tanks destroyed, 158 damaged, 392 abandoned and 533 captured by Ukraine, i.e. more than 4,000 tanks lost[3] (by way of comparison, the French Army has 220 Leclerc tanks). And the fate of towns such as Bakhmut, virtually destroyed after months of fierce fighting, bears witness to the sheer volume of fire on the battlefield. As mentioned in the introduction, this destructiveness has been a long-term trend since the end of the nineteenth century, and has effects not only on the preparation of forces for combat (encouraging camouflage and movement as means of protection), but of course on the armed forces themselves during the conflict.

Strategically, the decision to engage in combat can be based on different approaches: annihilation, dislocation, attrition and exhaustion. These four categories are obviously not disconnected, and can often be observed in the same conflict, but they allow us to distinguish, in principle, between several modalities for the use of force.[4]

Annihilation aims to destroy the opponent's military potential through one or two decisive battles. The near-pure model of this type of battle is the Battle of Cannae, in 216 BC, in which the Carthaginian Hannibal destroyed the Roman army of Gaius Varro in a double envelopment, killing 50,000 soldiers and capturing 20,000 men of the Roman Army, with only 10,000 escaping. The battle did not have the desired political effect, as the Roman Senate voted not to negotiate, but it did put the Carthaginians in a better strategic position, as several Greek colonies and Italian cities defected and joined the Carthaginian cause. In fact, as mentioned in the previous chapter, fascination with the notion of the decisive battle often masks the fact that they usually do not have the desired effect.[5]

Dislocation is intended to achieve a breakthrough, and to support the offensive as far as possible in order to retain the initiative and prevent the opponent from reconstituting an organized front. The aim is to pose multiple dilemmas to the opponent, who ends up paralyzed and dislocated owing to the combined effect of the pace of battle and his own indecisions.[6] Dislocation requires a high degree of coordination between ground and air elements, front and rear, as well as effective and secure communications. Logistics must also be able to support a high tempo of operations, and military leaders must be capable of initiative. The idealized version of this dislocation is the French campaign of 1940, in which the Wehrmacht, through a combination of daring, luck and French military incompetence, succeeded not only in breaking through the front line, but in continuing the offensive by collapsing the French military establishment.[7] This approach to warfare was romanticized in the US by proponents of "maneuver warfare," notably John Boyd,[8] who promoted it, particularly within the Marine Corps.[9] But here again, this approach risks being idealized: "Notions of out-thinking one's enemy using multiple dilemmas sound compelling in theory. Yet, for many reasons, they may be difficult to employ as they rely more on alluring ideas than harsh reality. Most importantly of all, many of maneuver warfare's assumptions challenge the most enduring reality of all: war's nature is fundamentally interactive. As such, one's efforts can only temporarily short circuit an enemy's ability to react."[10] In fact, "maneuver warfare" may well have been romanticized as a mode of force employment, and only very rarely achieves the dislocation hoped for.[11]

The third possible approach is attrition, which can be understood as the destruction of an adversary's capabilities faster than he can regenerate them. It should be noted that attrition occurs "naturally" in military organizations, as a result of wear and tear and accidents.

Obviously, this natural attrition is reinforced in the event of conflict, which puts men and equipment to a severe test. France's overseas operations in the post-Cold War period, for example, contributed to the accelerated deterioration in the condition of the equipment available to the armed forces, effectively eroding the country's military capital.[12] The fundamental idea behind attrition is that, if the aim of war is to break the enemy's will to fight, a good way of doing so is to deprive him of the very possibility of fighting.[13] The principle of attrition is simple, but its execution difficult: it requires the coordination of combat actions (to destroy the enemy's units), politico-strategic actions (to hinder the enemy's production capacity), and its own production apparatus. For example, one of the major factors in the Allies' victory in the Second World War was their ability to simultaneously destroy the production capacity of the Axis powers (in 1944, the Japanese lost 3,635 aircraft in combat, but 6,675 were destroyed outside direct engagement, in particular during transfer to bases in the Pacific),[14] while dominating industrial production. By the end of the war, the Allies had produced three aircraft for one of the Axis powers, four tanks for one, seven artillery pieces for one, and two and a half ships for one.[15]

From summer 2023 onward, the war in Ukraine entered a phase of attrition: the aim of the belligerents was to exhaust their adversary. Ukraine has thus been able to count on Western support to impose sanctions against Russia (aimed at weakening its industrial base) and supply weapons to Kyiv (compensating for the destructive effects of the fighting). For its part, Russia is trying to circumvent the sanctions (thanks to friendly countries such as China, North Korea and Iran), rebuild its stockpile (by buying back Russian equipment sold to third countries or by equipping itself with weapons from its supporters), and exploit its demographic advantage to impose battles on Ukraine that are costly in human terms.

Finally, the fourth approach is exhaustion, which can be thought of as a form of "psychological attrition":[16] the aim is to weaken troop morale and the population's confidence in its leaders. This approach can take many forms: scorched-earth tactics, economic blockades, sieges, even guerrilla tactics. Most approaches that involve trading space for time, i.e. refusing to fight but exhausting the opponent, fall under the heading of exhaustion. This is what Stephen Biddle calls the "Fabian strategy"—named after the strategy adopted by Fabius Maximus against Hannibal—which he contrasts with the "Napoleonic strategy" of decisive battle. These two approaches constitute the extremes of a spectrum of possible military actions.[17] Whatever the approach, the aim is to exert a constraining mechanism on the opponent.

Obviously, the destruction of their combat potential forces military organizations to make major reorganizations, and has effects on the continuation of the conflict. The dominant strategy of the First World War was fundamentally one of attrition, as actors such as Foch, Kitchener, Asquith and Joffre realized.[18] Within four years, attrition on the battlefield had eliminated Germany's strategic reserves. The manpower crisis that hit Germany in 1917 was the consequence of the intensified attrition of 1916, which was only partially alleviated by troops released by the collapse of Russia and redirected to the Western Front in a final attempt to annihilate the enemy.[19] This attempt was desperate because, by then, with the total mobilization of the Allies and the entry of the Americans into the war, the resources of the German Army were no longer sufficient to cope with the crisis. The battle for resources waged through home-front productivity and blockades and counter-blockades was decisively lost by Berlin.[20]

But the cost and stakes for the organizations were obviously terrible, imposing major reorganizations. For France, the first months of the conflict in 1914 were the deadliest: almost 7,000 French soldiers were killed on 22 August at Charleroi, and around 40,000 on the whole front between 21 and 23 August. In fact, the battle revealed the unpreparedness of the French Army for the conditions of modern warfare:

> These men are not the battle-hardened *poilus* of the Argonne or Champagne trenches. They all come from a 19th century in which war was imagined as a matter of courage and valor, where the offensive took precedence over defense, and lines of infantrymen over artillery. Neither the Germans nor the French had experienced a war on European soil since 1870—almost

fifty years. No soldier—apart from a few observers of the Russo-Japanese War of 1905 and the Balkan Wars of 1912–1913—had experienced the new fire of rifles, machine guns and cannons, so spectacularly perfected by the technical progress of the late 19th century. The deadly capacity of these new weapons was hard to anticipate for soldiers from town and country, whether they were peasants, workers, middle-class citizens, young lieutenants from Saint-Cyr or seasoned old generals. In the summer of 1914, they set off with images of 19th-century warfare that they knew were not yet outdated. Charleroi was their baptism of fire.[21]

The first consequence of the start of the campaign was a major turnover of French generals, starting in September 1914. In all, a third of them were dismissed between September and December of that year.[22] Between 2 and 6 September alone, two army commanders, nine corps commanders and thirty-three division commanders were replaced. Joffre recognized the need to renew his army leadership and acted accordingly (perhaps with the ulterior motive of minimizing his role in underestimating German intentions during the Battle of the Frontiers).[23] This command reform prefigured more substantial reorganizations of the French army's major units, which took place between 1914 and 1915. The first was the creation of the "army" level. This level was provided for in the established manuals, but only for wartime. An army comprised between three and five corps, but also controlled its own support elements, such as unique specialties, heavy equipment, or corps and divisional support and supply capabilities (which enabled the commands of these two structures to relieve themselves of this responsibility): "The Army thus becomes the highest level of employment in wartime, ensuring the unity and coherence of operations, and, thanks to its rear services, providing the structures necessary for the life and commitment of the corps and divisions assigned to it."[24]

However, the lengthening of the front from the winter of 1914–1915 onward complicated the exercise of the General Headquarters' authority over each of the armies, and the need emerged for an intermediate level of coordination: the Groupe d'Armées (GA, or Army Group). The principle was formally adopted in early 1915 with the creation of the Groupe d'Armées du Centre and the Groupe d'Armées de l'Est. Each army could command several army corps of around 40,000 men, initially composed according to a relatively identical model. However, the reality of combat meant that this model also evolved, with the composition of the corps changing according to requirements: the corps echelon was thus differentiated according to the evolution of the front. The function of the corps also evolved, from tactical pawn to command echelon. These corps commanded divisions, initially organized in 1914 around four regiments (grouped into two brigades of two regiments). Here, again, the conflict led to a change in the model, with the gradual disappearance of brigades and the creation of divisions with three regiments. Above all, the division evolved from a subordinate element of the corps to a fundamental tactical pawn. Thus, "at the top of the organization chart for armies in the field, we find successively the army group as the superior operational command body and relay of the Grand Quartier Général [General Headquarters], the army as the operational and supply echelon, the army corps as the tactical command level and the division as the basic joint unit with its own (but limited) support capabilities."[25] But even within the different branches, transformations took place. Probably the most notable was the gradual marginalization of cavalry, particularly on the Western Front. In 1915 and 1916, several hundred squadrons were disbanded, and several regiments (including cuirassiers, hussars and dragoons) were "dismounted" and transferred to the infantry.

Another example, at the operational level, is the evolution of British Army structures during the Desert War (1940–1943).[26] When General Montgomery arrived in Egypt in August 1942, he gave a new impetus to the British campaign by adapting operational objectives and reorganizing its structure. In particular, he directly challenged the force model encouraged by Churchill and his foremost adviser, Allan Brooke, based on "brigade groups," mobile columns of armored vehicles and light tanks, and decentralized command. On the contrary, Montgomery insisted that the elementary tactical unit should be the division, fighting as an organized unit: the effect was to confront Rommel with an organized front of divisions fighting side by side, rather than an assemblage of British-held areas, which he had hitherto regularly managed to dominate. In addition, the minimum level of command at which armor and artillery were concentrated was the division, thereby enabling better coordination of fire and movement. Finally, infantry, which until then had played an unclear role, was used as a means of occupying and holding the dominant points of the terrain. All in all, "these orders amounted to a revolution in desert warfare."[27] Here we can see the structuring effect of combat on institutional reorganizations related to innovation.

In addition to this pressure to adapt organizations, combat plays an important role in the structural wear and tear of military capital. Omer Bartov has famously documented the "demodernization" of the Wehrmacht on the Eastern Front during the Second World War due to the level of attrition suffered by the Nazi forces,[28] but many other examples exist. In 1916, the Battle of Verdun claimed almost 700,000 casualties (including 160,000 deaths on the French side and 140,000 on the German). This was not the deadliest battle of the First World War: the Battle of the Somme, for example, claimed almost 1,060,000 victims (killed and wounded) among British, French and German troops, and over a much shorter period of time. Cumulatively, however, these battles contributed to a significant erosion of armies, consistent with the strategy of attrition described above: "by the end of [1916] , the French and British armies were exhausted and out of breath, while the German Army was now outnumbered on the Western Front, with material resources dwindling as a result of the blockade."[29] This kind of destruction can have direct effects on soldiers, even at the lowest tactical level, with sometimes unforeseeable consequences.

A good example is provided by German reactions to Operation Overlord, the Allied landings in Normandy.[30] Firstly, the beginning of Allied operations created confusion in the dissemination of information and intelligence on the German side. Landings were announced in various sectors (Arromanches-les-Bains, the mouth of the river Vire), while parachutists and gliders were (falsely) reported in many parts of Brittany and upper Normandy. Together, the anxiety accumulated over several weeks in the face of the Allied threat, the fear aroused by the start of operations (leading to over-reporting or over-interpretation of events), and the partial alteration of communications created a distorted vision of the reality on the ground for the German command, preventing it from discerning accurately and rapidly the precise zone of the Allied offensive. Moreover, the sheer volume of fire necessarily reduced the German force, overloading the medical services. The latter had been under constant pressure as a result of the war itself, forcing the Waffen-SS to recruit medical students rather than qualified practitioners, for example, or general practitioners to improvise as surgeons. Against an ideological backdrop of fantasies of racial superiority,[31] this shortage encouraged the use of brutal medical practices, including operations without anesthesia and widespread recourse to amputation. Gradually, the pressure exerted by the Allies and the confusion of the battlefield led to a disjunction between the perception of the situation by the German General Staff and that of the commanders in the field, and thus to the issuing of orders deemed absurd by local commanders.

In fact, the war led to a rigidification of the Wehrmacht, and an impoverishment of the quality of officers:

> These officers were the pure products of a dictatorial regime that had selected them on the basis of their leadership, operational and tactical skills and endurance, but also on the basis of an obedience that left no room for reflection or doubt. This selection process gradually led to intellectual sclerosis: the only ones left were the leaders who lacked the breadth of vision, culture and ability to think that would enable them to analyze the issues at stake. They became mere cogs in the wheel. The system itself condemned all critical thinking. From early 1943, it was considered an offense for a divisional officer to express doubts about the outcome of the war to his subordinates.[32]

Reconciling the instructions received and the situation as perceived locally took the form of an institutionalization of order-avoidance strategies: either by not carrying them out or by providing deliberately misleading reports to headquarters. These lies were used particularly by unit commanders to avoid having to dispose of some of their troops: they got into the habit of over-reporting their losses in order to build up "secret reserves," thus giving them greater tactical flexibility. Of course, this practice further distorted the picture of the situation for the General Staff.

Finally, fire had a major morale-shattering effect on many soldiers. They adopted a range of strategies for escaping from combat: staying behind the lines, self-mutilation, voluntary exposure in the hope of being wounded, even suicide, although it seems that desertions were rare.

Ultimately, combat—and attrition in particular—functions as a kind of artificial selection mechanism: it creates an external constraint on the military organization, which is forced to change if it is to survive. But the effect of the pressure exerted by attrition resembles a bell curve: "too high a loss rate (too many killed and wounded in too short a time frame) can create such pressure so intense that the organization itself perishes. Likewise, too low a loss rate can generate insufficient pressure to spur innovation, so that the organization stagnates, stalling its adaptation."[33] So, paradoxically, there is a level of attrition that forces the organization to reform without putting it at risk of collapse, thus prolonging its fighting capacity: a belligerent would therefore in principle have every interest in using maximum force to ensure the collapse of its adversary, rather than encouraging its transformation. However, as we have seen, the reason wars often become wars of attrition is that this level of destruction is very difficult to impose on the adversary (except in the case of colossal asymmetry, which is ultimately quite rare), and the constraint exerted by attrition leads to military change according to mechanisms we discuss in the second part of this chapter.

Fire and practices

Combat can also contribute to the evolution of an organization's military culture and even the country's strategic culture. In the first place, combat experience can strongly influence the military culture of a young organization, providing inspiration, examples and strategic objectives. The military culture of the Chinese Navy, for example, is strongly influenced by the campaigns of 1949 and 1950. China's "people's war at sea" began in 1949 with the command of fishing boats and civilian cargo ships, organized into amphibious assault units against the offshore Chinese islands held by the Kuomintang (KMT). Having reached China's coastal cities and defeated the KMT in mainland China, the PLA turned to the sea but, trained in land warfare, it stopped short of the coast. Mao Zedong realized that he needed to raise a force to storm the nearby islands and Taiwan in order to achieve complete Communist hegemony over the country. Operations at sea began in August 1949 with the Zhoushan Islands, a group of small islands to the east of Ningbo. Communist forces seized four smaller islands, but initially failed to take Dengbu or Zhoushan. The following year, Nationalist forces on Zhoushan withdrew to Taiwan. Meanwhile, in October 1949, Communist forces launched a campaign to seize Xiamen Island, Kinmen Island and, from there, Taiwan. Mao's forces captured Xiamen but suffered a devastating defeat at Kinmen. In the spring and summer of 1950, Communist forces seized Hainan and the Wanshan Islands and, in a separate operation, Tanxushan Island near Shanghai, Dayangshan and Xiaoyangshan Islands and Shengsi Island. The success of these operations led to operations aimed at the Dachen Islands, Yijiangshan Island and Pishan, the main objective being to seize Pishan. The ultimate target of all these operations was Taiwan, but the planned invasion of the Nationalist island stronghold was cancelled when the US positioned the Seventh Fleet in the Taiwan Strait following the outbreak of the Korean War. This campaign, which literally laid the foundations for the modern-day Chinese Navy, has been extensively studied by Chinese strategists and still influences their naval thinking today, whether on the need for a deep-sea navy, the possibility of integrated fire (from the coast, from ships or from the air), the risks of amphibious assaults, or the strategic coherence of controlling the islands close to the mainland with Taiwan in their sights.[34]

Without necessarily being a founding experience serving as an inevitable reference point for the organization, combat can nonetheless shape the evolution of the military culture of the armed forces to some extent, as shown by the Bundeswehr's commitment in Afghanistan between 2001 and 2014.[35] The mission was presented by German politicians for years as positive and similar to peace operations in the Balkans, in contrast to the "bad" and "dangerous" Operation Enduring Freedom in the first stage of the war in Afghanistan, before the discourse exploded as a result of the deteriorating security situation in the north of the country (where the Bundeswehr was deployed) from 2006 onwards. To give new meaning to the intervention, forgotten words from the German military lexicon were brought back into use, such as the term *gefallen* to designate fallen soldiers, which had not been used since 1945; or the word *krieg* (war) instead of *kampfeinsatz* (combat mission). Other symbolic initiatives took place, such as the reinstatement of the Iron Cross as a military decoration. But the evolution was not only discursive, and was in part a response to the pressure experienced by Germany within NATO to reduce its military caveats (thereby showing how a multinational organization can influence a military culture), but also to pressure from the troops, who demanded training conditions consistent with the theater, and who thus contributed to shattering the myth of a peace operation. At the same time, the tactical behavior of Bundeswehr units changed, demonstrating a genuine shift in military culture from an overemphasis on armored cavalry combat to a new appreciation of infantry combat. The tactical behavior of German troops between Operation Harekate Yolo against the Taliban in 2007 and the fighting of 2011–2012 had (almost) nothing in common.[36] Of course, this adaptation of strategic culture has its limits, as shown by the German non-intervention in Libya and Mali (which is why it is an adaptation, not an innovation), but it illustrates the strain that combat puts on an organization, which forces it to question its military culture.

In the case of longer operations, the change in military culture can take place over time. Since independence, although the Indian Army has fought in three major wars and one limited conflict (in Kargil in 1999), it has suffered the most losses in long-term counterinsurgency operations. Although the Indian Army's primary mission remains territorial defense, and its military culture has long been dominated by conventional combat, the prevalence of counterinsurgency operations has, over several decades, come to influence the army's structures and doctrines.[37] The same applies to the Israeli Army, Tsahal, in the face of the long-term threat (and regular fighting) posed by Hezbollah.[38]

Another change linked to the constraints exerted by combat concerns practices, and in particular the development of indiscriminate violence. This can be of two kinds: unjustified violence against opposing soldiers, or deliberate violence against civilians in the conflict zone. These war crimes are violations of International Humanitarian Law (IHL), which today is based in particular on the Geneva Conventions of 1949 and their Additional Protocols, as well as on other treaties and customary law. But this IHL obviously has a history,[39] as it is fundamentally a prior agreement between states to mutually limit violence against their soldiers. In fact, IHL can be treated as an "international institution," which acts by reducing uncertainty about the preferences of actors. The preferences expressed by states when negotiating and ratifying international treaties provide information on the restrictions they are prepared to accept in wartime. In other words, IHL clarifies what is expected of states, and whether each of them is likely to comply with or violate established norms. Empirically, it seems that the ratification of a treaty by two states increases the likelihood of compliance with the norms of that treaty in the event of armed conflict between them, but it also increases the risk of reciprocal violation in the event of non-compliance by one of the parties.[40] War crimes therefore take on a strategic dimension: the violation of IHL by one party will prompt the other to react in retribution. Rape is a recurrent form of violence against civilians and thus has a strategic dimension, terrorizing populations and destabilizing the social environment of target communities: in fact, victims incur a double penalty, for they risk being ostracized within their groups (e.g. if a woman becomes pregnant by an enemy soldier).[41]

But we must not overlook the ideational and psychological factors that contribute to violations of IHL.[42] In the first place, the dehumanization of the adversary through propaganda facilitates the use of violence by soldiers, such as the killing of prisoners. The war waged by Nazi Germany against the USSR cannot be separated from the racialist thinking of Nazism and its vision of "Slavs" as inferior beings, and the criminal practices of both the Wehrmacht and the Waffen-SS against Red Army soldiers or Soviet civilians can be partly explained by a racist worldview and an eschatological conception of the conflict.[43]

Similarly, the war crimes committed by Russia in Ukraine since 2022 can be explained by a combination of propagandist rhetoric that has long dehumanized Ukrainians and soldiers' frustration at the proven limits of Russian military power. The indiscriminate use of violence, including that against prisoners of war, is a means of venting this frustration, which is the result of an ideological discourse that has existed in Russia for several years.[44] Indeed, combat itself exerts a pressure on individuals that can be released in violent impulses potentially seductive to the perpetrator by satisfying a desire for power: this is the fundamental idea behind Joseph Conrad's novel *Heart of Darkness* and its cinematic transposition by Francis Ford Coppola in *Apocalypse Now*. The most famous recent case is probably the My Lai massacre in 1968, in which a company of American soldiers massacred over five hundred Vietnamese civilians,[45] but we can also cite the torture inflicted by American soldiers on Iraqi detainees in Abu Ghraib prison between 2003 and 2004, or the war crimes committed by British soldiers in Afghanistan.[46] In these contexts, officers can play a paramount role in preventing violent behavior from becoming normalized and regular practice.

Generally speaking, exposure to the violence of combat can shock combatants, who may develop post-traumatic stress syndromes. Institutions react differently to this issue, but over the last twenty years or so there has been a growing awareness of the subject, particularly in Western forces, where screening and support procedures have been put in place for soldiers returning from operations. In contrast, and despite the much greater participation of African armed forces in peacekeeping operations on the continent due to the emphasis placed on the "Africanization of security," the problem seems to be underdiagnosed in African military organizations, either because of a lack of infrastructure (Democratic Republic of Congo, Ethiopia, Niger), a taboo around the subject of mental health and a preference for traditional medicines (Burundi, Gabon, Mali) or the prevalence of a norm of masculinity that associates post-traumatic stress with a weakness unworthy of a "real man" (Benin, Chad).[47]

Without necessarily leading to the normalization of war crimes, certain combat experiences can affect civil–military relations. For example, counterinsurgency campaigns (COIN) conducted by

Western countries have regularly been followed by tensions between civil and military authorities. The fundamental issue is the acquisition by military personnel engaged in counterinsurgency of an increasing number of civilian prerogatives, and ultimately the complete collapse of control mechanisms and the concentration of resources in the hands of the military. What COIN advocates, following Lyautey, applaud as a guarantee of effectiveness is in fact fraught with risk. Once back in the home territory, these military personnel tend to maintain the same mindset of merging powers for their own benefit and importing COIN against the population of their country. Douglas Porch traces this trend not only in France, but also in Britain and the US over nearly 200 years: each time, after a COIN campaign, there have been attempts (sometimes implemented, as in Northern Ireland) to use COIN against the country's own population.[48] Some military personnel, marked by their experience, thus develop a tendency to see civilians as inherently corrupt and blind to the risks of the "moral degradation" of the country, refuse civilian oversight and construe a part of the population as potentially insurrectional and, therefore, legitimately subject to coercive measures, possibly preventive ones. Combat experience can thus change the perception that some military personnel have of their own role within the state, thereby contributing to changes in civil–military relations. This evolution of civil–military relations in wartime is not only the result of the military: it can also come from the political authorities themselves. For example, Russia's invasion of Ukraine in 2022 led to a hardening of political–military relations in Moscow: the FSB allegedly modified the invasion plan in a manner contrary to Russian doctrine (thus calling into question the principle of military autonomy in operational planning established in Russia); and, faced with the Russian armed forces' difficulties in adapting, Vladimir Putin is said to have regularly intervened himself in the choice of operations and the promotion of commanders, thereby increasing the Kremlin's interference in the chain of command.

Finally, the ultimate case of combat pressure is obviously a major defeat, which leads to the collapse of the armed forces. In this event, their evolution is linked to the political and military context of the moment. A good example is the defeat of the French Army in

1940, which led, after various political upheavals, to a partition of the French armed forces between the Pétainists and the Free French Forces under General de Gaulle (even leading to fratricidal fighting in North Africa).[49] In such situations, the shock for the organization is so brutal that its evolution actually comes to depend on other entities belonging to configurations studied previously, notably the international system and civil–military relations.

The importance of the organization

As already mentioned, combat exerts a mechanism of constraint on the organization, prompting military change. But this change takes different forms depending on how the organization itself functions. Two mechanisms come into play: circumvention (of the adversary) and learning (to develop and disseminate best practices derived from combat experience). The effectiveness and implementation of these mechanisms depend on the intrinsic characteristics of the organization.

The importance of flexibility

Combat serves to reveal a military organization's prior weaknesses. The first challenge for the organization is to absorb and contain the initial shock of realizing that the combat it had prepared for is not the combat it is actually waging. How do armies that are surprised by an initial engagement manage to pull themselves together, or not? How, for example, can we explain the difference between the French Army of 1940, overwhelmed by a form of warfare it had not anticipated, and the Israeli Army of 1973, which, after an initial surprise, managed to adapt and reverse the course of events? The degree of flexibility of military organization is an important variable in understanding the resilience of forces. Military organizations therefore need to enhance flexibility factors at all levels upstream of a conflict:

- At a doctrinal and conceptual level, an army must create an environment conducive to the expression of opinions that

dissent from, and challenge, official doctrine. Doctrine must also be balanced to take into account all forms of warfare.
- At the technological and organizational level, flexibility means a balance between different capabilities (attack–defense, firepower and maneuvering, etc.), equipment redundancy to ensure rapid replacement in the event of failure of one of them, and the ability to use equipment in different situations.
- At command level, junior officers need to be encouraged to show initiative, while senior officers need to improve their creativity. This is probably the most difficult trait for a military organization to acquire.
- With regard to the circulation of information, the aim is to create mechanisms that make possible the rapid circulation of feedback, as well as the rapid learning of new situations. For example, the Tsahal had no culture of RETEX (experience feedback), and it was only very recently that brigade commanders required their junior officers to write down their accounts of operations.

Together, these four strata constitute an army's degree of flexibility and therefore influence its ability to recover from doctrinal or technological surprise.[50] Indeed, "rigid doctrine, inflexible technology and dogmatic leaders are a recipe for disaster, given the uncertainty, chaos and surprises that characterize every war."[51] This is why the incubators discussed in the previous chapter matter: the existence of a repertoire of doctrinal ideas, from which officers can draw when official doctrine has shown its limitations, is an important factor in creating flexibility while fighting.

Similarly, combat tests a military organization's ability to foster cohesion within its ranks. For example, an army's performance on the battlefield is partly determined by the country's pre-existing ethnic inequalities, whose reproduction within the army fosters soldiers' grievances and subversive behavior. Thus, military inequality (understood as discrimination against ethnic groups within the army, mirroring the society from which the army springs) poses significant problems on the battlefield. In armies characterized by greater inequality, soldiers seen as second-class citizens are more likely to identify with their ethnic group rather than their unit, organization or country. This, in turn, reduces motivation, degrades trust between ethnic groups, and increases casualties, thus influencing soldiers' choices and limiting how commanders use them on the battlefield. If armies reproduce the inequalities of society within them, there will be tensions within their ranks. Yet combat serves as a catalyst of these pre-existing tensions, leading to desertions on the part of victims of discrimination and quite simply a decline in military effectiveness.[52] Indeed, trust in superiors and interpersonal relations is an important factor in cohesion during armed conflict: to be accepted, discipline must be seen as fair and legitimate. During the Second World War, for example, the Red Army was faced with numerous avoidance strategies on the part of mobilized soldiers. The first response was coercive: a total of 158,000 soldiers were executed for desertion, cowardice or political deviance; 400,000 were condemned to serve in disciplinary battalions (serving as cannon fodder for the most dangerous missions); and 436,000 were sent to the Gulag. But this coercive response obviously couldn't work alone: from 1942 onwards, the Red Army began to promote a culture of military professionalism that made suffering more acceptable to soldiers: this involved the abolition of dual command, the dismissal of certain officers deemed incompetent (Voroshilov or Budyonny), and the reinstatement of the Tsarist Empire's military insignia.[53] In the absence of suchlike mechanisms to establish cohesion, the armed forces themselves may become fragmented as a result of combat. Some units may adopt avoidance strategies, defect or even, depending on the socio-political context, enter into open rebellion against the political authority (as shown by the examples of the Russian Revolution of 1917, or the attempted coups against Hitler in 1944, against Emperor Hirohito in 1945 and against Afghan President Najibullah in 1990).[54] As we can see, military organizations can be more or less successful in adapting to the constraints that combat places on their cohesion.

Circumventing the opponent

Once the initial shock has been absorbed, the circumvention mechanism plays an important role in military change. A recent example of circumvention may be the British campaign in Helmand, Afghanistan, between 2006 and 2011, which is detailed here.[55] At the start of the campaign, British forces adopted a kinetic approach, seeking to make contact with and destroy the enemy, but this only served to contain the insurgents. The 16 Air Assault Brigade was initially deployed from April to October 2006. For financial reasons, the British government decided to limit the number of troops deployed to 3,150, underestimating the threat posed by the Taliban. The 16 Brigade's main mission was to provide security and support development around Lashkar Gah, the provincial capital, and Gereshk, the economic center. The limited presence of International Security Assistance Force (ISAF) troops in Helmand province prior to the British deployment led to an underestimation of the dangers facing British troops. When the first British elements encountered strong resistance from the Taliban, it was decided to accelerate the deployment and send a further 1,500 troops. However, the Task Force took three months to fully deploy, which prevented it from capitalizing on the results of the first battles and pursuing the enemy. The dismissal of Helmand's governor, Sher Mohammad Akhundzada, was a prerequisite for British deployment, but his successor, Mohammad Daoud, had little local support. He quickly authorized the dispatch of British troops to the north of the province to protect the towns of Now Zad, Sangin and Musa Qala from the Taliban. However, he failed to realize that only a small part of the British contingent (600 soldiers) was deployable infantry. The British, for their part, considered it politically necessary for Daoud to consolidate his authority and therefore decided to send small garrisons to the northern towns of the province. These units soon found themselves under constant pressure from the Taliban, and 16 Brigade had to abandon Now Zad and Musa Qala, as it was impossible to resupply them. The brigade recognized that its concept of operations had undoubtedly contributed to the exhaustion of

Taliban forces, but that the emphasis on combat had hampered the development of Helmand.

In October 2006, 3 Commando Brigade took over with a different concept of operations. The Royal Marines wanted to concentrate on the economic and political centers of Helmand, which were now called the Afghan Development Zone (ADZ). To avoid being surrounded like their predecessors, the Royal Marines decided to give priority to mobility, creating mobile operations groups (MOGs) made up of 250 soldiers and 40 vehicles. Their mission was to patrol the desert, engaging and pursuing the Taliban to draw them away from the ADZ. This approach was intended to disrupt the enemy organization by operating behind their lines. However, the Taliban often engaged British forces on their own terms. While the Royal Marines understood that every engagement weakened the Kabul government and could be counterproductive, fighting in Helmand increased during their deployment, from 537 engagements under 16 Brigade to 821. The objective of engaging the Taliban in the desert, while successful in containing them, prevented British troops from concentrating on developing the ADZ.

In April 2007, the 12th Mechanized Brigade (a regular unit, as opposed to the parachute and commando units of 16 Air Assault Brigade and 3 Commando Brigade) arrived in Afghanistan. Observing the actions of the Royal Marines, the 12th Brigade concluded that they had neglected the local population and that the desert maneuvers had had little effect on the Taliban. The brigade officers decided to concentrate on the "green zone," in particular the area between Gereshk and the recently conquered town of Sangin. To this end, the brigade carried out a series of mopping-up operations, resulting in an increase in the number of engagements (1,096 during their deployment). General Lorimer, the brigade's commander, expected an increase in fighting during the deployment. The Taliban had planned a summer offensive, and Lorimer was determined to show that if an offensive did occur, it would be repelled by ISAF. The core of the 12th Brigade's concept of operations was to create security through a continuous presence, erecting physical protection and conducting patrols. The Afghan security forces (Afghan National Police (ANP) and Afghan National Army (ANA)) were to take over in the areas cleared by the British. Unfortunately, the 12th Brigade did not have sufficient human resources to achieve its ambitious goals. Most British soldiers were support troops, and cooperation with Afghan security forces was limited. Although the ANA had three battalions at Gereshk, Sangin and Camp Shorabak, which provided valuable support during offensive operations, they refused to hold the ground once operations were over, believing this to be the responsibility of the ANP. Unfortunately, the ANP was plagued by clan rivalries, widespread corruption and drug addiction. It was more a destabilizing factor than a reassuring one for the population. Despite their best efforts, the British were unable to maintain a permanent presence in the areas liberated from the Taliban, thereby allowing the latter to re-infiltrate.

The direction of the campaign underwent a significant change with the arrival of the 52nd Infantry Brigade in October 2007. General Mackay, the brigade's commander, had identified the local population as the focus of the campaign, rather than the enemy's ability and willingness to fight. As a result, the campaign concentrated on influence operations aimed at gaining the support of the population. In contrast to the rotation of 12th Brigade units within forward operating bases (FOBs), the 52nd Brigade decided to maintain a unit in the same FOB throughout its deployment to demonstrate to the locals a permanent presence, to which they could become accustomed. Influence operations became central to the 52nd Brigade's concept of operations.

When it was ordered to retake Musa Qala from the Taliban, the operation was designed to minimize civilian casualties. The aim was no longer to kill as many Taliban fighters as possible, but to force them out of the city. The British provided the population with plenty of information to give them time to find shelter. This population-centred approach was continued by 16 Air Assault Brigade during its second deployment to Afghanistan, from April to October 2008. To strengthen its influence, the brigade joined forces with the Provincial Reconstruction Team (PRT) based in Lashkar Gah. The brigade's planning section was physically relocated to the PRT building. Unlike in 2006, the aim was to counter the Taliban's influence rather than fight them.

The shift in Taliban tactics facilitated this evolution toward a population-based counterinsurgency. Between 2006 and 2007, the Taliban suffered heavy losses in combat with ISAF troops, making them less inclined to launch massive offensives against major cities and ISAF bases from 2008 onward. When the US Marines launched an attack on the Taliban stronghold in the Garmsir district in 2008, the enemy retreated without a fight. Similarly, when 16 Brigade carried out an air strike on Taliban villages south of Musa Qala, they found that the Taliban had fled. Tactics evolved toward the use of improvised explosive devices (IEDs) and the avoidance of large-scale engagements, although these still occurred occasionally. This change in tactics, although dangerous for British troops, enabled stabilization operations to be consolidated by avoiding major fighting near urban centers.[56]

A few days into its second deployment in October 2008, 3 Brigade discovered a force of 300 Taliban gathering to attack Lashkar Gah. As 3 Brigade did not have enough troops to repel the attack, it had to rely on the support of the Afghan police, backed up by British assault helicopters, to eliminate the attackers. This event made it clear that the British had lost control of the central region in 2007–2008, leading to a complete re-evaluation of the campaign plan. The new plan was approved by the 3 Brigade commander, the PRT director, the provincial governor and the 205th ANA Corps commander. The objective was to eliminate the Taliban from central Helmand. It was clear that this would require a series of operations involving several deployments of British brigades. The key district was Nad-e-Ali, west of Lashkar Gah, from where the Taliban could launch attacks on the provincial capital.

At the end of 2008, 3 Brigade launched Operation Sond Chara. The aim was to establish a governance structure from day one, while ensuring sufficient security to underpin development actions. The 19th Brigade followed this up with Operation Panchai Palang in June 2009, involving 3,000 British, Danish and ANA troops, which was aimed at eliminating the Taliban presence in the Babaji area, north of Nad-e-Ali. Civilians were widely informed and encouraged to flee the fighting in order to minimize the risks to themselves. The 11th Brigade then led Operation Tor Shpah in December 2009 and

Operation Moshtarak in February 2010 to eliminate the Taliban from central and northern Nad-e-Ali. Once again, these operations were carried out with a view to minimizing fighting and civilian casualties. During Operation Tor Shpah, the British favored negotiations with village elders to obtain the Taliban's departure, thus avoiding confrontation. This approach was used again during Operation Moshtarak, in the heart of the Chah-e-Anjir triangle, north of Nad-e-Ali. The Taliban were encouraged to flee, while civilians were assured that they would not be abandoned after the operation.

These operations benefited from the massive arrival of American forces in Helmand. The 1st and 2nd Marine Expeditionary Brigades (with a total of 20,000 soldiers) took responsibility for southern Helmand, enabling the British to free up their troops to support the effort in the center. In addition, operations were synchronized with those of the US Marines to reduce the Taliban's scope for maneuver in Helmand. For example, Operation Sond Chara was conducted at the same time as Operation Khanjar, during which the Marines took over the districts of Nawa, Garmsir and Khanashin. By spring 2010, the British had relatively secured central Helmand, while the Americans took responsibility for the south. The Americans were now deploying north of Helmand to relieve the British. As a result, the 4th Brigade, which replaced the 11th Brigade in May, focused on protecting communities and improving freedom of movement, rather than on major operations.

Here we see an adaptation of both tactics and approaches to the campaign, even if this evolution could not compensate for the fundamental strategic problems posed by Western intervention in the country.[57]

This military change, which took place on the scale of a modest, limited campaign, can be seen on much larger scales. The evolution of the French Army during the First World War provides an excellent illustration. Following the defeat of 1871, the French Army had to rebuild itself. The trauma of 1871 was so strong that it permeated all military thinking, which was split into several poles competing to redefine the French Army: the Conseil Supérieur de la Guerre (CSG), the École Supérieure de Guerre (ESG), the Forum (bringing together young commissioned officers), the army staff and the

Centre des Hautes Études Militaires (CHEM). On the eve of the war, the "intellectual aristocracy" came mainly from Saint-Cyr. Its sociological composition had a direct influence on conceptions of tactical evolution: interest in the technical aspect of warfare was neglected in favor of speculation on the importance of "moral forces." Maneuver regulations were not unanimously accepted, and there was a growing gap between the "practice" of units, i.e. their actual skills, and the proclaimed standards. Numerous shortcomings in the learning process plagued the French Army. Interest in tactical exercises was waning, generals were not sufficiently trained in the operational command of large units, artillery was neglected, and training was poor (shortage of men, courage, means). On the eve of the First World War, the French Army suffered from glaring contradictions between what was expected of men and the reality of what they knew how to do. The choice of weaponry also reflected the influence of a mentality blind to modern firepower. The obsession with the human offensive tended to favor large infantry battalions, while artillery was seen only as a direct support to infantry, and suffered from both bureaucratic compartmentalization and a lack of connection with large-scale industry.

The experience of fire led to numerous changes within the armed forces. Multiple sources of adaptation and innovation emerged, particularly on the part of genuine "military entrepreneurs": past experience was rediscovered, the adversary was imitated, existing equipment was diverted, new tactics were invented. The sum total of all these changes radically transformed the French Army, which by 1918 was the most effective army in the field, enabling the Allies to win.[58] A similar evolution in tactics took place for British troops, notably from 1916 onwards, with important improvements in trench assault, artillery barrages and counter-battery fire.[59] We could, in fact, multiply the examples: the evolution of US troop tactics in Iraq between 2003 and 2011,[60] the changes in the French Expeditionary Corps during the Indochina War,[61] and the evolution of the Soviet Air Force[62] and, more generally, of the Red Army during the Second World War.[63] In reality, all military organizations engaged in combat are caught up in a logic of circumvention that leads to military changes of varying intensity (adjustment, adaptation and innovation). This permanent circumvention is due to the dialectical logic of war as a clash of wills, and is therefore found in all conflicts.

Learning under fire?

Beyond the mere observation of this circumvention mechanism, the issue at stake is to know to what extent new tactics, techniques, procedures and technologies resulting from circumvention emerge, diffuse and become institutionalized. In other words, how does the military organization become a "combat learning organization." Indeed, while circumvention leads to a multitude of adjustments and adaptations, it is not uncommon for these to be lost, such as when units rotate in theater, in the absence of institutionalized processes.[64]

Learning is a particularly important topic in the academic literature on organizational science, and is also the subject of an increasingly large body of work in strategic studies. Organizations don't exist in a vacuum, so they need to keep in touch with their environment. By its very nature, an organization seeks to improve itself in order to ensure its continuity, and to be in a position to face up to the threats and opportunities of the environment: if it is unable to do so, the organization will ultimately fail. The stakes are clear for military organizations, which must adapt to the problems posed by combat. It should be noted, however, that, as we mentioned in the previous chapter, organizational learning does not invariably lead to better performance, although this is the objective. Organizations may learn lessons that are incorrect owing to a faulty analysis of the situation, or if the proposed solution does not work. Moreover, organizational responses to identified problems can be quickly rendered obsolete by changes in the organization's environment. This is particularly the case when learning takes place during a conflict, in which the adversary itself adapts and creates an environment of perpetual change.

Organizational learning is essentially made up of two interdependent, if sometimes discordant, processes: exploitation and exploration.[65] Exploitation means that an organization seeks to improve its existing skills. This enables the organization to increase efficiency in its normal operations for short-term success.

Exploration is the search for alternative modes of action in response to a changing environment, and is crucial to the organization's long-term survival. In simple terms, exploitation seeks reliability in experience, while exploration seeks variety in experience. Both exploitation and exploration are essential to an organization's ongoing success, and balancing the two is therefore a fundamental issue for the organization's leaders. One of the pioneers in the application of learning theories to military organizations was Richard Downie, who studied the learning process of US armed forces in low-intensity conflicts (counterinsurgency, stabilization operations and humanitarian interventions), arguing that learning was particularly weak.[66] However, there are many examples of learning during conflict, whether in irregular[67] or more conventional conflicts.

Here, we probably need to distinguish between the ways in which adaptations and innovations are disseminated, the actors responsible for this dissemination, and the learning sequence, which implies a particular timing. Firstly, it should be noted that a combat learning organization needs to be connected and traversed by a multiplicity of formal and informal networks. It is through these networks that the adaptations or innovations resulting from the circumvention process spread throughout the organization and become institutionalized. Informal, interpersonal networks are a first source of diffusion, involving written exchanges or face-to-face discussions between individuals who have established bonds of trust prior to the conflict. The search for solutions to tactical problems often involves seeking advice from recognized peers: the existence of these pre-war networks is thus a factor of resilience. In the British Army of the First World War, for example, officers' networks were formed on the benches of Sandhurst or the Staff College, by being posted to the same units during their careers, or by practices shared among a similar social class: marriages (some officers may have family ties) or membership of specific clubs.[68] Similarly, the drafting and adoption of counterinsurgency doctrine within the US Army and Marines at the instigation of General Petraeus, in reaction to the American failures in Iraq, was made possible by the creation of a community of practice through informal exchanges and discussions hosted by the professional journal *Military Review*, which enabled Petraeus to gather around him a group of experts who had accompanied him to Iraq and helped disseminate the doctrine in theater, with adaptation and dissemination following each other very rapidly.[69]

A second, more institutional type of network is the horizontal dissemination of adaptations and innovations within the armed forces. During the First World War, the decentralized decision-making structure of the German Army, combined with a well-established learning culture, produced a system of horizontal networks through which an ad hoc lessons-learned program was developed in the years 1916–1918.[70] The knowledge developed by junior officers was shared in open conversations, during which best practices could be established and then applied to all units. In addition, the knowledge generated by commanders in the field was codified and reapplied in decentralized training schools to teach these lessons to new units. A good example of the way of disseminating knowledge through horizontal networks was the use of tactical bulletins, which some commanders decided to publish. During the Second World War, Admiral Lockwood, commander of the American submarine fleet based at Pearl Harbor, adopted the practice of issuing tactical bulletins to promote best practices and highlight the successes of certain submarine commanders. This type of institutional dissemination allows the circulation of tried-and-tested knowledge among experienced military personnel, while saving time for young officers when they take up their duties.[71]

The form of these horizontal dissemination networks is important. If tactical units can largely solve the adaptation process on their own, such networks are less likely to form, as these units will not seek help elsewhere in the organization. Second, if the resulting network model is decentralized, good practices are less likely to diffuse. On the other hand, if the horizontal network model that emerges has a degree of centralization (e.g. around a body responsible for collecting and disseminating practices), then the circulation of adaptations and innovations within the army will be greater. For example, in both Vietnam and Iraq, American logistics convoys were targeted by their adversaries. In both cases, adaptations took place, initiated by the soldiers themselves and involving modification of the trucks (by fitting machine guns and armoring certain vulnerabilities) and the evolution of protection tactics. However, in the case of Vietnam, these adaptations had a limited diffusion and were forgotten by the end of the conflict, whereas in the case of Iraq, doctrine manuals were updated and the new tactics taught in the units. The difference in the institutionalization of adaptations between the two conflicts lies in the fact that in Iraq tactical development was centralized in a single location (in this case the Udairi firing range), which served as a base for experimentation and whose managers became the central node of a doctrinal development network involving the various units deployed in Iraq and the Army's training and feedback units.[72] We can see here how horizontal dissemination networks require a degree of centralization to be most effective as a means of disseminating adaptations and innovations. This is what Jon Lindsay calls "adaptive practice," combining the creation of horizontal networks to identify relevant adaptations with centralized management of dissemination.[73]

Another horizontal diffusion network is constituted by membership of an alliance or coalition, which makes it possible to draw inspiration from partners. During the First World War, British troops adopted a number of adaptations or innovations first developed by the French.[74] During the intervention in Afghanistan, both the Germans and the French drew inspiration from certain American military practices, acquiring British or American equipment off the shelf after observing its effectiveness within the NATO framework—a process I have termed "selective emulation."[75]

The third type of network is vertical, from the strategic command to the tactical echelons. For example, the dynamic of technical and tactical innovations within the French Army during the First World War led to a reorganization of the General Headquarters (notably in 1916, with Pétain), which became concerned with the ongoing training of troops and the experience of army group leaders. The General Headquarters understood that the assimilation of modern combat depended on the systematization of training.

In practice, these three types of networks combine and interact, and the challenge is to capitalize on the advantages of each of them.

Secondly, the diffusion actors themselves are important. Michel Goya distinguishes between three types of actors: experts, who identify a technical solution to a particular problem; entrepreneurs, who do not necessarily innovate themselves but are capable of bringing a project to fruition in the face of a reluctant bureaucracy; and commanders, often general officers who have to simultaneously lead operations and manage adaptations, and who can be seen as the benevolent protectors of the other two categories.[76] Here, we can see the importance for innovators of possessing specific skills, sometimes acquired outside the armed forces (particularly in conscript armies, which have to "militarize" civilians), in order to solve concrete problems. In addition, the question of leadership is essential, as it involves identifying, promoting and disseminating the changes proposed by innovators.

This brings us to the structural issue of officer selection, which has to do with organizational flexibility. First of all, the skills required of a senior officer or general in peacetime have little in common with those useful in wartime. In peacetime, generals develop budgets, manage limited resources, ensure soldiers' pay, develop new weapons systems or tactics, manage stocks and flows of materials and personnel, and maintain order and discipline in the ranks. The armed forces may conduct military operations of various kinds (as France has done since 1962), but these operations are only a minority of the organization's overall activities, most of which are actually routine. The skills required to run the organization in peacetime are therefore very different from those needed in wartime, when the very survival of the organization (or even the country it serves) is at stake. This is why general officer purges often take place at the start of a conflict, the contrast being too sharp between the skills used for promotion in peacetime and those needed to conduct military operations. The armed forces must therefore be capable (both in terms of organization and legitimacy) of absorbing a major replacement of their command. From this point of view, the very low replacement rate of Western general officers in post-Cold War military interventions in Iraq, Afghanistan or the Sahel, despite the now patent failure of these interventions, is another sure sign that these were mainly international police operations designed to manage risk, rather than wars involving an existential threat.[77]

Secondly, senior officers and generals were initially tactical leaders before being promoted, and were generally selected on the basis of their initial tactical performance. But "the skills they need to succeed at the operational level can be very different from the skills that they have already mastered at the tactical level. Effecting change throughout very large, complex organizations in the midst of combat is very different from issuing orders to a platoon or company and directly supervising their execution."[78] The same distinction can be made between the operational and strategic levels: compare Eisenhower and MacArthur. Eisenhower was an average tactical and operative leader, but he had the strategic and political intelligence to command a coalition in the most ambitious amphibious assault in history, while managing relations with political and military leaders as complicated as Truman, Churchill, de Gaulle, Patton, Bradley and Montgomery. MacArthur was an outstanding military leader, notably during the Philippines campaign, but eventually he lost sight of the political context of his actions, leading to his relief from command during the Korean War. In all this, we see the challenge, as well as the fundamental difficulty, of cultivating an officer corps capable of encouraging adaptation and innovation in wartime.

Thirdly, the learning sequence itself is important. In a recent book, Frank Hoffman synthesizes the literature on learning in military organizations, identifying several stages.[79] Firstly, there is the *investigation* stage, during which individuals at tactical level observe discrepancies between their expectations and actual experiences during operations. These discrepancies are then investigated by tactical units. The second step in the process is *interpretation*, which involves analyzing the perceived empirical data and making sense of it. This may lead to adjustments within units that do not require assistance or support from the wider organization. Next, the third stage, *investigation*, relies on experimentation, made possible by higher commands or even the institution as a whole, to fill identified performance gaps. It is during this stage that a decision is made as to whether or not the proposed solutions should be implemented by the institution, thereby creating the distinction between "single-loop" learning (which remains within the unit) and "double-loop" learning (which spreads throughout the institution). If the latter occurs, the fourth and final stage, *integration* and *institutionalization*, can take place. Corrective measures are taken to improve the institution's performance during operations, through organizational changes, the acquisition of new equipment, or the publication and dissemination of new doctrine. It is important to note that several iterations of the "single-loop" cycle may take place before moving into a "double loop," and the adaptation or innovation developed within a tactical unit is disseminated throughout the organization. Hoffman's summary of his observations appears in Figure 9.

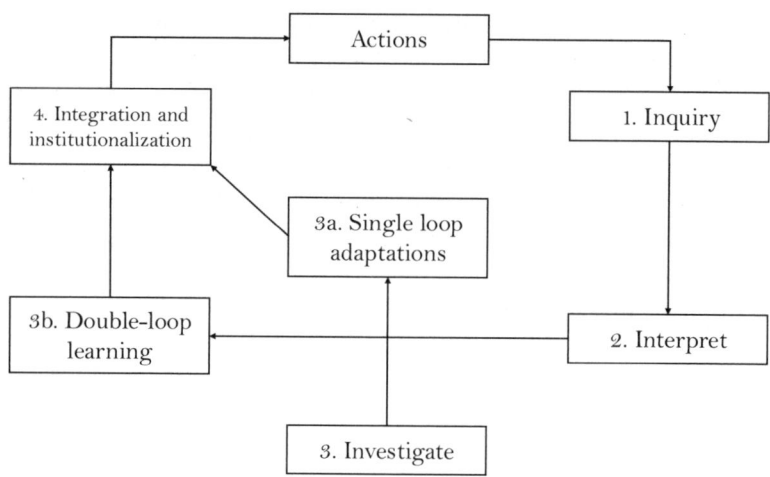

Figure 9. Learning sequence in the armed forces (Adapted from Frank G. Hoffman, *Mars Adapting: Military Change during War*, Annapolis, Naval Institute Press, 2021)

Studying learning in the armed forces during a conflict therefore requires attention to modes of dissemination (informal, horizontal or vertical networks); to the individuals contributing to learning (experts, entrepreneurial leaders); and, finally, to the learning cycle itself, whose course is shaped by the two preceding factors. Here, again, not all military organizations are equal when it comes to the challenge of learning in wartime, and their flexibility, the adaptability of their officers and the effective use of pre-existing networks are central factors in the degree of effective learning that occurs within the armed forces.

The importance of indicators

As already mentioned, for a learning cycle to take place, it must first be acknowledged that a problem exists. This acknowledgement can sometimes be resisted by the organization, for many different reasons. For example, the "Panzer generals" of the Second World War (such as Guderian, Hoepner or Reinhardt) were so infused with both the Nazi ideology (asserting the superiority of the will to fight over other elements) and the conviction that their own aggressiveness was a major military virtue,[80] that they blinded themselves to the dynamics of the campaign on the Eastern Front and the failure of the Wehrmacht to defeat the Red Army.

Moreover, the instruments chosen by organizations, in the form of indicators, can prove to be obstacles to change, or encourage a certain type of change to the detriment of others. In peacetime, military organizations develop quantitative measures of merit to assess the effectiveness of their strategies. Once war has begun, the strategy is regularly evaluated against these criteria and adjusted if necessary. The "leading indicators," which are the key measure of progress, are closely monitored to assess their evolution. In other words, when a situation deteriorates at an accelerated rate, a commander or organization may have to modify its strategy. However, organizations tend to keep their dominant indicators unchanged. So, even if a military organization chooses inappropriate criteria to measure its effectiveness, it is more likely to stick to them rather than change its strategy. Furthermore, it's important to note that dominant indicators can vary from one organization to another within the same country. This divergence means that two organizations, even when observing the same situation and examining the same data, may reach totally different conclusions as to the success of a war strategy, on account of the use of different measures of effectiveness.[81]

A significant example of this disparity can be found in the early years of the First World War, when the Royal Navy decided not to use convoys to protect merchant shipping from German U-boats. Despite heavy losses and pressure from the British government, the Admiralty refused to change its strategy of offensive patrols.

As maritime losses continued to mount, and Lloyd George's government increasingly called for change, the admirals resisted until April 1917, the worst month of the war. In this case, the Royal Navy's main measure of effectiveness was not the tonnage lost to enemy submarines (the criterion used by the government), but the number of German submarines destroyed. Admirals felt that aggressive patrols by the surface fleet offered the best chance of destroying German submarines, ideally at a faster rate than they were being built, and that this in turn would guarantee the safety of the merchant fleet. Interestingly, even as Allied merchant ships were being sunk at a steady and increasing rate in late 1916 and early 1917, the number of enemy submarines destroyed was also increasing.

However, in April 1917, a major change occurred. The tonnage of sunken merchant ships increased dramatically, at an unprecedented rate, prompting the government to demand a revision of strategy, while the number of enemy submarines destroyed fell dramatically. The dominant indicators for both the government and the Admiralty deteriorated at such a rate that both organizations were finally ready to change course. When the use of convoys began, casualties dropped significantly, and the Royal Navy discovered that convoys were actually more effective in destroying enemy submarines. The strategy was therefore modified and the dominant indicators stabilized.

This example vividly illustrates how two organizations in the same country can use different measures of efficiency. It highlights the fact that fluctuations in dominant indicators, as well as their rapid evolution, can influence strategic decision-making and lead to major adjustments. In the context of military organizations, these variations can have decisive consequences for the effectiveness of the strategies implemented.

A similar measurement problem arose during the Vietnam War.[82] The generation of senior American officers who commanded in Vietnam had come up through the Second World War and the Korean War, in which the measure of progress was simple: ground gained from the enemy was a tangible indicator of the progress of a military campaign. Obviously, the counter-guerrilla context of Vietnam made it impossible to measure progress in terms of ground gained or lost to the enemy, and so new indicators had to be developed that took into account the political nature of the conflict. At the outset of their involvement, American officers were still convinced that, with the right number of troops and the right amount of aggressiveness, the campaign would be relatively short. Faced with initial setbacks, the American forces developed a whole set of statistics designed to demonstrate the progress they had made.

However, it is possible that indicators are simply poorly constructed and reveal little of significance. For example, the body count revealed little about the real degree of control exercised by the government over remote villages in Vietnam. Secondly, indicators may be well constructed but difficult to measure, making them useless. For example, how could one quantitatively measure citizens' confidence in the Saigon government? Measurements of this indicator varied throughout the conflict (e.g. by counting information given by the population on enemy activities), but the American Army never succeeded in developing stable and effective measures of this type of indicator. The third potential problem is that indicators may be well constructed and well measured, but those in charge may choose to adopt an attitude of cognitive closure and deny the problems revealed. For example, the Battle of Ia Drang in 1965 was seen as an undeniable military success, seemingly validating the use of airborne cavalry, in particular thanks to Colonel Moore's exploits at LZ X-Ray, where he achieved an alleged kill ratio of 1,800 North Vietnamese for 75 Americans. However, this flattering analysis overlooked the fact that Moore had to call in B-52s to extricate himself and that, at the same time, Lieutenant-Colonel McDade of the 2nd Battalion, 7th Cavalry Regiment, was ambushed and lost 60% of his troops. While these events should have led to a reassessment of the role of airborne cavalry, the process of cognitive closure led to a preference for seeing the apparently positive facts rather than those calling into question the new tactical approach.

It should also be noted that the large mass of statistics produced could not be analyzed coherently and comprehensively, and there was indeed a situation of information overload. Finally, indicators can be politically counterproductive, for example when General

Westmoreland put forward apparently positive figures in a speech to the American press just before the start of the Tet offensive.

In fact, military organizations tend to make a permanent confusion between efficiency and progress: it's a natural tendency to think that the efficiency of a military troop necessarily leads to progress in the strategic objective, but the fundamental error was made at this level.[83] In Vietnam, the Americans developed an impressive battery of indicators of their military effectiveness (which was indubitable, since it was a mixture of firepower and the professionalism of the troops deployed), but these indicators could say nothing about the progress of the campaign. Indeed, in 1966, a CIA memo explicitly stated that the Agency was unable to determine whether the US was winning or losing the war.

The challenge of constructing relevant indicators of success or failure is thus important for understanding change in a military organization in combat, as it reveals what the organization knows, doesn't know, can't know or doesn't want to know about the situation on the ground.

Conclusion

During armed conflict, three mechanisms explain military change. The first is obviously constraint: fighting destroys the organization's military capital, forcing it to find ways of regenerating both its capabilities and its internal skills. If fighting goes on for any length of time at all, a circumvention mechanism operates: enemies adapt to each other and seek to gain a tactical, operative or strategic advantage. This interactionist dynamic is absolutely fundamental, and explains the multiplicity of adaptations and innovations observable in any conflict. One of the fundamental issues at stake is the organization's ability to institutionalize the innovations made possible by circumvention: this involves identifying and disseminating new practices or techniques that have proved effective, encouraging experimentation, and creating sufficient institutional memory to stabilize an organization under immense pressure. As we have seen, the characteristics of the organization established before the conflict, and in particular the existence of a repertoire of military ideas beyond official doctrine, internal cohesion and informal networks, both horizontal and vertical, are an important factor in this institutionalization.

CONCLUSION

TRANSFORMING MILITARY ORGANIZATIONS

At the end of this exploration of the mechanisms behind the transformation of the armed forces since 1870, can we identify a few key principles? As was mentioned in the introduction, organizational change occurs when there is a reorganization of three types of structures: cognitive, institutional and relational. However, there is a multiplicity of pathways leading to these reorganizations, depending on the articulation between entities and mechanisms at any given time.

Firstly, the different configurations of entities studied (international system, civil–military relations, technological developments, organizational logics and armed conflict) lead certain mechanisms to play a more or less important role, which are summarized in Table 6.

As mentioned, this is a simplification of a much more intertwined empirical reality: in practice, the different configurations interact with each other, and the mechanisms overlap. For example, Ian Bowers has shown how the transformation of the South Korean Navy from a naval force limited in its capabilities to a powerful fleet can be explained by a combination of North Korean threat perception, the alliance relationship established with the US, particular technological choices and the specific configuration of civil–military relations.[1] Indeed, empirical cases necessarily combine interactions between

Table 6. Dominant mechanisms of military change according to entity configurations

Entity configuration	Dominant mechanisms
International system	Circumvention Diffusion
Politico-military relations	Constraint
Technology	Constraint Learning Diffusion
Organization	Circumvention Learning
Armed conflict	Constraint Circumvention Learning

several mechanisms according to a particular temporal sequence: one configuration and one mechanism will be more important than others at specific times. But the aim of this book has been precisely to provide the conceptual vocabulary needed to disentangle entity configurations, understand the way in which they shape military change, and prioritize the relative importance of mechanisms depending on the context.

For academics, this conceptualization has the potential to bring together military historians, military sociologists and specialists in strategic studies. It allows us to focus empirically on certain dynamics in the study of military organizations by adopting a common vocabulary, and thus to prioritize the explanatory factors of change. However, for the purposes of this book, we were unable to establish firm correlations between configurations, mechanisms and degrees of change (adjustment, adaptation, innovation, rupture). The methodology employed did not allow us to do so (and this was not the objective), but other work, based on databases yet to be constructed, could, for example, attempt to identify correlations between entity configurations and degrees of military change. Another approach might be to employ qualitative comparative analysis (QCA), a

CONCLUSION

method particularly suited to taking into account causal complexity (the interaction of several factors causing an outcome) and the existence of several causal paths to the same outcome (equifinality).[2] In all cases, it will be necessary to set up a database, but this should be made easier by the conceptual vocabulary established in this book (even if the financial resources needed to establish such databases have yet to be found). We hope, however, that this work will open up new avenues of research, both empirical and conceptual.

For analysts studying the evolution of other countries' armed forces, who must therefore try to discern the dominant dynamics and prioritize factors, this book also offers a useful analytical grid, by means of a series of questions and factors to be analyzed. This approach is more comprehensive than simply observing and counting capabilities, and provides a better quality of analysis when studying the armed forces of a foreign country. Similarly, these questions can serve as a guide for military commanders and political leaders wishing to assess the capacity for change of the armed forces for which they are responsible.

Table 7. Criteria for analyzing the evolution of military organizations

International system	What are the main missions of the country's armed forces? Who are the identified enemies/adversaries? What alliance and cooperation networks does the country belong to?
Civil–military relations	What capacity do civilian authorities have to impose decisions on the armed forces? How familiar are civilians with military affairs? What is the level of civil–military cooperation in defense planning? How are the armed forces financed, and is it sustainable? What is the ideological zeitgeist? What are the lines of conflict within society, and are they reproduced in armies?

Technology	What are the operational challenges identified by the country's armed forces, and what are the plans to meet them? How much of acquisition plans involve seeking prestige? What is the force structure, and in particular the trade-offs between expensive and non-expensive equipment? How dependent is the procurement process on the needs of the local defense industry? What is the potential for the acquisition of a new technology to call into question the hierarchy of prestige within the armed forces? What is the potential for the acquisition of a new technology to challenge current military practices? What is the capacity of the armed forces to absorb the organic and practical transformations brought about by the introduction of new military technology? What is the timetable for the development and implementation of new equipment? What synergies are possible between old and new equipment in relation to this timetable?
Internal dynamics	What is the country's strategic culture? What are the military cultures of the country's armed forces? What is the degree of competition and cooperation between different armies? How does this affect military planning? How free is the military debate, and are there any incubators of military thought? What are the formal learning devices (exercises, wargames, LI/LL) and what is their value? Can they be used to reveal biases in the organization under study? How well trained are officers and soldiers?

CONCLUSION

War	What is the degree of attrition experienced by the organization, and is it sustainable? What is the effect on the organization's structures and practices? How flexible is the organization? What circumvention practices are used? What is the nature of the channels that enable these circumvention practices to be disseminated within the organization? What indicators does the organization use to measure its progress?

It should be noted that military change is no guarantee of success on the battlefield: contrary to a widespread myth, the US armed forces under General Westmoreland were able to define a globally relevant strategy and drive many changes and innovations during the Vietnam War, but the US still lost.[3] As mentioned, military change is a matter of strategy of means, and must be complemented by an operational strategy and a declaratory strategy to arrive at an overall military strategy. This military strategy must in turn be complemented by diplomatic, economic and other strategies as part of a national strategy (or "grand strategy").[4] On the other hand, the absence of change when it is necessary is a guarantee of failure. Military change is thus a necessary, but insufficient, condition for military effectiveness: a military organization incapable of implementing the relevant changes will certainly be defeated, but, conversely, this capacity for change is no guarantee of success. Military change must therefore be seen as one of the factors, but certainly not the only one, of military effectiveness and victory.[5] I hope this book can serve as a building block for a theory of military power in the twenty-first century that has yet to be established. Nevertheless, three major observations can be made about the conditions for successful military change: temporality, civil–military relations and the flexibility of military organizations.

Firstly, military organizations are part of complex, disjointed temporalities. An unforeseen catastrophe is always a possibility, and in such cases we have to fight the war with the army we have, not the one we'd like to have. But equipment programs, particularly for large-scale equipment, span several decades, and have an effect on human resources for many years to come. For example, the US Navy is currently recruiting the commanders of its aircraft carriers in 2048: they will have gone through a series of sea commands and shore posts to test their skills, in a trajectory that must reconcile both individual careers and capability development.[6] The problem is, as we have seen, the impossibility of predicting exactly which technology will be a real "game-changer" or when a combination of technologies will make possible the emergence of new military practices posing a major risk to existing organizations. In times of crisis, sudden accelerations can also occur, as shown by the evolution of aviation between the two world wars and especially during the Second World War. Decision-makers had to place bets on when to invest massively in the production of a certain type of aircraft, with the risk that it would quickly become obsolete, the alternative being that they would not have sufficient resources if the conflict came sooner than expected. The choice of timing was therefore partly a matter of luck.[7]

In any case, the longer a military model endures, the more likely it is to fall victim to a disruptive innovation that suddenly renders some of its equipment obsolete. As James Wirtz notes, the US Navy is currently planning capability development for its aircraft carriers until 2063, while "it's not clear what will be flying from these *Ford-class* aircraft carriers in 2063, even if anything will, and whether or not they will see the sea."[8] In fact, the more integrative a technology is (of other technological systems and human resource models), the more it creates dependencies on a military model that is likely to be circumvented. We can't rule out the element of chance in technological choices and, therefore, in the long-term relevance of army formats. On the other hand, it's important for planners to be aware of this, so as to design systems that are sufficiently modular to guarantee their use over time.

Secondly, civil–military relations are absolutely fundamental to the development of armed forces. First and foremost, a clear political strategy is a major guide to calibrating the size and scope of military organizations. Political leaders must be able to realistically articulate their level of international ambition, the resources to be devoted to it, and the place of the potential use of military force within this strategy. Moreover, depending on the configuration of civil–military relations, it is political leaders who can impose a completely new army format, as we have seen with the imposition of nuclear deterrence or the professional army by political power in France, or of "jointness" in the US. We have also seen several cases where the contribution of civilians to military thinking has led to changes in doctrine. This presupposes that civilians take an interest in military issues and do not offload their responsibilities onto the military themselves. After all, as Raymond Aron wrote, "in a democracy, national defense directly concerns the citizen. Why shouldn't the citizen strive to acquire enough knowledge to understand the issues? What is necessary in terms of economics is no less necessary in terms of strategy." He went on to argue that it was therefore necessary "to provide officers with political training, and not to leave politicians ignorant of the facts of strategy, if not of military art in practice."[9] The education of civilians in defense issues and the existence of mechanisms for civil–military coordination on military policy issues are indispensable factors in the positive evolution of armies, even if it is inevitable that this will give rise to concerns among some military personnel, particularly in countries where the military profession is associated with a specific (social or professional) status.

Thirdly, it is essential to create flexibility in military organizations, and this involves a multiplicity of factors. Organically, armed forces need density and mass to function, to absorb unforeseen blows, and therefore need redundancy (which accountants generally hate). This observation certainly runs counter to the precepts of new public management theory, but it recurs regularly in our study: redundancies are indispensable to organizations whose very nature dictates that they should be as resilient as possible. Secondly, intellectual flexibility is essential in the event of a surprise on the battlefield. This intellectual flexibility needs to be prepared well in advance, by creating incubators for military thought, encouraging debate on operational issues in dedicated journals, promoting posts in doctrine and think tanks, and ensuring that higher military education is not limited to training but includes a significant training component. It also implies the possibility of experimentation, in wargames or exercises. These aspects are sometimes secondary in organizations that may be focused on day-to-day operations and involved in military operations, but they are crucial in providing the organization with a repertoire of thoughts, reflections and practices from which to draw when the dominant practices are challenged (as they always are in a serious conflict). Finally, in combat, the military organization needs to be flexible enough to challenge itself, such as by replacing officers on a large scale if necessary, and by creating appropriate learning mechanisms.

Time management, the quality of civil–military relations and the encouragement of flexibility are thus three fundamental aspects that help to steer military change in a positive direction for the organization. This has important consequences for defense planning. In the short term (five years from the present), the framework advanced in this book suggests that defense planning must foster organizational responsiveness and adaptive capacity in the face of uncertainty. Rather than relying solely on equipment upgrades or new acquisitions, planners should consider internal processes of adaptation and experimentation, particularly at the operational and tactical levels. Given the intensifying pace of technological diffusion and the return of high-intensity conflict in Europe, military organizations must rapidly identify and address frictions between their cognitive, institutional and relational structures. Embedding iterative learning mechanisms, integrating commercial off-the-shelf technologies, and enabling bottom-up feedback from operational units will be essential to ensuring that armed forces remain relevant and effective in rapidly evolving environments.

Over the medium term (five to ten years), defense planning must transition from immediate adaptation to deeper institutional transformation. This period requires an explicit effort to align organizational structures, personnel systems and doctrinal frameworks with emerging strategic and technological trends. Drawing on the conceptual framework developed in this book, planners should focus on managing the mechanisms of diffusion and constraint: leveraging useful lessons and innovations from foreign partners while addressing internal resistance—whether bureaucratic, cultural or political. Crucial priorities will be investing in talent management strategies for future warfare domains, reforming professional military education to cultivate critical thinking and innovation, and establishing pathways for mid-level change agents to influence institutional direction.

In the longer term (beyond ten years), defense planning must confront the enduring challenge of preparing for major war—an event that remains both rare and systemically transformative. As this study has argued throughout, military organizations are tasked with preparing for conflict scenarios that may never materialize, and for which there is no empirical feedback until failure occurs. This condition demands a form of planning that privileges resilience, redundancy and strategic diversity over predictive certainty. Long-term force development should emphasize modularity in force design, depth in logistics and sustainment, and robust mechanisms for societal–military integration. At the same time, defense planning must grapple with global structural shifts—such as demographic change, climate disruption and the fragmentation of the international order—that will shape both the character of war and the political context in which military organizations operate.

Across all time horizons, the core implication of this book is that defense planning must be understood not merely as a technical exercise in force development, but as a strategic practice of managing institutional change.[10] Armed forces are shaped by the dynamic interaction of political imperatives, cultural norms, strategic assumptions and technological possibilities. Planning for future war, therefore, requires not just identifying the right capabilities, but cultivating the organizational conditions that allow those capabilities to emerge, evolve and be effectively employed. By clarifying the mechanisms and configurations that underpin military change, this book offers a framework for navigating the uncertainty that defines the contemporary and future security environment.

Finally, we can mention a few future challenges for military organizations, based on current international dynamics and trends.

The first challenge will obviously be the ongoing modernization of forces in a context of increasing diffusion of violent technologies to numerous state and non-state actors—what Audrey Kurth Cronin calls "lethal empowerment"[11] and Andrew Krepinevich the "democratization of destruction."[12] Depending on their missions and resources, armed forces will therefore have to adjudicate between capabilities at the high end of the conflict spectrum in order to conduct high-intensity confrontations, and technologies at the low end of the spectrum to counter this democratization of destruction, which strengthens the military capabilities of armed rebel or terrorist groups.[13] At the top end of the spectrum, Krepinevich thus imagines a duel between "combat networks" made up of various sensors and effectors, conducted over relatively long distances and made possible by a significant autonomization of decisions: victory will go to the one whose sensors and effectors prevail in a continuous duel between concealment and target identification.[14] Obviously, such a mode of warfare is beyond the reach of most of the world's countries, and even the few that have the means to develop military capabilities in this direction will still need to be able to operate across a broad spectrum of different modes of action: not every use of military force will be a duel between opposing combat networks. It is far more likely, therefore, that we will see the emergence of a multiplicity of hybrid models, integrating the technologies needed to operate combat networks to varying degrees, depending on strategic priorities and resources. From this point of view, the war in Ukraine certainly heralds other localized, high-intensity conflicts in Europe, Africa or Asia, which will also involve a confrontation, direct or by proxy, between Western countries and Russia and/or China. From this point of view, the ability to establish relatively versatile force models, capable of supporting partners over the long term but also with sufficient capacity to escalate (or threaten to escalate) into a high-intensity conflict if necessary, will be an important issue in maintaining the relevance of Western countries' armed forces in the twenty-first century.[15]

The second major challenge will be to adapt the armed forces to the three long-term trends of the twenty-first century: climate change, urbanization and aging. Climate change will obviously have serious effects on conflict risks (and therefore on the strategic planning of armies), as well as on the equipment and men themselves: we will

CONCLUSION

need to develop systems that are resilient to higher temperatures, and train military personnel accordingly. Urbanization is the other major trend: in 2023, around 55% of the world's population lived in cities, and this is projected to increase to 67% by 2050. Genuine megacities of several tens of millions of inhabitants have already emerged, with their own dynamics and geographical logic, and now constitute centers of economic and political power (and therefore natural stakes in a conflict). One can expect that this global urbanization will make cities a more than likely battleground for future conflicts, and armed forces need to prepare accordingly. This will require knowledge of human geography (to understand the flows of people, goods and resources that make up the dynamics of cities), training to operate in three dimensions (high up in buildings, in the street, and underground), and adapted technologies.[16]

Finally, aging populations will create recruitment problems for the armed forces of many countries: the global trend is toward aging populations, particularly in Asia and Europe (Africa should remain a young continent, as will North America thanks to immigration). The armed forces of these regions will have to compete with other types of public spending, notably the colossal expenses required to develop societies in which a quarter of the population will be over 65. Moreover, in economies under pressure from labor shortages, recruitment will also be more difficult if more attractive careers are available in the civilian sector. The armed forces will certainly have to take into account the expectations of rising generations in their recruitment, and in particular the need for flexibility in employment. We may need to think about career moves back and forth, allowing "lateral" entry into military organizations, at high ranks too, if the armed forces are to ensure that they maintain the skills they need so as to operate. There is likely to be a great deal of work to be done on what constitutes a "military" as opposed to a "civilian" identity in many countries. Overall, concerns about recruitments and casualties in aging societies may well create strong incentives for the robotization and automation of armed violence.

This leads to the final, and obvious, challenge: the degree to which emerging technologies are integrated into the armed forces, and the effect they will have on their day-to-day behavior. An initial challenge will be to adapt tactics to new military technologies. Under the impetus of the US, NATO member countries are now studying, to varying degrees, the concept of "multi-domain operations." The fundamental idea, linked to that of the "combat network" mentioned above, is to think about military operations not in terms of the equipment available for a specific mission, but in terms of the particular effects to be achieved by using the best-placed effector at a given moment, regardless of the effector's environment. Thus, instead of coordinating and synchronizing an air campaign with a ground campaign (the logic of domain), operations should be planned according to the desired effect. A target could be destroyed by an air strike, artillery fire or sabotage by special forces (or any other useful means), depending on the assessment of the tactical commander best placed on the ground and the availability and proximity of the relevant effectors. While the idea seems appealing, it requires a profound rethink of the way armies plan and command their operations (with delegation of command to lower tactical levels, which can pose problems of hierarchy); the foundations of their military cultures and therefore their cohesion (built according to land/air/sea logic of domains); and, finally, their doctrines (as well as the associated training and education).[17] The task of fully implementing this vision is immense and requires a revolution in military organizations: one can therefore expect that, in reality, what will be implemented in different countries will be gradations of this vision.

Furthermore, it is often mentioned that artificial intelligence will help with logistics or the coordination of a set of effectors, but there is much less discussion of the fact that AI, trained on a relevant database, will certainly be able to produce staff reports as well as a certified officer in the near future. These technologies will also require skills that are highly valued in the civilian world, with which the armed forces are already competing for recruitment and will increasingly do so in the future. In addition to the lateral entry routes mentioned above, should we also consider decoupling rank from income? Will it be acceptable for a senior officer to be paid less than a junior officer who has rare skills that are essential to the organization? On another note, so-called augmentation

CONCLUSION

technologies are being seriously studied by many armed forces around the world, with different possibilities for integration. Here again, the issue of the social acceptability of technology will intersect with the flexibility of military organizations, leading to results that will certainly vary greatly from one country to another. Finally, the war in Ukraine has illustrated the importance of private actors and individuals in capability development and the conduct of operations. For Western countries, the question of the scope and development of what constitutes a defense industrial and technological base is now acute, in a context in which the heart of technological innovation has shifted from the public to the private sector, and rival powers such as China make no secret of their desire to encourage dual use (civil and military) in their industrial development.

In any case, military change will be one of the fundamental dimensions of the distribution of military power and, therefore, of the strategic challenges of the twenty-first century.

NOTES

INTRODUCTION

1. Mick Ryan, *The War for Ukraine: Strategy and Adaptation under Fire*, Annapolis, Naval Institute Press, 2024.
2. Benjamin Tallis, "The End of the Zeitenwende," German Council on Foreign Relations. August 2024.
3. Keir Giles, *Who Will Defend Europe? An Awakened Russia and a Sleeping Continent*, London, Hurst, 2024.
4. Paul McLeary and Lee Hudson, "How Two Dozen Retired Generals Are Trying to Stop an Overhaul of the Marines," *Politico*, 1 April 2022.
5. Raymond Aron, *Paix et guerre entre les nations*, Paris, Calmann-Lévy, 1962, p. 28. For an introduction, see Olivier Schmitt (ed.), *Raymond Aron and International Relations*, Abingdon, Routledge, 2018.
6. Risa A. Brooks and Elizabeth A. Stanley (eds.), *Creating Military Power: The Sources of Military Effectiveness*, Palo Alto, Stanford University Press, 2007; Michael Beckley, "The Power of Nations: Measuring What Matters," *International Security*, 43/2, 2018, pp. 7–44; Jon R. Lindsay and Erik Gartzke, "Politics by Other Means: The Comparative Strategic Advantages of Operational Domains," *Journal of Strategic Studies*, 45/5, 2022, pp. 743–776; Thomas G. Mahnken (ed.), *Net Assessment and Military Strategy: Retrospective and Prospective Essays*, Amherst, Cambria Press, 2020.
7. Hervé Coutau-Bégarie, *Traité de stratégie*, 8th ed., Paris, Economica, 2011.
8. John G. Ikenberry, *A World Safe for Democracy: Liberal Internationalism and the Crisis of Global Order*, New Haven, Yale University Press, 2020.
9. Julian Fernandez and Jean-Vincent Holeindre (eds.), *Nations désunies? La crise du multilatéralisme dans les relations internationales*, Paris, CNRS Éditions, 2022.
10. John G. Ikenberry, "Three Worlds: The West, East and South and the

Competition to Shape Global Order," *International Affairs*, 100/1, 2024, pp. 121–138.

11. Olivier Schmitt, "La nouvelle crise des fondements. Repenser la défense de l'Europe," *Politique Étrangère*, 3, 2025.
12. Alexander Cooley and Daniel Nexon, *Exit from Hegemony: The Unraveling of the American Global Order*, Oxford, Oxford University Press, 2020.
13. The impossibility of predicting the effects of these different trends is linked to the fact that these effects will be conditioned by the way in which societies prepare for them, or not. They may therefore be more or less significant, depending on the context and situation.
14. Cornelia Baciu et al., "The Crisis of Liberal Interventionism and the Return of War," *Politics and Governance*, 12, 2024; Tanisha Fazal, "Is War in Decline?," *Annual Review of Political Science*, 28, 2025, pp. 58–73.
15. International Institute for Strategic Studies, *The Military Balance*, Abingdon, Routledge, 2022.
16. The notes in this book quote extensively from these works, which are therefore not mentioned here.
17. Brett Bennett and Gregory Barton, "Generalizations in Global History: Dealing with Diversity without Losing the Big Picture," *Itinerario*, 41/1, 2017, pp. 15–25.
18. Examples of this type of approach include Williamson Murray and Allan R. Millet (eds.), *Military Innovation in the Interwar Period*, Cambridge, Cambridge University Press, 1998; Harold R. Winston and David R. Mets (eds.), *The Challenge of Change: Military Institutions and New Realities, 1918–1941*, Lincoln, University of Nebraska Press, 2000; Emily O. Goldman and Leslie C. Eliason (eds.), *The Diffusion of Military Technology and Ideas*, Palo Alto, Stanford University Press, 2003.
19. Exceptions to this observation are Williamson Murray, *Military Adaptation in War: With Fear of Change*, Cambridge, Cambridge University Press, 2011; and Michel Goya, *S'adapter pour vaincre. Comment les armées évoluent*, Paris, Perrin, 2019.
20. Stuart Griffin, "Military Innovation Studies: Multidisciplinarity or Lacking Discipline?," *Journal of Strategic Studies*, 40/1–2, 2017, pp. 196–224.
21. Rob Sinterniklaas, *Military Innovation: Cutting the Gordian Knot*, Faculty of Military Sciences, Netherlands Defence Academy, 2018, p. 5.
22. See, for example, Tone Danielsen, *Making Warriors in a Global Era: An Ethnographic Study of the Norwegian Naval Special Operations Commando*, London, Lexington Books, 2018; Emmanuel Cardona Gil and Sébastien Jakubowski (eds.), *Les logiques de transformation des armées*, Lille, Presses Universitaires du Septentrion, 2020.
23. Theo Farrell and Terry Terriff (eds.), *The Sources of Military Change: Culture, Politics, Technology*, Boulder, Lynne Rienner, 2002.

24. Michael C. Horowitz and Shira Pindyck, "What Is a Military Innovation and Why It Matters," *Journal of Strategic Studies*, 46/1, 2023, pp. 85–86.
25. Bradley Graham, *By His Own Rules: The Ambitions, Successes, and Ultimate Failures of Donald Rumsfeld*, New York, Public Affairs, 2009.
26. Murray, *Military Adaptation in War*, p. 309. The same distinction based on a temporal criterion is taken up again in David Barno and Nora Bensahel, *Adaptation under Fire: How Militaries Change in Wartime*, Oxford, Oxford University Press, 2020. For a discussion of temporality in war, see Sten Rynning, Olivier Schmitt and Amelie Theussen (eds.), *Wartime: Temporality and the Decline of Western Military Power*, Washington DC, Brookings Institution Press, 2021.
27. Emilie Berthelsen, "Hybrid Times: War and Peace in Military Innovation Studies," *Journal of Strategic Studies*, 2025.
28. Jim Storr, *Something Rotten: Land Command in the 21st Century*, Havant, Howgate, 2022, p. 184.
29. Andrew Gordon, *The Rules of the Game: Jutland and British Naval Command*, Annapolis, Naval Institute Press, 2013.
30. For a historiographical synthesis, see Mark Charles Fissel, "Military Revolutions," *Oxford Bibliographies*, March 2022, online. Reference works include Geoffrey Parker, *The Military Revolution: Military Innovation and the Rise of the West, 1500–1800*, Cambridge, Cambridge University Press, 1988; Clifford J. Rogers (ed.), *The Military Revolution Debate: Readings on the Military Transformation of Early Modern Europe*, Boulder, Westview, 1995; MacGregor Knox and Williamson Murray, *The Dynamics of Military Revolution, 1300–2050*, Cambridge, Cambridge University Press, 2001; Peter A. Lorge, *The Asian Military Revolution: From Gunpowder to the Bomb*, Cambridge, Cambridge University Press, 2008; Tonio Andrade, *The Gunpowder Age: China, Military Innovation, and the Rise of the West in World History*, Princeton, Princeton University Press, 2016.
31. Ben Connable, *Ground Combat: Puncturing the Myths of Modern War*, Washington DC, Georgetown University Press, 2025, p. 26.
32. Michel Fortmann, *Les cycles de Mars. Révolutions militaires et édification étatique de la renaissance à nos jours*, Paris, Economica, 2009, p. 11.
33. Kendrick Kuo, "Dangerous Changes: When Military Innovation Harms Combat Effectiveness," *International Security*, 47/2, 2022, pp. 48–87.
34. For an overview of different theoretical approaches, see Heather A. Haveman, *The Power of Organizations: A New Approach to Organizational Theory*, Princeton, Princeton University Press, 2023; Marshall Scott Pool and Andrew van de Ven (eds.), *The Oxford Handbook of Organizational Change and Innovation*, 2nd ed., Oxford, Oxford University Press, 2021.
35. Nils Brunsson and Johan P. Olsen, *The Reforming Organization*, Abingdon, Routledge, 1993; Jens Beckert, "How Do Fields Change? The Interrelations of Institutions, Networks and Cognition in Dynamics of Markets,"

Organization Studies, 31/5, pp. 605–627. Beckert's approach is updated in Henri Bergeron and Patrick Castel, *L'organocène*, Paris, Presses de Sciences Po, 2024.

36. I here refer to Max Weber's distinction between behavior and action, the latter being a behavior to which the actors assign a specific meaning.
37. Göran Ahrne, Nils Brunsson and David Seidl, "Resurrecting Organization by Going beyond Organization," *European Management Journal*, 34/2, 2016, pp. 93–101.
38. David Baldwin, *Power in International Relations: A Conceptual Approach*, Princeton, Princeton University Press, 2016.
39. William H. Sewell Jr., *Logics of History: Social Theory and Social Transformations*, Chicago, University of Chicago Press, 2005.
40. See for example Joseph Soeters, *Management and Military Studies: Classical and Current Foundations*, Abingdon, Routledge, 2020.
41. Peter Feaver, "Civil–Military Relations," *Annual Review of Political Science*, 2, 1999, p. 214.
42. General Lucien Poirier, *Éléments de stratégique*, Paris, Economica, 2023, p. 466.
43. Nina Wilén and Lisa Strömbom, "A Versatile Organisation: Mapping the Military's Core Roles in a Changing Security Environment," *European Journal of International Security*, 7/1, 2022, pp. 18–37.
44. Kuehn and Croissant identify at least five missions and tasks shared by the armed forces, whatever the political regime: combat, counter-terrorism, peacekeeping, support for civilian authorities in the event of disaster (natural or otherwise), support for the police in the fight against crime. David Kuehn and Aurel Croissant, *Routes to Reform: Civil–Military Relations and Democracy in the Third Wave*, Oxford, Oxford University Press, 2023.
45. Paul Chambers and Napisa Waitoolkiat (eds.), *Khaki Capital: The Political Economy of the Military of Southeast Asia*, Copenhagen, NIAS Press, 2018.
46. Ben Connable et al., *Will to Fight: Analyzing, Modeling, and Simulating the Will to Fight of Military Units*, Santa Monica, RAND Corporation, 2018.
47. Kenneth L. Dion, "Group Cohesion: From 'Field of Forces' to Multidimensional Construct," *Group Dynamics: Theory, Research, and Practice*, 4/1, 2000, pp. 7–26.
48. Anthony King (ed.), *Frontline: Combat and Cohesion in the Twenty-First Century*, Oxford, Oxford University Press, 2015.
49. George Washington, *Letter of Instructions to the Captains of the Virginia Regiments*, 29 July 1759.
50. Claude Weber, *Un ethnologue dans les armées*, Paris, Pierre de Taillac, 2023.
51. Daniel Kahneman, Olivier Sibony and Cass R. Sunstein, *Noise: A Flaw in Human Judgement*, Boston, Little Brown Spark, 2021.
52. Jason Lyall, *Divided Armies: Inequality and Battlefield Performance in Modern War*, Princeton, Princeton University Press, 2020.

53. Dale C. Copeland, *The Origins of Major War*, Ithaca, Cornell University Press, 2000, p. 3.
54. Bear F. Braumoeller, *Only the Dead: The Persistence of War in the Modern Age*, Oxford, Oxford University Press, 2019.
55. Michael Howard, "The Use and Abuse of Military History," *RUSI Journal*, 107, 1962, p. 6.
56. Ibid.
57. Carl von Clausewitz, *On War*, translation by Michael Howard and Peter Paret, Princeton, Princeton University Press, 1976 (1832), p. 132.
58. Yosef Jabareen, "Building a Conceptual Framework: Philosophy, Definitions and Procedure," *International Journal of Qualitative Methods*, 8/4, 2009, p.51.
59. Giovanni Sartori, "Guidelines for Concept Analysis," in David Collier and John Gerring (eds.), *Concepts and Methods in Social Science: The Tradition of Giovanni Sartori*, Abingdon, Routledge, 2009, pp. 97–150.
60. The "scientific" approach uses concepts as methodological tools to measure and explain the social world. It differs from the "historical" approach, which traces the evolution of how a term is understood and used over time, and from the "critical" approach, which seeks to denaturalize concepts taken for granted and show their role in structuring power relationships within the social world. See Felix Berenskoetter, "Approaches to Concept Analysis," *Millenium*, 45/2, 2017, pp. 151–173.
61. This collective research project led by the author was conducted from 2017 to 2022 at the University of Southern Denmark (SDU) and was funded by the Danish Independent Research Fund, the Carlsberg Foundation and the Gerda Henkel Foundation.
62. Roy Bhaskar, *A Realist Theory of Science*, Leeds, Leeds Books, 1975; Roy Bhaskar, *The Possibility of Naturalism: A Philosophical Critique of Contemporary Human Sciences*, Brighton, Harvester Press, 1979.
63. For a discussion of critical realism in the field of International Relations, see Patrick Thaddeus Jackson, *The Conduct of Inquiry in International Relations: Philosophy of Science and Its Implications for the Study of World Politics*, 2nd ed., Abingdon, Routledge, 2016, pp. 83–122.
64. Berth Danermark et al. (eds.), *Explaining Society: Critical Realism in the Social Sciences*, Abingdon, Routledge, 2022.
65. Joe O'Mahoney and Steve Vincent, "Critical Realism as an Empirical Project," in Paul K. Ewards, Joe O'Mahoney and Steve Vincent, *Studying Organizations Using Critical Realism: A Practical Guide*, Oxford, Oxford University Press, 2014, p. 8.
66. Norbert Elias, *Qu'est-ce que la sociologie*, Paris, Pocket, 1981, p. 84.
67. Evelyn Micelotta, Michael Lounsbury and Ryston Greenwood, "Pathways of Institutional Change: An Integrative Review and Research Agenda," *Journal of Management*, 43/6, 2017, pp. 1–26.

68. Mike Dent et al. (eds.), *The Routledge Companion to the Professions and Professionalism*, Abingdon, Routledge, 2016.
69. Samuel Huntington, *The Soldier and the State: The Theory and Politics of Civil–Military Relations*, Cambridge MA, Belknap Press, 1957.
70. Jean Joanna, *Les armées contemporaines*, Paris, Presses de Sciences Po, 2012, p. 78.
71. Bernard Boëne (ed.), *La spécificité militaire*, Paris, Armand Colin, 1990.
72. As in English, "civil" in French has the dual meaning of "civilian" and "courteous." True to character, Talleyrand is of course softly insulting Augereau with this quip.
73. Laure Bardiès, "Du concept de spécificité militaire," *L'Année Sociologique*, 61, 2011, p. 279.
74. Wilén and Strömbom, "A Versatile Organisation."
75. André Thiéblemont (ed.), *Cultures et logiques militaires*, Paris, PUF, 1999.
76. Huntington, *The Soldier and the State*.
77. Morris Janowitz, *The Professional Soldier: A Social and Political Portrait*, New York, Macmillan, 1971.
78. Charles Moskos, "From Institution to Occupation: Trends in Military Organization," *Armed Forces and Society*, 4/1, 1977, pp. 41–50; John Allen Williams, "The Military and Society: Beyond the Postmodern Era," *Orbis*, 52/2, 2008, pp. 199–216.
79. Camille Trotoux, "La singularité militaire," *Brève Stratégique*, Irsem, no. 25, 23 July 2021.
80. Quoted in Vilhelm Stefan Holsting, "The Dynamics of Professional Values in Officership: A Study of 300 Years of Officer Performance Evaluation Systems," in Anne Roelsgaard Obling and Lotta Victor Tillberg (eds.), *Transformations of the Military Profession and Professionalism in Scandinavia*, Copenhagen, Scandinavian Military Studies, 2021, p. 209.
81. Peter Viggo Jakobsen and Sten Rynning, "Denmark: Happy to Fight, Will Travel," *International Affairs*, 95/4, 2019, pp. 877–895.
82. Holsting, "The Dynamics of Professional Values in Officership."
83. François Gresle, "La 'société militaire'. Son devenir à la lumière de la professionalisation," *Revue Française de Sociologie*, 44, 2003, pp. 777–798.
84. Detlef Bald, "The German Officer Corps: Caste or Class?," *Armed Forces and Society*, 5/4, 1979, pp. 642–668; Raoul Girardet, *La société militaire de 1815 à nos jours*, Paris, Perrin, 1998; Volker C. Franke, "Duty, Honor, Country: The Social Identity of West Point Cadets," *Armed Forces and Society*, 26/2, 2000, pp. 1175–1202; Peter H. Wilson, "Defining Military Culture," *Journal of Military History*, 72/1, 2008, pp. 11–41; Patrick Bury, "Barossa Night: Cohesion in the British Army Officer Corps," *British Journal of Sociology*, 68/2, 2017, pp. 314–335.
85. Feaver, "Civil–Military Relations"; Risa Brooks, "Integrating the Civil–Military Relations Subfield," *Annual Review of Political Science*, 22, 2019, pp. 379–398.

86. Sönke Neitzel, *Deutsche Krieger. Vom Kaiserreich zur Berliner Republik. Eine Militärgeschichte*, Berlin, Propyläen Verlag, 2020, p. 11.
87. Edward J. Drea, *Japan's Imperial Army: Its Rise and Fall, 1853–1945*, Lawrence, University Press of Kansas, 2009, p.166.
88. The literature on change in alliances and coalitions is still embryonic. See Heidi Hardt, *NATO's Lessons in Crisis: Institutional Memory in International Organizations*, Oxford, Oxford University Press, 2018; Sara Bjerg Moller, "Learning from Losing: How Defeat Shapes Coalition Dynamics in Wartime," *Journal of Strategic Studies*, 45/2, 2022, pp. 280–302.
89. On military change in rebel groups, see Jeremy Weinstein, *Inside Rebellion: The Politics of Insurgent Violence*, Cambridge, Cambridge University Press, 2007; Paul Staniland, *Networks of Rebellion: Explaining Insurgent Cohesion and Collapse*, Ithaca, Cornell University Press, 2014; Chad C. Serena, *It Takes More Than a Network: The Iraqi Insurgency and Organizational Adaptation*, Palo Alto, Stanford University Press, 2014; Peter Krause, *Rebel Power: Why National Movements Compete, Fight, and Win*, Ithaca, Cornell University Press, 2017; Theo Farrell, "Unbeatable: Social Resources, Military Adaptation, and the Afghan Taliban," *Texas National Security Review*, 1/3, 2018, pp. 58–75; Omar Ashour, *How ISIS Fights: Military Tactics in Iraq, Syria, Libya and Egypt*, Edinburgh, Edinburgh University Press, 2021; Antonio Giustozzi, *The Taliban at War, 2001–2021*, London, Hurst, 2022.
90. On military change in terrorist groups, see Brian A. Jackson, *Aptitude for Destruction*, vol. 1: *Organizational Learning in Terrorist Groups and Its Implications for Combating Terrorism*, Santa Monica, RAND Corporation, 2005; Assaf Moghadam, "How Al Qaeda Innovates," *Security Studies*, 22/3, 2013, pp. 466–497; Magnus Ranstrop and Magnus Normark (eds.), *Understanding Terrorism: Innovation and Learning*, Abingdon, Routledge, 2015; Louise Kettle and Andrew Mumford, "Terrorist Learning: A New Analytical Framework," *Studies in Conflict and Terrorism*, 40/7, 2017, pp. 523–538; Yannick Veilleux-Lepage, *How Terror Evolves: The Emergence and Spread of Terrorist Techniques*, Washington DC, Rowman and Littlefield, 2020.
91. For studies of change in intelligence agencies, see Michael Herman, "Counter-terrorism, Information Technology and Intelligence Change," *Intelligence and National Security*, 18/4, 2003, pp. 40–58; Amy B. Zegart, "September 11 and the Adaptation Failure of U.S. Intelligence Agencies," *International Security*, 29/4, 2005, pp. 78–111; Brent Durbin, *The CIA and the Politics of Intelligence Reform*, Cambridge, Cambridge University Press, 2017.
92. Michael Howard, *War in European History*, Oxford, Oxford University Press, 1976; William H. McNeill, *The Pursuit of Power: Technology, Armed Force, and Society since A.D. 1000*, Chicago, University of Chicago Press, 1984; Charles Tilly, *Coercion, Capital, and European States, A.D. 990–1992*, London, Blackwell, 1993; Azar Gat, *War in Human Civilization*, Oxford, Oxford University Press, 2008; Fortmann, *Les cycles de Mars*; Jacques Frémeaux and Michèle Battesti

(eds.), *Sortir de la guerre*, Paris, Presses de l'Université Paris-Sorbonne, 2014; Margaret MacMillan, *War: How Conflict Shaped Us*, New York, Profile Books, 2021. For an example of how war influences public policy, see Vincent Viet, *La santé en guerre, 1914–1918. Une politique pionnière en univers incertain*, Paris, Presses de Sciences Po, 2015.

93. Jürgen Osterhammel, *The Transformation of the World: A Global History of the Nineteenth Century*, Princeton, Princeton University Press, 2014, p. 483.
94. Antoine Bousquet, *The Scientific Way of Warfare: Order and Chaos on the Battlefield of Modernity*, 2nd ed., London, Hurst, 2022; Arnaud Guinier, "Une folle raison? Les lumières militaires et la crise de la rationalité géométrique," in Laurent Vissière and Marion Trévisi (eds.), *Le feu et la folie. L'irrationnel et la guerre (fin du Moyen-Âge – XIXe siècle)*, Rennes, Presses Universitaires de Rennes, 2016, pp. 217–230. For a study of European military thought between the eighteenth and nineteenth centuries, see Hervé Drévillon, *Penser et écrire la guerre. Contre Clausewitz (1780–1837)*, Paris, Passés Composés, 2021. For an analysis of the Western epistemological revolution brought about by the Napoleonic Wars, and in particular the notions of chance and contingency in the art of war, see Anders Engberg-Pedersen, *Empire of Chance: The Napoleonic Wars and the Disorder of Things*, Cambridge MA, Harvard University Press, 2015.
95. Robert M. Citino, *The German Way of War: From the Thirty Years War to the Third Reich*, Lawrence, University Press of Kansas, 2005, pp. 128–132.
96. Nathan W. Toronto, "Military Learning and Evolutions in Warfare in the Modern Era," *Oxford Research Encyclopedias*, 2021, online.
97. Karl Demeter, *Das Deutsche Offizierkorps in Gesellschaft und Staat 1650–1945*, 4th ed., Frankfurt am Main, Bernard & Graefe Verlag für Wehrwesen, 1965, pp. 29–33.
98. Gudrun Persson, *Learning from Foreign Wars: Russian Military Thinking 1859–1873*, London, Helion, 2011, p. 17.
99. The dates indicate the period of American participation in the war. There is a historiographical debate on the exact chronological boundaries of the Second World War, aimed at taking into account the Asian dimension of the conflict, and in particular Japan's invasion of Manchuria in 1931. The debate concerns the exact moment when a series of conflicts (having degenerated into wars or on the verge of doing so) cease to be regionally localized but "merge" into a global war. For an argument in favor of dating the start of the Second World War to 1931, see S. C. M. Paine, *The Wars for Asia, 1911–1949*, Cambridge, Cambridge University Press, 2012; for an argument in favor of 1939, see Gerard L. Weinberg, *A World at Arms: A Global History of World War II*, 2nd ed., Cambridge, Cambridge University Press, 2005; for an argument in favor of 1941, see Evan Mawdsley, *December 1941: Twelve Days That Began a World War*, New Haven, Yale University Press, 2012. For a historiographical synthesis,

see Pierre Grosser, *Pourquoi la seconde guerre mondiale*, 2nd ed., Brussels, André Versailles, 2022.
100. Christopher H. Hamner, *Enduring Battle: American Soldiers in Three Wars, 1776–1945*, Lawrence, University Press of Kansas, 2011.
101. Stephen Biddle, *Nonstate Warfare: The Military Methods of Guerrillas, Warlords, and Militias*, Princeton, Princeton University Press, 2021, p. 55.
102. Hamner, *Enduring Battle*, p. 47.
103. C. J. Dick, *From Victory to Stalemate: The Western Front, Summer 1944*, Lawrence, University Press of Kansas, 2016, p. 85.
104. Martin van Creveld, *Command in War*, Cambridge MA, Harvard University Press, 1985, p. 107.
105. Aurélien Rouquet, "Les racines oubliées de la logistique. La fonction de maréchal général des logis dans l'armée française entre le 16e et 18e siècle," *Revue Française de Gestion*, no. 297, 2021, pp. 35–52.
106. Annie Crépin, *Histoire de la conscription*, Paris, Gallimard, 2009, pp. 106–107.
107. For an argument in favor of the rupture brought about by the Revolution, see Lars-Erik Cederman, T. Camber Warren and Didier Sornette, "Testing Clausewitz: Nationalism, Mass Mobilization, and the Severity of War," *International Organization*, 65/4, 2011, pp. 605–638.
108. Massimiliano Gaetano Onorato, Kenneth Scheve and David Stasavage, "Technology and the Era of the Mass Army," *Journal of Economic History*, 74/2, 2014, pp. 449–481.
109. Robert M. Citino, *The Quest for Decisive Victory: From Stalemate to Blitzkrieg in Europe, 1899–1940*, Lawrence, University Press of Kansas, 2002.
110. Howard, *War in European History*.
111. B. A. Friedman, *On Operations*, Annapolis, Naval Institute Press, 2021, p. 5.
112. Osterhammel, *The Transformation of the World*, p. 484.
113. Stephen Biddle, *Military Power: Explaining Victory and Defeat in Modern Battle*, Princeton, Princeton University Press, 2006; Ryan Grauer and Michael Horowitz, "What Determines Military Victory? Testing the Modern System," *Security Studies*, 21/1, 2012, pp. 83–112.
114. Tommy Jamieson, "Taking the 'Modern System' to Sea: The Past and Future of Naval Power in Industrial War," *Comparative Strategy*, 41/3, 2022, pp. 261–281.
115. Antonio Calcara et al., "Why Drones Have Not Revolutionized War: The Enduring Hider-Finder Competition in Air Warfare," *International Security*, 46/4, 2022, pp. 130–171.
116. Dierk Walter, *Colonial Violence: European Empires and the Use of Force*, London, Hurst, 2016.
117. Stéphanie Soubrier, *Races guerrières. Enquête sur une catégorie impériale*, Paris, CNRS Éditions, 2023.
118. Heather Streets, *Martial Races: The Military, Race and Masculinity in British*

Imperial Culture, 1857–1914, Manchester, Manchester University Press, 2010.

119. Alessandro Monsutti, "Anthropologizing Afghanistan: Colonial and Postcolonial Encounters," *Annual Review of Anthropology*, 42, 2013, pp. 269–285.
120. Paul Pandolfi, "La construction du mythe Touareg. Quelques remarques et hypothèses," *Ethnologies Comparées*, Montpellier III, 2004; Rémi Carayol, "Le mythe (écorné) de 'l'homme bleu,'" *Afrique XXI*, 19 January 2021.
121. Montgomery McFate, *Military Anthropology: Soldiers, Scholars and Subjects at the Margin of Empire*, London, Hurst, 2018.
122. Stuart Creigton Miller, "*Benevolent Assimilation*": *The American Conquest of the Philippines, 1899–1903*, New Haven, Yale University Press, 1984, pp. 164, 208–210.
123. Robert Wooster, *The American Military Frontiers: The United States Army in the West, 1783–1900*, Albuquerque, University of New Mexico Press, 2009.
124. Some authors have argued that this conflict constituted the "first genocide" of the twentieth century, and have seen it as one of the origins of Nazi practices. See, for example, Casper Erichsen and David Olusoga, *The Kaiser's Holocaust: Germany's Forgotten Genocide and the Colonial Roots of Nazism*, London, Faber and Faber, 2011. Most historians, without denying the brutality of this colonial conflict, are reluctant to establish such a filiation. See, for example, Isabel V. Hull, *Absolute Destruction: Military Culture and the Practice of War in Imperial Germany*, Ithaca, Cornell University Press, 2006; or Volker Langbehn and Mohammad Salama (eds.), *German Colonialism: Race, the Holocaust, and Postwar Germany*, New York, Columbia University Press, 2011, especially the introduction.
125. Douglas Porch, *Counterinsurgency: Exposing the Myths of the New Way of War*, Cambridge, Cambridge University Press, 2013; Stuart Schrader, *Badges without Borders: How Global Counterinsurgency Transformed American Policing*, Oakland, University of California Press, 2019. On the continuity between British "sky policing" operations in Iraq in the interwar period, theories of strategic bombing and contemporary air operations (which tends to obscure the underlying strategic rationality), see Thomas Hippler, *Le gouvernement du ciel. Histoire globale des bombardements aériens*, Paris, Les Prairies Ordinaires, 2014.
126. Thomas Rid, "The Nineteenth Century Origins of Counterinsurgency Doctrine," *Journal of Strategic Studies*, 33/5, 2010, pp. 727–758; Elie Tenenbaum, *Partisans et centurions. Histoire de la guerre irrégulière au XXe siècle*, Paris, Perrin, 2018.
127. John France, *Perilous Glory: The Rise of Western Military Power*, New Haven, Yale University Press, 2011.
128. J. Bradford DeLong, *Slouching towards Utopia: An Economic History of the Twentieth Century*, London, Basic Books, 2022.

129. Tor Hernes, *A Process Theory of Organization*, Oxford, Oxford University Press, 2014, p. 159.
130. Harald Høiback, "What Is Doctrine?," *Journal of Strategic Studies*, 34/6, 2011, p. 897.
131. Pascal Vennesson, "Penser les guerres nouvelles. La doctrine militaire en questions," *Pouvoirs*, 125/2, 2008, p. 81.
132. Søren Sjøgren, "What We Disagree about When We Disagree about Doctrine," *Journal of Strategic Studies*, 47/4, 2024, pp. 474–497.
133. Davide Nicolini, *Practice Theory, Work and Organization*, Oxford, Oxford University Press, 2012, p. 10.
134. The term "organizational routines" is sometimes used in the literature with a meaning very close to that which we adopt here for practices. See, for example, Cornelius Friesendorf, *How Western Soldiers Fight: Organizational Routines in Multinational Missions*, Cambridge, Cambridge University Press, 2018.
135. I thank Isabelle Dufour for her invaluable comments, which helped define the degrees of military change presented here.
136. Kuo, "Dangerous Changes."
137. Barno and Bensahel, *Adaptation under Fire*.
138. Horowitz and Pindyck, "What Is a Military Innovation?
139. For an example of conceptualizing innovation as a process, see Tai Ming Cheung, "A Conceptual Framework of Defence Innovation," *Journal of Strategic Studies*, 44/6, 2021, pp. 775–801. For an example attempting to combine process and outcome, see Horowitz and Pindyck, "What Is a Military Innovation?"
140. Edward N. Luttwak, *Strategy: The Logic of War and Peace*, Cambridge MA, Belknap Press, 2002.
141. Knus Illeris (ed.), *Contemporary Theories of Learning: Learning Theorists in Their Own Words*, Abingdon, Routledge, 2018.
142. Kendrick Kuo, "On Military Restoration: How Militaries Recover from Battlefield Surprises," *Journal of Strategic Studies*, 2025. Kuo establishes "restoration" as a distinct type of military change, but I would argue that it is a subtype of the "learning" mechanism.
143. Olivier Sibony, *Vous allez commettre une terrible erreur*, Paris, Flammarion, 2019.
144. James G. March, *The Ambiguities of Experience*, Ithaca, Cornell University Press, 2010, p. 114.
145. This definition is a variation on the classic definition of diffusion of innovations by Everett Rogers, for whom it is "the process by which (1) an innovation (2) is communicated through certain channels (3) over time (4) among the members of a social system." See Everett Rogers, *Diffusion of Innovations*, 5th ed., New York, Free Press, 2003, p. 11.
146. David Benson and Andrew Jordan, "What Have We Learned from Policy

Transfer Research? Dolowitz and Marsh Revisited," *Political Studies Review*, 9/3, 2011, pp. 366–378.
147. Rogers, *Diffusion of Innovations*, Chapter 6.
148. Michael Horowitz, *The Diffusion of Military Power: Causes and Consequences for International Politics*, Princeton, Princeton University Press, 2010.
149. These three categories refer to the three types of institutional isomorphism (coercive, mimetic and normative) identified in Walter W. Powell and Paul J. DiMaggio (eds.), *The New Institutionalism in Organizational Analysis*, Chicago, University of Chicago Press, 1991.

1. THE CONFIGURATION OF THE INTERNATIONAL SYSTEM AND MILITARY CHANGE

1. David A. Lake, *Hierarchy in International Relations*, Ithaca, Cornell University Press, 2011; Vincent Pouliot, *International Pecking Orders: The Politics and Practices of Multilateral Diplomacy*, Cambridge, Cambridge University Press, 2016; Ayse Zarakol (ed.), *Hierarchies in World Politics*, Cambridge, Cambridge University Press, 2017.
2. Kenneth M. Waltz, *Theory of International Politics*, Reading, Addison-Wesley, 1979. See also Kenneth M. Waltz, *Man, the State, and War: A Theoretical Analysis*, New York, Columbia University Press, 1954.
3. This is a debate between proponents of balancing powers and those of balancing threats. For the second position, see Stephen M. Walt, *The Origins of Alliances*, Ithaca, Cornell University Press, 1984.
4. Waltz, *Theory of International Politics*, p. 127.
5. Laure Bardiès, "Le raisonnement stratégique," in Taillat, Henrotin and Schmitt, *Guerre et stratégie*, pp. 43–57.
6. Barry Posen, *The Sources of Military Doctrine,* Ithaca, Cornell University Press, 1984.
7. Barry Posen, "Military Doctrine and the Management of Uncertainty," *Journal of Strategic Studies*, 39/2, 2016, pp. 159–173.
8. This argument is based on the theory of offense and defense, which essentially postulates that international conflict is more likely when military technologies favor offensive operations, and that cooperation is more likely when military technologies favor defense. This theory is hotly debated within the (neo)realist movement. For an overview of the debate, see Stephen Van Evera, "Offense, Defense, and the Causes of War," *International Security*, 22/4, 1998, pp. 5–43; Charles L. Glaser and Chaim Kaufmann, "What Is the Offense–Defense Balance and How Can We Measure It?," *International Security*, 22/4, 1994, pp. 44–82; Keir A. Lieber, *War and the Engineers: The Primacy of Politics over Technology*, Ithaca, Cornell University Press, 2005; Corentin Brustlein, "Innovation militaire, équilibre de l'offensive et de la défensive, et distribution de la puissance," *Les Champs de Mars*, 17, 2005, pp.

183–211; Tang Shiping, "Offence–Defence Theory: Towards a Definitive Understanding," *Chinese Journal of International Politics*, 3, 2010, pp. 213–260.
9. Winston and Mets, *The Challenge of Change*.
10. Michel Goya, "Une révolution africaine dans les affaires militaires," *Annuaire Français de Relations Internationales*, 21, 2020, pp. 669–682.
11. Olivier Schmitt, "Wartime Paradigms and the Future of Western Military Power," *International Affairs*, 96/2, 2020, pp. 401–418; David Kilcullen, *The Dragons and the Snakes: How the Rest Learned to Fight the West*, London, Hurst, 2020. For Russia, see Dimitri Minic, *Pensée et culture stratégiques russes. Du contournement de la lutte armée à la guerre en Ukraine*, Paris, Editions de la Maison des Sciences de l'Homme, 2023.
12. Rush Doshi, *The Long Game: China's Grand Strategy to Displace American Order*, Oxford, Oxford University Press, 2021.
13. Michael Schuman, *Superpower Interrupted: The Chinese History of the World*, New York, Public Affairs, 2020.
14. Joseph Henrotin, *Les fondements de la stratégie navale au XXIe siècle*, Paris, Economica, 2011.
15. Joel Wuthnow et al. (eds.), *The PLA beyond Borders: Chinese Military Operations in Regional and Global Context*, Washington DC, National Defense University Press, 2021.
16. Fiona S. Cunningham, *Under the Nuclear Shadow: China's Information-Age Weapons in International Security*, Princeton, Princeton University Press, 2025.
17. Adam R. Grissom, Caitlin Lee and Karl P. Mueller, *Innovation in the United States Air Force: Evidence from Six Cases*, Palo Alto, RAND Corporation, 2016, p. vii.
18. Schmitt, "Wartime Paradigms"; Mikkel Vedby Rasmussen, *The Risk Society at War: Terror, Technology and Strategy in the 21st Century*, Cambridge, Cambridge University Press, 2006.
19. Bastian Giegerich and Maximilian Terhalle, *The Responsibility to Defend: Rethinking Germany's Strategic Culture*, Abingdon, IISS and Routledge, 2021, p. 67.
20. Jeremy Stöhs, *The Decline of European Naval Forces: Challenges to Sea Power in an Age of Fiscal Austerity and Political Uncertainty*, Annapolis, Naval Institute Press, 2018.
21. Anthony King, *The Transformation of Europe's Armed Forces: From the Rhine to Afghanistan*, Cambridge, Cambridge University Press, 2011.
22. Storr, *Something Rotten*.
23. Richard Rosecrance, "Review: Overextension, Vulnerability, and Conflict; The 'Goldilocks Problem' in International Strategy," *International Security*, 19/4, 1995, pp. 145–163.
24. Randal L. Schweller, *Unanswered Threats: Political Constraints on the Balance of Power*, Princeton, Princeton University Press, 2006; Ellis Mallet and Thomas

Juneau, "A Neoclassical Realist Theory of Overbalancing," *Global Studies Quarterly*, 3/2, 2023.
25. Drea, *Japan's Imperial Army*.
26. Michael A. Hunzeker and Alexander Lanoszka, *A Question of Time: Enhancing Taiwan's Conventional Deterrence Posture*, Schar School of Policy and Government, 2018.
27. William E. Odom, *The Collapse of the Soviet Military*, New Haven, Yale University Press, 2000, p. ix.
28. Tanisha Faizal, *Wars of Law: Unintended Consequences in the Regulation of Armed Conflict*, Ithaca, Cornell University Press, 2018.
29. Janina Dill, *Legitimate Targets? Social Construction, International Law, and US Bombing*, Cambridge, Cambridge University Press, 2015.
30. Nicole Deitelhoff and Lisbeth Zimmermann, "Norms under Challenge: Unpacking the Dynamics of Norm Robustness," *Journal of Global Security Studies*, 4/1, 2019, pp. 2–17.
31. Philippe Boulanger, *La géographie, reine des batailles*, Paris, Perrin, 2020.
32. Adrien Estève, *Guerre et écologie. L'environnement et le climat dans les politiques de défense*, Paris, PUF, 2022; Nicolas Regaud, Bastien Alex and François Gemenne (eds.), *La guerre chaude. Enjeux stratégiques du changement climatique*, Paris, Presses de Sciences Po, 2022.
33. Duncan Depledge, "Low-Carbon Warfare: Climate Change, Net Zero and Military Operations," *International Affairs*, 99/2, 2023, pp. 667–685.
34. Andrea Gilli et al., "Climate Change and Military Power: Hunting for Submarines in the Warming Ocean," *Texas National Security Review*, 7/2, 2024, pp. 16–41.
35. Goldman and Eliason, *The Diffusion of Military Technology and Ideas*; Walter Bruyère-Ostells and François Dumasy (eds.), *Pratiques militaires et globalisation*, Paris, Bernard Giovanangeli, 2014.
36. João Resende-Santos, "Anarchy and the Emulation of Military Systems: Military Organizations and Technology in South America, 1870–1930," *Security Studies*, 5/3, 1996, pp. 193–260; João Resende-Santos, *Neorealism, States, and the Modern Mass Army*, Cambridge, Cambridge University Press, 2007.
37. Barry Posen, "Nationalism, the Mass Army, and Military Power," *International Security*, 18/2, 1993, p. 82.
38. David B. Ralston, *Importing the European Army: The Introduction of Military Techniques and Institutions into the Extra-European World, 1600–1914*, Chicago, University of Chicago Press, 1996.
39. Michael A. Bonura, *Under the Shadow of Napoleon: French Influence on the American Way of Warfare from the War of 1812 to the Outbreak of WWII*, New York, New York University Press, 2012.
40. Niall Barr, *Yanks and Limeys: Alliance Warfare in the Second World War*, London, Jonathan Cape, 2015.

41. Lucien Bély and Isabelle Rochefort (eds.), *L'invention de la diplomatie: Moyen-Âge–Temps modernes*, Paris, PUF, 1998; Lucien Bély, *L'art de la paix en Europe. Naissance de la diplomatie moderne*, Paris, PUF, 2007.

42. Alfred Vagts, *The Military Attaché*, Princeton, Princeton University Press, 1967; Maurice Vaïsse, "L'évolution de la fonction d'attaché militaire en France au XXe siècle," *Relations Internationales*, 31–32, 1982, pp. 507–524; Philippe Vial, "Une place à part. Les militaires et les relations extérieures de la France en temps de paix depuis 1870," *Matériaux pour l'Histoire de Notre Temps*, 65–66, 2002, pp. 41–47.

43. Gudrun Persson, *Learning from Foreign Wars: Russian Military Thinking, 1859–73*, London, Helion and Company, 2010.

44. Thomas G. Mahnken, *Uncovering Ways of War: U.S Intelligence and Foreign Military Innovation, 1918–1941*, Ithaca, Cornell University Press, 2001.

45. Martha Finnemore and Kathryn Sikkink, "International Norm Dynamics and Political Change," *International Organization*, 52/4, 1998, p. 891.

46. Theo Farrell, "World Culture and Military Power," *Security Studies*, 14/3, 2005, pp. 448–488.

47. Joelien Pretorius, "The Security Imaginary: Explaining Military Isomorphism," *Security Dialogue*, 39/1, 2008, pp. 99–120.

48. Theo Farrell, "Professionalization and Suicidal Defence Planning by the Irish Army, 1921–1941," *Journal of Strategic Studies*, 21/3, 1998, pp. 67–85. See also Theo Farrell, "Transnational Norms and Military Development: Constructing Ireland's Professional Army," *European Journal of International Relations*, 7/1, 2001, pp. 63–102.

49. Peter Westwick, *Stealth: The Secret Contest to Invent Invisible Aircraft*, Oxford, Oxford University Press, 2020.

50. Andrea Gilli and Mauro Gilli, "Why China Has Not Caught Up Yet: Military-Technological Superiority and the Limits of Imitation, Reverse Engineering, and Cyber Espionage," *International Security*, 43/3, 2019, pp. 141–189.

51. Gregory Barber, "The J-20's Role in Modern Chinese Airpower," *Vortex*, no. 5, 2023, pp. 181–194.

52. Horowitz, *The Diffusion of Military Power*.

53. Michael Raska, *Military Innovation in Small States: Creating a Reverse Asymmetry*, Abingdon, Routledge, 2016.

54. Gerhard Krebs, "World War Zero? Re-assessing the Global Impact of the Russo-Japanese War, 1904–05," *Asia-Pacific Journal*, 10/2, 2012.

55. Barton C. Hacker, "The Weapons of the West: Military Technology and Modernization in 19th-Century China and Japan," *Technology and Culture*, 18/1, 1977, pp. 45–54; Pierre-François Souyri, *Moderne sans être occidental. Aux origines du Japon d'aujourd'hui*, Paris, Gallimard, 2016.

56. D. Eleanor Westney, *Imitation and Innovation: The Transfer of Western Organizational Patterns to Meiji Japan*, Cambridge MA, Harvard University Press, 1987.

57. Vagts, *The Military Attaché*.
58. Yigal Sheffy, "A Model Not to Follow: The European Armies and the Lessons of the War," in Rotem Kowner (ed.), *The Impact of the Russo-Japanese War*, Abingdon, Routledge, 2006, pp. 253–268.
59. William Philpott, *War of Attrition: Fighting the First World War*, New York, Harry Abrams, 2014.
60. Schweller, *Unanswered Threats*.
61. Tor Bukkvoll and Volodymyr Solovian, "The Threat of War and Domestic Restraints to Defence Reform: How Fear of Major Military Conflict Changed and Did Not Change the Ukrainian Military, 2014–2019," *Defence Studies*, 20/1, 2020, pp. 21–38.
62. Colin Elman, "Horses for Courses: Why Not Neorealist Theories of Foreign Policy?," *Security Studies*, 6/1, 1996, pp. 7–53; Kenneth N. Waltz, "International Politics Is Not Foreign Policy," *Security Studies*, 6/1, 1996, pp. 54–57.
63. Peter D. Feaver et al., "Correspondence: Brother Can You Spare a Paradigm (or Was Anybody Ever a Realist?)," *International Security*, 25/1, 2000, pp. 165–169.
64. David A. Baldwin, *Power and International Relations: A Conceptual Approach*, Princeton, Princeton University Press, 2016; Fabrice Argounès, *Théories de la puissance*, Paris, CNRS Éditions, 2018.
65. Hans J. Morgenthau, *Politics among Nations*, New York: Alfred A. Knopf, 1973 (1948).
66. Aron, *Peace and War between Nations*, p. 65. Italics in original.
67. Ibid.
68. John J. Mearsheimer, *The Tragedy of International Politics*, New York, W. W. Norton, 2001.
69. William C. Wohlforth, *The Elusive Balance: Power and Perceptions during the Cold War*, Ithaca, Cornell University Press, 1993.
70. Biddle, *Military Power*, p. 2.
71. Patricia L. Sullivan, *Who Wins: Predicting Strategic Success and Failure in Armed Conflict*, Oxford, Oxford University Press, 2012, p. 7.
72. Michael Beckley, "The Power of Nations: Measuring What Matters," *International Security*, 43/2, 2018, pp. 7–44; Caleb Pomeroy and Michael Beckley, "Correspondence: Measuring Power in International Relations," *International Security*, 44/1, 2019, pp. 197–200; Robert J. Carroll and Brenton Kenkel, "Predictions, Proxies, and Power," *American Journal of Political Science*, 63/3, 2019, pp. 577–593.
73. Mahnken, *Uncovering Ways of War*.
74. Williamson Murray and Allan R. Millett, "Net Assessment on the Eve of World War II," in Williamson Murray and Allan R. Millett (eds.), *Calculations: Net Assessment and the Coming of World War II*, New York, Free Press, 1992, p. 1.
75. Peter Jackson, *France and the Nazi Menace: Intelligence and Policy-Making*,

1933–1939, Oxford, Oxford University Press, 2000; Simon Catros, *La guerre inéluctable. Les chefs militaires français et la politique étrangère, 1935–1939*, Rennes, PUR, 2020; Simon Catros, "Un cas de surinterprétation du renseignement. L'évaluation du potentiel militaire allemand en mars 1936," *Guerres Mondiales et Conflits Contemporains*, 252, 2013, pp. 61–79.

76. Klaus H. Schmider, *Hitler's Fatal Miscalculation: Why Germany Declared War on the United States*, Cambridge, Cambridge University Press, 2022.
77. Keren Yarhi-Milo, *Knowing the Adversary: Leaders, Intelligence, and Assessment of Intentions in International Relations*, Princeton, Princeton University Press, 2014.
78. Philip Towle (ed.), *Estimating Foreign Military Power*, Abingdon, Routledge 1982.
79. James Fearon, "Rationalist Explanations for War," *International Organization*, 49/3, 2017, pp. 379–414; Kristopher W. Ramsay, "Information, Uncertainty, and War," *Annual Review of Political Science*, 20, 2017, pp. 505–527; Christopher Blattman, *Why We Fight: The Roots of War and the Paths to Peace*, New York, Viking, 2022.
80. Tom Dyson, *Neoclassical Realism and Defence Reform in Post-Cold War Europe*, Basingstoke, Palgrave Macmillan, 2010.
81. Zack Cooper, *Tides of Fortune: The Rise and Decline of Great Militaries*, New Haven, Yale University Press, 2025.
82. Frédéric Mérand (ed.), *Coping with Geopolitical Decline: The United States in European Perspective*, Montreal, McGill-Queen's University Press, 2020.
83. Not to mention that they don't know what they don't know. This tripartition refers to a famous speech by Donald Rumsfeld.
84. John Kay and Mervyn King, *Radical Uncertainty: Decision-Making beyond the Numbers*, New York, W. W. Norton, 2020.
85. Per Jacob Lindgaard, "The Challenges of Multiple Doctrines: Evidence from the Danish Army," PhD thesis, University of Southern Denmark, 2023.
86. For summaries of the literature on alliances, see Sten Rynning and Olivier Schmitt, "Alliances," in Alexandra Gheciu and William C. Wohlforth (eds.), *Oxford Handbook of International Security*, Oxford, Oxford University Press, 2018, pp. 653–667.
87. For the challenges facing alliances in the twenty-first century, see Olivier Schmitt, "La recomposition des alliances au XXIe siècle," *La Vie des Idées*, 13 April 2022; Alexander Lanozska, *Military Alliances in the 21st Century*, London, Polity, 2022.
88. James D. Morrow, "Alliances and Asymmetry: An Alternative to the Capability Aggregation Model of Alliances," *American Journal of Political Science*, 35/4, 1991, pp. 904–933.
89. Glenn H. Snyder, *Alliance Politics*, Ithaca, Cornell University Press, 1997.
90. Holger Herwig, "Disjointed Allies: Coalition Warfare in Berlin and Vienna, 1914," *Journal of Military History*, 54, 1990, pp. 265–280; Richard F. Hamilton

and Holger Herwig (eds.), *War Planning 1914*, Cambridge, Cambridge University Press, 2014.
91. Philpott, *War of Attrition*, especially Chapter 2, "Into Battle," pp. 37–60.
92. Elizabeth Greenhalgh, *Victory through Coalition: Britain and France during the First World War*, Cambridge, Cambridge University Press, 2005.
93. Jeffrey W. Taliaferro, Norrin M. Ripsman and Steven E. Lobell, *The Challenge of Grand Strategy: The Great Powers and the Broken Balance between the World Wars*, Cambridge, Cambridge University Press, 2012.
94. Simon Berthon, *Allies at War*, London, Thistle Publishing, 2013 (2001); Mark A. Stoler, *Allies and Adversaries: The Joint Chiefs of Staff, the Grand Alliance, and U.S. Strategy in World War II*, Chapel Hill, University of North Carolina Press, 2003.
95. Jonathan Adelman (ed.), *Hitler and His Allies in World War II*, Abingdon, Routledge, 2007.
96. Hubert Van Tuyll, *Feeding the Bear: American Aid to the Soviet Union, 1941–1945*, Westport, Greenwood Press, 1989.
97. In recent years, the Putin regime's historical revisionism has endeavored to play down the importance of the Lend-Lease program in the USSR's victory, highlighting the 25 million dead suffered by Moscow (who are often presented as Russians, whereas a large proportion came from other USSR territories). It should be noted that witnesses from the period, notably Nikita Khrushchev in his memoirs and Marshal Zhukov in a conversation recorded by the KGB in 1965, both insist on the major role played by American aid in the Soviet victory on the Eastern Front. For the importance of the USSR in the final Allied victory, see Phillips O'Brien, *How the War was Won: Air–Sea Power and Allied Victory in World War II*, Cambridge, Cambridge University Press, 2015; David M. Glantz and Jonathan M. House, *When Titans Clashed: How the Red Army Stopped Hitler*, Lawrence, University Press of Kansas, 1995. For the USSR's creation of the memory of the "Great Patriotic War," see Jonathan Brunstedt, *The Soviet Myth of World War II: Patriotic Memory and the Russian Question in the USSR*, Cambridge, Cambridge University Press, 2021. For the Putin regime's instrumentalization of the memory of the Second World War, see Mark Edele, "Who Won the Second World War and Why Should You Care? Reassessing Stalin's War 75 Years after Victory," *Journal of Strategic Studies*, 43/6–7, 2020, pp. 1039–1062; Jade McGlynn, *Memory Makers: The Politics of the Past in Putin's Russia*, London, Bloomsbury, 2023.
98. Vojtech Mastny, Sven G. Holtsmark and Andreas Wenger (eds.), *War Plans and Alliances in the Cold War: Threat Perceptions in the East and West*, Abingdon, Routledge, 2006.
99. Christopher Jones, "Reflections on Mirror Images: Politics and Technology in the Arsenals of the Warsaw Pact," in Goldman and Eliason, *The Diffusion of Military Technology and Ideas*, pp. 117–145.

100. James Sperling and Mark Webber (eds.), *The Oxford Handbook of NATO*, Oxford, Oxford University Press, 2025.
101. Lucie Béraud-Sudreau and Olivier Schmitt, "Alliance Politics and National Arms Industries: Creating Incentives for Small States?," *European Security*, 33/4, 2024, pp. 711–31.
102. Jenny Raflik-Grenouilleau, *La IVe République et l'Alliance atlantique. Influence et dépendance (1945–1958)*, Rennes, PUR, 2013; Olivier Schmitt, "France and NATO," in Sperling and Webber, *The Oxford Handbook of NATO*, pp. 671–686.
103. Gérard Bossuat, *Les aides américaines économiques et militaires à la France, 1938–1960. Une nouvelle image des rapports de puissance*, Paris, IGPDE, 2011. For the French navy, see Hugues Canuel, *The Fall and Rise of French Sea Power: France's Quest for an Independent Naval Policy, 1940–1963*, Annapolis, Naval Institute Press, 2021.
104. Wallace J. Thies, *Why NATO Endures*, Cambridge, Cambridge University Press, 2009.
105. Thomas-Durrell Young, *Anatomy of Post-Communist Defense Institutions: The Mirage of Military Modernity*, London, Bloomsbury, 2017.
106. Kjell Inge Bjerga and Torunn Laugen Haaland, "Development of Military Doctrine: The Particular Case of Small States," *Journal of Strategic Studies*, 33/4, 2010, pp. 505–533.
107. Srdjan Vucetic and Atsushi Tago, "Why Buy American? The International Politics of Fighter Jet Transfers," *Canadian Journal of Political Science*, 48/1, 2015, pp. 101–124; Stéfanie von Hlatky and Jeffrey Rice, "Striking a Deal on the F-35: Multinational Politics and US Defence Acquisition," *Defence Studies*, 18/1, 2018, pp. 19–38.
108. Frank Maas, *The Price of Alliance: The Politics and Procurement of Leopard Tanks for Canada's NATO Brigade*, Vancouver, UBC Press, 2017.
109. The "lethality" of a weapon is incredibly difficult to measure, and depends on the criteria used for evaluation (penetration, bullet trajectory stability, projectile diffusion, etc.). In addition to the question of lethality, the manufacture of a weapon is a series of trade-offs between several parameters (range, simplicity, accuracy, weight, recoil), which means that the choice of one weapon over another is the result of a social process of determining what constitutes "military effectiveness" at a given moment, rather than of technical characteristics: the same armies may at different times prioritize the accuracy of their shooters, the speed at which to pour a volume of fire (to the detriment of accuracy), or the simplicity in handling the weapon. On this subject, see Matthew Ford, "The Epistemology of Lethality: Bullets, Knowledge Trajectories, Kinetic Effects," *European Journal of International Security*, 5/1, 2020, pp. 77–93.
110. An in-depth history can be found in Matthew Ford, *Weapon of Choice: Small Arms and the Culture of Military Innovation*, London, Hurst, 2017. See

Chapter 6: "Alliance Politics and NATO Standardisation: Interests, Power, Rationality," pp. 117–140.

111. Ulrich Krotz, *Flying Tiger: International Relations Theory and the Politics of Advanced Weapons*, Oxford, Oxford University Press, 2011.
112. Alice Pannier, *Rivals in Arms: The Rise of UK–France Defence Relations in the Twenty-First Century*, Montreal, McGill-Queen's University Press, 2020.
113. James S. Corum, *The Luftwaffe: Creating the Operational Air War, 1918–1940*, Lawrence, University Press of Kansas, 1997; Robert Citino, *The Path to Blitzkrieg: Doctrine and Training in the German Army, 1920–39*, Boulder, Lynne Rienner, 1999.
114. Ian Ona Johnson, *Faustian Bargain: The Soviet–German Partnership and the Origins of the Second World War*, Oxford, Oxford University Press, 2021, p. 4.
115. Abraham Rabinovich, *The Boats of Cherbourg: The Secret Israeli Operation That Revolutionized Naval Warfare*, London, Seaver Books, 1988; Justin Lecarpentier, *Rapt à Cherbourg. L'affaire des vedettes israéliennes*, Louviers, L'Ancre de Marine, 2010.
116. Bruce A. Elleman, *A History of the Modern Chinese Navy, 1840–2020*, Abingdon, Routledge, 2021, p. 101.
117. Terrence G. Peterson, "Networking the Counterrevolution: The École Supérieure de Guerre, Transnational Military Collaboration, and Cold War Counterinsurgency, 1955–1975," *Journal of Social History*, 2022. See also Tenenbaum, *Partisans and Centurions*.
118. Niagalé Bagayoko, "Explaining the Failure of Internationally-Supported Defence and Security Reforms in Sahelian States," *Conflict, Security and Development*, 22/3, 2022, p. 244.
119. Eitan Shamir and Eyal Ben-Ari, "The Rise of Special Operations Forces: Generalized Specialization, Boundary Spanning and Military Autonomy," *Journal of Strategic Studies*, 41/3, 2018, pp. 335–371.
120. Nina Wilén, "The Impact of Security Force Assistance in Niger: Meddling with Borders," *International Affairs*, 98/4, 2022, pp. 1405–1421.
121. Kristen A. Harkness, "Security Force Assistance to Cameroon: How Building Enclave Units Deepens Autocracy," *International Affairs*, 98/6, 2022, pp. 2099–2117.
122. Whitney Grespin and Matthew Marchese, "Things Fall Apart: Soviet Assistance to the Somali Armed Forces, 1960–1977," *Journal of African Military History*, 2022.
123. Renanah Miles Joyce, "Soldiers' Dilemma: Foreign Military Training and Liberal Norm Conflict," *International Security*, 46/4, 2022, pp. 48–90.
124. Derek S. Reveron, *Exporting Security: International Engagement, Security Cooperation, and the Changing Face of the US Military*, Washington DC, Georgetown University Press, 2016; Greg Kennedy (ed.), *Defense Engagement since 1900: Global Lessons in Soft Power*, Lawrence, University Press of Kansas, 2020.

2. THE CHALLENGE OF CIVIL–MILITARY RELATIONS

1. Posen, *The Sources of Military Doctrine*.
2. Bastien Irondelle, "Démocratie, relations civilo-militaires, et efficacité militaire," *Revue Internationale de Politique Comparée*, 15, 2008, pp. 117–131.
3. Deborah Avant, *Political Institutions and Military Change: Lessons from Peripheral Wars*, Ithaca, Cornell University Press, 1994.
4. Risa Brooks and Peter M. Erickson, "The Sources of Military Dissent: Why and How the US Military Contests Civilian Decisions about the Use of Force," *European Journal of International Security*, 7/1, 2022, pp. 38–57.
5. James R. Locher III, *Victory on the Potomac: The Goldwater–Nicholas Act Unifies the Pentagon*, College Station, Texas A&M University Press, 2002.
6. Theo Farrell, *Weapons without a Cause: The Politics of Weapons Acquisition in the United States*, Basingstoke, Palgrave Macmillan, 1997.
7. Daniel Nasaw, "Why Is America Still Flying the A-10 Warthog, a Cold War Relic?," *Wall Street Journal*, 13 April 2023.
8. David Morgan-Owens and Alex Gould, "The Politics of Future War: Civil–Military Relations and Military Doctrine in Britain," *European Journal of International Security*, 7/4, 2022, pp. 551–571.
9. Anit Mukherjee, *The Absent Dialogue: Politicians, Bureaucrats and the Military in India*, Oxford, Oxford University Press, 2019.
10. Samy Cohen, "Monarchie nucléaire, dyarchie conventionnelle," *Pouvoirs*, 38, 1986, pp. 13–20; Delphine Dulong, *Premier ministre*, Paris, CNRS Éditions, 2021.
11. Raoul Girardet, "Pouvoir civil et pouvoir militaire dans la France contemporaine," *Revue Française de Science Politique*, 10/1, 1960, p. 3.
12. Olivier Schmitt, "Accompagner les mutations de la puissance française. De 1962 à nos jours," in Hervé Drévillon and Olivier Wieviorka (eds.), *Histoire militaire de la France II. De 1870 à nos jours*, Paris, Perrin, 2018, pp. 623–624.
13. Pierre Messmer, *Après tant de batailles … Mémoires*, Paris, Albin Michel, 1992.
14. Alain Peyrefitte, *C'était de Gaulle*, Paris, Éditions de Fallois, 1997, vol. 2, p. 119.
15. Frédéric Turpin, *Pierre Messmer*, Paris, Perrin, 2020.
16. Sten Rynning, *Changing Military Doctrine: Presidents and Military Power in Fifth Republic France, 1958–2000*, Westport, Praeger, 2002.
17. Bastien Irondelle, *La réforme des armées en France. Sociologie de la décision*, Paris, Presses de Sciences Po, 2011, p. 29.
18. Sébastien Jakubowski, *La professionnalisation de l'armée française. Conséquences sur l'autorité*, Paris, L'Harmattan, 2007.
19. Sümbül Kaya, "Vers une hybridation idéologique au sein de l'armée turque?," *Confluences Méditerranée*, no. 122, 2022, pp. 183–196.
20. Nicole Jenne and Rafael Martínez, "Domestic Military Missions in Latin America: Civil–Military Relations and the Perpetuation of Democratic Deficits," *European Journal of International Security*, 7/1, 2022, pp. 58–83.

21. Massensen Cherbi, "L'armée algérienne face à la revendication d'un 'état civil, non-militaire,'" *Confluences Méditerranée*, no. 122, 2022, pp. 77–98.
22. Sara Tonsy, "The Egyptian Army in the Political and Economic Fields since 2013: A Neo-military Society," *Confluences Méditerranée*, no. 122, 2022, pp. 129–142.
23. Fabrizio Coticchia, and Marco Di Giulio, "What Makes Paradigms Last? A Study of Defense Policy Change in Germany and Italy (1989–2022)," *Journal of European Public Policy*, 32/7, 2024, pp. 1831–1860.
24. M. Taylor Fravel, *Active Defense: China's Military Strategy since 1949*, Princeton, Princeton University Press, 2019.
25. Thomas M. Nichols, *The Sacred Cause: Civil–Military Conflict over Soviet National Security, 1917–1992*, Ithaca, Cornell University Press, 1993. See also Kimberley Marten Zisk, *Engaging the Enemy: Organization Theory and Soviet Military Innovation, 1955–1991*, Princeton, Princeton University Press, 1993.
26. Alfred J. Rieber, *Stalin as Warlord*, Yale, Yale University Press, 2022.
27. Zoltan Barany, *Democratic Breakdown and the Decline of the Russian Military*, Princeton, Princeton University Press, 2007.
28. Olivier Schmitt, "How to Challenge an International Order: Russian Diplomatic Practices in Multilateral Security Organisations," *European Journal of International Relations*, 26/3, 2020, pp. 922–946; Mark Galeotti, *Putin's Wars: From Chechnya to Ukraine*, Oxford, Osprey, 2022.
29. Roger N. McDermott, *The Reform of Russia's Conventional Armed Forces: Problems, Challenges, and Policy Implications*, Washington DC, Jamestown Foundation, 2011.
30. Kirill Shamiev, "Against a Bitter Pill: The Role of Interest Groups in Armed Forces Reform in Russia," *Armed Forces and Society*, 47/2, 2021, pp. 319–342.
31. Aleksandr Golts, *Military Reform and Militarism in Russia*, Washington DC, Jamestown Foundation, 2018.
32. Lawrence Freedman, *Command: The Politics of Military Operations from Korea to Ukraine*, London, Allen Lane, 2022, p. 514.
33. Kirill Shamiev, "Civil–Military Relations and Russia's Post-Soviet Military Culture: A Belief System Analysis," *Armed Forces and Society*, 2022.
34. Sally W. Stoecker, *Forging Stalin's Army: Marshal Tukhachevsky and the Politics of Military Innovation*, Boulder, Westview Press, 1998.
35. Jean Lopez and Lasha Otkhmezuri, *Joukov: L'homme qui a vaincu Hitler*, 2nd ed., Paris, Perrin, 2019, p. 183.
36. Richard Overy and Andrew Wheatcroft, *The Road to War*, London, Vintage Books, 2009; Peter Whitewood, *The Red Army and the Great Terror: Stalin's Purge of the Soviet Military*, Lawrence, University Press of Kansas, 2015.
37. Caitlin Talmadge, *The Dictator's Army: Battlefield Effectiveness in Authoritarian Regimes*, Ithaca, Cornell University Press, 2015.

38. Pierre Razoux, *La guerre Iran–Irak. Première guerre du Golfe, 1980–1988*, Paris, Perrin, 2013.
39. Thomas Crosbie (ed.), *Military Politics: New Perspectives*, London, Berghahn, 2023.
40. Adam Smith, *An Inquiry into the Nature and Causes of the Wealth of Nations*, 1776, online, p. 396, available at http://gesd.free.fr/smith76bis.pdf.
41. Tilly, *Coercion, Capital, and European States, AD 990–1992*; Fortmann, *The Cycles of Mars*.
42. Chin-Hao Huang and David C. Kang, *State Formation through Emulation: The East Asian Model*, Cambridge, Cambridge University Press, 2022.
43. Priya Satia, *Empire of Guns: The Violent Making of the Industrial Revolution*, New York, Penguin Press, 2018.
44. See the four volumes of Michael Mann's powerful synthesis, *The Sources of Social Power*, Cambridge, Cambridge University Press, 2012, as well as Brian D. Taylor and Roxana Botea, "Tilly Tally: War-Making and State-Making in the Contemporary Third World," *International Studies Review*, 10/1, 2008, pp. 27–56; Cameron Thies and David Sobek, "War, Economic Development, and Political Development in the Contemporary International System," *International Studies Quarterly*, 54/1, 2010, pp. 267–287; Sebastián Mazzuca, *Latecomer State Formation: Political Geography and Capacity Failure in Latin America*, New Haven, Yale University Press, 2021; Jean-François Bayart, *L'énergie de l'état. Pour une sociologie historique et comparée du politique*, Paris, La Découverte, 2022.
45. Rosella Cappella Zielinski, *How States Pay for Wars*, Ithaca, Cornell University Press, 2016.
46. Jurgen Brauer and Hubert van Tuyll, *Castles, Battles, and Bombs: How Economics Explains Military History*, Chicago, University of Chicago Press, 2008.
47. Lindsay P. Cohn and Nathan W. Toronto, "Markets and Manpower: The Political Economy of Compulsory Military Service," *Armed Forces and Society*, 43/3, 2016, pp. 436–458.
48. Lindsay P. Cohn, "Who Will Serve? Labour Markets and Military Personnel Policy," *Res Militaris*, 3/2, 2013, online.
49. Obviously, the average voter is an abstraction that can be used to construct explanatory models of voting. For an overview of this literature and its critics, see Torun Dewan and Kenneth A. Shepsle, "Political Economy Models of Elections," *Annual Review of Political Science*, 14, 2011, pp. 311–330.
50. Jonathan D. Caverley, *Democratic Militarism: Voting, Wealth, and War*, Cambridge, Cambridge University Press, 2014.
51. Sarah Kreps, *Taxing Wars: The American Way of War Finance and the Decline of Democracy*, Oxford, Oxford University Press, 2018.
52. G. C. Peden, *Arms, Economics, and British Strategy: From Dreadnoughts to Hydrogen Bombs*, Cambridge, Cambridge University Press, 2007.
53. Joseph L. Votel, Francis A. Finelli and Samuel Cole, "Leveraging U.S. Capital

Markets to Support the Future Industrial Network," *War on the Rocks*, 11 January 2023.
54. Charlotte Halpern, Pierre Lascoumes and Patrick Le Galès, "Instrument," in Laurie Boussaguet, Sophie Jacquot and Pauline Ravinet (eds.), *Dictionnaire des politiques publiques*, 5th ed., Paris, Presses de Sciences Po, 2019, p. 321; Pierre Lascoumes and Patrick Le Galès (eds.), *Gouverner par les instruments*, Paris, Presses de Sciences Po, 2005.
55. Fabien Cardoni, "La lente 'civilianisation' des finances de la défense, XIXe–XXIe siècle," in Fabien Cardoni, Matthieu Conan, Etienne Douat and Céline Viessant (eds.), *Singularité des finances de la défense et de la sécurité*, Paris, Mare et Martin, 2021, pp. 23–40.
56. The land component was later abandoned.
57. Fabien Cardoni, *Le futur empêché. Une histoire financière de la défense en France (1945–1974)*, Paris, Éditions de la Sorbonne, 2022, p. 233.
58. Josselin Droff and Julien Malizard, "Cohérence entre politique budgétaire et budget de défense en France," *Revue Défense Nationale*, 769, 2014, pp. 116–121.
59. Catherine Hoeffler and Jean Joana, "The Impact of Austerity: Spending Cuts, Coping Strategies and Institutional Change in the Case of French Defense Policy," *Defence Studies*, 22/3, 2022, pp. 448–463.
60. Bastien Irondelle, "Qui contrôle le nerf de la guerre? Financement et politique de défense," in Philippe Bezes and Alexandre Siné (eds.), *Gouverner (par) les finances publiques*, Paris, Presses de Sciences Po, 2011, pp. 491–523.
61. Schmitt, "Accompagner les mutations," p. 614.
62. Interview with the author, June 2021.
63. Jennifer Mittelstadt and Mark R. Wilson, "The Politics of US Military Privatizations, 1945–2000," in Jennifer Mittelstadt and Mark R. Wilson (eds.), *The Military and the Market*, Philadelphia, University of Pennsylvania Press, 2022, p. 13.
64. Aaron L. Friedberg, *In the Shadow of the Garrison State: America's Anti-statism and Its Cold War Grand Strategy*, Princeton, Princeton University Press, 2000.
65. Mittelstadt and Wilson, "The Politics of US Military Privatizations," p. 15.
66. Philippe Bezes, *Reinventing the state: Les réformes de l'administration française (1962–2008)*, Paris, PUF, 2009.
67. Violette Larrieu, "La mise en oeuvre des préceptes du New Public Management dans les soutiens des armées françaises. Échec ou réussite?," *Les Champs de Mars*, 30, 2018, pp. 67–75.
68. Léo Péria-Peigné, "Stocks militaires. Une assurance-vie en haute intensité?," *Focus Stratégique*, no. 113, IFRI, 2022.
69. Patrick Bury, "Conceptualizing the Quiet Revolution: The Post Fordist Revolution in Western Military Logistics," *European Security*, 30/1, 2021, pp. 112–136.

70. Claude Weber, *À genou les hommes. Debout les officiers. La socialisation des Saint-Cyriens*, Rennes, Presses Universitaires de Rennes, 2012.
71. Heinrich Hartmann, *The Body Populace: Military Statistics and Demography in Europe before the First World War*, Cambridge MA, MIT Press, 2011.
72. "Marching on Their Stomachs," *The Economist*, 21 January 2023.
73. Tom Phuong Le, *Japan's Aging Peace: Pacifism and Militarism in the Twenty-First Century*, New York, Columbia University Press, 2021.
74. March Bloch, *L'histoire, la guerre, la résistance*, Paris, Gallimard, 2006, pp. 548–549.
75. Mathieu Merly, *Distinguer et soumettre. Une histoire sociale de l'armée française (1872–1914)*, Rennes, Presses Universitaires de Rennes, 2019, p. 250.
76. General Patton is quoted as saying, "If they don't fuck, they don't fight."
77. Emma Moore, "Women in Combat: Five-Year Status Update," *Center for a New American Security*, 31 March 2020.
78. See chapters in Beth Bailey et al. (eds.), *Managing Sex in the U.S. Military: Gender, Identity, and Behavior*, Lincoln, University of Nebraska Press, 2022.
79. Elyamine Settoul, "Un regard sur la présence des descendants de l'immigration au sein des institutions sécuritaires françaises," *Migrations Société*, no. 169, 2017, pp. 13–24.
80. Frédéric Jonnet, "Diversifier les élites militaires. Réalités et défis," *Migrations Société*, no. 169, 2017, pp. 53–68.
81. René Backmann, "L'armée israélienne en danger de 'théocratisation'?," *Confluences Méditerranée*, no. 122, 2022, pp. 167–182.
82. Amit Ahuja, "India," in Ron E. Hassner (ed.), *Religion in the Military Worldwide*, Cambridge, Cambridge University Press, 2013, pp. 159–178.
83. Sanna Strand, "The Reactivation and Reimagination of Military Conscription in Sweden," *Armed Forces and Society*, 2023.
84. Vincent Rubio, "Le regard sociologique sur la foule au XIXe siècle," *Mil Neuf Cent. Revue d'Histoire Intellectuelle*, no. 28, 2010, pp. 13–33.
85. Title of Chapter 1 of Jan-Werner Müller, *Difficile démocratie. Les idées politiques en Europe au XXe siècle, 1918–1989*, Paris, Alma Éditeur, 2013.
86. Azar Gat, *Fascists and Liberal Visions of War: Fuller, Liddell Hart, Douhet and Other Modernists*, Oxford, Oxford University Press, 1998.
87. Quoted in A. J. Echevarria II, *War's Logic: Strategic Thought and the American Way of War*, Cambridge, Cambridge University Press, 2021, p. 45.
88. Olivier Schmitt, "Penser les effets. L'importance des sciences sociales pour la pensée stratégique aérienne," *Vortex*, no. 2, 2021, p. 113.
89. Dmitry Adamsky, *Russian Nuclear Orthodoxy: Religion, Politics, and Strategy*, Palo Alto, Stanford University Press, 2019.
90. Mahsa Rouhi, "Iran," in Hassner, *Religion in the Military Worldwide*, pp. 143–158; Stéphane A. Dudoignon, *Les gardiens de la révolution islamique d'Iran*, Paris, CNRS Éditions, 2022.
91. Adamsky, *Russian Nuclear Orthodoxy*, pp. 10–11.

3. TECHNOLOGY AND MILITARY CHANGE

1. Jeremy Black, *War and Technology*, Bloomington, Indiana University Press, 2013.
2. Martin van Creveld, *Technology and War: From 2000 B.C. to the Present*, 2nd ed., New York, Free Press, 1991, p. 1.
3. W. Brian Arthur, *The Nature of Technology: What It Is and How It Evolves*, London, Allen Lane, 2009.
4. Jeffrey Ding and Allan Dafoe, "Engines of Power: Electricity, AI, and General-Purpose, Military Transformations," *European Journal of International Security*, 8/3, 2023, pp. 377–394.
5. Wiebe E. Bijker, Thomas P. Hughes and Trevor Pinch (eds.), *The Social Construction of Technological Systems*, Cambridge MA, MIT Press, 1990.
6. Daniel R. McCarthy (ed.), *Technology and World Politics: An Introduction*, Abingdon, Routledge, 2018.
7. Bruno Latour, *Changer de société. Refaire de la sociologie*, Paris, La Découverte, 2006.
8. Alvin and Heidi Toffler, *War and Anti-War: Survival at the Dawn of the 21st Century*, New York, Warner Books, 1995, p. 30.
9. François Furet, *Le passé d'une illusion. Essai sur l'idée communiste au XXe siècle*, Paris, Robert Laffont, 1995, p. 53.
10. Buzan and Herring call this stage "maintenance." See Barry Buzan and Eric Herring, *The Arms Dynamics in World Politics*, Boulder, Lynne Rienner, 1998.
11. Hedley Bull, *The Control of the Arms Race: Disarmament and Arms Control in the Nuclear Age*, London, Weidenfeld and Nicolson for the Institute for Strategic Studies, 1961, p. 5.
12. Geoffrey Till, *Asia's Naval Expansion: An Arms Race in the Making?*, Abingdon, Routledge, 2012.
13. Joseph A. Maiolo, "Course aux armements, désarmement et contrôle des armements," in Taillat, Henrotin and Schmitt, *Guerre et stratégie*, pp. 397–423.
14. Ken Booth and Nicholas Wheeler, *The Security Dilemma: Fear, Cooperation, and Trust in World Politics*, Basingstoke, Palgrave Macmillan, 2008.
15. Thomas Mahnken, Joseph A. Maiolo and David Stevenson (eds.), *Arms Races in International Politics: From the Nineteenth to the Twenty-First Century*, Oxford, Oxford University Press, 2016.
16. Avi Kober, "Arms Races and the Arab–Israeli Conflict," in Mahnken, Maiolo and Stevenson, *Arms Races in International Politics*, pp. 205–224.
17. Steven A. Pomeroy, *An Untaken Road: Strategy, Technology and the Hidden History of America's Mobile ICBMs*, Annapolis, Naval Institute Press, 2016.
18. Michael Horowitz, Joshua Schwartz and Matthew Fuhrmann, "Who's Prone to Drone? A Global Time-Series Analysis of Armed Uninhabited Aerial Vehicle Proliferation," *Conflict Management and Peace Science*, 39/2, 2022, pp. 119–142.

19. Lilach Gilady, *The Price of Prestige: Conspicuous Consumption in International Relations*, Chicago, University of Chicago Press, 2018.
20. Susan Turner Hayes, "The Power of Prestige: Explaining China's Nuclear Weapons Decisions," *Asian Security*, 16/1, 2020, pp. 35–52.
21. We won't go into detail here about "hybrid" systems such as maneuvering ballistic missile warheads (MaRV) and fractional orbit bombardment systems (FOBS).
22. David Pappalardo, "Hypersonique. Entre rhétorique et réalité," *Vortex*, no. 3, 2022, pp. 41–54.
23. Dominika Kunertova, "Hypersonic Weapons: Emerging, Disruptive, Political," in Brian G. Carlson and Oliver Thränert (eds.), *Strategic Trends 2022*, Zürich, ETH Center for Security Studies, 2022, pp. 43–67.
24. David Edgerton, *The Shock of the Old: Technology and Global History since 1900*, London, Profile Books, 2006.
25. Center d'Étude de Politique Étrangère, Report of the Study Committee of the Atlantic Organization, "NATO and the Rearmament of the West," *Politique Étrangère*, 18/5, 1953, pp. 406–407.
26. Norman Augustine, *Augustine's Laws*, London, Penguin, 1987.
27. Keith Hartley, "Rising Costs: Augustine Revisited," *Defence and Peace Economics*, 31/4, 2020, pp. 434–442.
28. Edward Luttwak, "Les armements peuvent-ils devenir 'abordables,'" *Politique Étrangère*, 4, 2007, pp. 773–786.
29. John A. Alic, *Trillions for Military Technology: How the Pentagon Innovates and Why It Costs So Much*, Basingstoke, Palgrave, 2007.
30. William C. Martel, *Victory in War: Foundations of Modern Strategy*, 2nd ed., Cambridge, Cambridge University Press, 2012.
31. Michel Goya, "Dix millions de dollars le milicien. La crise du modèle occidental de guerre limitée de haute technologie," *Politique Étrangère*, 1, 2007, p. 191.
32. Jon R. Lindsay and Eric Gartzke, "Politics by Many Other Means: The Comparative Strategic Advantages of Operational Domains," *Journal of Strategic Studies*, 5, 2022, pp. 743–776.
33. Audrey Kurth Cronin, *Power to the People: How Open Technological Innovation Is Arming Tomorrow's Terrorists*, Oxford, Oxford University Press, 2019.
34. T. X. Hammes, *Deglobalization and International Security*, Amherst, Cambria Press, 2019.
35. Michael C. Horowitz, "Battles of Precise Mass: Technology is Remaking War – and America Must Adapt," *Foreign Affairs*, 103/6, 2024.
36. Simona R. Soare, Pavneet Singh and Meia Nouwens, *Software-Defined Defense: Algorithms at War*, International Institute for Strategic Studies, 2023.
37. Jacquelyn Schneider and Julia Macdonald, "Looking Back to Look Forward: Autonomous Systems, Military Revolutions and the Importance of Cost," *Journal of Strategic Studies*, 47/2, 2024, pp. 162–184.

38. Antoine Bousquet, *The Scientific Way of Warfare: Order and Chaos on the Battlefield of Modernity*, London, Hurst, 2009, p. 3.
39. Sean T. Lawson, *Nonlinear Science and Warfare: Chaos, Complexity and the US Military in the Information Age*, Abingdon, Routledge, 2014. Alan Beyerchen's article, "Clausewitz, Non-linearity and the Unpredictability of War," *International Security*, 17/3, 1992–3, pp. 59–90 is a milestone in the adoption of complexity theories by US defense circles.
40. Joseph Henrotin, *The Art of War in the Network Age*, London, ISTE Editions, 2017.
41. Thomas G. Mahnken, *Technology and the American Way of War since 1945*, New York, Columbia University Press, 2008; Joseph Henrotin, *La technologie militaire en question. Le cas américain*, Paris, Economica, 2008; Lake, *The Pursuit of Technological Superiority*.
42. Rebecca Slayton, *Arguments That Count: Physics, Computing and Missile Defense, 1949–2012*, Cambridge MA, MIT Press, 2013.
43. Westwick, *Stealth;* Adam B. Young, "The Genesis of the First Strategic Stealth Bomber: Understanding the Interactions between Strategy, Bureaucracy, Politics, and Technology," *Journal of Strategic Studies*, 46/6–7, 2023, pp. 1364–1382.
44. Julie Le Gac and Nicolas Patin, *Guerres mondiales. Le désastre et le deuil, 1914–1945*, Paris, Armand Colin, 2022, p. 55.
45. Olivier Razac, *Histoire politique du barbelé*, Paris, La Fabrique, 2000.
46. Joanna Spear, *The Business of Armaments: Armstrongs, Vickers and the International Arms Trade, 1855–1955*, Cambridge, Cambridge University Press, 2023
47. Friedberg, *In the Shadow of the Garrison State*.
48. This theme is the subject of a voluminous literature. See, for example, Warren Chin, "Technology, War and the State: Past, Present and Future," *International Affairs*, 95/4, 2019, pp. 765–783; M. Susan Lindee, *Rational Fog: Science and Technology in Modern War*, Cambridge MA, Harvard University Press, 2020.
49. Christoph Bluth, "The Soviet Union and the Cold War: Assessing the Technological Dimension," *Journal of Slavic Military Studies*, 23/2, 2010, pp. 282–305.
50. Evan A. Feigenbaum, *China's Techno-Warriors: National Security and Strategic Competition from the Nuclear to the Information Age*, Palo Alto, Stanford University Press, 2003; Tai Ming Cheung, *Innovate to Dominate: The Rise of the Chinese Techno-Security State*, Ithaca, Cornell University Press, 2022.
51. Richard A. Bitzinger, "China's Shift from Civil–Military Integration to Military–Civil Fusion," *Asia Policy*, 28/1, 2021, pp. 5–24.
52. Yaakov Katz and Amir Bohbot, *The Weapon Wizards: How Israel Became a High-Tech Military Superpower*, New York, St Martin's Press, 2017; Edward N. Luttwak and Eitan Shamir, *The Art of Military Innovation: Lessons from the Israel Defense Forces*, Cambridge MA, Harvard University Press, 2023.

53. Klaus Schwab, *The Fourth Industrial Revolution*, New York, Crown Publishing, 2016.
54. Morten Skumsrud Andersen and Erik Reichborn-Kjennerud, "The Unsolicited Rocket: A Story of Science, Technology, and Future Wars," *Critical Military Studies*, 9/3, 2023, pp. 364–383.
55. Matthew Ford, *War in the Smartphone Age: Conflict, Connectivity, and the Crisis at Our Fingertips*, London, Hurst, 2025.
56. The "agent–principal problem" refers to a set of problems encountered when the action of one economic actor, referred to as the "principal," depends on the action or nature of another actor, the "agent," over which the principal is imperfectly informed and has limited control.
57. Marc R. De Vore, "The Arms Collaboration Dilemma: Between Principal–Agent Dynamics and Collective Action Problems," *Security Studies*, 20/4, 2011, pp. 624–662.
58. Antonio Calcara, *European Defence Decision-Making: Dilemmas of Collaborative Arms Procurement*, Abingdon, Routledge, 2020.
59. Josselin Droff and Julien Malizard, "50 Shades of Procurement: The European Defense Trilemma in Defense Procurement Strategies," *Economics of Peace and Security*, 18/1, 2023.
60. Samuel B. H. Faure, *Avec ou sans l'Europe. Le dilemme de la politique française d'armement*, Brussels, Éditions de l'Université de Bruxelles, 2020.
61. Detlef Puhl, "La coopération en matière d'armement entre la France et l'Allemagne. Une entente impossible?," IFRI, *Visions Franco-Allemandes*, no. 31, 2020, p. 13.
62. Ronan Le Gleut and Hélène Conway-Mouret, *2040, l'odyssée du SCAF. Le système de combat aérien du futur*, Rapport d'Information no. 642 (2019–2020), made on behalf of the Senate Committee on Foreign Affairs, Defense and Armed Forces, submitted on 15 July 2020, pp. 57–58.
63. Calestous Juma, *Innovation and Its Enemies: Why People Resist New Technologies*, Oxford, Oxford University Press, 2016.
64. Frédéric Chauviré, *Histoire de la cavalerie*, Paris, Perrin, 2013.
65. Roman Jarymowycz, *Cavalry from Hoof to Track*, Westport, Praeger, 2008.
66. See, for example, David E. Johnson, *Fast Tanks and Heavy Bombers: Innovation in the U.S. Army, 1917–1945*, Ithaca, Cornell University Press, 1998; Mary R. Habeck, *Storm of Steel: The Development of Armor Doctrine in Germany and the Soviet Union, 1919–1939*, Ithaca, Cornell University Press, 2003.
67. Steven A. Fino, *Tiger Check: Automating the US Air Force Fighter Pilot in Air-to-Air Combat, 1950–1980*, Baltimore, Johns Hopkins University Press, 2017.
68. Michael W. Hankins, *Flying Camelot: The F-15, the F-16, and the Weaponization of Fighter Pilot Nostalgia*, Ithaca, Cornell University Press, 2021.
69. Terry C. Pierce, *Warfighting and Disruptive Technologies: Disguising Innovation*, Abingdon, Routledge, 2004.
70. Timothy S. Wolters, *Information at Sea: Shipboard Command and Control in the*

U.S. Navy, from Mobile Bay to Okinawa, Baltimore, Johns Hopkins University Press, 2013, p. 225.
71. Henrotin, *La technologie militaire en question*.
72. Jon R. Lindsay, *Information Technology and Military Power*, Ithaca, Cornell University Press, 2020, p. 7.
73. "Find, fix, finish, exploit and analyze." The central idea was to create a very rapid cycle of target identification and near-immediate exploitation of intelligence found on the site of intervention to identify new targets, thus creating a very high tempo of operations aimed at weakening and ultimately dismantling insurgent networks. See Stanley McChrystal, "It Takes a Network: The New Front Line of Modern Warfare," *Foreign Policy*, 21 February 2011.
74. Jon R. Lindsay, "Target Practice: Counterterrorism and the Amplification of Data Friction," *Science, Technology, and Human Values*, 42/6, 2017, pp. 1061–1099.
75. Lindsay, *Information Technology and Military Power*.
76. Chris C. Demchak, *Military Organizations, Complex Machines: Modernization in the U.S. Armed Services*, Ithaca, Cornell University Press, 1993.
77. Christopher G. Pernin et al., *Lessons from the Army's Future Combat Systems Program*, Santa Monica, RAND Corporation, 2012.
78. Benjamin M. Jensen, Christopher Whyte and Scott Cuomo, *Information in War: Military Innovation, Battle Networks, and the Future of Artificial Intelligence*, Washington DC, Georgetown University Press, 2022, p. 55.
79. Colin S. Gray, "Dowding and the British Strategy of Air Defense, 1936–1940," in Williamson Murray and Richart Hart Sinnreich (eds.), *Successful Strategies: Triumphing in War and Peace from Antiquity to the Present*, Cambridge, Cambridge University Press, 2014, pp. 241–279.
80. Barry Watts, *Six Decades of Guided Munitions and Battle Networks: Progress and Prospects*, Center for Strategic and Budgetary Assessments, 2007.
81. Jensen, Whyte and Cuomo, *Information in War*.
82. Tor Bukkvoll, "Iron Cannot Fight: The Role of Technology in Current Russian Military Theory," *Journal of Strategic Studies*, 34/5, 2011, pp. 681–706.
83. Minic, *Russian Strategic Thought and Culture*.
84. Rebecca A. Adelman, "Security Glitches: The Failure of the Universal Camouflage Pattern and the Fantasy of 'Identity Intelligence,'" *Science, Technology, and Human Values*, 43/3, 2018, pp. 431–463.
85. Markus Pöhlmann, *Der Panzer und die Mechanisierung des Krieges. Eine Deutsche Geschichte, 1890 bis 1945*, Paderborn, Schöningh, 2016; Alaric Searle, *Armoured Warfare: A Military, Political and Global History*, London, Bloomsbury, 2017.
86. O'Hara and Heinz, *Innovating Victory*.
87. Timothy P. Schultz, "Remote Warfare: A New Architecture of Air Power," in Phil M. Haun, Colin F. Jackson and Timothy P. Schultz (eds.), *Air Power*

in the Age of Primacy: Air Warfare since the Cold War, Cambridge, Cambridge University Press, 2022, p. 29.
88. Murray and Millet, Military Innovation in the Interwar Period.
89. H. Christian Breede, Stéphanie A. H. Bélanger and Stéfanie von Hlatky (eds.), Transhumanizing War: Performance Enhancement and the Implications for Policy, Society and the Soldier, Montreal, McGill-Queen's University Press, 2020.

4. THE INTERNAL DYNAMICS OF MILITARY ORGANIZATIONS

1. Christophe Wasinski, "La notion de culture stratégique dans les études stratégiques," in Taillat, Henrotin and Schmitt, Guerre et stratégie, pp. 131–147.
2. Jack Snyder, The Soviet Strategic Culture: Implications for Limited Nuclear Operations, Santa Monica, RAND Corporation, 1977, p. 8.
3. Alastair I. Johnston, Cultural Realism: Strategic Culture and Grand Strategy in Chinese History, Princeton, Princeton University Press, 1995.
4. Colin S. Gray, "Strategic Culture as Context: The First Generation of Theory Strikes Back," Review of International Studies, 25/1, 1999, pp. 49–69.
5. Alan Bloomfield, "Time to Move On: Reconceptualizing the Strategic Culture Debate," Contemporary Security Policy, 33/3, 2012, pp. 437–461.
6. Olivier Schmitt, "Strategic Users of Culture: German Decisions for Military Action," Contemporary Security Policy, 33/1, 2012, pp. 59–81.
7. Olivier Schmitt, "Les spécificités de la culture stratégique française," Défense et Sécurité Internationale, Special Edition 31, 2013, pp. 38–42.
8. Quoted in Christian Malis, Raymond Aron et le débat stratégique français, Paris, Economica, 2005, p. 578.
9. Olivier Schmitt, "Opérations extérieures et 'culture stratégique' française," in Julian Fernandez and Jean-Baptiste Jeangène Vilmer (eds.), Les opérations extérieures de la France, Paris, CNRS Éditions, 2020, pp. 48–49.
10. Chiara Ruffa, Military Cultures in Peace and Stability Operations: Afghanistan and Lebanon, Philadelphia, University of Pennsylvania Press, 2018, p. 3.
11. Jeffrey W. Donnithorne, Four Guardians: A Principled Agent View of American Civil–Military Relations, Baltimore, Johns Hopkins University Press, 2021.
12. Peter R. Mansoor and Williamson Murray (eds.), The Culture of Military Organizations, Cambridge, Cambridge University Press, 2019.
13. Brian McAllister Linn, The Echo of Battle: The Army's Way of War, Cambridge MA, Harvard University Press, 2007.
14. Peter Lorge, Sun Tzu in the West: The Anglo-American Art of War, Cambridge, Cambridge University Press, 2022. For an introduction to non-Western strategic thought, see Delphine Allès, Sonia le Gouriellec and Mélissa Levaillat (eds.), Paix et sécurité. Une anthologie décentrée, Paris, CNRS Éditions, 2023.

15. On the projection of cultural biases onto the adversary, see Ken Booth, *Strategy and Ethnocentrism*, Abingdon, Routledge, 1979. On the tendency to "exoticize" non-Western adversaries and the illusion of finding the "key" to understanding their reasoning, see Patrick Porter, *Military Orientalism: Eastern War through Western Eyes*, London, Hurst, 2010.
16. Ilya Yabolokov, *Fortress Russia: Conspiracy Theories in the Post-Soviet World*, London, Polity, 2018.
17. Martin Kragh, Erik Andermo and Liliia Makashova, "Conspiracy Theories in Russian Security Thinking," *Journal of Strategic Studies*, 45/3, 2022, pp. 334–368.
18. Stéphane François and Olivier Schmitt, "L'extrême droite française contemporaine et le monde. Une vision 'alternative' des relations internationales," *Interrogations*, 21, 2015, online.
19. Minic, *Pensée et culture stratégique russe*.
20. Elizabeth Kier, *Imagining War: French and British Military Doctrine between the Wars*, Princeton, Princeton University Press, 1997.
21. Craig M. Cameron, *American Samurai: Myth, Imagination, and the Conduct of Battle in the First Marine Division, 1941–1951*, Cambridge, Cambridge University Press, 1995.
22. Dima Adamsky, *The Culture of Military Innovation: The Impact of Cultural Factors on the Revolution in Military Affairs in Russia, the U.S., and Israel*, Palo Alto, Stanford University Press, 2010.
23. Terry Terriff, Frans Osinga and Theo Farrell (eds.), *A Transformation Gap? American Innovations and European Military Change*, Palo Alto, Stanford University Press, 2010; David J. Galbreath, "Western European Armed Forces and the Modernisation Agenda: Following or Falling Behind?," *Defence Studies*, 14/4, 2014, pp. 394–413.
24. Ina Wiesner, *Importing the American Way of War? Network-Centric Warfare in the UK and Germany*, Berlin, Nomos Verlag, 2013.
25. Ben Zweibelson, *Beyond the Pale: Designing Military Decision-Making Anew*, Maxwell, Air University Press, 2023.
26. Ben Zweibelson, *Understanding the Military Design Movement: War, Change and Innovation*, Abingdon, Routledge, 2023.
27. Captain Jeremy Stocker, *Architects of Continental Seapower: Comparing Tirpitz and Gorshkov*, Abingdon, Routledge, 2021, p. 183.
28. Kerry Longhurst, *Germany and the Use of Force*, Manchester, Manchester University Press, 2004.
29. David Collier and Gerardo L. Munck (eds.), *Critical Junctures and Historical Legacies: Insights and Methods for Comparative Social Science*, London, Rowman and Littlefield, 2022.
30. Ruffa, *Military Cultures in Peace and Stability Operations*. Ruffa also details the subcultures of specific units, such as the Ariete and Alpini in Italy, or the 1st

Régiment de Tirailleurs and the 8th Régiment Parachutiste d'Infanterie de Marine in France.
31. Finnemore and Sikkink, "International Norm Dynamics and Political Change."
32. Eric Hobsbawm and Terence Ranger, *The Invention of Tradition*, Cambridge, Cambridge University Press, 1983.
33. Oleg Benesch, *Inventing the Way of the Samurai: Nationalism, Internationalism, and Bushido in Modern Japan*, Cambridge, Cambridge University Press, 2014.
34. Garren Mulloy, *Defenders of Japan: The Post-Imperial Armed Forces, 1946–2016*, London, Hurst, 2021; Christopher Hughes, *Japan as a Global Military Power: New Capabilities, Alliance Integration, Bilateralism-Plus*, Cambridge, Cambridge University Press, 2022.
35. Robert Farley, *Grounded: The Case for Abolishing the United States Air Force*, Lexington, University Press of Kentucky, 2014.
36. Gary Sheffield and Peter Gray (eds.), *Changing War: The British Army, the Hundred Days Campaign and the Birth of the Royal Air Force, 1918*, London, Bloomsbury, 2013.
37. General Sir William Jackson and Field Marshal Lord Bramall, *The Chiefs: The Story of the United Kingdom Chiefs of Staff*, London, Brassey's, 1992.
38. John Grigg, *Lloyd George: War Leader, 1916–1918*, London, Faber and Faber, 2003.
39. Richard Overy, *The Birth of the RAF, 1918*, London, Allen Lane, 2018.
40. John Sweetman, "Crucial Months for Survival: The Royal Air Force, 1918–19," *Journal of Contemporary History*, 19/3, 1984, pp. 529–547.
41. Ross Mahoney, "Trenchard's Doctrine, Organisational Culture, the 'Air Force Spirit,' and the Foundation of the Royal Air Force in the Interwar Years," *British Journal for Military History*, 4/2, 2018.
42. Phillip S. Meilinger, "Trenchard, Slessor, and Royal Air Force Doctrine before World War II," in Phillip S. Meilinger (ed.), *The Paths of Heaven: The Evolution of Airpower Theory*, Maxwell, Air University Press, 1997, pp. 41–78.
43. Allan D. English, "The RAF Staff College and the Evolution of British Strategic Bombing Policy, 1922–1929," *Journal of Strategic Studies*, 16/3, 1993, pp. 408–431.
44. Malcolm Smith, *British Strategy between the Wars*, Oxford, Clarendon Press, 1984.
45. Aaron O'Connell, *Underdogs: The Making of the Modern Marine Corps*, Cambridge MA, Harvard University Press, 2012; Heather Venable, *How the Few Became the Proud: Crafting the Marine Corps Mystique, 1874–1918*, Annapolis, Naval Institute Press, 2024; Mark Ryland Folse, *The Globe and Anchor Men: U.S. Marines and American Manhood in the Great War Era*, Lawrence, University Press of Kansas, 2024.
46. Owen R. Cote, "The Politics of Innovative Military Doctrine: The U.S. Navy and Fleet Ballistic Missiles," PhD thesis, MIT, 1996.

47. Lawrence Freedman and Jeffrey Michaels, *The Evolution of Nuclear Strategy*, 4th ed., Basingstoke, Palgrave, 2019.
48. Frederic A. Bergerson, *The Army Gets an Air Force: Tactics of Insurgent Bureaucratic Politics*, Baltimore, Johns Hopkins University Press, 1980.
49. Phil Haun, "Peacetime Military Innovation through Inter-Service Cooperation: The Unique Case of the U.S. Air Force and Battlefield Air Interdiction," *Journal of Strategic Studies*, 43/5, 2020, pp. 710–736.
50. Andrew F. Krepinevich Jr, *The Origins of Victory: How Disruptive Military Innovation Determines the Fates of Great Powers*, New Haven, Yale University Press, 2023, p. 434.
51. Colin S. Gray, *Strategy and Defence Planning*, Oxford, Oxford University Press, 2014.
52. Ann Hironaka, *Tokens of Power: Rethinking War*, Cambridge, Cambridge University Press, 2017.
53. Jon Tetsuro Sumida, *Decoding Clausewitz: A New Approach to "On War,"* Lawrence, University Press of Kansas, 2008, p. 189.
54. Hugh Smith, *On Clausewitz: A Study of Military and Political Ideas*, Basingstoke, Palgrave, 2004.
55. Jean-Luc Leleu, *Combattre en dictature. 1944 – La Wehrmacht face au débarquement*, Paris, Perrin, 2022, p. 257.
56. Larry E. Cable, *Conflict of Myths: The Development of American Counterinsurgency Doctrine and the Vietnam War*, New York, New York University Press, 1986, p. 113.
57. Cathal J. Nolan, *The Allure of Battle: A History of How Wars Have Been Won and Lost*, Oxford, Oxford University Press, 2017.
58. Howard, "The Use and Abuse of Military History."
59. Pierre Grosser, *L'autre guerre froide? La confrontation États-Unis/Chine*, Paris, CNRS Éditions, 2023, p. 12.
60. Francis J. Gavin, "Unspoken Assumptions," *Texas National Security Review*, 6/2, 2023, p. 4.
61. Zachary Shore, *A Sense of the Enemy: The High-Stakes History of Reading Your Rival's Mind*, Oxford, Oxford University Press, 2014.
62. Daniel Kahneman, *Thinking Fast and Slow*, New York, Farrar, Straus and Giroux, 2011.
63. I would like to thank Michael S. Neiberg for this analogy, which he develops in "Reflections of Change: Achieving Intellectual Overmatch through Historical Mindedness," US Army War College, unpublished.
64. Yuen Foong Khong, *Analogies at War: Korea, Munich, Dien Bien Phu, and the Vietnam Decisions of 1965*, Princeton, Princeton University Press, 1992.
65. Rémi Carayol, *Le mirage sahélien. La France en guerre en Afrique. Serval, Barkhane et après*, Paris, La Découverte, 2023, Chapter 1: "Papa Hollande et Oncle Lyautey."

pp. [209–213] NOTES

66. Jean-Pierre Olivier de Sardan, *La revanche des contextes. Des mésaventures de l'ingénierie sociale, en Afrique et au-delà*, Paris, Karthala, 2021.
67. Andrew Mumford, *The Counter-Insurgency Myth: The British Experience of Irregular Warfare*, Abingdon, Routledge, 2012.
68. Eric Sangar, "The Pitfalls of Learning from Historical Experience: The British Army's Debate on Useful Lessons for the War in Afghanistan," *Contemporary Security Policy*, 37/2, 2016, pp. 223–245.
69. Simon Akam, *The Changing of the Guard: The British Army since 9/11*, London, Scribe, 2021.
70. Toshi Yoshihara, *Chinese Lessons from the Pacific War: Implications for PLA Warfighting*, Center for Strategic and Budgetary Analysis, 2023, p. 79.
71. Anders Engberg-Pedersen, *Martial Aesthetics: How War Became an Art Form*, Palo Alto, Stanford University Press, 2023.
72. Tom Clancy, *Red Storm Rising*, New York, G. P. Putnam's Sons, 1986.
73. P. W. Singer and August Cole, *Ghost Fleet: A Novel of the Next World War*, Boston, Houghton Mifflin Harcourt, 2015.
74. Red Team, *Ces guerres qui nous attendent, 2030–2060*, Paris, Éditions des Équateurs, 2022.
75. Lawrence Freedman, *The Future of War: A History*, London, Allen Lane, 2018.
76. It goes without saying that the author can neither confirm nor deny what the CIA knows, or doesn't know, about the J-20.
77. Philip E. Tetlock and Dan Gardner, *Superforecasting: The Art and Science of Prediction*, New York, Random House, 2015.
78. Theo Farrell, "Figuring Out Fighting Organisations: The New Organisational Analysis in Strategic Studies," *Journal of Strategic Studies*, 19/1, 1996, pp. 122–135.
79. Stephen Peter Rosen, *Winning the Next War: Innovation and the Modern Military*, Ithaca, Cornell University Press, 1991.
80. Kimberly Marten Zisk, *Engaging the Enemy: Organization Theory and Soviet Military Innovation, 1955–1991*, Princeton, Princeton University Press, 1993.
81. The coalition was preparing to attack an enemy that had just waged a long war of attrition against Iran, and that most observers agreed was battle-hardened and competent, with the added advantage of being able to defend itself. Most military experts, notably American, predicted a conflict lasting several months, with between 10,000 and 30,000 deaths in the coalition's ranks. Apparently, only the Indian experts had correctly anticipated the dynamics of the campaign. On this last point, see Krepinevich, *The Origins of Victory*, p. 8.
82. Kai Liao, "The Future War Studies Community and the Chinese Revolution in Military Affairs," *International Affairs*, 96/5, 2020, pp. 1327–1346.
83. Anders Klitmøller and Anne R. Obling, "Organizing for Future War and

Warfare: Complexity as 'Folk Theory' in NATO Policy," *Security Dialogue*, 55/6, 2024, pp. 535–551.

84. Alex Waterman and James Worrall, "Know Thy Enemy? Generating, Negotiating and Codifying Knowledge of Insurgencies into US Counterinsurgency Doctrine, 2004–2006," *Journal of Strategic Studies*, 2025.

85. Sarah P. White, "The Organizational Determinants of Military Doctrine: A History of Army Information Operations," *Texas National Security Review*, 6/1, 2022–2023, p. 76.

86. Benjamin M. Jensen, *Forging the Sword: Doctrinal Change in the U.S. Army*, Palo Alto, Stanford University Press, 2016.

87. Andrew Krepinevich and Barry Watts, *The Last Warrior: Andrew Marshall and the Shaping of Modern American Defense Strategy*, New York, Basic Books, 2015.

88. Matthieu Chillaud, "Le centre de prospective et d'évaluations. Un outil prospectiviste au service de la planification stratégique," *Stratégique*, no. 113, 2016, p. 141.

89. Alex Abella, *Soldiers of Reason: The RAND Corporation and the Rise of the American Empire*, New York, Houghton Mifflin Harcourt, 2008.

90. Lawrence Freedman, "Academics and Policy-Making: Rules of Engagement," *Journal of Strategic Studies*, 40/1–2, 2017, pp. 263–268.

91. Michael Desch, *Cult of the Irrelevant: The Waning Influence of Social Science on National Security*, Princeton, Princeton University Press, 2019.

92. Matthieu Chillaud, *Les études stratégiques en France sous la Ve République. Approche historiographique et analyse prosopographique*, Paris, L'Harmattan, 2020.

93. Jörg Muth, *Command Culture: Officer Education in the U.S. Army and the German Armed Forces, 1901–1940, and the Consequences for World War II*, Denton, University of North Texas Press, 2011.

94. These paragraphs are based on Muth's book *Command Culture*, to illustrate the importance of education in the learning mechanism. But it should be stressed that Muth is part of a historiographical tradition that takes for granted German tactical and operational excellence, and in contrast American mediocrity, during the Second World War. This is an idea developed, for example, in Martin van Creveld, *Fighting Power: German and U.S. Army Performance 1939–1945*; Russell Weigley, *Eisenhower's Lieutenants: The Campaigns of France and Germany, 1944–45*; or John Ellis, *Brute Force: Allied Strategy and Tactics in the Second World War*. However, many recent works, which Muth does not take into account, challenge this idea of supposed American mediocrity, such as Michael Doubler, *Closing with the Enemy*, Keith Bonn, *When the Odds Were Even*, and Peter Mansoor, *GI Offensive in Europe*. The idea of the importance of the training system remains valid, but Muth's interpretations probably need to be moderated.

95. Geoffrey P. Megargee, *Inside Hitler's High Command*, Lawrence, University Press of Kansas, 2000.

96. Peter J. Schifferle, *America's School for War: Fort Leavenworth, Officer Education, and Victory in World War II*, Lawrence, University Press of Kansas, 2010.
97. Nathan W. Toronto, *How Militaries Learn: Human Capital, Military Education, and Battlefield Effectiveness*, Lanham, Lexington Books, 2018.
98. Anit Mukherjee, "Educating the Professional Military: Civil–Military Relations and Professional Military Education in India," *Armed Forces and Society*, 44/3, 2018, p. 477.
99. Simon Batten, *Futile Exercise? The British Army's Preparations for War, 1902–1914*, Warwick, Helion, 2018, p. 210.
100. Brian D. Laslie, *The Air Force Way of War: U.S. Tactics and Training after Vietnam*, Lexington, University Press of Kentucky, 2015.
101. Damien Baldin and Emmanuel Saint-Fuscien, *Charleroi. 21–23 août 1914*, Paris, Tallandier, 2012, p. 162.
102. Beatrice Heuser, Tormod Heier and Guillaume Lasconjarias (eds.), *Military Exercises: Political Messaging and Strategic Impact*, Rome, NATO Defense College, 2018.
103. Antoine Bourguilleau, *Jouer la guerre. Histoire du wargame*, Paris, Passés Composés, 2020.
104. John M. Lillard, *Playing War: Wargaming and U.S. Navy Preparations for World War II*, Lincoln, Potomac Books, 2016.
105. Bourguilleau, *Jouer la guerre*, p. 223.
106. Thibault Fouillet, *Wargaming. Un outil de recherche stratégique*, Paris, L'Harmattan, 2022; Erik-Lin Greenberg, Reid B. C. Pauly and Jacquelyn G. Schneider, "Wargaming for International Relations Research," *European Journal of International Relations*, 28/1, 2022, pp. 83–109.
107. Lopez and Otkhmezuri, *Joukov*, p. 284. See also Robert Kirchubel, "Wargaming Operation Barbarossa," *Journal of Slavic Military Studies*, 37/3–4, 2024, pp. 310–337.
108. Leleu, *Combattre en dictature*, p. 271.
109. Tom Dyson, *Organisational Learning and the Modern Army: A New Model for Lessons-Learned Processes*, Abingdon, Routledge, 2021.
110. Stendhal, *The Chartreuse of Parma*, Appleton and Company, 1901, pp. 44–45. Author's emphasis.
111. David Pappalardo, "Guerre aérienne en Ukraine. Le problème de Diagoras," *Le Rubicon*, 5 August 2022, online.
112. Jean Lopez, *Guderian. Le maître des Panzers*, Paris, Perrin, 2024.
113. Jeannie L. Johnson, *The Marines, Counterinsurgency and Strategic Culture: Lessons Learned and Lost in America's Wars*, Washington DC, Georgetown University Press, 2018.
114. Quoted in Michel Goya, *Les vainqueurs. Comment la France a gagné la Grande Guerre*, Paris, Tallandier, 2018, p. 301.
115. François Cochet, "Des outils militaires en reconversion, 1919–1925," in

François Cochet (ed.), *Les guerres des années folles, 1919–1925*, Paris, Passés Composés, 2021, p. 293.
116. Joshua Rovner, "History Is Written by the Losers: Strategy and Grand Strategy in the Aftermath of War," *Journal of Strategic Studies*, 48/1, 2025, pp. 5–35.
117. Brent L. Sterling, *Other People's Wars: The US Military and the Challenge of Learning from Foreign Conflicts*, Washington DC, Georgetown University Press, 2021.
118. Ryan Evans, "Bind Ukraine Closer to American Military Learning," *War on the Rocks*, 20 April 2023, online.
119. JALLC, *NATO Lesson Learned Handbook*, 4th ed., 2022.
120. Tom Dyson, "The Military as a Learning Organisation: Establishing the Fundamentals of Best-Practice in Lessons Learned," *Defence Studies*, 19/2, 2019, pp. 107–129.
121. William E. DePuy, *Selected Papers of General William E. DePuy*, Fort Leavenworth, Combat Studies Institute, 1994, p. 194.
122. Conrad C. Crane, *Avoiding Vietnam: The US Army's Response to Defeat in Southeast Asia*, Carlisle Barracks, Strategic Studies Institute, 2002.
123. BDM Corporation, *A Study of Strategic Lessons Learned in Vietnam*, McLean, BDM Corp, 1979.
124. Harry G. Summers, *On Strategy: The Vietnam War in Context*, Honolulu, University of the Pacific Press, 1981.
125. David Fitzgerald, *Learning to Forget: US Army Counterinsurgency Doctrine and Practice from Vietnam to Iraq*, Palo Alto, Stanford University Press, 2013, pp. 56–57.
126. Rudolph C. Barnes, "The Politics of Low Intensity Conflict," *Military Review*, 68/2, 1988; Andrew Krepinevich, *The Army and Vietnam*, Baltimore, Johns Hopkins University Press, 1988.
127. Trent Hone, *Learning War: The Evolution of Fighting Doctrine in the U.S. Navy, 1898–1945*, Annapolis, Naval Institute Press, 2018.

5. WAR

1. Fearon, "Rationalist Explanations for War"; Ramsay, "Information, Uncertainty, and War"; Blattman, *Why We Fight*.
2. Margaret Atwood, "The Loneliness of the Military Historian," Poetry Foundation, https://www.poetryfoundation.org/poems/47788/the-loneliness-of-the-military-historian.
3. According to the countdown on the Oryx website: https://www.oryxspioenkop.com/2022/02/attack-on-europe-documenting-equipment.html (accessed 15 July 2025).
4. Antulio J. Echevarria II, *Military Strategy: A Very Short Introduction*, Oxford, Oxford University Press, 2017. See also Joseph Henrotin, *Précis de stratégie militaire*, Paris, Economica, 2018.

5. Nolan, *The Allure of Battle*.
6. Christian Malis (ed.), *Guerre et manœuvre*, Paris, Economica, 2009.
7. Karl-Heinz Frieser, *The Blitzkrieg Legend: The 1940 Campaign in the West*, Annapolis, Naval Institute Press, 2012 (1996); Lloyd Clark, *Blitzkrieg: Myth, Reality and Hitler's LightningWar; France, 1940*, London, Atlantic Books, 2016; Philip Nord, *France 1940. Défendre la République*, Paris, Perrin, 2017.
8. However, Boyd has a "naive" relationship with military history, which leads him, for example, to accept without the slightest critical distance the discourse on Blitzkrieg and the existence of a so-called German operative art during the Second World War, to unconvincingly apply his OODA loop to the Battle of Cannes, or to interpret the Mongolian art of war as an example of cognitive maneuver. See Stephen Robinson, *The Blind Strategist: John Boyd and the American Art of War*, Wellington, Exisle Publishing, 2021. For a more positive view of Boyd's contribution to strategic thinking, see Frans Osinga, *Science, Strategy and War: The Strategic Theory of John Boyd*, Abingdon, Routledge, 2007.
9. Ian T. Brown, *A New Conception of War: John Boyd, the U.S. Marines, and Maneuver Warfare*, Quantico, Marine Corps University Press, 2018
10. Heather Venable, "Operation Enduring Effect? Why Maneuver Warfare Works Better in Theory Than Reality," *Vortex*, no. 2, 2021, p. 95.
11. Amos C. Fox, "Manoeuvre is Dead? Understanding the Conditions and Components of Warfighting," *RUSI Journal*, 166/6–7, 2021, pp. 10–18; Franz-Stefan Gady, "Manoeuvre versus Attrition in US Military Operations," *Survival*, 63/4, 2021, pp. 131–148.
12. Josselin Droff, Julien Malizard and Olivier Schmitt, "When Military Interventions Decrease Military Power: Evidence from the French Case," *Defence and Peace Economics*, 36/1, 2025, pp.102–125.
13. Carter Malkasian, *A History of Modern Wars of Attrition*, Westport, Praeger, 2002.
14. O'Brien, *How the War Was Won*.
15. Williamson Murray and Allan Millet, *A War to Be Won: Fighting the Second World War*, Cambridge MA, Harvard University Press, 2001, p. 252.
16. Echevarria, *Military Strategy*, p. 27.
17. Biddle, *Nonstate Warfare*.
18. Philpott, *War of Attrition*.
19. Jack Sheldon, "The German Manpower Crisis," *Douglas Haig Fellowship Records*, 15, 2011, pp. 35–49.
20. David Stevenson, *With Our Backs to the Wall: Victory and Defeat in 1918*, London, Allen Lane, 2011.
21. Baldin and Saint-Fuscien, *Charleroi*, pp. 11–12.
22. Jean-Jacques Becker, *L'Année 14*, Paris, Armand Colin, 2013.
23. Historians debate this point. See, for example, Jean-Claude Delhez, *La bataille*

des frontières. Joffre attaque au centre. 22–26 août 1914, Paris, Economica, 2013; Rémy Porte, *Joffre*, Paris, Perrin, 2014.

24. François Cochet and Rémy Porte, *Histoire de l'armée française. 1914–1918*, Paris, Tallandier, 2017, p. 68.
25. Ibid., p. 75.
26. Nicola Labanca, David Reynolds and Olivier Wieviorka (eds.), *La guerre du désert, 1940–1943*, Paris, Perrin, 2019.
27. Robin Prior, *Conquer We Must: A Military History of Britain, 1914–1945*, New Haven, Yale University Press, 2022, p. 436.
28. Omer Bartov, *Hitler's Army: Soldiers, Nazis, and War in the Third Reich*, Oxford, Oxford University Press, 1994.
29. Michaël Bourlet, *Verdun, 1916. La guerre de mouvement dans un mouchoir de poche*, Paris, Perrin, 2023, p. 270.
30. This section is based on Leleu, *Combattre en dictature*, in particular chapters 13, 20, 22, 26 and 34.
31. Johann Chapoutot, *La loi du sang. Penser et agir en Nazi*, Paris, Gallimard, 2014.
32. Leleu, *Combattre en dictature*, p. 194.
33. Kilcullen, *The Dragons and the Snakes*, p. 41.
34. Toshi Yoshihara, *Mao's Army Goes to Sea: The Island Campaigns and the Founding of China's Navy*, Washington DC, Georgetown University Press, 2023.
35. Carolin Hilpert, *Strategic Cultural Change and the Challenge for Security Policy: Germany and the Bundeswehr's Deployment to Afghanistan*, Basingstoke, Palgrave, 2014.
36. Thomas Rid and Martin Zapfe, "Mission Command without a Mission: German Military Adaptation in Afghanistan," in Theo Farrell, Frans Osinga and James A. Russel (eds.), *Military Adaptation in Afghanistan*, Palo Alto, Stanford University Press, 2013, pp. 192–218.
37. Vivek Chadah, "The Indian Army Adapting to Change: The Case of Counter-Insurgency," in Inge Bekkevold, Ian Bowers and Michael Raska (eds.), *Security, Strategy and Military Change in the 21st Century: Cross-Regional Perspectives*, Abingdon, Routledge, 2015, pp. 115–132.
38. Raphael Marcus, *Israel's Long War with Hezbollah: Military Innovation and Adaptation under Fire*, Washington DC, Georgetown University Press, 2018.
39. Ruti Teitel, *Humanity's Law*, Oxford, Oxford University Press, 2013.
40. James D. Morrow, *Order within Anarchy: The Laws of War as an International Institution*, Cambridge, Cambridge University Press, 2014.
41. Jonathan Gottschall, "Explaining Wartime Rape," *Journal of Sex Research*, 41/2, 2004, pp. 129–136.
42. Benjamin A. Valentino, "Why We Kill: The Political Science of Political Violence against Civilians," *Annual Review of Political Science*, 17, 2014, pp. 89–103; Laia Balcells and Jessica A. Stanton, "Violence against Civilians

during Armed Conflict: Moving beyond the Macro- and Micro-Level Divide," *Annual Review of Political Science*, 24, 2021, pp. 45–69.
43. Christian Ingrao, *La promesse de l'Est. Espérance nazie et génocide (1939–1943)*, Paris, Seuil, 2016.
44. Sarah Fainberg and Céline Marangé, "Entre intentionnalité et inévitabilité. Aux sources des crimes de guerre russes en Ukraine," *Le Rubicon*, 24 February 2023.
45. Howard Jones, *My Lai: Vietnam, 1968, and the Descent into Darkness*, Oxford, Oxford University Press, 2017.
46. Akam, *The Changing of the Guard*.
47. Sonia Le Gouriellec, "Managing Post-traumatic Stress Disorder in African Armed Forces Participating in Peace Operations," forthcoming.
48. Porch, *Counterinsurgency*.
49. Douglas Porch, *Defeat and Division: France at War, 1939–1942*, Cambridge, Cambridge University Press, 2022.
50. Meir Finkel, *On Flexibility: Recovery from Technological and Doctrinal Surprise on the Battlefield*, Palo Alto, Stanford University Press, 2011.
51. Barno and Bensahel, *Adaptation under Fire*, p. 22.
52. Jason Lyall, *Divided Armies: Inequality and Battlefield Performance in Modern War*, Princeton, Princeton University Press, 2020.
53. Masha Cerovic, "Le front germano-soviétique (1941–1945). Une apocalypse européenne," in Alya Aglan and Robert Frank (eds.), *1937–1947. La guerre-monde*, vol. 1, Paris, Gallimard, 2015, pp. 913–962.
54. Naunihal Singh, *Seizing Power: The Strategic Logic of Military Coups*, Baltimore, Johns Hopkins University Press, 2017.
55. See Theo Farrell, "Improving in War: Military Adaptation and the British in the Helmand Province, Afghanistan, 2006–2009," *Journal of Strategic Studies*, 33/4, 2010, pp. 567–594.
56. Giustozzi, *The Taliban at War*; Rudra Chaudhuri and Theo Farrell, "Campaign Disconnect: Operational Progress and Strategic Disconnect in Afghanistan, 2009–2011," *International Affairs*, 87/2, 2011, pp. 271–296.
57. M. L. R. Smith and David Martin Jones, *The Political Impossibility of Modern Counterinsurgency: Strategic Problems, Puzzles and Paradoxes*, New York, Columbia University Press; Theo Farrell, *Unwinnable: Britain's War in Afghanistan, 2001–2014*, London, Bodley Head, 2017.
58. Michel Goya, *La chair et l'acier. L'invention de la guerre moderne*, Paris, Tallandier, 2004; William Philpott, "France's Forgotten Victory," *Journal of Strategic Studies*, 34/6, 2011, pp. 901–918; Elizabeth Greenhalgh, *The French Army and the First World War*, Cambridge, Cambridge University Press, 2014; Goya, *Les vainqueurs*.
59. Paddy Griffith, *Battle Tactics of the Western Front: The British Army's Art of Attack, 1916–1918*, New Haven, Yale University Press, 1994.
60. Stéphane Taillat, "Adaptation et apprentissage. Les forces terrestres

américaines et la contre-insurrection en Irak," *Revue Française de Science Politique*, 58, 2008, pp. 773–793; James A. Russell, *Innovation, Transformation, and War: Counterinsurgency Operations in Anbar and Ninewa Provinces, Iraq, 2005–2007*, Palo Alto, Stanford University Press, 2011.
61. Maurice Vaïsse (ed.), *L'armée française dans la guerre d'Indochine (1946–1954). Adaptation ou inadaptation*, Brussels, Complexe, 2000.
62. Von Hardesty and Ilya Grinberg, *Red Phoenix Rising: The Soviet Air Force in World War II*, Lawrence, University Press of Kansas, 2012.
63. David M. Glantz, *Colossus Reborn: The Red Army at War, 1941–1943*, Lawrence, University Press of Kansas, 2005; David M. Glantz and Jonathan M. House, *When Titans Clashed: How the Red Army Stopped Hitler*, Lawrence, University Press of Kansas, 2015.
64. Chad C. Serena, *A Revolution in Military Adaptation: The US Army in the Iraq War*, Washington DC, Georgetown University Press, 2011; Sergio Catignani, "Coping with Knowledge: Organizational Learning in the British Army?," *Journal of Strategic Studies*, 37/1, 2013, pp. 30–64.
65. James G. March, "Exploration and Exploitation in Organizational Learning," *Organization Science*, 2/1, 1991, pp. 71–72.
66. Richard Downie, *Learning from Conflict: The U.S. Military in Vietnam, El Salvador, and the Drug War*, Westport, Praeger, 1998.
67. John A. Nagl, *Learning to Eat Soup with a Knife: Counterinsurgency Lessons from Malaya and Vietnam*, Westport, Praeger, 2002.
68. Aimée Fox, *Learning to Fight: Military Innovation and Change in the British Army, 1914–1918*, Cambridge, Cambridge University Press, 2018.
69. Fred Kaplan, *The Insurgents: David Petraeus and the Plot to Change the American Way of War*, New York, Simon and Schuster, 2013.
70. Robert T. Foley, "A Case Study in Horizontal Military Innovation: The German Army, 1916–1918," *Journal of Strategic Studies*, 35/6, 2013, pp. 799–827.
71. Clay Blair, *Silent Victory: The U.S. Submarine War against Japan*, Annapolis, Naval Institute Press, 2001.
72. Nina Kollars, "War's Horizon: Soldier-Led Adaptation in Iraq and Vietnam," *Journal of Strategic Studies*, 38/4, 2015, pp. 529–553.
73. Lindsay, *Information Technology and Military Power*.
74. Fox, *Learning to Fight*.
75. Olivier Schmitt, "French Military Adaptation in the Afghan War: Looking Inside or Outside?," *Journal of Strategic Studies*, 40/4, 2017, pp. 577–599.
76. Goya, *Flesh and Steel*. The typology is taken up by Fox, *Learning to Fight*.
77. Schmitt, "Wartime Paradigms."
78. Barno and Bensahel, *Adaptation under Fire*, p. 76.
79. Frank G. Hoffman, *Mars Adapting: Military Change during War*, Annapolis, Naval Institute Press, 2021.

80. David Stahel, *Hitler's Panzer Generals: Guderian, Hoepner, Reinhardt and Schmidt Unguarded*, Cambridge, Cambridge University Press, 2023.
81. Scott Sigmund Gartner, *Strategic Assessment in War*, New Haven, Yale University Press, 1997.
82. Gregory A. Daddis, *No Sure Victory: Measuring U.S. Army Effectiveness and Progress in the Vietnam War*, Oxford, Oxford University Press, 2011.
83. Leo J. Blanken, Hy Rothstein and Jason J. Lepore, *Assessing War: The Challenge of Measuring Success and Failure*, Washington DC, Georgetown University Press, 2015.

CONCLUSION

1. Ian Bowers, *The Modernisation of the Republic of Korea Navy: Seapower, Strategy and Politics*, Basingstoke, Palgrave, 2018.
2. Patrick A. Mello, *Qualitative Comparative Analysis: An Introduction to Research Design and Applications*, Washington DC, Georgetown University Press, 2021.
3. Gregory A. Daddis, *Westmoreland's War: Reassessing American Strategy in Vietnam*, Oxford, Oxford University Press, 2014.
4. Thierry Balzaq and Ronald R. Krebs (eds.), *The Oxford Handbook of Grand Strategy*, Oxford, Oxford University Press, 2021.
5. Brooks and Stanley, *Creating Military Power*.
6. James Wirtz, "Innovation and Navy-Time", in Alessio Patalano and James A. Russell (eds.), *Maritime Strategy and Naval Innovation: Technology, Bureaucracy, and the Problem of Change in the Age of Competition*, Annapolis, Naval Institute Press, 2021, pp. 187–202.
7. Richard Overy, "Aircraft and the Arms Race between the World Wars," in Mahnken, Maiolo and Stevenson, *Arms Races in International Politics*, pp. 115–133.
8. Wirtz, "Innovation and Navy-Time," p. 200.
9. Raymond Aron, *Le grand débat. Initiation à la stratégie atomique*, Paris, Calmann-Lévy, 1963, pp. 8 and 10.
10. Henrik Breitenbauch and André Ken Jakobsson (eds.), *Defence Planning as a Strategic Fact*, Abingdon, Routledge, 2020.
11. Audrey Kurth Cronin, *Power to the People: How Today's Technological Innovation Is Arming Tomorrow's Terrorists*, Oxford, Oxford University Press, 2020.
12. Krepinevich, *The Origins of Victory*.
13. Joseph Henrotin, *Techno-guérilla et guerre hybride. Le pire des deux mondes*, Paris, NUVIS, 2014.
14. Krepinevich, *The Origins of Victory*.
15. C. Anthony Pfaff, *Coercing Fluently: The Grammar of Coercion in the Twenty-First Century*, Carlisle, Strategic Studies Institute, 2022.
16. Anthony King, *Urban Warfare in the Twenty-First Century*, London, Polity, 2021.
17. Davis Ellison and Tim Sweijs, *Breaking Patterns: Multidomain Operations and*

NOTES

Contemporary Warfare, The Hague Center for Strategic Studies, September 2023; Amos Fox and Franz-Stefan Gady (eds.), *Multidomain Operations: The Pursuit of Battlefield Dominance in the 21st Century*, Havant, Howgate Publishing, 2025.

INDEX

Note: Page numbers followed by "*n*" refer to notes, "*f*" refer to figures and "*t*" refer to tables.

A-10 (aircraft), 223
A-10 "Warthog", 105
A-4K Skyhawks, 157
Abu Ghraib prison, 249
Acre War, 70
Adamsky, Dmitry, 137–8
ADZ (Afghan Development Zone), 255
Afghanistan, 29, 158, 209, 246–7, 249, 254–5
 British campaign in, 254–60
Africa, 99, 282
agricultural mechanization, 172
AI. *See* artificial intelligence (AI)
Air Combat Command, 223
Air Ministry, 199–200
Akhundzada, Mohammad, 254
Aldwych, 200
Algeria, 99, 110
American Army, 104
American Civil War (1861–1865), 33, 34–5
American fighter jets, 173
American Joint Staff, 86

American Reaper drone, 170
Americans, 46, 59–60, 71, 85, 87, 89, 91, 93, 104–5, 111, 128, 133, 240, 269, 270
American soldier, 34
ANA (Afghan National Army), 255–6
Anbar, 176
Andropov, 113–14
Anglo-Afghan wars, 209
Anglo-Irish war (1919–1921), 72
Anglo-Japanese alliance, 64
Annapolis Naval Academy, 32
annihilation, 237–8
ANP (Afghan National Police), 255–6
anti-aircraft defenses, 145
anti-aircraft weapons, 145–6
anti-submarine warfare, 181
Apocalypse Now (film), 249
Arab–Israeli war (1973), 111
Arabs, 149
Argentina, 70
Arizona, 105

INDEX

armament policies, 148
armed forces, 1–4, 6, 8–12, 15–16, 17–21, 33, 42, 44–5, 46–9, 57–8, 62–70, 99–101, 103–4, 181, 185–6, 190, 195–6, 197*t*, 218, 221, 237–9, 259, 262, 275–7*t*, 279, 281–5
   adopting and implementing new technologies, 172–4
   challenge of international cooperation, 168–72
   and civil society, 129–32
   civil–military relations, 278
   evolution of, 148–9, 211–12, 246, 275
   importance of political preferences, 111–16
   importance of technology, 141–2
   learning, 264–6, 266*f*
   military history and defense planning, 206–10
   military power, unintended diffusion of, 70–83
   object of study, 26–31
   political economy of military change, 119–29
   political power, role of, 104–110
   pressure of combat on, 250–1, 253
   rise in equipment costs, 153–9
   technological development, 144–5, 147, 163–8, 183
Armstrongs, 164
Army Aviation, 205
Army War College, 220, 230, 231
Aron, Raymond, 2, 55, 78–9, 188, 279
Arthur, W. Brian, 142
Article 125 (Uniform Code of Military Justice), 133–4

artificial intelligence (AI), 167, 184, 284
   See also technology
Artillery School, 230
Asia, 60, 282, 283
Asia-Pacific, 62
Assault Breaker, 193
Atlas program, 202
atomic bomb, 151
Atomic Energy Commission, 164
attrition significance of, 237–45
Atwood, Margaret, 236
Auftragstaktik, 219
Augereau, Pierre François Charles, 27
augmentation technologies, 284–5
Augustine, Norman, 154–5, 157
Australia, 194
Austria-Hungary, 77
automation, 166
Avant, Deborah, 104

B-2 (aircraft), 163
B-47 (aircraft), 203
B-70 (aircraft), 203
Balkans, 246–7
Barany, Zoltan, 114
Bartov, Omer, 243
bases de défense (BDD), 127
Batten, Simon, 222
Beaufre, André, 46
Beijing, 60–2, 73
Beirut airport, 97–8
Bekaa Valley, 193
Berger, David, 2
Bergerson, Frederic, 204
Berlin crisis (1958), 87–8
Berlin Wall, 2
Berlin, 81, 170, 240
Bhaskar, Roy, 23
Biddle, Stephen, 37–8, 80, 240

INDEX

biotechnology, 166
Bloch, Marc, 131
"blunting" (1989–2008), 59, 60
Boer War, 39, 104, 106, 123, 222
Bolivia, 70
Bolsheviks, 95, 117
Bonaparte, Napoleon. *See* Napoleon Bonaparte
Boshin Civil War (1868–1869), 75
Bowers, Ian, 273
Boyd, John, 173, 223, 238, 325n8
Bradley, Frank, 265
Brasilia, 150
Brazil, 5, 70, 150
Brexit, 59
"brigade groups", 242
Britain, 106, 123, 250
Britain, Battle of, 180
British Army, 64, 93, 106, 209, 261
large-scale exercises, 222
British Expeditionary Corps (1914), 77
British Expeditionary Corps 108, 77
British Royal Air Force (RAF), 199–201
Brittany, 243
Brooke, Allan, 242
"building" (2008–2016), 59
Bulgarian Army, 36–7
Bundeswehr, 2, 92–3, 246–7
Burke, Arleigh, 203
bushido ("samurai way"), 196

Cameron, Craig, 192
Cameroon, 100
Camp Shorabak, 256
Canada, 91, 194
Canadian armed forces, 92

Cannae, Battle of, (216 BC), 237–8
Carter, Jimmy, 150
Carthaginians, 238
CARVER (criticality, accessibility, recuperability, vulnerability, effect, recognizability), 194
Centre de Prospective et d'Évaluations (CPE), 216
Centre des Hautes Études Militaires (CHEM), 259
Centre Terre pour le Partenariat Militaire Opérationnel, 101
CGSS (Command and General Staff School), 220
Charleroi, 240
Charterhouse of Parma, The (Stendhal), 226
"Cherbourg missile boats", 97
Chernenko, 113–14
Cheyenne (armed helicopter), 204–5
Chiang Kai-shek, 98
Chile, 70
China, 2, 5, 6, 59–62, 66–7, 69, 71, 83, 146–7, 149, 151–2, 196, 285
alliances and military cooperation, 84–101
techno-nationalist development strategy, 165–6
Chinese Communist Party, 111, 213
Chinese J-20 fighter jet, 211
Chinese Navy, 245–6
Chirac, Jacques, 109
Churchill, Winston, 39, 242, 265
CIA, 164, 211
CIC, 175
"civil–military relations", 103

333

INDEX

armed forces and civil society, 129–32
importance of political preferences, 111–16
political economy of military change, 119–29
political power, role of, 104–110
Clancy, Tom, 211
Clausewitz, Carl von, 22, 31, 36, 46, 206–7, 211, 231
Climate and Defense strategy, 69
climate change, 282–3
Clinton, Bill, 134
cognitive structures, 14–15
COIN (counterinsurgency campaigns), 249–50
Cold War (1990–2001), 29, 56, 59, 63–4, 73, 90, 99, 126, 137, 148, 164
Cole, August, 211
Colombian–Peruvian War (1932–1933), 70
"color revolutions", 191
Command and General Staff College, 230
Commodore Perry, 75
computing, 164
Congress, 104–5, 134
Conseil Supérieur de la Guerre (CSG), 258–9
Constructions Mécaniques de Normandie (CMN), 97
Convention on Cluster Munitions, 68
Coppola, Francis Ford, 249
Council of Ministers, 165
"coup d'oeil", 211
Crimean War (1854), 182
Cronin, Audrey Kurth, 282
Cuban population, 39

Cuban War of Independence, 38–9
cultural factors, 186
cultural norms, 281
Cultural Revolution, 111
Cunningham, Fionna S., 61–2
Cybernetics, 160–1
Czech Republic, 90
Czechoslovakia, 88

d'Annunzio, Gabriele, 137
d'Estrées, Victor Marie, 36
Dachen Islands, 246
DADT (don't ask, don't tell) policy, 134
Danish Army, 83
Daoud, Mohammad, 254
Dassault Aviation, 91
Davis-Monthan Air Force Base, 105
Dayangshan (Island), 246
de Gaulle, Charles, 97, 108, 139, 188, 190, 251, 265
de Négrier, François Oscar, 77
decision-makers, 217–18
Defence and Security Accelerator (DASA), 167
Defense Innovation Agency (AID), 167
Defense Innovation Marketplace (DIM), 167
DEG (Délégation aux Études Générales), 216
DeLong, J. Bradford, 39–40
Democratic Control of Armed Forces (DCAF), 99
Deng Xiaoping, 111, 166
Dengbu, 246
Denmark, 29
Depledge, Duncan, 69
DePuy, William E., 215, 229–30
Desert War (1940–1943), 242
detection devices, 145

INDEX

Devil Pups, 201
discipline, 18–19, 29, 32, 160, 162, 208, 253, 264
  intellectual discipline, 22
disruptive technology, 46
divergent incentives, 217
Djibouti, 61
Doshi, Rush, 59
"double-loop" learning, 265–6
Doughty, Robert, 227–8
Douhet, Giulio, 136
Downie, Richard, 261
Duruy, Victor, 130

École Navale, 32
École Spéciale Militaire de Saint-Cyr, 32
École Supérieure de Guerre (equivalent to the Kriegsakademie), 32
École Supérieure de Guerre (ESG), 258–9
École Supérieure de Guerre, 99
economic blockades, 239
Edgerton, David, 153
Edwardian period, 164
Egypt, 33, 71, 98, 110, 242
Egyptian Army, 110
863 Plan, 166
Eisenhower, Dwight D., 265
El Dorado Canyon operation, 223
11th Brigade, 257–8
Elias, Norbert, 25
environmental constraints, 162
esprit de corps, 17–19
EU Capability Building Mission (EUCAP), 99
Europe, 33, 38, 63–4, 83, 89, 91–2, 120, 123, 129–30, 192, 215
  aging populations, 283

high-intensity conflict, 280, 282
Europe, concert of, 56
European A400M (aircraft), 170
European Defence Agency, 168
European Task Force Takuba, 99
European Union Training Mission, 99
European Union, 168
exhaustion, 237, 239–40
"expansion" phase (2016–), 59–60
expected kinetic energy (EKE), 93
exploitation, 260–1
exploration, 260–1

F-117 (aircraft), 163, 223
F-15 (fighter aircraft), 151
F-16 (fighter aircraft), 151, 223
F-20 (fighter aircraft), 151
F3EA. *See* "find, fix, finish, exploit, and analyze"
"Fabian strategy", 240
Fabrique Nationale, 93
Farrell, Theo, 10
Faure, Samuel, 169–70
FCAS program, 170–1
Feaver, Peter D., 15, 78
Ferry, Jules, 130
52nd Infantry Brigade, 256
Fighter Weapons School, 223
"find, fix, finish, exploit, and analyze", 176
Fitzgerald, David, 231
FM 100-20, 230, 232
FM 100-5, 230, 232
FM 31-16, 230
FM 31-23, 230
FM 3-24, 214
FOBs (forward operating bases), 256
Foch, Ferdinand, 86
Fokker Eindecker E.1 aircraft, 199

335

INDEX

"folk theories", 213
Force Design 2030, 2
Fort Bragg, 230
Fort Leavenworth, 220, 221
Fortmann, Michel, 13
4th Brigade, 258
"Fourth Industrial Revolution", 184
France, 32, 58, 69, 77, 78, 85, 89, 94, 98, 101, 107, 124–5, 128, 152, 169–70, 179–80, 192
  change in military culture, 195
  conflict in, 240–1
  project "Red Team", 211
  See also military change
France, John, 39
Franco-Israeli affair, 97
Fravel, Taylor, 111
Free French Forces, 251
FREMM multi-purpose frigates, 126
French Air Force, 156
French Army, 36, 37, 129–30, 191–2, 225, 240–1
  defeat of, 250–1
  evolution of, 258–9
French Expeditionary Corps, 259
French military intelligence, 81
French Navy, 180
French Revolution, 36
French Second Empire, 70
French, 263
Friedberg, Aaron L., 128
Frunze, Mikhail, 113
Future Combat Systems program, 178

Gaius Varro, 237
Garmsir, 257, 258
Gaullism, 125
Gazelle helicopter, 156

Geddes, Eric, 199
General Reform of Public Policies (RGPP), 128
genetic engineering, 167
Geneva Conventions (1949), 248
George, Lloyd, 199, 268
Gereshk, 254, 255–6
German Army, 95–7, 207, 240, 243, 262
German Leopard 1, 91
Germans, 29–30, 46–7, 77, 81, 85–6, 93, 95–8, 263
Germany, 2, 39, 46–7, 58, 71, 73, 85, 96, 171, 179, 247
  defeat in World War II, 219
  manpower crisis, 240
Gladiator (fighter aircraft), 155
Gneisenau, 31
"Golden Division", 100
"Goldilocks problem", 64
Goldwater-Nichols Act (1986), 105
Gorbachev, Mikhail, 114, 213
Gordon, Andrew, 12
Gorshkov, Sergey, 195
Goya, Michel, 157–8, 263–4
Gray, Colin, 187
Great Britain, 78, 147
Greece, 30
Grierson, James, 222
Griffin, Stuart, 8–9
Grissom, Adam, 7–8, 7*f*
Grosser, Pierre, 208
Groupe d'Armées de l'Est, 242
Groupe d'Armées du Centre, 242
Groupe d'Armées, 241–2
GrouPES (Groupement Permanent de Planification et d'Études Stratégiques), 216
"groupthink", 19
Guadalcanal, Battle of, 210

INDEX

Guderian, Heinz, 227
guerrilla tactics, 239
Guizot law (1833), 130
Gulag, 253
Gulf War (1991), 60, 111, 213, 223
Guttenberg, Karl-Theodor zu, 63

Haig, Douglas, 222
Hamburg War College, 63
Hastenbeck, Battle of, 36
Hauptkadettenanstalten, 219
HCMs. *See* hypersonic cruise missiles (HCMs)
Heart of Darkness (Conrad), 249
Helmand, 254–5, 258
Herero, 39
Hezbollah, 247
HGVs. *See* hypersonic glide vehicles (HGVs)
Hirak protest movement, 110
Hitler, Adolf, 95–7
Hoffman, Frank, 265–6
Horowitz, Michael, 11
Howard, Michael, 208
Howze, Hamilton, 204
Hungary, 90
Huntington, Samuel, 27–8, 31–2
Hussein, Saddam, 119
hydrogen bomb, 151–2
hypersonic cruise missiles (HCMs), 152
hypersonic glide vehicles (HGVs), 152
hypersonic weapons, 152–3

Ia Drang, Battle of (1965), 269
ICBMs. *See* intercontinental ballistic missiles (ICBMs)
IEDs (improvised explosive devices), 257

IHL (International Humanitarian Law), 248
IISS (International Institute for Strategic Studies), 217
Imperial Germany, 147
Imperial Japanese Army, 30, 65
Imperial Policing operation, 39
India, 5, 146–7
Indian Army, 247
Indian-style Goldwater-Nichols Act, 107
indicators, 267–70
Indochina War, 259
Indonesia, 5
Industrial Revolution, 35, 39, 163–4
industrial warfare, 145
"information operations", 214
information technology, 166
institutional structures, 14
Instruction sur l'emploi tactique des grandes unités (Instruction on the tactical employment of large units), 227
Intelligence School, 230
intercontinental ballistic missiles (ICBMs), 149–50, 151–2, 203
international cooperation, 168–72
international humanitarian law (IHL), 68
International Institute for Strategic Studies, 6
international relations, 55
international system, distribution of power
  alliances and military cooperation, 84–101
  factor of change, 57–70
  military power, unintended diffusion of, 70–5

337

power distribution, limits of, 75–83
Iran, 118–19, 149, 162, 321n81
Iran–Iraq War, 118
Iraq, 119, 158, 176, 209, 223
    American logistics, 262–3
    US troop tactics in, 259
Irish Army, 72
Iron Cross, 247
ISAF (International Security Assistance Force), 254, 255, 257
Israel, 97, 122–3, 149, 166, 192, 194
Israeli Army, 247, 251
Israeli intelligence services, 98
Israeli–Palestinian conflict, 149
Israelis, 149, 158
Italian Navy, 180
Italy, 195

JALLC. *See* Joint Analysis and Lessons Learned Centre (JALLC)
jamming systems, 145
Janowitz, Morris, 28, 29
Japan, 33, 64–6, 71–5, 146–7, 196, 210
Japanese Army, 66
Japanese Self-Defense Forces, 130
JFK Special Warfare Center and School, 230
Joffre, Joseph, 241
Johnson, Jeannie, 227
Johnston, Alastair, 187
Joint Analysis and Lessons Learned Centre (JALLC), 228
Journal of Strategic Studies, 8
JSOC (Joint Special Operations Command), 176
Jumper, John, 223

Jutland, Battle of, 12

Kahneman, Daniel, 208
kampfeinsatz (combat mission), 247
Kansas, 220
Kennedy administration, 106
"khaki capitalism", 16
Khanashin, 258
Khrushchev, Nikita, 113
Kier, Elizabeth, 182, 191–2
Kyiv, 1, 239
King's College London, 217
Kingsway, 200
Kinmen Island, 246
KMT (Kuomintang), 246
"known knowns", 211
"known unknowns", 211
Korean War, 111, 123, 201, 202, 246
Krepinevich, Andrew, 232, 282
krieg (war), 247
Kronstadt, 182
Ku Klux Klan, 137
Kursk submarine tragedy, 115

Lancaster House Treaties (2010), 94
"The Land Ironclads", 182
large-scale wars, 149
Lashkar Gah, 254, 256, 257
Latin America, 33, 110
Lebanon, 158
Leclerc tank, 126–7
Lecointre, François, 28–9, 209
legal advisors (LEGADs), 68
Leleu, Jean-Luc, 207
"Lend-Lease" program, 86–7
LI/LL (lessons identified/lessons learned), 225–9
liberal democracy(ies), 5

INDEX

Libya, 223, 247
LICs ("low intensity conflicts"), 232
Lindsay, Jon, 263
Linn, McAllister, 190
Lockheed (the angular F-117), 73
Lockheed Martin, 162–3
Lockwood, Henry Hayes, 262
London, 123
Lorimer, John, 255
Louis XII, King, 119
Louis XIV, 36
Louis XV, 36
"low-carbon warfare", 69
Luttwak, Edward, 46
Luyang-III, 61
Lyautey, Hubert, 250
Lyautey, Marshal, 209
LZ X-Ray, 269

M-1 Abrams, 177–8
MacArthur, Douglas, 265
machine guns, 145–6
Mackay, Iven, 256
Maghreb, 134
Malaya, 104, 106
Mali crisis (2012), 99
Mali, 99–100, 247
Manchuria, 75
"maneuver warfare", 238
Mao Zedong, 111, 246
Marine Corps, 227, 238
Marshall, Andrew, 215–16
Marten, Kimberly, 213
"martial aesthetics", 211
Marxist-Leninist science, 113
Maximus, Fabius, 240
McChrystal, Stanley, 176
McDade, Robert, 269
McNamara, Robert, 204

Mearsheimer, John J., 79
mechanical refrigeration, 172
Meiji era, 196
Meiji government, 75
Membership Action Plan, 90
Merkava tank, 166
Merly, Mathieu, 131
Messmer, Pierre, 108–9
MGCS project, 170–1
Middle East, 148–9
Midway, Battle of, 210
military change, 1–6, 149, 235–7, 274*t*, 285
  alliances, 85–94
  circumvention mechanism, 212, 254–60
  conceptualizing, 40–53, 43*f*, 47*f*, 52*f*
  conditions for, 277–81
  culture and, 191–6
  Defense cooperation, 95–101
  inter-service competition and, 197–205
  mechanisms, 270–1
  political economy of, 119–29
  structures, 14–21
  studying, 7–14, 7*f*, 10*t*
  theory and concepts, 22–26
  See also technology
Military Council, 88
military culture, 8, 32, 185, 214, 233–4
  evolution of, 191–6
  role of combat, 245–7
  strategic culture and, 186–90, 189*f*
"military geography", 68
military innovations, 11, 59
"military isomorphism", 72
military magazines, 216
military organizations, 6, 7, 9, 9*t*,

339

INDEX

10t, 14, 15, 17, 23, 26, 27–30, 41–3, 48–51, 58, 66–9, 72, 80, 83, 104, 110, 267, 270, 275–7t
  adopting and implementing new technologies, 172–4
  armed forces impact on, 163–4
  bureaucratic struggles and theory of victory, 212–14
  culture and military change, 191–6
  flexibility factors, 251–3
  flexibility issues, 277–80
  future challenges, 281–5
  imagination, foresight and science fiction, 210–12
  learning phase, 183–4
  LI/LL process, 225–33
  military history and defense planning, 206–10
  military incubators, 214–18
  stages of, 265–6
  strategic culture and military culture, 186–90, 189f
  training and education, 219–22, 222t
  training and experimentation, 222–5
  trial of combat, 235, 240, 259–60
Military Programming Law (LPM), 124–5
Military Review (journal), 231, 261–2
"military revolution", 12–13
"military societies", 29, 30
military strategy, 82, 111
  operational strategy, 4–5, 4f
military technology (ies), 4, 49, 50, 60, 73–5, 95, 96
  cost, 153–9

military
  circumvention mechanism, 254–60
  experimentation and training, 222–5
  history and defense planning, 206–10
  importance of flexibility factors, 251–3
  incubators, 214–18
  inter-service competition, 197–205
  modernization, 145–50
  strategy, 82, 111
  technological cost, 153–9
  technology (ies), 4, 49, 50, 60, 73–5, 95, 96
  training and education, 219–22
  See also military change; military culture; military organizations; "military revolution"
Military-Industrial Commission (VPK in the Russian abbreviation), 165
"military-industrial complexes", 147
Military modernization, 145–50
military-technical revolution (MTR), 13
Milyutin, D. A., 71
Minic, Dimitri, 191
Ministry of General Machinery Construction, 165
Ministry of Medium Machinery Construction, 165
Mirage 2000 fighter jet, 156
missile defense, 161–2
Mitchell, William (Bill), 136–7
MOGs (mobile operations groups), 255

340

INDEX

Montgomery, Bernard, 242–3, 265
Morgenthau, Hans J., 78–9
Moscow, 81, 87, 250
Moskos, Charles, 28
Mukden, Battle of (20 February – 10 March 1905), 77
Mukherjee, Anit, 221
"multi-domain operations", 284
Murray, Williamson, 11–12
Musa Qala, 254, 256
Muslim populations, 134–5
My Lai massacre (1968), 249

Nad-e-Ali, 257–8
Nama, 39
Namibia, 39
Napoleon Bonaparte, 36, 226
Napoleonic France, 31
"Napoleonic strategy", 240
NASA (National Aeronautics and Space Administration), 164
National Defense University, 231
Navaho, 203
Naval War College, 32–3, 224, 231
Nawa, 258
Nazi Germany, 78, 80–1, 179, 225
  war against USSR, 248
Nazism, 248
NDSTC (National Defense Science and Technology Commission), 166
neorealism, 76–8
neutron bomb, 151–2
New Zealand Air Force, 157
NH-90 helicopter, 156
Nicolau, Valeriano Weyler y, 39
Nie Rongzhen, 166
Niger, 100
Nigeria, 5, 38
19th Brigade, 257
Ningbo, 246

Nolan, Cathal J., 207
non-aggression treaty ("Ribbentrop–Molotov Pact") (1939), 96
Normandy, 243
North Africa, 221
North Atlantic Treaty Organization (NATO), 51, 84–5, 128, 171, 192–4, 247
  importance of alliances, 85–9
North Korea, 152, 162
North Vietnamese, 269
Northrop (the rounded B-2), 73
Northrop, 162–3
Norway, 167
Norwegian Defense Research Establishment (FFI), 167
Norwegian Navy, 167
Now Zad, 254
nuclear power, 164
nuclear weapons, 148

O'Connell, Aaron, 201
Obama, Barack, 115, 134
October Revolution, 117
Office for Naval Research, 164
Office of the Secretary of Defense (OSD), 203
Offiziers-Kriegsschule, 31
Okinawa, Battle of, 210
On Strategy, 231–2
ONA (Office of Net Assessment), 215–16
128 Leopard 1 tanks, 92
Operation Barbarossa, 117
Operation Barkhane, 38, 99
Operation Enduring Freedom, 246–7
Operation Harekate Yolo, 247
Operation Khanjar, 258

341

INDEX

Operation Moshtarak, 258
Operation Overlord, 243
Operation Panchai Palang, 257
Operation Sond Chara, 257, 258
Operation Tor Shpah, 257–8
operational concepts, 174
organizational culture, 8, 12, 184, 192
organizational learning, 260–6
OSD. *See* Office of the Secretary of Defense (OSD)
Ottawa, 91–2
Ottoman Empire, 33, 71

Pacific campaign, 201, 210
Pacific War (1879–1884), 70
"Painlevé" law, 191
Palestinians, 135
Panzer I, 96
Panzer II, 96
Panzer III, 96
Panzer IV, 96–7
Paris, 99, 170
Parker, Geoffrey, 13
"path dependency", 183
Patton, George S., 265
Pearl Harbor, 262
Pentagon officials, 11
Pentagon, 186, 215–16
People's Republic of China. *See* China
Peru, 70
Pétainists, 251
Petraeus, David, 261–2
Peyrefitte, Alain, 108
Philippine Sea, Battle of the, 175
Philippines, 39
Pierce, Terry, 173–4
Pindyck, Shira, 11
Piper Cubs, 204
Pishan, 246

PLA (People's Liberation Army), 210, 213, 246
PME (professional military education), 221, 222*t*
Poirier, Lucien, 16, 216
Poland, 88, 90
Polaris missile, 201–2, 203
political imperatives, 281
Politico (newspaper), 2
Porch, Douglas, 250
Port Arthur, 75
Posen, Barry, 58–9, 70–1
professional military education (PME), 31, 33
PRT (Provincial Reconstruction Team), 256
Prussia, 32, 37, 70, 224
"psychological attrition", 239
Puma helicopter, 156
Putin, Vladimir, 114–15, 138, 190, 250

QCA. *See* qualitative comparative analysis (QCA)
qualitative comparative analysis (QCA), 274–5
quantum computing, 167

R&D (research and development), 168
"racetracks", 150
racial superiority, 244
radar, 178–80
"radical uncertainty", 82
RAF Staff College, 200
RAF. *See* British Royal Air Force (RAF)
Rafale (fighter jet), 156, 170
ranco-Prussian War, 31, 39
RAND Corporation, 217
Rapallo, Treaty of (1922), 95

INDEX

Reagan, Ronald, 150, 162
Red Army, 86–7, 95–6, 113, 117, 253, 259, 267
Redstone Arsenal, 202
régie rationalisée optimisée (RRO), 128
Reichswehr, 51, 95
relational structures, 14–15
research ecosystems, 144
Resende-Santos, João, 70
RETEX, 252
Revolutions in military affairs (RMAs), 13, 194
RGPP. *See* General Reform of Public Policies (RGPP), 128
"right to sexual relations", 132
RMAs. *See* Revolutions in military affairs (RMAs)
RNAS (Royal Naval Air Service), 199
Roberts, Michael, 13
robotics, 167
Rogers, Everett, 50
Roman Army, 237–8
Rommel, Erwin, 242–3
Rosen, Stephen, 212, 213, 215
Royal Flying Corps (RFC), 199
Royal Marines, 255
Royal Navy, 12, 73, 267–8
Ruffa, Chiara, 195
Rumsfeld, Donald, 11, 211
RUSI (Royal United Services Institute), 217
Russia, 5, 33, 69, 71, 78, 85, 112, 137, 149, 152–3, 180–1, 237, 239
  invasion of Ukraine, 250
  war crimes in Ukraine, 249
Russian Army, 1, 36, 81, 116
Russian Civil War, 117
Russian Orthodox Church, 137–8

Russian Revolution (1917), 253
Russians, 59, 65, 85–6, 115–16, 182
Russo-Japanese War (1904–1905) 36–7, 75, 76–7, 182

SAC (Strategic Air Command), 223
Sahel region, 38
Sahel, 158, 264
Saint-Cyr, 129, 259
Sangin, 254, 255–6
Sarkozy, Nicolas, 128
Sartori, Giovanni, 22–3
satellites, 164
Satsuma Rebellion (1877), 75
Saudi Arabia, 5
Scharnhorst, 31
Schleswig War I (1848–1851), 182
"Schöningen spears", 141
science and technology (STS), 144
scientific communities, 162
scorched-earth tactics, 239
SEAD (suppression of enemy air defenses) (1975–1985), 62–3, 146
2nd Battalion, 269
"secret reserves", 244–5
Security Assistance Force Brigades, 101
security force assistance (SFA), 98
Sedan, 75, 76
Serdyukov, Anatoly, 116
Seven Years War, 36
7th Cavalry Regiment, 269
sexually transmitted infections (STIs), 132
Shanghai, 246
Shengsi Island, 246
Shock of the Old, The (Edgerton), 153

INDEX

Shogun, 76
Sicily, 221
sieges, 239
Singer, Peter, 211
"single-loop" learning, 265–6
Sino-Japanese War, 66
Sissi, Marshal, 110
Six Day War (1967), 88, 97
16 Air Assault Brigade, 254–5, 256
Skybolt, 203
SLBMs. *See* submarine-launched ballistic missiles (SLBMs)
Smart Weapons Program, 193
smartphones, 167
Smith, Adam, 119
Smuts, Jan, 199
Snark, 203
Snyder, Jack, 186
Social cohesion, 17
Social Democrats, 95
Somali "Danab", 100
Sources of Military Change, The (Farrell and Terriff), 10
South Africa, 5, 39
South African regime, 72
South Korea, 146–7
South Korean Navy, 273
Soviet air defenses (1960–1970), 63
Soviet Air Force, 259
Soviet Army, 193
Soviet General Staff, 87
Soviet Union, 96, 112, 148
Soviets, 193–4, 215
Spain, 171
Spanish Civil War (1936), 227
Special Operations Command, 100
Specialised Infantry Group, 101
Spitfire (fighter aircraft), 155
Stalin, Joseph Vissarionovich, 113

STANAG 4172, 94
STANAGs (standardization agreements), 89, 92
steam propulsion, 174–5
Strasbourg, 108
strategic culture, 185
  evolution of, 191–6
  military culture and, 186–90, 189*f*
Strategic Defense Initiative, 162
strategic precision strikes (1990–1999), 63
Strategic Studies Institute, 230–1
STS. *See* science and technology (STS)
submarine-launched ballistic missiles (SLBMs), 150, 152, 203
Sullivan, Patricia, 80
Summers, Harry, 231–2
Sun Tzu, 190
Supreme Soviet Commander, 88
surface-to-air missiles, 145–6
SWOT (strengths, weaknesses, opportunities, threats), 194
Syria, 149

TAC (Tactical Air Command), 223
Tacit Blue, 163
Taipei, 66–7
Taiwan Strait crisis (1995–1996), 62
Taiwan Strait, 246
Taiwan, 66–7, 246
Talent Management 2030, 2
Taliban, 247, 254–5
  British attack on, 254–60
Talleyrand-Périgord, Charles Maurice de, 27
Talmadge, Caitlin, 117, 118–19
Tanaka, Shizuichi, 65
Tanxushan Island, 246

INDEX

Task cohesion, 17
"technological blocks", 143
technology, 10, 68, 74, 122
    adapting and implementing of new, 172–4
    development stages, 159–63, 160*t*
    force employment theory and, 178–83
    interactions between civilian and military, 163–8
    mastery of, 174–5
    organizational consequences, 176–8
    quest for prestige, 150–3
    role in military change, 143–4, 274*t*
    significance in armed forces, 141–2
    See also armed forces; military
Teller, Edward, 162
Terne anti-submarine missile, 167
Terriff, Terry, 10
"theory of victory", 212–14
third dimension, 198
Third Reich, 81, 86
3 Commando Brigade, 255
Tiananmen Square massacre, 111
Tiger helicopter (M-51 missile), 126
Tiger helicopter, 156
Tilly, Charles, 120
Tirpitz, Alfred Peter Friedrich von, 46, 195
Tokyo, 76
Toys for Tots, 201
TRADOC (Training and Doctrine Command), 193, 215
Trafalgar, 77
Transforming Armed Forces, 23
Trenchard, Hugh, 136, 200

"Triomphe", 129
Trivulzio, Gian Giacomo, 119
Trotsky, Leon, 113
Trudeau, Pierre, 91
Truman, Harry S., 265
Trump, Donald, 5, 59, 134
Tsahal, 247
Tsarism, 117
Tsarist Empire, 253
Tsushima, Battle of (27–28 May 1905), 77
Tucson, 105
Turkey, 16, 149
Turkish armed forces, 110
Türkiye. *See* Turkey
12th Mechanized Brigade, 255–6
Twenty-First Century project, 23
2008 financial crisis, 59
Type 071 landing ships, 61
Type 075 helicopter, 61
Type 055 Renhai, 61

Uehara, Yūsaku, 64
Ufimtsev, Pyotr, 163
Ugaki, Matome, 65, 66
UK (United Kingdom), 58, 71, 86, 155, 164, 179, 194
    alliances and military cooperation, 84–101
    Avant on, 104
Ukraine, 5, 78, 128, 153, 158, 237
    Russia's failures in, 181
    Russian invasion, 1, 250
    Russian war crimes in, 249
    war in, 239
Ukrainians, 1–2, 237, 249
Uniform Code of Military Justice, 133–4
United Nations Mission for Mali (MINUSMA), 99
University of Berlin, 32

345

INDEX

University of Oxford, 217
urbanization, 282–3
US (United States), 56, 58, 59, 69, 146–7, 148, 149–50, 179–80
   Avant on, 104
   defense budget, 155, 155*f*
   entry into World War II, 201
   NATO and, 171
   withdrawal from Vietnam, 229
US Air Force (USAF), 62, 105, 149–50, 189, 204
   ballistic missile program, 202–3
US armed forces, 127
US Army War College, 33
US Army, 106, 130, 132, 177–8, 181–2, 189, 220–1, 230–1
   airborne combat development, 204–5
   military subcultures, 190
US Congress, 2
US Department of Defense, 163
US Marine Corps, 189, 200
US Marines
   launched attack on Taliban, 257
   Taliban vs, 258
US Navy Special Forces, 176–7
US Navy, 150, 174–5, 189, 203–4
   Polaris missile launch, 201–2, 210, 224, 278
USSR (Union of Soviet Socialist Republics), 1, 46, 56, 67, 112, 192
   alliances and military cooperation, 84–101
   Chinese strategic thinking, 60
   Nazi Germany war against, 248

van Creveld, Martin, 142
Verdun, Battle of, (1916), 243

Versailles, Treaty of, 51, 67, 95–6
Vickers, 164
Vietnam War, 88, 123, 160, 201, 209, 223, 268, 277
Vietnam, 104, 106, 205, 215, 231, 268–9
   American logistics, 262–3
   American withdrawal from, 229–30
Virginia Military Institute, 32

Waffen-SS, 244, 248
Waltz, Kenneth, 78
War Ministry, 199
War of Independence (1775–1783), 33
Warden, John, 223
Warsaw Pact, 51, 192–3
   alliances and military cooperation, 84–101
Washington Agreement (1922), 64
Washington, 81, 86
Washington, George, 18–19
Waterloo, 35
Waterloo, Battle of, 225–6
Wealth of Nations, The (Smith), 119
Wehrmacht, 225, 238, 243, 244, 248, 267
Wellington, 35
Wells, H. G., 182
West Africa, 38
West Germany, 92
Western Front, 240, 242, 243
Westmoreland, William, 269–70, 277
Weyand, Fred C., 230
Whampoa Military Academy, 98
Whampoa, 98
Williams, John, 28
Wirtz, James, 278

INDEX

Wohlforth, William, 79
Wohlstetter, Albert, 142
World War I, 51, 65, 67, 74, 123, 131–3, 147, 164, 181–2
  importance of alliances, 85–9
World War II (1941–1945), 12, 33–5, 37, 63, 71, 86–7, 124–5, 127, 133, 153, 175, 181–2, 196, 219, 239
  alliances and military cooperation, 84–101
  US entry into, 201

Xiamen Island, 246

Xiaoyangshan Island, 246

Yeltsin, Boris, 114
Yijiangshan Island, 246
Yokohama language school, 75
Yom Kippur War (1973), 215, 230
"Young Turks", 213

Zeppelin airships, 199
Zhang Zuolin, 30
Zhou Enlai, 98
Zhoushan Islands, 246
Zhoushan, 246
Zweibelson, Ben, 194